# THE MIDDLE CLASSES 1900–1950

# THE
# MIDDLE CLASSES
# 1900–1950

Alan A. Jackson

DAVID ST JOHN THOMAS PUBLISHER

Is this to be the type of all civilizations, when the whole western world is to become comfortable and tranquil, and progress finds its grave in a universal suburb? – C. F. G. Masterman, *The Condition of England* (1909)

**British Library Cataloguing in Publication Data**

Jackson, Alan A.
  The middle classes 1900–1950.
  I. Title
  305.50941082

  ISBN 0–946537–67–4

Printed in Great Britain
by Redwood Press Ltd   Melksham
for David St John Thomas Publisher
PO Box 4   Nairn   Scotland IV12 4HU

# CONTENTS

# AUTHOR'S PREFACE

An alternative title for this book was *Privacy and Comfort*, derived from a phrase once cherished by the copywriters of mail order advertisements: 'Examine these goods in the privacy and comfort of your own home' (to which was sometimes added 'All our goods are delivered in plain vans'). Encapsulated in this are some crucial elements of the lifestyle of the British middle classes in the first half of the 20th century, a lifestyle which is portrayed and examined here, together with all that went with it.

The period is a significant one, in which this important section of British society, building upon the strong base it had established for itself in the latter part of the Victorian era, expanded and advanced to new levels of prosperity and security whilst remaining a distinct and recognisably separate minority. For the British middle classes, these fifty years saw further refinements in comfort and privileges as their increasingly pervasive influence rose to new strength. And for the lower middle class in particular, it was an era of growth and consolidation, in which living standards improved as many moved into the bright modernity of the small houses so plentifully supplied between the wars by private enterprise.

1950 may seem a convenient but artificial limit; yet, as will be seen, there is some evidence that the years around the middle of the century really did mark a turning point, after which things would never be quite the same again for the middle classes, their values and their way of life, even though some of the characteristics mentioned in this book have endured. After the early fifties, the high standards of comfort were no longer the privilege of a visibly disparate minority, becoming much more widely spread; within few more years, as one of Alan Ayckbourn's characters points out, almost everyone not already middle class appeared to be striving for that status in some degree. Masterman's 1909 prophecy of a western world transformed to a comfortable 'universal suburb' seemed on the way to fulfilment, at least so far as Britain was concerned.

The reader will quickly notice that a great deal is said in this book about London and southern England and that many of the illustrative examples are taken from that region. No apology is made for this; it is to a large extent inevitable since, in the period under consideration, that was where the action was and where the larger part of the middle classes lived and worked. There is little if any evidence that middle class life and ways were greatly different elsewhere in Britain, only that change occurred somewhat later and more slowly, reflecting the distance from metropolitan influence.

Another small caveat should be entered. Even before our period began, the distinctions between the middle and upper classes were already blurring; and this trend continued through the five decades covered by this book. Thus what is mentioned here as an aspect of middle class life or behaviour might also frequently be found, with little alteration, in the relatively small upper class group, though the latter also had special features of its own, which survived in greater or lesser degree throughout the fifty years and these are of course not explored here. At the other end of the spectrum, the differences between the middles and the working classes remained obvious and easily recognisable right through to the end of the 1940s, though by then they were at last showing signs of decay.

Much of the content of this book is derived from personal experience from the late 1920s onwards, or from the recollection of others who have shared these years, or were old enough to remember the first decades of the century. I am especially grateful to my wife, who contributed a great deal from her own memories and discussed my early drafts critically and patiently when they were thrust upon her; also to my sister, who talked in a lively manner about her Hertfordshire schooldays and experiences as a young teacher in the 1940s. Mrs Eva Simmonds contributed valuable reminiscences of her private school and early adulthood in the 1920s, and Miss Edith and Miss Doris Mercer, who grew up in the 1910s and 1920s, genially talked me through a fascinating collection of family photographs extending back to that period. Oscar T. Hill and J. H. Price offered helpful comments and suggestions on travel history matters; G. Harry Guilmartin kindly gave permission for use of material from his *Bare Empty Sheds* and Doug Cluett, Heritage Officer, London Borough of Sutton, agreed to a quotation from Eileen Whiteing's *Anyone for Tennis?* I am also grateful to the Royal Statistical Society of London for allowing me to use material published in their *Journal*. Lucy Bramwell-Jones, Miss S. P. Stott (Assistant Archivist of the Girl Guides' Association) and A. M. Eserin (Assistant Librarian, Hertfordshire Libraries, Welwyn Garden City) were all helpful regarding photographs. Many others have assisted (often unwittingly) with recollections and reflections on particular aspects of middle class life, some of them in conversations over the last forty years or so, since this is a book I have long had in mind to write.

I should be very pleased to hear from readers whose memories are stirred, especially if they feel able to elaborate on items of detail, or wish to discuss my generalisations and conclusions (which I shall stoutly defend). Such correspondence may be addressed to me care of the publisher.

ALAN A. JACKSON
Dorking, May 1990

---

# Note Regarding the Illustrations

All the illustrations are from the author's own collection except the following:

Plate 20: *London Transport Museum*
Plate 27: *Lucy Bramwell-Jones*
Plate 28: *Miss Edith and Miss Doris Mercer*
Plate 29: *J. H. Price collection*

# ABBREVIATIONS

| | |
|---|---|
| BBC | British Broadcasting Corporation |
| BUF | British Union of Fascists |
| c | circa |
| C19, C20 | 19th Century, 20th Century |
| EDA | British Electrical Development Association |
| EN | *The Evening News* (London) |
| GLRO | The Greater London Record Office |
| GPDS | Girls' Public Day School Trust |
| LCC | London County Council |
| m | million |
| nco | non-commissioned officer |
| nd | no date |
| PRO | Public Record Office (Kew) |
| RSS | Royal Statistical Society |
| RAF | Royal Air Force |
| RU | Rugby Union |
| WRAF | Women's Royal Air Force |
| WRNS | Women's Royal Naval Service |
| WRVS | Women's Royal Voluntary Service |

# MONEY

For amounts under £1 the contemporary costs in shillings (s.) and old pence (d.) are given. Guineas (one guinea = £1 1s) were also used in prices in the period covered by the book. The equivalents advised by the Decimal Currency Board in 1970 were one penny (¹⁄₂₄₀th of £1) = 00.417p, sixpence = 2½p, one shilling (¹⁄₂₀th of £1) = 5p, but of course such conversions are meaningless without taking into account the very substantial decrease in purchasing power of the pound which has occurred in the last forty years, particularly since 1971. Some deductions can however be drawn about the real value of the money amounts quoted in the text by referring to the information given in Chapter 2 and Appendix A on net incomes at various periods for different occupations and making cross references to the contemporary costs of goods and services, using the index. Up to date information on the internal purchasing value of the pound sterling over the years since 1914, based on official indices, may be obtained from the Central Statistical Office.

CHAPTER 1

# MORE IN THE MIDDLE

The subject of social class continues to obsess the British, particularly the English. It has confused and irritated some modern social historians, who, wishing to ignore it, realise they cannot. Concern has been expressed at the inability of some people to describe themselves in class terms and undue import given to the differing responses evoked by alternative descriptions such as 'upper/middle/lower', 'governing/middle/working' or 'bourgeois/petit bourgeois/protelariat'. The sheer size and variety of the middle and working classes has stimulated several fascinating attempts to break down the traditional tripartite division into sub-groups. Others have sought refuge in a more radical approach, seeking to deny the importance of social class as a concept, even its very existence.

Yet the evidence of social distinctions and disparate lifestyles is irrefutable and, for want of anything better, the doubters, the confused, and the would-be innovators can occasionally be caught relapsing into use of the traditional terms. In particular the middle classes remain obstinately present, a recognisable element even today. In the first half of the twentieth century, which is our concern here, their status, appearance and attitudes were much more sharply defined.

This was a period which witnessed a rapid expansion and growth in importance of the British urban middle classes, a section of the population which A. J. P. Taylor has suggested 'set the standards of the community . . . were its conscience and did its routine work'[1]. Others have called them the backbone of the nation. Masterman, in 1909, went so far as to say 'It is the middle class which stands for England in most modern analyses'[2].

A large group, which does indeed present some problems of definition, the British middle classes of these years formed not one-tight band but a many-layered conglomerate of sub-classes or categories, sharing some common attitudes and principles and mostly working for a living, although working in a way which clearly distinguished them from the proletariat. They stood between the upper classes of aristocrats and plutocrats (with which they were increasingly merging and intermarrying) and the manual workers and the very poor. Income and wealth cannot be used to identify them; unless large enough to produce and sustain the level of wealth that brings power, this factor has almost no relevance in the definition of social class, and confusion can arise because the incomes of the middles spanned a wide spectrum from the marginally adequate to the comfortably affluent.

The writers of a statistical survey of English and Welsh society in the late 1930s, looking at this scene and apparently anxious to dismiss the importance of social class, described the middle classes as never having been anything more than 'a heterogeneous assemblage of disparate elements'[3]. This is an assertion which touches only part of the truth, ignoring the shared ethos and characteristics which this book sets out to examine in some detail.

But enough of generalities. Let us break open this multi-layered cake and try to identify the specific elements of the middle classes.

Prominent of course were the established professionals: the clergy, lawyers, doctors, architects and others with appropriate qualifications; into this broad category we may also admit regular officers of the armed services, senior central and local government officials, academics and public school masters and railway officers. There were a fortunate if declining group not gainfully employed but living on dividends and rents. Also we must include medium and small employers engaged in all kinds of trades and businesses, including small shopkeepers and independent farmers, although many of these (apart from the last) continued to be held in low regard by those who did not taint their fingers with commerce. Others in the 'heterogeneous assemblage' were artists, musicians and full time writers of all kinds; senior managers and operators in banking and insurance and other financial institutions; and newspaper and periodical editors and journalists. Successful actors and other entertainers and professional sportsmen present a problem; whilst some came from a middle class background, others were clearly working class in origin. Of the latter, some but not all would tend to adopt many aspects of middle class lifestyle as their rewards grew. If permanent success eluded them, they would soon return to working class ways.

Nor were these all. As the twentieth century dawned, coming up in the rear was the rapidly growing army of the lower middle class, with incomes below most of those just mentioned. For the purposes of this book, all salary earners and wage-paid non-manual workers will be regarded as middle class. Some readers may wish to argue about this, but for the majority of this group, attitudes, way of life and the character of their daily work all point to this classification, even though their incomes were often no more than many in the working class and sometimes less.

In today's terminology, these lower middle 'white collar workers' were all potentially 'upwardly mobile'. A salary implied higher status, expectation of advancement, 'respectability', stability of employment and in many cases a pension, not necessarily all of these in every case, but each of them tending to confirm the recipient into unmistakeable middle class behaviour and lifestyle. We shall look a little more closely at these lower middles later in this chapter.

Together with the upper class, the middle classes formed the 'respectable society', with a way of life, education and housing, and (for many years), dress, accents and behaviour which readily distinguished them from the manual working class. As the century advanced, this cleavage between the working classes and the rest, so deep in the first two decades, (and still discernible in the 1940s) was gradually to become blurred and dislocated.

Having tried to clear the reader's mind on what is meant by the middle classes, it remains to dismiss some features which might seem to present themselves as class indicators. The first of these is liability to income tax. Virtually no members of the manual working class paid this tax at least until 1915 but large numbers of the lower middle class were also exempted; their salaries were not high enough to attract it, especially if they had children.[4].

Servant-keeping is another aspect that has sometimes been selected as marking a social distinction[5], especially in the 1900s and 1910s. Although it is probable that the majority of the middle classes kept living-in servants in the first two decades of the century, by no means all did so. As we shall see when we come to look at incomes and expenditure in the next chapter, some simply could not afford it, nor did they have the necessary accommodation in their houses. On the other hand, at least up to the late 1910s, there was a limited amount of servant-keeping in the upper echelons of the working class. In the 1920s and 1930s living-in servants became difficult to obtain, so much so, that especially in the south-east, even those who could afford this amenity learned to manage with fewer, or with none. And by the mid 1940s the reservoir of men and women prepared to live in a middle class household as maids, cooks and nannies had all but dried up.

Lastly there is the ownership of what the Americans call real estate. Before the 1920s it was by no means always the case, even among the wealthiest section of the middle classes, that the head of household owned the main residence. However, from the twenties, home ownership did become an increasingly reliable, although not infallible, indicator of class, simply because, as a result of the continuation of statutory wartime rent restrictions, very few houses were built to rent after World War I and there was a growing shortage of such property at a time of vastly increased housing demand. And, by and large, purchase by mortgage, usually the sole practical means of house acquisition, was only available to those with secure incomes. However, whilst home ownership remained beyond the reach of most working class people until the 1950s, it would not be entirely correct to say that it was the sole prerogative of the middle and upper classes. Before the First World War, the artisan and tradesman elements of the working class frequently invested their savings in the purchase of small cottage type properties, taking the rents as a supplement to their normal income or as means of saving and support in old age, whilst continuing to live in rented houses themselves. And some working class families, especially in south east England, also bought small plots of depressed agricultural land for as little as £5 or £10, on which, often with their own hands, they put up simple shacks to serve as holiday or retirement homes[6].

## A Prosperous and Expanding Middle

Even before the century opened, the increasing complexity of British society had set off an expansion of the middle classes, a growth which was to continue strongly. Census figures showed that in Great Britain civil and local government and railway officials, council schoolteachers, clerks of all kinds and commercial travellers had grown from a total of 534,622 (5.5 per cent of all employed adult males) in 1891 to 918,186 (7.1 per cent) in 1911. For reasons not unconnected with the social upheaval of 1914–18, the number of salaried workers in private employment in the UK almost tripled from 1.7 to 2.75 million between 1911 and 1921, representing a rise from twelve to twenty two per cent of the occupied population[7]. There was a comparable growth in the same period in the salaried employees of central and local government, stimulated in particular by the enlargement of the armed services, the Liberal Government's social welfare measures of 1909 onwards and the unprecedented expansion in government control and hence bureaucracy under war and immediate post war conditions. The thousands of additional staff recruited for the defence departments and the new Ministry of Munitions were of course a temporary feature but a group of new government departments formed in 1916–20 proved long-lasting and the civil service numbered 116,241 in 1923 compared with 57,706 in 1914. The 'professional classes', as defined by the census compilers, grew from 796,000 in 1911 to 875,000 in 1921.

Middle class numbers continued to expand throughout the 1920s and

1930s as rising material and social standards increased the strengths of the professions and central and local government white collar staffs. By 1930 the civil service total was 120,418 and from the mid 1930s preparations for a new war brought further growth. Simultaneously, the requirements of new large scale industries created many more managerial and clerical posts. New areas of middle class activity such as advertising agencies, work measurement and work study, industrial psychology and industrial welfare were enthusiastically developed after the end of World War I.

Census figures of 1931 showed there were by then in the UK over four and a half million in the white collar category, representing 23.5 per cent of the employed population, including 968,000 professionals, 1.4 million employers, 770,000 managers and administrators and 1,465,000 clerks. This last total showed an increase of almost half a million over comparable 1921 figures, the latter still inflated by the administrative aftermath of the war. Perhaps more significant, those categorised as being salaried were 1.4 million higher than the 1911 figure.

A further boost to middle class managerial, sales, advertising and office jobs arose with the great boom in private enterprise house building of 1934-37[8]. And also in the 1930s, other employment openings were created by prosperity in the retail sector (notably in expansion of multiples) and by the proliferation of service and entertainment industries of all types. By 1938 salaries represented 24 per cent of national incomes compared with 10.5 per cent in 1911. In her careful analysis of the numbers in salaried employment in Great Britain & Northern Ireland in the 1920s and 1930s,[9], Agatha Chapman indicates that the largest increase between 1924 and 1938 was in the distributive trades (552,600 more salaried posts, making a total of 1.6m). There was also a significant growth in the same period in salaried jobs in the manufacturing industries (an increase of 267,100 to 897,900) and in professional services (151,000 to 767,500). In Miscellaneous Services, which included entertainment, sport, catering and hotels, Chapman estimates the number of salaried jobs in the same period expanded by 97,900 to 236,200. Another interesting salaried growth area was in gas (10,600 new jobs) and electricity (24,200). Taken together, these estimates show that whilst salaried jobs comprised 17.8 of the total numbers employed in 1924, the proportion had reached twenty per cent in 1938.

The numbers of those in non-manual occupations continued to expand through the 1940s. By 1951 they constituted 30.4 per cent of the employed population compared with only 20.3 per cent in 1911. Another continuing trend was the increase of women in middle class occupations, something we shall look at in detail in Chapter 6.

As the new consumer durable, service and entertainment industries and the house building boom were all largely concentrated in the south east, adding to the business and financial prosperity already existing in London, a high proportion of the new and the established middle classes were to be found there. By the end of the 1930s, almost one third of those with incomes of £400 and over were living in and immediately around the capital.

Other factors were at work. From the early years of the century, with infant mortality falling and the expense of child-rearing increasing, birth control in various forms was increasingly practised. The crude birth rate began to fall, declining from 28.2 per thousand in 1901–5 to 15.8 in 1931 and 15.5 in 1951, the latter figure inflated by the postwar baby boom[10]. Between 1901 and 1931 the average number of children per family fell from 3.5 to 2.2. That the middle and upper classes were pioneers in family limitation (with or without the contraceptives they could more readily afford) is shown by the smaller number of children per family of non-manual workers compared to those of manual fathers (eg in the years 1925–9, 1.93 compared with 2.49). Even before 1914, two children at most was becoming the norm for a middle class family. The Registrar General's figures for 1911 and 1921[11] show a marked drop in fertility with ascent in the social scale in both years. When, in 1930 the Anglican bishops gave a cautious blessing to the use of contraceptives, this merely had the effect of making the middle classes feel more comfortable about what most of them had been doing for thirty years or more. Together with the decline in servant keeping, smaller families stimulated a general reduction in the new house size when building recommenced around 1920. Smaller houses and smaller families were an important factor underpinning the improvement of middle class living standards, an improvement particularly seen in London and south east England as wealth and prosperity increasingly concentrated in that region.

Another significant trend was the increase in the number of people living beyond sixty, a large proportion of whom were middle class since their lifestyle and occupational environment up to that age tended to give them better chances of survival against those of manual workers. The numbers in the age group sixty-five to seventy-four in England & Wales grew from 1,076,000 in 1901 to 2,141,000 in 1931 and by the middle of the century it was around three million[12].

The steady improvement in middle class living standards which fuelled the prosperity of the consumer and service industries was evident from the first decade of the century. The Edwardian years saw the rich growing richer whilst the poor could afford even less than before. Inland Revenue returns between 1899 and 1913 showed a rise of 55 per cent in the gross value of unearned incomes (profits and interest). Much of the new capital wealth created in these years went overseas to secure the higher profits available from the opening up of new territories, using cheap native labour. This in turn tended to create pressure for higher dividends from the investment-starved domestic British companies, returns which could only be achieved by clamping down labour costs, a feature that led to industrial unrest in the early 1910s which was serious enough to frighten the middle classes.

Many middle class people continued to do well during the 1914–18 war. Organisation and management of the military effort and restrictions of many kinds on civilian activities and consumption all engendered growth in the central bureaucracy. Lawyers prospered from the proliferation of regulations, doctors from wartime stresses and strains. Most small businessmen and tradesmen were unable to ignore the temptations offered by price inflation and supply shortages. Savings were built up which were to help cushion the effects of postwar inflation and the subsequent economic depression, events which tended to hit hardest those in the middle and upper sections of the middle classes.

In the later 1920s and the 1930s conditions for the middle classes again improved, returning living standards to near pre-1915 levels. This will be examined further in the next chapter.

## Expansion at the Base

As already indicated, much of the numerical growth described above was attributable to the rise of the lower middles. These council school teachers, technicians, shop managers, sales managers, commercial travellers and above all, clerks, usually came from a working class background[13] but once on the first rung of the middle class ladder, they managed their financial affairs with care and frugality, so that they were able, ever more successfully, by saving and salaried job holding, to achieve secure middle class status. And in the 1920s and above all in the 1930s, most were able to confirm it with home ownership. The general rising trend in disposable income, in which smaller family size played such an important part, enabled these people to live cheaply and pleasantly in new suburbs from which they could commute cheaply over expanded and improved public transport systems to reach the better-paid jobs in city centres. Signs of this social change appeared quite early. Between 1901 and 1914, in a town as much as 22 miles from London, 'another new community' appeared – junior clerical workers and book keepers who could afford a second or third class season ticket between their London jobs and 'a house on the lower slopes of the hill'[14].

The evolving pattern of publicly-financed education was another potent factor in sustaining this new sub-class and promoting its expansion. As early as 1891, in his report on the census, the Registrar General had noted that 'The increased diffusion of education has apparently flooded the country with candidates for clerkships'. Following the Education Act of 1902 (and a similar statute for London in 1903), which transferred the power to provide primary and secondary education to the elected county councils and some large borough councils, larger amounts of public money were spent on free working class education. Although the elementary school child unable to gain a secondary place had to leave at age twelve (fourteen from 1918) and a few of these did find their way into lowly office jobs, it was the significant expansion of secondary education which followed this legislation which provided a steadily increasing supply of recruits for the growing white collar army as well as some for the better middle class jobs. The number of pupils in grant-aided secondary schools rose from 94,000 in 1905 to around 200,000 in 1914 and after 1907 state grants were cut unless these schools reserved at least a quarter of their places free of fees for elementary school children. Further opportunities for secondary education were opened up by the steady expansion of local council secondary schools and legislation of 1918 and 1921. By 1939 there were 470,000 children enjoying wholly or partly publicly-financed secondary education compared with only 174,000 in 1913[15]. Providing a mainly academic education for around fifteen per cent of the children in any of the eleven to eighteen age groups, the county and county borough secondary schools and the state-aided independent grammar schools turned out boys and girls suitable, if not over-educated, for the greatly expanded salaried job market of the 1920s and 1930s, most of this simple office work of one kind or another.

The author, who attended one of these schools in the 1930s, recalls his chemistry master repeatedly emoting in a strong Welsh accent that he wanted his pupils 'to become *chemists*, not seven and sixpenny clerks'[16]. But he was fighting a hopeless battle: in the circumstances of the time, as we shall see later, the majority of secondary school leavers were to move from school to routine desk jobs at sixteen and seventeen without the further education needed for scientific, technical or professional qualification. In January 1939 the national examinations for the Civil Service Clerical Class (today's 'Administrative Officers') attracted no less than 7,159 candidates, a high proportion of whom gained posts. It was a telling climax to two decades in which thousands of secondary school leavers had donned cheap lounge suits, white shirts and semi-stiff collars to work in offices of many kinds. The stark truth was that despite some modest expansion in university education since the beginning of the century, by the 1930s only a small minority of the English secondary school output (around six to seven per cent, or about 14,500) possessed parents with sufficient means to sustain them at university until their early twenties or later[17].

Most of the secondary school leavers, having achieved a starting salary of £50-90, aspired to move upwards until they were well-established members of the middle class. They had already been indocrinated at school (and often in their church life as well) to look in that direction for standards of conduct, dress and taste, even if their family background and some of their parents' neighbours and friends were 'respectable working class'. Many had vague aspirations, engendered by reading, personal contact and observation, of attaining a position in society above that achieved by their parents. Others entered service trades and industries catering for the middle class life style and so doing, secured it for themselves and their families.

## The Rural Seam also Strengthened

Whilst the middle classes of the period were predominantly urban and suburban in their location and influence and the growth and changes touched upon in this chapter were mainly confined to them, this survey would be incomplete if we were to overlook the extensive if thin seam of middle class running through the countryside and the small country towns. The established sector – the owner-farmers, the clergy and the doctors, the country solicitors and auctioneers and market town business-men – were a very stable element, forming local society, dominating local government . For them the changes were few and slow in the first half of the new century but they were increasingly supplemented by new arrivals who fell into two distinct categories. From around the turn of the century but more intensively after 1919, improvements in public utilities and public and private transport encouraged the urban middle classes to set up permanent and weekend homes in the countryside at some distance from the larger cities and towns. Many of these newcomers, with their urban roots and interests well-established, were only marginally involved in rural life and could hardly be considered part of it, but there were others, who may be termed the 'new countrymen', who did try very hard to integrate themselves and their families into the rural communities. In general, this middle class invasion had the effect of heightening rural class distinctions and accelerating the breaking-up of the traditional peasant culture which was already under way.

Bourne writes of the changes brought about by the arrival of the leisured classes in Bourne, Farnham Common (39 miles from London) between 1900 and 1911:

> the village is an altered place . . . the old comfortable seclusion gone. Even the obscurity of winter night does not veil that truth; for where, but a few years ago, the quiet depths of darkness were but emphasised by a few cottage lights, there is now a more brilliant sparkling of lit-up villa windows, while northwards the sky has a dull glare from the new road lamps which line the ridge. . .

The labourer, sweating in his cottage garden, hears the sound of piano-playing, or the 'affected excitement of a tennis-party; the braying of a motor car informs him that the rich are the masters of the road'[18].

True representatives of the new countrymen preferred full-time rural living and the rural environment, finding the means, one way or another, to sustain themselves in reasonable middle class comfort in bucolic seclusion, not feeling any need to return even temporarily to taste urban pleasures and excitements. Most of them were inspired by the middle class Englishman's romantic love of the countryside, an emotion not shared or appreciated by the rural labourers and their families on whom the effects of the middle class invasion were not always entirely beneficial[19]. The progressive decay of agriculture and the disappearance of the old self-sufficient rural way of life and its traditions, well evident by 1920, only served to heighten this romanticised and often sanitised middle class view of the countryside and all that went with it. The flow of related art, fiction and documentary writing, the attempts to revive or preserve rural crafts, all increased at a great pace under the encouragement and enthusiasm of the invaders. Influential in this respect was the work of J. Robertson Scott, who founded the quarterly magazine *The Countryman* in 1927, editing it over the ensuing twenty years from his home in the small west Oxfordshire village of Idbury.

This new element of the rural middle class was composed of retired officers, professionals and businessmen and others with sufficient private means to make them independent of urban ties. There were also those who could earn a living from home, notably artists and writers. Many deliberately tried very hard to involve themselves and their families in their adopted surroundings, often making a substantial contribution. In community life generally and in church and council affairs in particular they took over the role of the Victorian rural minor gentry, the village school teachers and the intellectual clergymen with private means. Their ladies were often the leading lights in the Women's Institutes, founded in 1915 'to improve and develop conditions of rural life'.

In the countryside and villages, the resident land-owning upper class and the established rural middle classes had long drifted together for mutual support, mixing socially in the local hunts and associated events and for other activities such as shooting and hare-coursing. Amongst them class snobbery was perhaps at its least prevalent, although the middle class farmer and his family did not normally participate in the leisure activities of their labourers or pay regular visits to the village inn. Although often supported by at least one servant, the middle class farmer's household bore little resemblance to its urban equivalent, principally because the mistress of the house was inevitably involved in a great deal of physical activity which left her little time to play the leisured lady. In general these characteristics of rustic middle class life persisted in many areas at least until the 1940s.

On the other hand the small country towns continued to harbour what were perhaps the severest manifestations of social snobbery on the part of the middle classes, a characteristic which had provided grist for many Victorian novels. Here those from all walks of life found themselves thrust together in a confined area, their houses by no means as nicely segregated as in the larger towns and cities. Everyone knew everyone else and watched their activities closely, a situation which, for those who considered themselves on the way up, called for exaggerated attention to the subtleties of manners, dress and attitudes perceived to be correct for the desired social status. Women were the generators of this behaviour; for them gossip was a leisure activity and it was they who presided over the attempts to secure the right invitations, to make and maintain the right contacts and generally operate the nicer social distinctions, which in such circumstances assumed great sharpness and sensitivity.

In the little market towns, a rise in both the prosperity and numbers of the lower middle classes and the professionals faithfully reflected the national trend. It was assisted by the development of road motor transport after 1920, which brought with it a small boom in retail and leisure activity, since it became easier to get into such towns from the surrounding countryside, or to visit them from further afield.

World War 2 brought shattering changes. A large number of army and air force bases were established, many in the remotest areas, soon to be peopled with American, Commonwealth and other allied forces as well as the native soldiers and airmen. Thousands of evacuees, children and adults, of all social classes, sought refuge in the countryside from air attacks on cities. Farmers faced the problem of adapting themselves to a new labour force: a Women's Land Army recruited from every social class, then Italian and German prisoners of war. All this changed attitudes and accelerated social mixing to an unprecedented degree; entertainments, dances and similar activities, in which local civilians participated, became weekly instead of annual events. Soldiers and airmen were billeted on middle class households since these were most likely to have spare space; many more were given generous hospitality in middle class homes. Middle class country people who had not left for war service elsewhere found themselves with opportunities and excitement far headier than those available at any events organised by the Women's Institutes or the vicar's wife. For many, the 1940s saw an ending to much of the old unchanging and often narrow way of life, although the 'new countrymen' continued much as before, growing in number and influence.

## NOTES

1. Taylor, A. J. P., *English History 1914–1945*, (1970)
2. Masterman, C. F. G., *The Condition of England*, (1909)
3. Carr-Saunders, A. M., and Jones, D. Caradog, *A Survey of The Social Structure of England & Wales as illustrated by Statistics* (Second Edition 1937).
4. Before 1915, even for those unable to claim allowances, there was no tax on incomes below £160, a level which exempted over ninety three per cent of the occupied population. For the one million affected, the direct tax rate before 1915 was 1s 2d in the £ above £3,000 a year, 9d from £160 to £3,000. There was also a supertax of 2d in the £ on incomes over £5,000.
5. eg by Rowntree, B. Seebohm, in his *Poverty: A Study of Town Life*, (1901).
6. For a thorough study of the plotlands phenomenon see Hardy, Dennis and Ward, Colin, *Arcadia for All: The Legacy of a Makeshift Landscape*, (1984)
7. Bowley, A. L., and Stamp, J., *The National Income 1924* (1927).
8. See the author's *Semi-Detached London*, (1973).
9. Chapman, Agatha L., *Wages & Salaries in the United Kingdom 1920–38*, (1953).
10. Marsh, David C., *The Changing Social Structure of England and Wales 1871–1961*, (1965).
11. Quoted by Saunders and Jones, op cit (note 3)
12. Marsh, op cit (note 10).
13. Although firm data about the origins of recruits to these occupations in the 1900s and 1910s is hard to find, family history research and Hugh McLeod's analysis of the occupations of fathers of lower middle class grooms in marriage registers (see Cossick, Geoffrey, (ed.) *The Lower Middle Classes*

*in Britain 1870–1914*, (1977), both suggest that the majority came from the 'respectable' working class.

14. Dunlop, Sir John, *The Pleasant Town of Sevenoaks* (1964)
15. Cole, G. D. H., and Postgate, Raymond, *The Common People 1746–1946* (1949).
16. His reference to a clerk's starting salary of 7s 6d a week (£19.50 a year), whilst poetically expressed, was well behind the times. In the 1930s a secondary school leaver could expect at least £50 a year in London, perhaps £35–40 outside. In London, male civil service clerks started at £85.
17. Saunders and Jones, op cit (note 3).
18. Bourne, George, *Change in the Village* (1912).
19. Bourne (op cit) attempts an assessment of these and carefully notes the attitudes of each group to the other.

CHAPTER 2

# PAYING FOR THE LIFE STYLE

From the start of the century up to World War 1, when average adult male industrial earnings rose only to £75 a year, the incomes of the middle classes ranged from that level to around £5,000*. The highest rewards went mostly to judges and the best barristers and were not typical; by around 1913 the predominant salaried groups were averaging only £340 a year.

The group with incomes up to around £500 formed the majority and it is possible to look at their outlay in some detail. In London, where housing costs always tended to be higher than elsewhere, substantial four-bedroom, two/three-reception room suburban houses in lower middle class areas like Eltham Park, Bowes Park, Wanstead, Ilford or Lewisham could be had at rents of £35–52 a year inclusive of local authority rates. Such houses could also be purchased on a four and a half per cent mortgage with annual payments of £26–35 after handing over an initial cash deposit of a similar amount. Before 1914 the furnishing of a small three-bedroomed house might be decently achieved for no more than £100.

From such places as those just mentioned, Third Class railway season tickets to the West End or City would cost between £7 and £9 a year, Second Class £9–13 and First £11.5s to £17. For a family with two children and a living-in maid, lighting, cooking and heating costs would absorb another £10–11 a year, house repairs perhaps £6, food and household items a minimum of say £63 (but flexible upwards), clothes (another flexible item) a minimum of £22 to £25, doctor, dentist and holiday extras say £4 to £6 (in the hope that all three would not make demands in the same year), insurance (of life and effects) £8–10, the living-in maid around £12–£16 in wages, plus her food at about £26. From this we arrive at a minimum total outlay of £193. Assuming an income of £300 a year, such a family would pay no income tax, so there would be a substantial margin for such options as private education, more expenditure on food and clothes, a living-in cook (say £16–30 a

---

* Some details of typical earnings are given at Appendix A

year), more comfortable Second or First Class commuting and such unallocated items as reading matter, entertainment, gifts, tobacco and drink, and lunches in town. Even after providing for such extras, the £300 a year man would have something left to put aside for contingencies or major purchases.

At £500 and above, a better house, perhaps detached, with four or more bedrooms as well as a maid's room, could be had at a rental of £60–£120 a year. Those receiving £800 or more could contemplate even larger houses; a full time gardener with boy helper and garden supplies (say £150 in all); and such potent status symbols as a carriage and groom (£130–150). With the latter, they would attain the enviable classification 'carriage folk'.

Those families with incomes of £150 a year or less, a group which included most clerks, could reduce their outlay by taking more modest accommodation. In the London area this ranged from two-bedroom 'half houses' at £18 a year to two-and three-bedroom terrace houses in mixed lower middle class and working class areas such as Tottenham, Edmonton, Lewisham, Willesden, or Walthamstow at £24 to £26 a year[1]. Outside London, rents would be a few pounds lower than those mentioned.

It will be appreciated that households on the very lowest rungs of the middle class ladder (say those with incomes under £200 a year) might not be able to afford, let alone accommodate, a living-in servant. Nor could they find money for private education. Many such people would be newly-wed and childless couples able to improve their financial situation by taking in a lodger who would use the second bedroom and share their breakfasts and dinners, contributing perhaps another £26–30 a year. This arrangement was of course facilitated by the fact that the wife was almost always at home all day.

## Middle Class Money: 1915–40

By 1926, with the domestic economic disturbance caused by the war settling down, the cost of living index was falling, although still at 172 compared with 100 in 1914. Salaries, stipends and professional fees had by no means always been adjusted in line with the higher prices of the 1920s. Since the first war budget of late 1915, taxation was also hitting the middle class harder; those paying 1s 2d in the £ in 1913–14 were having to find six shillings by 1918–19. The tax threshold had been lowered to £130 despite inflation and almost eight million had been brought into the tax net by 1919–20. Those on £2,000 a year or more suffered the worst punishment. These high rates of tax were modified during the 1920s, the take falling after 1923 to an average of 4s 3d in the £. By 1938 a man on £500 a year was still only paying just under ten per cent of his income in direct taxation. From the mid 1920s until the end of the 1930s married men with three children paid no tax at all for earned incomes up to £350 and even at £1,000 a year were called upon to sacrifice only about eight per cent. Indirect taxes on tobacco, alcohol etc as well as death duties rose steeply after 1915. When the shoe did pinch, economies tended to be made in two treasured areas of the middle class life style – servant keeping and private education.

In the mid to late 1920s, as Appendix A shows, typical middle class salaries ranged from around £180 (starting salaries for junior clerks were as low as £45 to £60) to £10,000 or more. This was at a time when unskilled labourers were averaging £130–145 a year and skilled workers up to £200 or more.

| | *LONDON* | *Towns over 50,000 population* | *Towns under 50,000* |
|---|---|---|---|
| | £ | £ | £ |
| Rent and rates | 82 (18.4%) | 60 (14.3%) | 60 (13.6%) |
| Fuel and lighting | 18 (4%) | 19 (4.5%) | 22 (5%) |
| Food, housekeeping, service | 186 (41.8%) | 180 (42.9%) | 186 (42%) |
| Clothes | 41.10s (9.3%) | 48 (11.4%) | 50 (11.3%) |
| Doctor, dentist, chemist | 7 (1.6%) | 10 (2.4%) | 10 (2.3%) |
| Insurance | 23 (5.2%) | 25.10s (6.1%) | 25 (5.6%) |
| Holiday, clubs, car, leisure | 39.10s (8.9%) | 35 (8.3%) | 46.10s (10.5%) |
| Subscriptions, charities | 4.10s (1%) | 5 (1.2%) | 6 (1.4%) |
| Alcohol & tobacco | 7.10s (1.7%) | 10 (2.4%) | 13 (2.9%) |
| Newspapers, stamps | 4 (0.9%) | 4 (0.9%) | 5 (1.1%) |
| Fares (excluding holidays) | 17 (3.8%) | 8.10s (2%) | 4 (0.9%) |
| Repairs, renewals, sundries | (3.4%) | 15 (3.6%) | 15 (3.4%) |
| | £445 | £420 | 442.10s |

It will be noticed that there is no mention of expenditure on education. Jones admitted that no safe general conclusion could be drawn on this category since the returns in his sample were so few and the experience so varied. A very high proportion had no children of school age.

If married but without children, those at the top of the tree, earning say £10,000 a year would retain just over two thirds (£6,986.5s) after paying income tax. But the number with large incomes fell slightly between the wars. In the £2,000–5,000 bracket there were 63,275 taxpayers in 1924–5 but only 61,849 in 1933–4; in the same period the £5,000–£10,000 group fell from 16,940 to 13,715 [2].

How was this middle class money spent? In his 1928 paper[3], D. Caradog Jones shows that in 1926, the average annual expenditure of a group of married professional men with salaries around £455 was distributed as shown in the table opposite.

A major item of interest in these figures is the variation under different heads according to location. Whilst it is no surprise to see the relatively high cost of housing and fares in London compared to elsewhere, it is interesting that expenditure on other items in small towns brings the total annual cost of living in this category close to that of London. This Jones ascribes to higher distribution costs, lack of retail competition and a difference in the standard of living (more 'keeping up appearances' under the closer social scrutiny of small town life). With the growth of the multiples and an increase in the efficiency of retail trading and distribution, it seems likely that the first two factors were already becoming weaker by the late 1930s.

Individual late 1920s budgets for incomes of £300 and £500 are given in detail at Appendix A2. As usual, after food and household expenses, the repayments on the house purchase loan show up as the next largest item. During the 1920s building societies generally adhered to the 'safe rule' that these, together with local authority rates, should not exceed a quarter of the borrower's regular net income. The minimum salaries to sustain owner occupation in London and the south east were those in the group £4.10s–£5.10s a week, just enough to meet mortgage repayments of 18s to £1 a week (£46.16s–£52 a year plus rates of say £7.16s to £15.12s). Such an outlay would procure a small semi or terrace block unit selling at £500 to £575. Those earning around £350 (say a male teacher) could afford to repay at £1.8s a week (£72.16s a year), a sum which would secure a reasonably spacious semi priced at £850. Furniture, still relatively low in real cost because it was produced by cheap labour intensively-used, might require between £230 and £300 for such houses, and was now generally available on the easy payment system[4].

There is some evidence that during the 1920s, the upper and middle sections of the middle classes were not living quite so well as they were in the early 1910s, at any rate in London and the south east. The years between 1919 and 1932 brought what seemed to some a degree of hardship compared to their pre 1914 experience. Those affected were in the income bracket £300 – £600 a year, people such as head and senior teachers, bank managers, accountants, civil service Executive Officers, and chemists and professional engineers in mid career. Writing in 1928, Mrs C S Peel demonstrates[5] that a £300 a year London family with two young children, although still paying no income tax, were almost £146 a year worse off than a family with the same income in 1914. The reason for this was mostly the steep rises in the cost of food, clothes and housing. That she was able to make such a comment is evidence that incomes of this group had fallen behind price inflation. In a similar comparison of the purchasing power of a £500 income in 1914 and 1928, she shows the latter as just over £234 worse off. Neither of her specimen 1928 budgets (Appendix A) allows any margin for a living-in servant or school fees. Her comments on the latter omission provide an interesting reflection of middle class sensitivity on this issue:

> . . . it would not be fair to ignore this question, for it is one which falls very heavily on the middle class, for it must be remembered that a sound education to at least matriculation standard is required if the children are to maintain themselves in the same social grade as their parents.

She concludes that up to 1914 the children of a £300 a year family would have been educated at a 'good secondary or grammar school' with tuition fees of £9.9s a year, although these could have been avoided if the child won a scholarship. Up to 1914 those with 'various social or other objections' to state primary schools would have been able to afford what she calls the 'dubious' educational advantages of a private preparatory school. She adds that up to 1914 the children of a £500 a year family 'went naturally to a good [private] preparatory school, thence to a second class public school' (i.e. a second rank private school for children over 12–13). In 1928, we are told, the £300 a year family would have no margin for educational purposes and private schools were out, especially as 'the struggle to keep them during holidays and clothe them respectably is terrific'. Similarly, the £500 family in 1928 could not afford the 'preparatory-second class public school' education route for their children. She tells us that as 'The school fees are up 70 to 100 per cent, and the margin of income for this purpose is extremely small', the children must attend state schools, the universities being 'absolutely barred to them unless they are exceptionally brilliant and can earn their fees in scholarships'. Even then, some education authorities 'make the grave mistake of refusing scholarships to the children of parents whose incomes are above working class standards'. Her conclusion is that this squeezing of middle class budgets was leading to a very definite lowering of the educational standards of 'a very important section of the community . . . that used to supply a good, solid, well-educated core to the centre of society'. All this had to be seen against the background of another problem – 'enormously increased doctor's fees – ' illness could be 'a nightmare which may cripple them financially for years'.

With hindsight we can see that Mrs Peel's assessment of a fall in middle class living standards was perhaps a little overdrawn – it overlooks for example the accumulation of wartime savings, which could have been used to pay for private education; such savings were receiving a generous rate of interest from the Treasury through the 1920s. In any case, her 'hardships' were short-lived. Matters were improving even as she wrote. By 1929 average real income per head was ten per cent higher than in 1924 and the cost of living index (1914 = 100) stood at 164 compared with 249 in 1920. These improvements continued: taking 1929 as 100, the cost of living index had dropped to 85 by 1933 and the prices of consumption goods and services stood at 90. By 1937 the standard of living of those employed was thirty per cent higher than in 1914. But for those in the middle class dependent on fees which related directly to the level of their professional activity there was another bad patch in the peak depression years 1929–32. After 1932 things began to look up for all who were working. Prices fell more quickly than salaries, even taking into account that central and local government and railway employees suffered pay cuts between 1928 and 1935. With the onset of the world economic depression, imports, including food, became very cheap and because there were still substantial British investments overseas, there was no need to cut imports of cheap food when British exports declined. In a few words, from the beginning of the 1930s, more could be bought with less money. In another book, written in 1933, Mrs Peel was thus able to suggest that 'given clever management' it was possible to 'provide plain food of the kind to which middle class people are now accustomed' at 10s per head per week, which meant that costs in this important area were again comparable with the pre-World War I years[6].

The rise in real income was an important factor in the boom in private house construction which took off at this time. Although the cost of living again advanced after 1933 as world prices rose with economic recovery, and although domestic prices were pushed up by rearmament after 1936, real wages fell only slightly.

Within this general picture of middle class prosperity, there were some who were not doing so well. Small shopkeepers had first felt the wind of competition from large stores and food and footwear multiples at the beginning of the century and this threat continued to grow in strength. In 1932 it was estimated that the average annual turnover of small shops in Britain was below £2,000[7]. From this it can be assumed that there were shopkeepers with a smaller net income than the lowest paid workers (the agricultural labourers) although unlike them, the tradesman could live on overdrafts. Again this situation needs to be viewed in the light of the substantial savings many would have accumulated in 1914–18, savings which, if invested in Government bonds and loans, were receiving generous rates of interest through the 1920s. Even so there is little doubt that here we have a depressed category of the lower middle class; and as the 1930s advanced, many of these small shopkeepers were to face increasing pressure from the expanding multiples. There were other hard cases, not least those so damaged mentally and physically in the carnage of World War I that they were unable to realise their full earning potential.

In the middle and late 1930s, when unskilled labour was commanding around £135 a year, middle class incomes were not significantly different from those of the previous decade (Appendix A), ranging from the clerks' average of around £190–217 to £15,000 or more. At this time only some twenty two per cent of the population earned over £250 a year, and a mere 500,000 or so received over £685 gross. This last privileged group included the experienced general practitioners and all civil servants in the 'First Division' (Principals and above), but not members of parliament. The latter, most of them, then as now, with other sources of income, had to rub along on their original 1911 salary of £400 until 1937, when they voted themselves an increase to £500.

Although the continuation of the wartime freezing of rents had virtually killed the construction of small houses for renting, thousands of new houses were being erected for sale, at a time when building costs were low, when cheap capital for construction was available and mortgages were easily obtained at very low rates of interest. Between 1919 and 1939, according to Marian Bowley's careful calculations, 3,997,700 new houses were erected in England & Wales, 2,886,000 of them by private enterprise. Almost all the latter were for the middle class owner-occupier. This building boom, reaching its peak in 1935, met a rising demand stimulated by the increased real income per head in the middle classes and the upsurge in the number of (smaller) households after 1920. Although the bulk of new construction was concentrated in prosperous London and the south east, similar new suburbs or estates of speculatively-built small middle class houses were appearing in the 1930s around cities and towns throughout the United Kingdom, all in much the same building styles and with similar room sizes and levels of accommodation.

30

In the London area, in 1934–7, typical mortgage repayments were £26 a year for a tiny two reception room, two bedroomed terrace property (sale price £395); £54.12s for a £799 semi with three bedrooms, two reception rooms and garage space; £66.11s 2d for a spacious £995 semi with three bedrooms, two reception rooms and a garage; and £70.4s for a small detached three-bedroomed house selling at £1,099[8]. Very broadly, by the early 1930s, the building society mortgage system had been developed, thanks to favourable economic circumstances, to the point where anyone with a secure salary of around £190 or above could aspire to house ownership[9]. An advertisement of 1934 suggested that a salary of £234 would secure a £675 three-bedroom, one-reception room house; £260 one with three bedrooms and two reception rooms selling at £699; £312 a semi costing £799 with three bedrooms, two reception rooms and garage space; and £364 a spacious semi with similar accommodation plus a garage[10].

Most of those with regular incomes under £500 a year used the speculative builder/building society mortgage route to home ownership, those with the lower range of salaries securing terrace block units and semis and those with incomes of £350–400 small detached houses selling at prices up to around £1,200. With an income of £500–600 or above, a detached house of some quality could be obtained, costing £1,500 or more in the London area and £1,000 upwards elsewhere.

The enormous output of private enterprise house builders between the wars, almost three millions, and some seventy two per cent of the total build, was thus readily accessible to the expanding middle classes and a very substantial shift into home ownership resulted, especially among the lower middles and most notably in London and the south east and the midlands. By 1950, 29 per cent of the housing stock of England & Wales was owner-occupied, compared with 10 per cent in 1914. The vast majority of these house owners at both dates can be regarded as middle class.

Budgets in the 1930s and 1940s reflected the relatively low real cost of housing. In 1938 a speculative house-building firm suggested a feasible budget for a married lower middle class couple without children receiving £221 a year and purchasing a £625 London suburban semi-detached house with a £65 cash deposit. The house had two reception rooms, a tiny kitchen, two main bedrooms and a single bedroom and it was apparently assumed that basic furniture had already been bought at say £160–200[11]). The details given were as follows (shillings and pence have been decimalised to facilitate comparisons) –

31

|  | £ |
| --- | --- |
| Mortgage | 37.96 |
| Rates, local & water | 12.48 |
| Electricity & Gas | 5.20 |
| Coal (for house heating) | 6.50 |
| Fares to work and newspapers | 19.76 |
| Housekeeping (food etc) | 91.00 |
| Clothes | 19.50 |
| Cinema and leisure | 9.10 |
| Savings for holidays, doctors etc | 19.50 |
| Total | 221.00[12] |

Even allowing for the fact that a new house would incur minimal upkeep costs, this is a very tight budget indeed and the arrival of children would impose a severe strain. Steady advancement of salary in real terms would be an essential factor in maintaining even this modest standard of living. The fact that such a budget could be presented as realistic is evidence of the significant reductions in the real cost of housing, food and clothes that had occurred since the 1920s.

An analysis of expenditure patterns at higher levels of income, using returns from a sample of approximately equal numbers of civil servants, local government officers and teachers with salaries over £250 a year, a group described as 'broadly representative of the middle class and in particular of salary earners as a whole', was carried out in 1938–9 by Philip Massey[13]. Some details from this survey are given at Appendix A2 and it is of particular interest in showing how the higher income groups diverted their additional marginal expenditure into such items as private education, alcoholic drinks, reading matter, insurance and pension provision and domestic help, thereby providing a useful confirmation of the lifestyle aspirations of the middle class of the period.

## NOTES

1. Figures in this and the two preceding paragraphs from Peel, Mrs C. S., *How We Lived Then, 1914–1918* (1929) ('Pre-war' budget); also oral evidence of the author's father, W. A. Jackson, and EN, 4 September 1912.
2. Reports of the Commissioners of HM Inland Revenue (Great Britain & Northern Ireland) 1924–5 and 1933–4, quoted by Saunders & Jones, *op cit* (note 3, Chapter 1).
3. Jones, D. Caradog, *The Cost of Living of a Sample of Middle-Class Families*, a paper read before the Royal Statistical Society, 15 May 1928 (Journal of the RSS, xci, part iv).

4. For example in 1927 the well-known central London furniture store of Hamptons offered to furnish a small house for £235. At the same time they were selling a dining room suite in carved oak, consisting of pull-out table, sideboard, six chairs and carver chair, for just under £34 (advertisement in *The Play Pictorial* July 1927).

5. Peel, *op cit* (note 2).

6. Peel, Mrs C. S., *Life's Enchanted Cup: An Autobiography (1872–1933)* (1933).

7. Neal, Lawrence E., *Retailing and The Public*, (1932).

8. Figures from advertisements in EN 1934–7. House prices (and consequently mortgages) were a little lower outside south east England, principally because house building was labour-intensive and labour costs were lower.

9. For more on the economic and financial background to the private enterprise housing boom and details of house prices and mortgage facilities, see the author's *Semi-detached London: Suburban Development, Life and Transport 1900–39* (1973).

10. G. T. Crouch Ltd (London), EN, 13 June 1934.

11. In 1938 the West London department store of Whiteleys suggested they could furnish two reception rooms, two bedrooms, hall, bathroom and kitchen of a small house, including cutlery, crockery, bed linen, curtains and carpets for £160, or £10.10s deposit and twenty four monthly payments of £7 (advertisement in EN, 20 August 1938).

12. Figures from New Ideal Homesteads advertisement, EN 13 July 1938.

13. Massey, Philip, *The Expenditure of 1,360 Middle Class Households in 1938–9*, a paper read before the Royal Statistical Society, 16 June 1942 (Journal of the RSS, cv, part iii).

CHAPTER 3

# NOT PROPERLY DETACHED
# BUT TRYING

In this and the following chapter we touch upon a matter of supreme importance for the middle classes, one to which, as we have seen, they were prepared to allocate a significant part of their income. To them the house was a principal status symbol, a matter deserving of financial sacrifice, carefully chosen in relation to the occupier's estimate of his present and potential social standing. It was seen as a refuge and sanctuary from the cares and stresses of the world outside, a place of security for wife and children, which symbolised the central importance of family and home life in the class ethos. As one writer for a middle class readership in the mid 1930s put it: 'a modern well-equipped home is a worthwhile possession . . . it gives a sense of security and comfort and intimacy essential to real family life'[1].

Segregation, privacy and individuality were the principal priorities for the ideal middle class home. If possible it should also be placed in a rural-romantic setting, or at least stimulate the imagination in that direction.

These feelings and priorities about the family house were accepted just as enthusiastically by the lower middles as by the rest, in their case creating demands which could only be met by compromises. It is primarily with this sub-class and those compromises that this chapter will be concerned.

Above all, the middle classes desired to dwell surrounded by their social equals (or slight betters), separated from all others. An important attraction of outer suburban and extra-urban life was the possibility of escape from the shoulder-rubbing proximity with the less attractive aspects of the working class, something which could not be avoided in the central streets of the cities and towns and many of the older inner suburbs. And that escape achieved, they wanted an environment comfortingly free from the embarrassments and discomforts of living among any but those they saw as being of the social standing they wished themselves to maintain, whose behaviour would be predictable and understood. Developers were well aware of this and planned accordingly. At Ruislip Manor, Middlesex in 1912, Associated Garden Estates Ltd., clothing their policy in the language of architecture, avowed,

... although the company aims at introducing all classes into the community, it is not intended to indiscriminately mix all classes of houses together; different portions of the estate lend themselves to different types and sizes of houses. Thus one of the neat village houses which are being erected near Ruislip station would be completely lost amid the wooded heights of Northwood, which demand more stately architecture, with its more massive setting.[2]

The desire to be apart, unsullied by contact with lower orders, was often most strongly felt at the lower end of the spectrum, the one in which people, particularly women, experienced the highest degree of insecurity as to status. It occasionally manifested itself in extreme measures. In 1926 the residents of a lower middle class estate at Bromley, Kent erected a 2.14 metre high wall topped by broken glass to prevent access into their area by the working class inhabitants of the London County Council's new Downham cottage estate. Eleven years later at Cutteslowe, a northern suburb of Oxford, the proximity of a lower middle class estate to council housing, and the fact that it provided a short cut to local amenities for the council tenants, led to the erection of high brick walls across two of the middle class residential roads. Both sets of barriers disappeared during or shortly after World War 2, crumbling beneath the pressures of wartime expediency and changing social attitudes. During the late 1940s and early 1950s there were many examples of council housing projects filling up vacant land on middle class estates where work had stopped at the outbreak of war. Although no more barriers appeared, those middle class houses nearest the newcomers, or overlooking them, would sell less readily and at figures well below the price of similar houses further away. An experienced estate agents never tire of repeating, there are three things which guarantee the sale of a middle class house at a good price: position, position and position.

Whilst segregation at various social levels was not a problem, and was widely available, individuality and privacy were more difficult and more expensive to provide. They could only be satisfactorily achieved with detached houses, set well apart, preferably in spacious parkland type layouts. However, as we shall see, some attempt was made by those catering for the cheaper end of the market to pay at least some superficial attention to these demands.

The innate desire for individuality, proclaiming 'this is my home and no-one else has anything quite like it' was particularly important for the insecure lower middles, who did not want their house to have about it any hint or suggestion of the standardised and plain-faced council 'dwelling', nor, in the twenties and thirties, anything to remind them of the dreary repetitiveness of the inner suburban terraces which they were abandoning to the respectable element of the working class.

Privacy was of course basic to the vision of the home as a means of withdrawal from the harsh realities of the outside world into a familiar, controllable and secure environment. It was also important in relation to the need to demonstrate outward decorum, respectability and perceived social status, whatever the true state of affairs within. Once again these were matters of particular concern for the lower middles. In the 19th century many of the prosperous and successful in the middle classes had successfully achieved both privacy and individuality to a substantial degree; in the 20th, for the majority, compromises were necessarily the order of the day, especially for the numerous and impecunious lower middles.

Compromises and deceits were also much in evidence for this group in relation to the last of the middle class home-seeker's priorities: the nostalgic longing for a rural-romantic, cottagey setting. The origins of this perhaps deserve rather lengthier consideration.

## The Country Home Image

Many of the early 20th century urban lower middles grew up and began their married lives in terrace housing of one type or another, most of it rented rather than owner-occupied. But even before 1914, new types of terrace and semi-detached houses were appearing for this market. Owner occupation of units in short terrace blocks (providing more of the superior end-terrace houses) and above all, of semis, became the general rule after 1920. The ubiquity and popularity of the cottagey 2½ bedroomed semi-detached house design[3], which became an attainable ideal for many thousands of lower middles in the between-war years, cannot be ascribed simply to a revulsion for the dull, dark monotony and gregarious proximity of the inner suburban terrace units of 1890–1914, or even to a reaction against the greyness and horror of World War I. It went deeper than that.

In their emigration from the drab inner ring terraces to the bright new suburbs of the 1920s and 1930s, the lower middles were emulating those further up the social ladder who, as the railways had begun to provide the necessary umbilical chords in the 19th century, had set out to acquire 'a place in the country' within easy reach of the expanding urban centres. Around London in particular, this movement of the more prosperous members of the middle class to the outer suburbs and beyond had perceptibly accelerated in the first decade and a half of the new century, when erosion of inner suburban business by the newly-arrived electric tramcar and motor omnibus drove the railway companies to develop longer-distance residential services.

Encouraged by several influences, the old dream of having a country home whilst retaining contact with all the pleasures and conveniences of urban life, having taken hold in the minds of the lower middle class, soon came to be seen as a practical possibility. Many of their parents or grandparents were country people who had drifted into the cities in search of wider employment choice and higher pay. As domestic servants for the upper middle class or the aristocracy, some had gained first hand experience of the delights of comfortable and civilised living in semi-rural or rural surroundings. At the fireside or on summer walks, the children who were to become the lower middle class homeseekers of the twenties or thirties heard their grandparents' or parents' recollections of country life, memories rendered all the more attractive by the passage of time. When holidays came round, few lower middle class families of the turn of the century period were able to afford more than the briefest breaks away from home but at Bank Holidays and weekends, and on days taken off from work, many trips were made to the countryisde by wagonette, train, open-top motor bus or electric tram, for fruit-picking, picnics, cottage teas, rambles, haymaking and other rural delights. Sunday and day school children were taken out to the rural fringes of the large cities for summer 'treats' and as they grew up, they too ventured into the country around the city edges on their bicycles or by public transport. Such trips to the rural edges were also a natural favourite with lovers, who shared dreams of 'let's live here' as they gazed about them through a romantic mist. And at weekends, office and shop workers invaded the semi-rural fringes to play football, cricket and tennis on the sports grounds provided by their employers.

All this proved a powerful formative influence. Much of the city-edge countryside visited in a happy and relaxed mood was already thinly populated by the more privileged early middle class settlers. Their spacious villas, red-bricked and red-tiled, or plain light-washed, set in generous plots of a half-acre or more, surrounded by shrubberies and lawns, excited the romantic imagination of the pleasure-seeking lower middles and potential lower middles. Such delightful private retreats, half-hidden from the road, with their fine views of distant hills and woods, generated images and aspirations not easily subdued. Here indeed was something to dream of achieving; if not a villa, at any rate a small house or cottage?

And, from around 1905, if any further stimulation was required, the desire to move to a country home with all modern conveniences within easy reach of the workplace in large town or city was sedulously fostered by the publicity of those railway companies anxious to build up their outer suburban traffic, particularly on routes around London and beyond into Buckinghamshire, south Essex, outermost Surrey, west Kent, and much of Sussex.

## Tunnel Backs and Better

So much for the dream; but if we look at the reality, we find the majority of lower middle class housing in the decade and a half before 1915 was still being built to the urban style terrace designs of the last decades of the 19th century, although increasingly a bathroom and indoor w.c. were now being included. In places where land was relatively cheap, streets of identical 'double-fronted' houses with four to six bedrooms and frontages of 9.14–16.46 metres were erected, usually in terraces, occasionally semi-detached. Such houses sold at £330–665 freehold in London, rather less elsewhere. There were also cheaper versions, with a central front entrance into a narrow hall, dining room and kitchen on one side and drawing room and scullery on the other, the two main reception rooms looking on to the street. Above, these had a bathroom and w.c. and four bedrooms, two of them quite small, but enough for a family of three or four children and a maid. Around the edges of London in the 1900s this terrace type could be bought for as little as £285, or £298 leasehold (999 years ground rent at £5.16s a year), according to whether the customer wanted a bay window one side or both, two bays providing a significant increase in social status. For £303 and a ground rent of £6.20 the purchaser secured all the advantages of an end of terrace position, with side passage to the garden and back door[4].

Far more common were the hundreds of miles of dull terraces built to the 'tunnel back' plan, equally monotonous in their ceaseless repetition of a standard design and elevations but ingenious in providing the maximum number of houses in the available space, using the narrowest possible plot width (4.88–5.18 metres). This optimisation of land use and profit was achieved by placing the main rooms one behind the other, extending the house lengthways to the maximum extent.

Entrance to this very common type of lower middle class house was through a glazed tile porchway into a narrow hall, lit only by the stained glass in the front door, from which the stairs rose after some 1.53–1.83 metres. Alongside this hallway was the sitting room and behind it a dining room. Normally of approximately equal size, these two rooms were frequently separated by a folding partition which enabled them to be thrown into one should occasion demand. In the author's grandfather's house in North London this happened only once in some forty years, for a wedding reception, but in others nearby the two rooms were always used as one large sitting room, the extra space proving useful for the near-obligatory piano.

Next to the dining room was a dark and narrow passage, leading to a living room or kitchen. This room was starved of natural light and had a depressing outlook, since its windows faced those of the same room of the neighbouring house across a very narrow yard (the 'tunnel' of 'tunnel-back'). Behind the kitchen, and in line with it, there was a scullery equipped with pantry and coal cupboard, these flanked on the yard side by an outside w.c., intended for the servant's use. Such houses often had a transverse passageway between the dining room and kitchen which gave access to the yard and garden, also reached by a door in the scullery. Refuse bins could be removed and coal delivered through this passage, avoiding any invasion of the kitchen/living room.

Upstairs, at the front, the tunnel-back houses had either one large bedroom across the full width of the house or two smaller ones side by side. A narrow landing served two further bedrooms, a bathroom, a w.c. and a boxroom, all placed one behind the other, with one of the bedrooms at the back over the scullery. The front garden, necessarily minute, had little room for anything but a privet hedge screen to discourage passers-by from peeping into the sitting room. At the rear, the plot conformation gave a narrow chicken-run of a garden, usually a small patch of grass bordered by flower beds retained by wooden planks.

Such houses were very adaptable; they could be operated with or without one living-in servant and were not too difficult to divide to accommodate two small households, one upstairs and one down. With slight variations of plan, they were built in large numbers for the lower middle class in London and other cities, selling at £250–£300 leasehold (annual ground rent £5–£6) or up to £450 freehold. Many were also available to rent.

There were other varieties of terrace housing, including more spacious types, with an additional attic floor, suitable for servants' bedrooms or a children's nursery. Landlords building to this pattern in Streatham, south London, in 1902–6 strictly controlled the middle class tone of their estate by refusing tenancies to anyone in 'a uniformed occupation'[5] (presumably other members of the working classes were not considered likely to apply).

A few words should be said about the interior use and appearance of these terrace houses. Most families would keep the sitting room immaculate, reserving its use to weekends when visitors were expected, or special occasions. This room was 'front' in more than one sense; it was into here that important visitors such as a doctor or clergyman would be invited to step and it strove to demonstrate the social status to which the family aspired. To this end, builders helpfully installed battery-operated bell pushes by the fireplace, to give the impression that a servant was employed or would soon be recruited. Furniture would normally consist of a sofa, two armchairs and perhaps two or three upright matching chairs, sold as a suite, together with a piano, occasional tables and a china cabinet, the latter displaying the family's best tea set and other treasures, most of them acquired as wedding presents. Although some firms, such as Heal's were beginning to sell furniture influenced by the Arts & Crafts movement, most families living in these houses chose reproduction; 'Sheraton', 'Queen Anne', or 'Adams' were all obtainable on hire-purchase.

The use made of the adjacent dining room, with its distant view of the garden through the gloomy passage-like yard, depended to some extent on the size of the family and of the kitchen and whether a servant was kept. Where there was no skivvy and the kitchen was of reasonable dimensions, it often served as the family living room, warmed by a coal fire for much of the year, its back-boiler heating water for the scullery and perhaps the bathroom, thus economising in coal. Especially if a servant were kept, the dining room would be used as the family eating and living room, furnished with heavy reproduction table, sideboard and chairs. Even if there were no maid, had the builder placed the back-boiler fire in this room and a solid fuel cooking range in the kitchen, this pattern of use would be confirmed.

Furnishing these lower middle class houses was not expensive. Manufactured by cheap labour, tables, chairs, beds and other items were sold competitively. To supplement what could be afforded, surplus items were handed down by the previous generations. In the decade and a half up to World War I, a dining room suite in solid fumed oak, including six chairs, table and sideboard, could be had for seven to ten pounds. Jacobean dark oak designs, which continued to be popular up to the 1940s, cost a little more, say around £15 for the same items, but for real quality, it would be necessary to pay up to £30 or more to furnish a dining room. An oak bedroom suite consisting of one chair, single wardrobe, washstand and dressing table could be obtained for eight to twelve pounds; another five pounds would be needed for a double bed, mattress, pillows and linen.

In general the internal decorations of these houses were in dark hues, chosen to hide grime and wear. Brown was a popular colour and deal woodwork was usually varnished and grained to disguise its appearance. Heavy cream or off-white lace curtains were draped over all the main windows, supplemented in the sitting room by velvet, damask or brocade drapes to add style. Curtains had particular importance here and in the front bedrooms in that they could be seen from the road and provided the astute lower middle class female eye with a ready means of judging the taste, income and status of the occupants. Half-dropped green Venetian blinds contributed further to the atmosphere of gloom, which was tolerated in the interests of maintaining the strictest privacy. No matter how close the house might be to the road, it was virtually impossible for an outsider to look in. Heavily-curtained windows, the almost unlit internal passage and the dark tunnel-back area, all tended to make these houses depressing in summer, if cosy in winter.

Not surprisingly, with their repetitive monotony and restricted outlook across a narrow street or yard (only two windows upstairs and one down had any sort of view of the garden), the tunnel-back terrace houses and their slightly larger terraced sisters offered no satisfaction to those hankering to fulfil the rural-romantic dream and lifestyle, even though some of them were briefly situated at the edge of the built-up area of a town or city.

It was the disappointment and discontent of the lower middles with this monotonous and dreary urban-style housing that caused them to give an enthusiastic welcome to the garden city and garden suburb movement, whose architects challenged the prevailing trend by providing informally-grouped, cottagey styles in a semi-rural setting. Between 1900 and 1914 some sixty garden city and garden suburb developments appeared in Britain, mainly inspired by the pioneer work of the architects Barry Parker and Raymond Unwin at Letchworth, the world's first garden city. Many of these developments were organised on a tenants' co-partnership basis and the majority were populated by the middle classes[6].

By the late 1900s the middle class marketing success of the garden city type of house was inspiring speculative builders to produce lighter, brighter and more attractive designs, both in the terrace and semi-detached styles. Although local authority byelaws caused these to be arranged in regular rows along the streets, there was occasionally an attempt to provide at least a nominal grass verge and some trees, in pale imitation of the garden city layouts. These houses had pebble-dashed or cement-washed walls and generous amounts of painted external soft wood to replace the dark bricks and stone copings and mullions of their predecessors. Art nouveau coloured glass and leaded panes sometimes appeared in their windows. Instead of tunnel-backs, their internal plan provided the main reception and bedrooms with a full and open outlook to the garden or road frontages. This rearrangement could only be achieved within economic limits by eliminating both the scullery and servant's outside w.c.; it was also necessary to reduce the size of the kitchen, move the coal shed to a separate structure near the back of the house and limit the bedroom accommodation to two rooms of medium size and one which would take only a single bed. With these changes commercial success as a lasting saleable design was therefore closely linked to the demand for smaller, 'servantless' lower middle class houses, something which did not appear in strength until the 1920s[7].

## The Classic Lower Middle Class Semi

This new plan thus became almost universal for the speculative builders' four, six, or eight-block terraces and the semi-detached houses of the between-war years. Architects were rarely involved in lower middle class housing but with a remarkably perceptive assessment of what would sell, builders settled for the new plan, providing elevations with varying degrees of cottagey charm in obeisance to the rural-romantic dream, making the product readily distinguishable from the stripped neo-Georgian of the architect-designed council cottage estates. As for the interior, the private enterprise providers of small houses in the 1920s and 1930s sought to offer a convenient layout with all modern amenities, the whole constructed in such a way that it could be marketed at a competitive price. Using the more or less standard plan, they succeeded well in achieving these objectives.

Facing the street and embellished by a tiny porch, the entrance hall of these houses was often smaller than that of the Edwardian tunnel-back predecessor and embraced the rise of the staircase. There was usually just about enough room to park baby's perambulator and squeeze around it. In some of the larger semis, builders would manage a slightly more spacious hall capable of being opened into one of the two reception rooms by pulling back glazed double doors, a refinement that was a pale reflection of the open-plan, 'central living-space' idea found in some contemporary detached houses.

Behind the hallway was an extremely small half-tiled kitchen, equipped with a larder cupboard. A room disarmingly called a 'kitchenette' in sales brochures and publicity, its dimensions were frequently such that it could not comfortably accommodate a busy mother and an active toddler at the same time. The two main reception rooms, often of more or less equal size, were set alongside hall, staircase and kitchen, that at the front normally selected to serve as what was by this time becoming known as the 'lounge'. The other, overlooking the garden, was the 'dining' or 'living' room. Very occasionally the scullery and outside servant's w.c. survived, incorporated in a single-storey extension jutting into the garden beyond the kitchen, which was then sometimes renamed the 'breakfast room'.

From the front door, the stairs led up to a constricted landing serving two main bedrooms placed directly above the reception rooms, reproducing the same equal size. There was a bathroom over the kitchen, space and cost limitations often requiring it to include the only w.c. in the house – an inconvenient compromise. At the front, over the hall, was a tiny third bedroom, often more accurately referred to as 'the boxroom'.

If their financial prospects possibly allowed, buyers would try to avoid the new short terrace block houses built to this plan, since despite some variety of decoration, lighter interiors and in some cases service roads providing rear access for coal deliveries and refuse removal, this type with its 4.57–4.88 metres frontage, was too closely reminiscent of its predecessors in the inner suburbs, particularly as regards proximity to immediate neighbours. Terrace blocks of the twenties and thirties were also often unattractively sited alongside main roads, where they could cheaply make use of existing service mains and sewers, and were also frequently to be found close to new industrial areas. Scope for individuality of design treatment was virtually non-existent. In contrast, the semi offered much: the possibility of superficial differences in design amongst adjacent houses; often a more spacious environment; and subtle indications of a perceptibly higher social status.

For both builder and purchaser, the interwar semi was an economical compromise and a brilliant design success, avoiding much of the gregarious intimacy of terrace life whilst providing some remnants of those characteristics of the detached house so much valued by the middle class – separation, individuality and privacy. It even provided scope for some slight realisation of the widely-shared romantic dream of a little country house of one's own, its extra plot width (a minimum of six metres to as much as 11 metres with garage space) providing a more ample garden, which the proud owner could just conceivably regard as his very own miniature country park. Sadly, although the new suburban estates of the twenties and thirties might at first have rural surroundings, these were often quickly built over, leaving the occupier encircled by street after

*Compact Furniture*
*for Bungalows, Flats*
*and Small Houses*

# WHITELEYS

*Furnish*
*from Income*
*at*
*Whiteleys*

**F**URNISHING Goods over £20 in value are supplied at actual CASH prices. Deposit— one tenth of the total value. Interest at 2% per annum only is added to the balance. Instalments are spread over 1, 2, or 3 years, according to the value of the goods selected. Furniture, Carpets, Linens, Curtains, China, Ironmongery, Turnery, etc., are all included under these favourable terms.

**T**HE search for furniture best suited for Bungalows, Flats, and the smaller houses now being built ends at Whiteleys, where a huge selection of compact yet "roomy" designs is available in our usual reliable quality.

**THE WARWICK.** New model Oak Bedroom Suite, finished rich Brown rubbed effect. Comprising 3-ft. Wardrobe, excellent carving, interior fitted shelf for hats; 3-ft. Dressing Chest, new design, drop centre, two long and two short drawers, upright oval swing mirror; 3-ft. Washstand, enclosed bottom, marble top, tile back. Also one cane-seated chair.

THE SUITE COMPLETE **£17 : 19 : 6**

*The Dressing Chest & Washstand may be had without the Wardrobe. Two Pieces £13 : 7 :6*

**THE CLEVEDON.** Solid Oak Bedstead, finished Dark Brown shade, substantially built and fitted wire spring mattress bottom. Single size, 3 ft. wide **£3 : 10 : 0**

**THE AVONDALE.** Reproduction Chair, finished Mellow Brown shade, wheel back, caned seat fitted with loose cushion, covered in Cretonne of pretty design **£2:17:6**

**CATALOGUE POST FREE** Write *for* Whiteleys Complete Furnishing Catalogue, the wonderful guide to house furnishing for every station in life—profusely illustrated and priced throughout.

*Carriage Paid on £5 orders in England or Wales; £10 orders to Scotland or Ireland*

**WM. WHITELEY LTD., QUEENS ROAD, LONDON, W.2**

Whiteley's bedroom furniture for the smaller middle class house, 1922 street of houses very similar in size and amenities to his own, so that he was left to make the best of any country or garden views he could get from his upstairs back windows.

With its slightly more generous frontage, the semi allowed the inclusion of wide bay windows to the front reception and bedroom and these were often separated by tile-hanging over a wood or breeze block partition. This design provided the builder with scope for a cheap, partly mass-produced form of construction; for the purchaser it made the house instantly distinguishable from the local authority designs of the period, the tile-hanging suggesting the vernacular rural architecture of Surrey, Sussex and Kent. Leaded lights in at least the front windows and creosoted barge boards nailed to the front gables were widely found, again providing distinction from the council dwelling and adding to the cottagey, nostalgic image at little cost to the builder. False half-timbering, seen everywhere on the new estates, proved immensely popular. It fulfilled the rural-romantic yearning as nothing else affordable could have done. Its potency had been identified as early as 1922 in *The Ideal Home* magazine, with the comment that 'The English half-timbered homestead seems to epitomise the traditions of the race'.

Lastly but by no means least, the semi was able to offer complete separation from the neighbour on one side, including a passageway through to the garden. This sideway had great social significance in that it perpetuated the hallowed middle and upper class practice of separating the family and social entrance from that used by servants, tradesmen and other lesser breeds within the law. Indeed it was normal in the twenties, thirties and forties to see quite modest semis and small detached houses with side gates conspicuously labelled 'Tradesmen', just in case such callers forgot their place and were tempted to go to the main door. On the other side of the house however, the usual design of semi brought the neighbour into the same close proximity as the terrace unit, often with an inadequately sound-proofed party wall which formed one side of both main reception and bedrooms. Only the tiny kitchen and third bedroom enjoyed complete isolation. In an effort to overcome this defect, for a slightly higher price, some builders provided a 'hallway to hallway' plan which left only one reception and one bedroom sharing the party wall[8]. An even better arrangement, frequently combined with a four bedroom plan, was the placing of the garages of each house in the centre of the block, giving complete 'detachment' to all rooms on the ground floor, with the party wall restricted to only two of the bedrooms.

Freehold prices of conventional 2½ bedroom semis varied considerably according to room sizes and to a lesser extent, location. There was also a considerable amount of competitive price-cutting amongst estate developers in new districts at the expense of quality. The price range in south east England in the 1920s was broadly £550–£1,250 and in the 1930s £450 to £1,200, whilst terrace block units of 2½ bedrooms sold at £395 upwards in the 1930s. In other areas of the country, prices were a little lower.

Whilst a few semis were built with four, five and even six bedrooms, commanding prices up to around £2,500, such very large designs were exceptional and their occurrence was related to the high price of land in those areas (usually in and around London) which the developers, wishing to maximise profit by building as many units to the acre as possible, judged the wealthier purchaser might find socially acceptable whilst being willing to sacrifice the advantages of a fully detached house for locational convenience (eg proximity to an Underground station), or some other attraction. Although these very large semis were sometimes advertised as having specific accommodation for a maid[9], by the mid 1920s the idea of a living-in servant in a semi was beginning to seem slightly incongruous.

Design variations of the semi arrangement included the 'chalet', which some speculative developers dotted about amidst standard semis; others, such as New Ideal Homesteads, planted them in monotonous rows along the building line each side of their estate roads. Although the conventional semi would frequently be given superficial elevational treatments to accentuate the difference between one house pair and the next, this was rarely attempted with chalets, perhaps because the design itself was thought sufficiently unusual. Chalets, with their characteristic roofs reaching down from the ridge to ground floor ceiling level, were a development of the 'semi-bungalow' (a bungalow with one room in its roofspace). They normally had two medium-sized bedrooms in the roofspace, one each side of a central staircase leading up from an entrance hall and main door at right angles to the roadway. The bathroom and w.c. were either placed in the roofspace or, inconveniently, alongside the hall. Many chalets had a small room on the ground floor in addition to the two equally-sized reception rooms and small kitchen. Where only two bedrooms were required by the occupiers, this room often served as a tiny study or 'den' for the head of the household. By the nature of their design, chalets incorporated large cupboard spaces under the sloping roofs at the outer sides of the bedrooms and in recent years they have proved much more amenable than the semi to easy extension, since extra rooms can be inserted by building above and around the long and steeply pitched roof. Such reconstruction, carried out in varying styles with little or no visual

46

appeal, tended to damage what was previously a slightly more pleasing elevation than that offered by the average pair of semis.

Until around 1920, bungalows (noticed in more detail in the next chapter) were normally detached buildings, used for a holiday or seaside retirement home, but in the next two decades, they found considerable popularity as a suburban house type and were frequently seen on new estates in semi-detached form, often with only two bedrooms and one reception room. Where land was cheap, some builders erected nothing else, finding that they sold well.

Another form of low cost middle class home, mostly confined to the London area, was the 'maisonette', usually sold freehold in the 1930s from £355 upwards. In external appearance not unlike large semis or spaciously-built short terrace blocks, these units contained two completely self-contained residences (normally with only two bedrooms and one reception room), one on each floor, the upper one usually reached by an external fireproof staircase at the side. Maisonettes were a development of the Edwardian 'half house'[10], a version of the tunnel-back which had the staircase partitioned off to give segregated access to a separate front door alongside that for the ground floor unit. Both half-houses and maisonettes necessarily had to make do with a narrower than normal back garden, little more than an untidy laundry-drying area. Along with the small blocks of conventional flats with communal porterage and central heating which are considered in the next chapter, maisonettes were popular with newly-weds, the childless and singles. Although up to date, bright and convenient, they were rarely given any cottagey treatment and with backs and sides made hideous by open staircases, they were almost as far from the Country Home Dream as the Edwardian terraces.

Before leaving the small lower middle class houses of the inter-war years, something must be said about how they were used and decorated. It was normal for the dining room to be adopted as the main living room, furnished with one or two armchairs and perhaps a small writing bureau as well as the usual dining table, chairs and sideboard. This room saw much activity, including the ironing and folding of laundry, which could not be easily accomplished in the confines of the little kitchen. Virtually no between-wars lower middle class houses had central heating and since this was the only room likely to be heated by a coal fire, the family would be found in it for much of the day during cold weather. At first, the fireplace in this room would have a back-boiler for the hot water supply, causing a fire to be kept burning for the greater part of the year (the alternatives were a gas geyser, or electric immersion heater in the hot water storage tank) but from around 1930, new houses of the type described were increasingly provided with solid-fuel slow-combustion hot water stoves made small enough to be placed in a corner of the kitchen.

Through to the 1940s or even later, many lower middle class households continued to restrict use of the sitting room to weekends and special occasions. With its plumply-upholstered 'three-piece suite' of two chunky armchairs and three-seater settee, it still served as a 'public' room, displaying status items and prized possessions (including family photographic portraits) to special visitors. Another function of this room was to provide an ostensibly vulnerable (and therefore 'respectable') refuge for teenage children when closeted with their current friend of the opposite sex.

Upstairs, the unheated bedrooms saw little daytime use, especially in winter, but as children grew older, they tended to retreat there, converting them into bed-sitting rooms and causing fuel bills to rocket upwards as they attempted to keep warm with electric or gas fires. Except for those rare cases where there was a good view at the front, the 'best' bedroom was usually that overlooking the garden, since its occupants were insulated to some extent from street noise.

In most types of middle class houses, detached as well as those considered here, 'period' designs of furniture, notably Jacobean and Georgian, remained popular because they tended to reinforce and complement the rural-romantic idiom of the exterior. More adventurous purchasers chose the simpler, 'functional' furniture styles of the Modern Movement, widely sold from 1928 onwards. 'Easy purchase' by instalments after optional payment of a small cash deposit (which would reduce the payments) became common practice in the retail furniture trade in the late 1920s, some large firms such Drage's building up their business entirely on this basis. With showrooms in London, Manchester and Birmingham, this firm advertised in 1929 that £75 worth of furniture (a sum just covering the main items for the sitting and dining rooms and one bedroom) could be had for fifty monthly payments of £1.10s, and would be delivered on first payment. No references were required and there was a 'free insurance policy'[11]. Despite the spread of such arrangements, there were still many in the middle classes who regarded anything but outright cash purchase as vaguely immoral, although strangely most were prepared to make exceptions when buying a house or a gas or electric cooker (the instalments for the latter items were painlessly extracted in the normal quarterly bills).

Graining of interior woodwork continued to be a feature of new houses up to 1940 though towards the end of the period it was often executed on a lighter base. Paint shades also tended to be lighter than hitherto, both on walls and woodwork, beige, ivory, sand and eau-de-nil becoming very popular. A combination of cream and black was regarded as the very latest in decor for internal woodwork in the late 1930s. For ease of cleaning, those areas of the condensation-prone kitchen and bathrooms not covered in white ceramic tiles were coated in glossy oil paints. The heavily-patterned wallpapers of the 1910s and 1920s gave way in the thirties to plain creams and browns, highlighted by jazzy 'art deco' borders and corners. Except in the hall, which in all but the cheapest houses was given a floor of polishable hardwood, the rough deal boards provided by the builder were covered with shiny linoleum, usually patterned, and resting on a base of old newspapers. On top of this, rugs and carpet squares were arranged. Since virtually all the houses had small casement windows, new designs of curtains had to be produced, usually in thin rayon, cotton or linen, and unlined, hanging close for privacy below a pelmet and drawn together at night.

Whilst the thousands of lower middle class families occupying these new suburban terrace blocks, semis, chalets and bungalows in the twenties and thirties often found themselves in less spacious accommodation than the Victorian and Edwardian housing they had left, the benefits of the move were substantial. They enjoyed vastly improved standards of living and hygiene, thanks to a healthier environment and to important amenities most experienced for the first time. These included electric light, heating and power for cleaning and other gadgets; an indoor w.c.; some built-in furniture; and a modern bathroom and kitchen with a constant supply of hot water. Gardens were larger than those of the older inner area terraces, with lengths normally from twenty five to thirty-one metres. The challenge of transforming a plot from rough grass and builder's rubble to something worthwhile tempted most new home owners at least temporarily into greater open air activity, satisfying creative drives suppressed in the dull routines of office life. Inside, these houses were altogether brighter and more cheerful than those that had been left behind in the Edwardian and Victorian suburbs; rooms were sunnier and much easier to keep tidy and clean.

At the time they were built, much derision and disdain was directed at the new interwar private sector lower middle class suburbs and their house designs by writers such as D. H. Lawrence, George Orwell, Osbert Lancaster and John Betjeman, although the latter eventually changed his view[12]. The town planners and architects, who were not consulted, also voiced their contempt in their professional journals and elsewhere. An architect's motor trip along the Uxbridge–London road in 1937 stirred him into patronising remarks about its 'occasional new cinemas, its characterless "pubs" and cheap little shops', its scenery generally reflecting 'the misery of the lower middle class'[13]. More recently, writers such as John Osborne[14] have described without much affection what they saw as the narrowness and dullness of life in these between-wars estates of semis, chalets and bungalows.

Yet, for all its faults – occasional jerry-building, unimaginative layouts, lack of community spirit and an environmental impact rarely better than negative, and often disastrous – the new provision by speculators for the lower middle class in the years 1921–40 was an outstanding popular and market success. In large measure it met, at an affordable outlay, the needs and aspirations of an important section of the community. And the oft-derided semis of which these new developments were largely composed have proved so adaptable to the demands of later generations that, re-roofed, double-glazed, wall- and loft-insulated and centrally-heated, their popularity endures sixty years on to a surprising degree.

## NOTES

1. Anon, *The Home of Today – Its Choice, Planning, Equipment & Organisation* (nd but c 1935)
2. EN 6 May 1912
3. For a full and careful, if occasionally controversial, analysis of the success of the interwar speculative builders' semi-detached house, its decoration and the lifestyle of its occupants, see Oliver, Paul; Davis, Ian; and Bentley, Ian, *Dunroamin: The Suburban Semi and Its Enemies* (1981).
4. Corbett Estates leaflets for Ilford and Lewisham estates, January 1896). All other house prices quoted in this chapter are taken from contemporary advertising.
5. Rockett, Dorothy, and Hargreaves, Brenda, *Two Streatham Childhoods*, (1980).
6. For a discussion of the lower middle class and the garden city/suburb up to 1914 see Crossick, Geoffrey (ed.), *The Lower Middle Class in Britain 1870–1914* (1977), Chapter 6, 'Housing and The Lower Middle Class' by S. Martin Gaskell. On co-partnership schemes, see the author's *Semi-Detached London: Suburban Development, Life, and Transport, 1900–39*, (1973).
7. Some architects attempted to improve the tunnel-backs. In 1907 one-room width terrace houses by S. Jackson at Newbury Park, Ilford had the sitting room in the conventional position at the front alongside the entrance hall but behind this were the kitchen, scullery, and outside w.c. with the dining room placed at the very back, looking on to the garden and reached by

a separate side corridor running from the hall behind the scullery. (*The Builder's Journal*, 4 December 1907).

8. Hall-to-hall semis appeared as early as 1908 at the Grass Park Estate, Church End, Finchley, London (architects W. Bennett and F. E. Stratton). (*The Builder's Journal*, 10 March 1909).

9. eg £1,180 semi-detached houses with 'Four double bedrooms and maid's room' at Upper Selsdon Road, Sanderstead, Surrey, advertised by R. Costain & Sons in EN 20 March 1932.

10. 'Maisonnettes' (sic) at Streatham Hill, London with one bedroom, one reception room and kitchen at £72 a year appeared in advertisements as early as 22 October 1902 (EN).

11. EN advertisements 1929.

12. For a detailed factual account and more sympathetic assessment of this environment, see the author's op cit, (note 6) and Oliver, Paul etc., op cit, (note 3).

13. 'Murus', "Diary of an Architect", in *The Builder*, 17 December 1937.

14. Osborne, John, *A Better Class of Person: An Autobiography 1929–1956*, (1981).

# CHAPTER 4

# SUFFICIENTLY DETACHED

Ownership of a detached house reasonably aligned to the personal needs of the occupier and his family, properly separated from neighbours, in conditions affording a measure of quiet and seclusion, had long been a middle class aspiration. The widely-shared desire to escape to a rural environment, or at any rate a suggestion of it, which we noticed in the previous chapter, ideally required that such a house should overlook open countryside, or if that were not feasible, at least provide a glimpse of it. Easy access to urban civilisation was for most a prerequisite, whilst elevations different from those of adjacent houses and segregation from those not of equal social status were essential requirements.

In the first half of the 20th century none of this was unduly difficult to achieve for those in moderately comfortable circumstances. Planning restrictions were virtually non-existent and building land could be found readily in most 'desirable' areas. Thus many members of the comfortable middle class were able to select a site of their own choice, hiring an architect who would translate their accommodation requirements and whims into a buildable design, within the financial limits laid down. In the 1920s and 1930s, if the more popular suburban areas were avoided, this process could be completed for a minimum of around £1,000 (say a year's average earnings for a general practitioner or a civil service Principal). For this the client would secure a small two- or three-bedroom cottage on a quarter of an acre or so. Before 1914, the same might be obtained for as little as £500. What could be had for various higher levels of outlay will be considered later in this chapter but first we shall look at the alternative course of buying a ready-made detached house from a speculative developer.

## Speculators' Detached

Such properties appealed to those who preferred to buy a house which could be seen in completed form, one they did not have to wait for, or worry over its planning and construction. To many this would be the obvious and most sensible course; it would not even occur to them to commission an architect or look for a site. They would also observe that, thanks to economies of scale, the price was lower than the alternative and they were ready to forego the extra thought an architect would give to design and use and to his client's particular needs and prejudices.

During the 1900s and 1910s small speculatively-built detached houses were obtainable at between £500 and £1,000 but more usually they were rented for an annual sum of about one twentieth of the sale price. In style they were often debased versions of the larger Arts & Crafts houses designed by such architects as C. F. A. Voysey, C. R. Ashbee and M. H. Baillie Scott, featuring pronounced gables, wide eaves, dormer windows and a great deal of external softwood.

Between the wars speculatively-built detached houses at the lower end of the market were merely detached versions of the ubiquitous semi already described, with the identical 2½-bedroom, kitchenette arrangement, offering little more than the advantage of separation from neighbours on both sides at the cost of loss of heat insulation on one wall. From the middle 1920s they could be bought at £750 to just over £1,000. Dropped into estate developments which consisted mainly of semis, they were often on corner plots where slightly more space could be provided. With only a little more land, their detachment tended to be distinctly minimal. Occasionally a whole estate or section of an estate would be composed of such small detached houses, in which case the separation might be slightly more generous. Such lower density would probably be dictated by one of the few effective planning controls of the 1901–47 period, a restriction which sought to enhance the status of a designated residential zone by limiting the number of houses which could be built to the acre.

In common with almost all semis, most speculatively-built detached houses were erected without the direct aid of a professional architect. Builders would copy plans published in magazines and journals, or simply adopt the layout and form of existing houses they had studied, adding their own personal touches. Plans sold at the annual Ideal Home Exhibition organised by *The Daily Mail* newspaper from 1908 onwards were another ready and cheap source of inspiration. Examination of plans deposited with local authorities shows that builders did not always follow them exactly once they had started work.

The use of plans drawn up for him by architects, surveyors or quasi-professional designers enabled a builder to put an edge on his publicity. 'Which is Your Choice?' demanded an advertisement for houses at Watford, Hertfordshire costing £1,095 upwards in 1926:

# IFIELD, SUSSEX

### (1½ miles from Crawley)

**THIS ESTATE IS SITUATED MIDWAY BETWEEN LONDON AND BRIGHTON ON THE BORDER OF SUSSEX AND SURREY, THE MOST BEAUTIFUL OF THE HOME COUNTIES.**

## PRICE £2,150 FREEHOLD

**Comprising 5 bedrooms, 3 reception rooms, separate kitchen and scullery, bathroom, 2 w.c.'s, Loggia or garage, etc.**

Each house is individually planned with large rooms, easy to work, and embodies every modern labour-saving device. Built under the supervision of an architect on the most modern methods of brick construction with the finest materials obtainable and built to last.

### RESIDENCES BUILT TO PURCHASERS' REQUIREMENTS OR SPECIAL DESIGNS.

Finance can be arranged for the bulk of Purchase Price at a low rate of interest.

The newly constructed 18-hole Golf Course at Ifield is already a proven success. This Course covering an area of 130 acres and measuring 6,300 yards offers every attraction to the keen golfer and is indeed an asset to this beautiful Estate.

A selection of Plans of Houses, Prices from £1,000 to £2,500 with Fullest Particulars on Application to

## The IFIELD ESTATE OFFICE

### 7, HANOVER SQUARE, LONDON, W.1
'Phone: Mayfair 0368

Advertisement for large detached houses at Ifield, Sussex, 1929

'The "Suburban Villa" – a stereotyped mass-produced home in which sickly-looking stucco and sham half-timbering make one wonder what is underneath OR Houses of Character and Distinction designed by Architects and constructed by true Craftsmen in good honest brickwork – brickwork that is a pleasure to see?'[2].

By the beginning of the 1930s, some of the more reputable speculative developers were discovering that the small extra cost of employing architects to draw up designs specifically for their use provided a dash of style and quality that benefited sales. Whilst there were examples of this policy being applied to semis, most of this architectural effort went into detached house design. In general, the results, although pleasing enough to the eye, were unadventurous and uninspired. This did not matter, indeed it was a positive advantage, since middle class housebuyers, and especially their wives, were very conservative. They wanted their future home 'to look like a house' ie conform with their mental image of how a house should look. There were, it is true, occasional forays into the new International Modern style, with its flat roofs, plain cement-rendered walls, and curved metal windows, when young architects were able to influence speculative builders to follow what was the very latest trend in the early 1930s. But the minute number of such designs amidst oceans of 'Tudorbethan', and neo-Georgian tends to confirm their unpopularity with purchasers in the speculatively-built house market. Other departures from the two most popular general styles were even rarer.[3]

E & L Berg, building speculatively from the late twenties, employed an architect to produce a range of cottagey plans and elevations which enabled the firm to scatter its Surrey estates with a satisfying variety of designs of semis and detached houses (mostly the latter). At Hinchley Wood in 1931 these three, four and five bedroom detached houses, every one 'different – distinctive' sold at £1,195 to £1,800, including 'artistic fencing' and a garage[4]. Here and elsewhere in 1934 Bergs put up a few International Modern detached houses by A. Wells Coates, but the average purchaser scorned them and the experiment was soon dropped.

Another patron of professional architects amongst the large speculative builders was John Laing & Son, a firm which erected thousands of small houses in the 1930s. From about 1934 designs were produced by a team of five architects, one of them a woman. Their contributions, although somewhat lack-lustre and plain, were dignified and well-mannered, and were described at the time as 'embracing modern features without being ultra-modern' (this being an apology for not using International Modern). Selling at just over £1,000, these houses have stood the test of time well[5]. Employment of architects to design speculatively-built estate houses was largely confined to London and the south east or large London-based firms (such as Laing) operating in the provinces. Otherwise private enterprise speculative estate developments were not on a scale large enough to justify such an extravagance.

Moving further up-market, we find a slightly different process on what were usually the more attractive sites. Here, the developer would lay out the roads, provide the main services and divide up the ground into large plots. A choice of suitable plans, the services of a builder, or completed houses ready to occupy, would be available to the purchaser not wishing to employ his own architect. All houses would be detached, usually with four or five bedrooms and up to three reception rooms. Architect-designed or built to professionally-drawn plans and elevations, they sold in the late 1920s and the 1930s at between £1,500 and £3,000, including plot. Before 1915, within the same price range, such houses would be larger, with loft bedrooms for servants or children's nurseries. Sales at such locations were often slow since the number of potential buyers at this level was very limited and it could take as much as twenty years before all the available plots were filled. Many of these developments were on private parkland, secured at low prices after the breaking-up of the country estates of the landed gentry or disposal of more modest mansioned estates established or improved by the Victorian upper middle class. In contrast to the normal practice when laying out estates of semis or terrace blocks, great care was usually taken at such sites to preserve as many of the existing trees as possible and to retain other parkland features such as lakes and sinuous carriage drives[6].

On one estate of this type, the 800-acre Moor Park, Hertfordshire, where house building began in 1923, plots of a quarter of an acre or more were on offer in a 1925 advertisement which made much of the existence of country club facilities (with tennis, golf and croquet) situated on the estate itself. Houses here, with two reception rooms and five bedrooms, were available at £3,200; with three reception rooms, four bedrooms and a boxroom at £2,600; or with two reception rooms and four bedrooms at £2,500. All were built to the designs of the architect George E. Clare MSA, 'constructed to last a century without the need for anything more than minor repairs'. It was claimed that the design made these houses so easy to run that purchasers could manage with at least one less servant. Local rates were quoted as 11s 9d in the £, gas as 1s 2d a therm and electricity as nine pence a unit[7].

Such developments with their medium- to large-sized detached houses, well-separated on their tree-girt plots, were virtually middle class ghettos, forming an apparently unfriendly environment for the less fortunate not there on legitimate business. A Surrey man recently recalled how, as a youth in the 1940s, he and his companions kept out of one such area, with its cul-de-sac private roads, knowing from experience that if a policeman were encountered, they would be tapped on the shoulder and asked, 'Now mate, what are you doing up here?'. And despite the existence of footpaths leading out at the far side, the ordinary townspeople would be reluctant to walk through the private roads here, rightly feeling they might be regarded as intruders.

By the early 1930s, with supply beginning to exceed a demand damaged by the effects of economic depression, speculative builders and developers were finding it difficult to sell detached houses of this class[8] but there was some recovery in the later 1930s and many found a quick sale in the panic for a home in 'safe' areas that occurred in 1939–40.

# A Made-to-Measure Home

Commissioning an architect to design a house on a selected plot, preferably out of sight of other buildings, enabled the privileged middle class client to obtain the maximum expression of personal choice, coming close to all the desirable objectives. As mentioned earlier, this procedure need not be unduly expensive. Once a suitable district had been selected, building land was not difficult to obtain, whether for a weekend or holiday country or seaside cottage, or main residence, and there were few if any restrictions as to what might be built. Outside the large towns and cities and even on many suburban sites, the cost of land represented only a very small proportion of the total outlay on a new house.

By engaging his architect before finally deciding where to build, the prudent client would obtain wise advice on site selection. Once the plot was secured, the architect would design a house within a stated building cost (say £850 upwards), taking as his fee six per cent of this figure if the final cost was £2,000 or more. His percentage for a more modest house was fixed by arrangement but for a £1,000 house an architect would normally charge £80[9]. Should the total cost of the house exceed £2,000, there would be a further 2½ per cent of the finished cost payable for the preparation of the bill of quantities. The accommodation required by the client for his family's needs, both existing and prospective, and those of his servants, taking into account any special interests and hobbies, would form the basis of the design, the architect accepting the delicate task of arriving at the best compromise between these requirements and the money available.

It should be noted that resort to an architect was not necessarily related to the size of the sum to be spent on the house. In the mainstream of the middle class, employment of another professional would be taken for granted, whereas most lower middles were not accustomed to using the services of professionals (other than doctors and dentists) if this could be avoided.

As with the speculatively-built houses, only a small proportion of those commissioning an architect chose non-traditional designs. In the late twenties and more so in the 1930s, some were indeed persuaded, perhaps against their better judgement, to have a 'functional' house built in the contemporary International Modern style. Such decisions often led to grievous disappointment, since however well-built, these houses, with their flat roofs, sun balconies, smooth light-painted elevations and vast expanses of single sheet glass proved remarkably ill-suited to the vagaries of the British climate. Many commissioned houses emerged from the architect's desk as 'safe' designs in the Elizabethan/Jacobean rural vernacular revival styles pioneered by the Arts & Crafts architects around the turn of the century. Their rooflines featured gables, deep eaves, and often dormers. Exposed beams showed in red brickwork which was frequently varied with herringbone patterns. Some architects heightened the atmosphere by making ingenious use of building materials (including tiles complete with their coating of moss) taken from ancient rural buildings, even producing falsely distorted roof lines and leaning gables by using a steel framework beneath, to give the finished product the appearance of great age. Instead of old tiles, some of these designs incorporated elaborately-thatched roofs in local styles. Such 'houses desirable', to use the title of a book which featured them[10], were furnished with inglenooks, miniature minstrels' balconies, varied floor levels, stained glass, heavy natural oak doors and other goodies. When it came to the crunch, a professional architect could outdo any speculative builder at this sort of fakery, though it goes without saying he did it with panache. But by the time Osbert Lancaster was mocking what he called 'Stockbroker Tudor' in the late 1930s the fashion for fake 'ye olde' was already dying out.

There was also a more honest, plainer style, loosely classifiable as neo-Georgian, which paid some lip service to the clean proportions of the original Georgian house. In dignified, pleasing designs, often carried out in local brick or stone, models of English restraint, such houses looked soberly out through square-paned or lead light casements, windows and main door symmetrically-placed on the elevation. Expensive facing bricks were carefully used on all four external walls and there were sometimes rural-vernacular revival touches such as tile-hanging. Hipped roofs prevailed. More cottagey variations on this plainer style featured mansard roofs and gabled dormers for the upper floor. Other favoured styles included Dutch Colonial and Hollywood/Spanish Colonial, the latter popular in the 1930s and often given hideous green roof tiles.

Excluding the cost of land and architect's fee, a pleasant and minimally adquate house with three bedrooms and two reception rooms could be erected in the 1920s for £850 to £1,200. This would have a main bedroom around 16.7 square metres and a living room of about 19.5 sq. metres. A four-bedroom house with two or three reception rooms could be built for £1,000–£1,500, five bedrooms and three reception rooms for £2,300 to £3,000. In this decade only the most expensive houses would include a garage. On the same basis, in the 1930s, prices were a little higher, mainly because all now included a garage as a matter of course. At this time it was possible to build a three-bedroom, two-reception room house for £1,100 to £1,800, four bedrooms and two reception rooms for £1,700 to £2,000, four bedrooms and three reception rooms together with cloakroom and maid's room for £2,000–£2,500 and five bedroom and three reception rooms with all desirable trimmings from £2,500 to £3,500[11].

# Beyond the Front Door

When considering middle class detached houses it is not possible, as with the semi, to identify anything like a standard plan. Even the double-fronted design, with its central hall and main reception rooms either side was capable of layout variation by changing the position of the staircase and the relative location of the main rooms. Instead of dining room on one side of the entrance hall and sitting room on the other, some had the kitchen at one side of the front door to allow a through sitting room on the other side and a dining room behind the kitchen overlooking the garden. Others featured a long and narrow hall running through the house to a garden door. We can however attempt to describe in general terms the sort of accommodation most likely to be encountered in 1920s and 1930s detached houses in the price range £1,500 to £3,000, in other words the sort of house likely to be occupied by the median groups of the middle classes. We shall also look at the way in which it would be used.

Houses of this type would usually be set well back from the road on a generous frontage of 24–25 metres or more, separated from it by an ample lawn, shrubs and mature trees. However, in the popular suburban areas, closer to city and town centres, particularly around London, to extract the maximum profit from expensive land, they might well be squeezed more closely together and brought nearer to the road. A drive was arranged to bring cars close to the main entrance and into the garage; if this did not sweep around the front and back to the road to afford an exit without reversing, there would often be a separate path from the road for those on foot. All approaches would be closed by gates, normally in oak, each carrying the house name. It should be noted that houses of this class were usually identified solely by name, with slight regard for problems created for strangers, delivery men and the fire brigade. Their occupants regarded the use of both names and road numbers as suburban and lower middle class, whilst houses with just numbers were quite beyond the pale.

On reaching the front door, the visitor might find this protected by a large porch with quarry-tiled floor and, if compatible with the style of the house, a tiled roof supported by heavy hardwood timbers resting on a base of facing bricks to match the elevations, church lych-gate style. Otherwise the porch might be inset into the house itself. It would usually be spacious enough to shelter a perambulator, also forming a useful parking place for wet clothes and umbrellas and muddy footwear. Windows each side of the front door might be of pebbled glass to protect the privacy of the hall beyond. Since architects would differ as to the priority of lighting the hall and the extra security provided by omitting glass, some front doors had an oval or rectangle of pebbled glass or stained glass, others none. The door itself would certainly be heavily-made, probably in solid oak.

In the larger houses, the hall served as an anteroom where visitors could be detained whilst the family members prepared themselves to meet the caller or decided not to be at home. If funds allowed, there might be an outer hall or vestibule. Ideally the latter would be given direct access to the servants' quarters to protect the privacy of the main hall when servants were called to attend to the front door. Since its appearance dominated the hall and gave the visitor some early clues as to the owner's taste and social status, builders and architects would provide a handsome staircase. Writing in *The Ideal Home* magazine in 1929, Leslie Lewis suggested the hall was 'perhaps the most important part of the house, for it is here that visitors gain their first and last impressions. And those impressions, whether favourable or unfavourable, are always long lasting'[12]. An impeccably middle class sentiment indeed, as might be expected from this magazine. Lewis went on to advise against creating an atmosphere of coldness or severity in the hall, recommending primrose or sunshine yellow walls, brightly coloured mats and curtains in warm tones. He made the rather obvious suggestion that there should be a 'comfortable seat' and advised a wardrobe cupboard rather than the hat and coat stand much favoured in the lower middle class houses of the period. In his view the staircase (which should have a plain carpet) was one of the most intriguing features of the home since it imparted an air of mystery and, he added, ignoring the perils of ambiguity, 'a promise of undiscovered beauties on the floor above'.

Heavy oak joinery, often of high quality, was a common feature of staircases in this type of house, where the stairs themselves would be of more generous width than those in the average semi. In the hall and perhaps up to the top landing, the walls might be oak panelled, possibly with a china rail along the top. Such panelling might also be extended into the dining room. Parquet flooring was commonly found in halls, otherwise there would generally be good quality, closeboarded oak flooring, kept highly polished. Again, these refinements would often be extended into the main reception rooms.

A fashionable concept amongst some contemporary domestic architects, which they would be eager to put into commissioned houses if sufficient funds were available, was to enlarge the hall to create a central room of considerable size complete with its own fireplace which they saw as a focal point for the whole interior[13]. It was thought that if this were done successfully it would evolve into the room that was most lived-in, a gathering place for the family and visitors at all times of the day. Alas, like so many architectural fads, this was a fantasy doomed to become wrecked on the rocks of reality. The so-called 'lounge-hall', fitted with a fireplace and perhaps opening into one of the main reception rooms through glazed double doors, was a toned-down version of this concept, provided on a modest scale by some speculative builders, even in semis, but it needed some sort of lobby to protect it from the opening of the front door and even then was apt to be draughty. Kitchen odours were another problem, since that room often opened directly into the hall. Not surprisingly the lounge-hall was out of fashion by the mid 1930s. Where a large central space was provided, other uses for it were usually found after making suitable alterations to the original plan. Nevertheless, a hall of reasonable size, say 2.4 by 4.6 metres including the lower flight of stairs, was a feature of these middle class detached houses. This provided enough space to take one or two chairs and a small table or bench to accommodate letters and parcels or facilitate the writing of a hasty note. Perhaps the best summary of its function in this type of house was given by a writer of the 1920s who saw it as serving as 'a pleasant little ante-room to the more generous hospitality of the comfortable living-room'[14].

Lewis's mention of a hall wardrobe is a little surprising since houses of the character with which he and his magazine were concerned would almost invariably have a cloakroom off the hall. Large enough to hold outdoor clothing and footwear for family and visitors as well as golf clubs, tennis racquets and other accessories of middle class outdoor life, it would also include a wash-basin and w.c. or provide access to a closet containing these. This last facility led some architects to advise against having a cloakroom next to the front door, since it was considered the sound emanating from its interior might offend the sensibilities of lady visitors standing in the porch.

## Sitting, Dining or Just Living

Until the 1930s, virtually all houses of this type had at least two good-sized reception rooms leading off from the hall, described as a sitting room (or lounge) and a dining room. At the higher end of the price range there would usually be a third, variously designated study, library, morning or breakfast room according to the whims and needs of the owner. Having lost the battle to impose the enlarged hall on the middle class, around the mid 1930s architects sought to incorporate a single 'living space' in their ground floor plans, anxious as they were to make at least one room in the house as interesting and spacious as possible. Designers such as Anthony Bertram argued that the house should be a 'machine for living in', with this large multi-functional area as its chief feature. Such rooms, measuring around 7.6 by 4.6 metres or even more, appeared in plans for both modest and quite expensive houses, normally with a 'dining recess' or dining space separated from the rest by arrangements that were little more than symbolic. This 'living space' can be seen as an extreme version of the 'flow of space' concept, using interconnecting rooms with wide, door-free openings, adopted by M. H. Baillie Scott in a small suburban detached house at Gidea Park, Essex as early as 1911. The cult of single large living rooms, with and without 'dining recesses' survived long enough to be carried over into small lower middle class house designs of the 1950s, as many will know to their cost.

Not all architects were oblivious to the practical disadvantages of such 'functionalism'. Martin Briggs wrote in 1937 'Today the middle class is asked to accept a single room in which people will listen to the wireless (whether they want to or not), play bridge, eat fried onions and bask in the afterglow that onions leave, talk against the gramophone, and read anything up to the standard of the Daily ----'[15]. A sensible man, he found it difficult to understand that such an arrangement could be tolerated when in any household there were always a number of disparate activities in progress at any given time, so that least two reception rooms were necessary to provide the requisite separation, three if there were someone whose occupation involved desk work at home. He was of course writing in an era when central heating was still relatively uncommon and insulation was very poor, making bedrooms virtually unusable in daytime for much of the year.

Whilst two reception rooms (three, in the larger houses) and a smallish kitchen remained the popular norm, in the 1930s the middle classes were already moving towards a greater flexibility in the use of ground floor rooms, even to the extent of eating some meals in the kitchen, a labour-saving custom they were beginning to see in US cinema films. This new informality in the use of rooms had to await the disappearance of living-in servants in the late 1930s and the 1940s – the presence of servants had always caused the English middle classes to emphasise social distinctions and separation within the house. Families behaved with a certain stiffness and affectation when domestics were in earshot, following set routines and usages which emphasised class differences. Once they had gone, there was scope for much less formality in the entertainment of guests, the reception of callers, parent-child relationships and behaviour with the opposite sex. Nor was there any further need to maintain distinctive areas in the house for family use, for servants and for visitors. This opened the way for a more relaxed, multi-functional approach to the use of rooms, although its full flowering had to await the all-over warmth provided by central heating.

But we must return to the sitting room, or drawing room as some old-fashioned people still called it in the early years of the century. Whilst servants were still kept, this was very much part of the 'public' space of the house, the only room on whose door servants did not knock before entering. With the morning room if one existed, it formed the reception area into which the maid would invite callers of importance and recognised social standing (all others would be requested to wait in the hall). Understandably some inexperienced servants found difficulty over this distinction, so that someone announced as 'a gentleman in the drawing room' might turn out to be nothing more exalted than an insurance man with a smart air or even a superior-looking tradesman.

In detached houses of the quality we are considering the sitting room would be at least six by 4.25 metres and many were larger. Edwardian architects and builders frequently filled the side facing the garden with glazed doors opening into a conservatory in which the owner would place potted plants and ferns. Other features of that period were 'cosy corners' and irregular bays for bookshelves.

A tendency to remove some of the Victorian clutter and fussiness of decoration was already apparent before 1914 and by the mid 1920s greater simplicity was the general rule. Writing in 1929, Lewis proposed that the modern sitting room should demonstrate a revolt against the stuffy

Victorian drawing room, combining 'comfort and beauty, informality and real utility'. He called it the 'lounge' (a term still fashionable at that time but soon to fall from grace as its use slipped down the social scale) and suggested the room should be used simply as that, or as 'primarily a smoking room, music room, a study, a library or a combination of all these'[16]. Most architects of the 1920s and 1930s would try to ensure this room had a major south or south western aspect with windows providing a low glass line so that those seated in its armchairs had not only a chance of some sunlight but a comfortable view of the garden. Outlook to the garden was often enhanced by incorporating French doors which led on to a recessed, sheltered patio or loggia, where meals might be taken in good weather. Side walls were often fenestrated to give a pleasing cross light, combining both south and south-west aspects. Recesses and alcoves were frequently introduced to vary the fall of light and add interest to the shape of the room. To afford the spaciousness the multiple functions of the room demanded, it was often taken across the full depth of the house from the front to the back. Architects also sought to secure ample draught-free space around the fireplace, which formed the focal point. Furniture would principally consist of a large sofa and two ample armchairs, supplemented by a pouffe and one or two occasional tables. The more affluent households collected antique furniture, beginning with small 'occasional' items. One newcomer threatening to intrude was questioned by Briggs: '. . . the provision of a cocktail cabinet, derived like so many other fashions from America, is said to be essential among the best people and among all social climbers at the present time [1937], but it is doubtful whether it will form a permanent feature of our national life'[17]. Eight years earlier, Lewis had been more confident when he noted: 'In the corner of the modern lounge is frequently a little bar'[18].

Even when one or more further reception rooms were available, the sitting room was usually the largest room in the house, or at any rate equal in size to the main bedroom, since it not only had to accommodate parties of guests but bulky furniture, including a piano. Demanding much space, especially if it were a baby grand, the latter was normally decorated with silver-framed photographs of members of the family. From around 1930 it had to compete with, and in many cases give way to, a radiogram and by the end of that decade, in homes around London, a television. Such valuables as the family possessed, together with holiday souvenirs and books would be on show to visitors in this room as evidence of the owners' taste and social and economic status.

A picture rail round the top of the wall, 23–30.5cm below the ceiling of the principal rooms, was seen in most middle class houses built before the mid-1930s. Although the strings which suspended the pictures themselves were ugly, the rail itself did give some unity to the appearance of a room since it was usually in line with the tops of the window openings. This feature was abolished by the modernists of the 1930s as superfluous clutter, in common with decoration of skirting rails. In the 1930s the latter were also reduced in height and ground floor ceiling heights came down from the 2.8 metres or so usual in many middle class houses, eventually reaching the late 1940s minimum of 2.29. All these changes took some time to filter through to architects and builders remote from the modern ideas and tastes first generated and initiated in the London region.

The fireplace formed a central feature and focal point in the sitting room. Even before 1914 the grandiose Victorian overmantel, with its little range of ornament shelves and mirrors, was giving way to simpler painted mantlepieces. The 1920s brought rustic brick or tiled surrounds with a painted or varnished wooden framework supporting the mantlepiece, whilst the following decade saw the arrival of glazed tileware fire surrounds, projecting slightly from the wall, some with plain wooden frames, others with no mantlepiece as such but simply offering the ledge formed by the top, which was often stepped in Aztec style at the sides.

Though smaller than the sitting room, the dining room needed to be at least 4.27 by 3.66 metres if it were to accommodate a sideboard and allow space for serving all round a table seating six. A south-east or east aspect was considered advisable as providing cheerful sunlight at breakfast and avoiding slanting rays from the setting sun at dinner, a meal for which artificial light was considered more suitable. Electric lamps were arranged, sometimes with elaborate pulleys, to throw light on the table at a low level, leaving the rest of the room in shadow, so creating a romantic and relaxing atmosphere for dinner. Some importance was attached to this matter of lighting the table. Lady Troubridge suggests in her 1926 guide 'there may be candles or some form of electric light on the table which should be carefully shaded to make it becoming to the complexions of the ladies and pleasant to the eyesight'. An oriental carpet was often chosen for this room because its complicated patterns tended to hide stains produced by the inevitable accidents.

Many dining rooms were fitted with a serving hatch opening directly into the kitchen, a feature also frequently seen in the smaller houses of the lower middle class. Whilst this saved some running around, it had the disadvantage when open of bringing kitchen noises and smells into the dining room and allowing table gossip to be overheard by any servants in the kitchen. In 1927 the Universal Housing Company was offering a 'soundproof' service hatch but the ideal solution, found only in the most expensive houses, was for the hatch to open into a lobby, servery or maid's pantry placed between the dining room and the kitchen, or, better still, between the kitchen and all the main rooms, including the hall. In any case full value was only obtained when the household could afford to have two servants in action at mealtimes, one waiting at table and remaining in the dining room whilst the other stayed in the kitchen, passing and receiving dishes through the hatch. With anything less, this feature was little more than a pretentious gesture.

Ideally the use of the dining room would be restricted to meal times, so allowing it to be furnished in a simple, plain and uncluttered way. In practice it often had to double as a study, in which case space had to be found at one end for a bookcase and a desk.

Should there be a third reception room, pressure on space and overall cost usually meant that it was fairly small, its wall area too limited to accommodate the bookshelves and cupboards required if it were to serve adequately as a study or library. When asked to include a study in the plan, architects would try to place it near the front door so that visitors did not unduly intrude on the life of the rest of the household, and space sacrifices sometimes had to be made in the two main rooms so that it could be made a reasonable size. At first the third reception room was frequently designated a breakfast or morning room but this provision disappeared almost completely from new middle class houses of medium size after 1920. Were such a room available and of adequate size, it would normally be occupied by the family until afternoon tea, when they would move to the sitting room. Ideally, its aspect would be east or south east.

# Domestic Quarters

Almost all middle class houses built before 1915 had both a kitchen and a scullery, the latter devoted to washing dishes and clothes. After World War 1, both were usually combined into one well-planned room which formed the workshop of the house, surrounded by its associated annexes. A reasonable minimum size for a middle class kitchen would be about 3.65 by 3.05 metres, this space containing a deep white 'butler' sink and wooden draining boards, cooking stove (normally by then gas or electric), hot water boiler, a table and a chair and various cupboards for cooking utensils and crockery. Until the early 1950s, washing machines, dishwashers, food mixers, clothes dryers, freezers and refrigerators were of course either not invented or, in their early and costly forms, rarely found in middle class kitchens.

The design and manner of use of the kitchen quarters depended very much on whether servants were kept. Those providing houses costing £1,500 upwards in the interwar period normally fitted electric bell call systems, assuming at least one living-in maid. Pushes in each of the main rooms, the bathroom and on the outside doors were wired to an indicator board in the kitchen. In such houses there would usually be a servants' w.c. somewhere near the kitchen door. Despite these features, kitchens were often too small to afford much daytime comfort for a maid or cook-general.

If an architect were told there would be a servant he would endeavour to provide a kitchen capable of doubling up as her sitting and eating room, setting aside a recess for these purposes, or at any rate providing enough space for a table and chair to be placed out of cross-draughts. In the more expensive houses there would normally be a separate maids' sitting-room next to the kitchen, a modestly-sized provision still grandly designated 'servants' hall' on some architects' plans as late as the 1930s.

Victorians and Edwardians preferred a kitchen to face north, since it was considered sunshine might create hot weather discomfort for the servants in what was already the warmest room of the house, with its continuously-burning coal range cooking all the food and heating water the year round. But in the 1920s and 1930s, as more households became servantless, or managed with only one domestic who might leave at any time, and as gas or electricity began to replace the coal-fired range, it was thought better to have the kitchen environment as bright and cheerful as possible, so a southerly aspect with a pleasing view became the ideal. The heat from the coal range was also used to dry and air clothes, which were hung on an arrangement of wooden rails raised and lowered by means of ropes and pulleys attached to the ceiling.

Leading off the kitchen there was normally a garden door and tradesmen's entrance, preferably with a lobby to enable transactions to proceed under protection from the weather and without encroaching into the kitchen itself. In a well-designed detached house of medium to large size it was usual to arrange around the kitchen and its outer lobby a walk-in larder, (if possible facing north), a coal store, and the servants' w.c., all accessible without going outdoors. In the larger houses there might also be a parlourmaid's pantry, the 20th century version of the butler's pantry. This would include a sink with plate and cup rack alongside, cupboards for dusters and cleaning materials, and drawers for table linen and cutlery. There would also be a wine bin and a cupboard for the cakes, biscuits, jams etc. required for afternoon tea, a meal prepared here, using an electric kettle or gas ring. Silver cleaning would also be done in this pantry. For the convenience of the parlourmaid, there would be a mirror and roller towel.

Perusal of illustrations in contemporary magazines clearly demonstrates the rapid improvements made between 1920 and 1940 in the design of kitchen equipment, notably in that of gas and electric cookers. By the 1930s, what had been a muddle of tables and dark-hued cupboards of various sizes was being replaced by purpose-designed 'kitchen-cabinets' or built-in equipment bright with hygienic white and cream vitreous enamel and chromium plate, all arranged for easy working. Stainless steel sink units with cupboards beneath were another new feature of the 1930s. As it became ever more difficult to obtain and keep satisfactory servants, much energy was devoted to kitchen planning with the objective of making the housewife's work easier. In the mid-1930s a Kitchen Centre was opened in London's Bond Street to dispense pamphlets and general advice on the arrangement and equipment of this important room. It was claimed that a properly-planned kitchen could reduce the amount of labour by as much as 70 per cent.

## Upstairs Rooms

From the 1910s most middle class houses were designed without an attic storey, the maids' bedrooms being placed on the same floor as those of the family, thus providing extra flexibility of use. In those few cases where attic rooms were still provided, they now tended to be used for hobbies, as children's playrooms, or simply as stores for lumber.

Whilst bathrooms were virtually universal in middle class houses built after 1900, at first some had only a cold water supply, the hot water brought up from the kitchen in cans by the maids. Since most middle class houses built before 1950 lacked full central heating, bathrooms were apt to be very chilly places in winter. Architects would often place the unlagged hot water tank in a corner airing cupboard, thus making the room a little more comfortable for the bather. Even in the larger houses it was not at all uncommon to find only one bathroom, although maids' rooms might be given wash-basins fitted with running hot and cold water. Sharing of a single bathroom by family and maids was a matter to be handled with delicacy; some employers obliged servants to make do as best they could with wash-basins or portable baths.

As with kitchens, the design and appearance of bathrooms improved significantly from around 1930. Until that time, the Victorian wooden

68

bath casings having been declared unhygienic, bathrooms were ugly with exposed piping and the unconcealed underparts of the bath itself. Then the porcelain, brass and nickel-plated taps and fittings began to be replaced by neat and bright chromium-plated labour-saving designs and plumbing was increasingly concealed behind pedestal wash-basins and marbled or tiled bath surrounds. New patterns of tap brought hot and cold flows into one mixer outlet and baths and wash-basins were given built-in soap dishes and toothbrush holders. Ceramic tiling to shoulder height (usually in white relieved by black patterns), a chromium-plated heated towel rail, a cork-seated stool or chair and a mirrored cupboard for cosmetics, medicines and shaving gear completed the furnishings. As for size, this room was normally large enough for the owner to perform a modest morning ritual of physical jerks were he so inclined. Bidets were unknown, except in houses occupied by those brought up in Continental Europe.

For convenience and comfort, the upstairs w.c. was normally located in its own closet, this also quite often tiled to shoulder height. Here the innovations were, in the late 1920s, the low-level, lever-flush suite, and in the early 1930s, the plastic (originally bakelite) seat, which replaced the traditional mahogany. Although the latter was perhaps more hygienic and certainly was cheaper, many thought it less welcoming.

In houses costing £1,750 or more, four bedrooms were the minimum. It was normal for all to be sufficiently large to take a double bed, so that one of the smaller bedrooms was sufficiently spacious to make a comfortable base for the maid. Given the general absence of domestic central heating, bedrooms could only double as sitting rooms if the expense of burning an electric or gas fire for long periods in cold weather could be tolerated and this was something that, as they became more difficult to get between the wars, servants could insist upon having. As the 1930s advanced, some builders of small and medium sized houses began to provide electric wall fires instead of coal fireplaces in the main bedrooms but architects generally continued with the latter, which could of course be readily adapted to include a gas fire. It was customary for one or perhaps two of the bedrooms to be of significantly larger dimensions than the others, the main one perhaps as big as the sitting room. Ideally this would face south-east or east, to benefit from any early morning sun.

Should a day nursery be provided, the architect would normally place this on the first floor so that it could be used as an ordinary bedroom when no longer required. For this room a south-west aspect was favoured. A night nursery would ideally face south-east.

Patterned wallpaper and friezes in bedrooms had long been frowned upon as an irritant to the restless invalid confined to bed. To Leslie Lewis in 1929, the essentials for a middle class bedroom were 'peace, restfulness, comfort and cheerfulness', a room in which 'there is nothing to irritate the mind or strike a discordant note'[19]. To achieve these ideals, he advocated large unbroken plain surfaces with an overall effect of simplicity, all unnecessary ornamentation being banished. He considered beds looked better without foot and head boards and during the 1930s bed design was gradually simplified in this way, a development which increased the sense of spaciousness in the room at the expense of certain practical disadvantages. Bateman[20] was of the opinion that 'no room in the house reflects the taste and character of its owner so completely as the bedroom'. He considered the general effect should be 'bright and restful' and thought the housewife would want to devote special care to what he saw as 'her own personal sanctum in particular'. It was a room normally large enough for her to use for reading and writing, and so sometimes contained a small desk or bureau and a comfortable chair or two; but once again this would require an electric or gas fire for comfort during the winter months. A pleasant feature of some of the larger houses was a balcony overlooking the garden, reached from the main bedroom through doors or French windows which could be flung open on hot nights. Some of these balconies were spacious enough to be used for sleeping in the open air when the weather was suitable[21]. Sunbathing balconies at first floor level or doors leading on to flat roofs adapted for the same purpose were a feature of many of the International Modern houses of the 1930s.

After 1920, to relieve the pressure on the single bathroom, wash-basins with running hot and cold water were frequently installed in bedrooms, although some architects and designers considered this item introduced a jarring, clinical note to a room which had been furnished and decorated with care. This problem was solved by concealing basins in alcoves, or by providing a small dressing room off the bedroom which could accommodate this useful feature. Dressing rooms had their origins in the need to give the husband privacy whilst his wife was being dressed by her maid, but by the 1910s that particular ritual was becoming rare in all but the most affluent middle class families. Later generations were able to convert such alcoves and dressing rooms to the *en suite* shower cubicles and bathrooms which house builders and equipment manufacturers were to generate into profitable fashionable necessities in the 1970s.

Ever conscious of the middle class obsession with privacy, especially in the servanted house, architects would pay careful attention to the arrangement of bedroom doors. These were usually placed in the corner of the room so that even when ajar, anyone passing outside could not see the bed or very far into the room.

By the 1930s, as in kitchens, the vogue for built-in bedroom furniture was emerging. Large wardrobe units with flush-fitting doors often faced with tall mirrors, took the place of the bulky and heavy free-standing wardrobes which generations of removal men had struggled to carry up staircases. With the advent of bathrooms and the plumbed bedroom wash-basin, the Victorian bedroom washstand with its large basin and jug had all but disappeared by the end of the 1920s. Another change of this period, the fashion for replacing double beds with twin divans, may well have been influenced by the cinema. When stricter censorship codes for Hollywood films were introduced in 1934, shots of couples in bed together were forbidden, so twin beds became *de rigueur* for filmed bedroom scenes.

## Garages and Gardens

Outside the house, a garage was a prominent feature almost invariably provided for medium to large detached houses after the late 1920s. Architects soon began to integrate garages with the house, providing weatherproof access from the rest of the building, though this required careful attention to fireproofing, especially for the accommodation above. In the early years of motoring it had been the custom to place the garage at a distance from the house, following the precedent of stable and coach-house blocks, a practice which assumed a chauffeur, housed in a loft room, over his charge. But from the 1920s, unless the lie of the ground made it difficult, garages were almost invariably placed alongside the house or even within the main ground floor plan. If the garage were detached, care had to be taken to ensure it was in harmony with the main elevations. That this created problems for those designing Tudoresque and revived rural-vernacular houses is evident from the slightly absurd oak half-timbered and thatched roofed garages illustrated in Barron's 1929 book[22]. Sufficient room was made available in most garage interiors to accommodate a work bench and the bicycles of family and servants but well-designed houses often had storage lofts, garden tool sheds and fuel stores built around and over the garage itself.

Architects preferred to be involved in general garden planning and would of course take the shape and broad arrangement of the garden area into consideration when designing a house. Close examination of estates of detached houses of the interwar period can sometimes reveal which houses were erected without the advice of an architect. Thus one can find a house built to a commercially-sold plan, intended for a narrow suburban plot, looking somewhat lost on a site with some 25 metres of frontage, or a house with its sitting room facing a back garden on the north side instead of enjoying the sunny and open aspect of a spacious front garden.

A plot of half an acre or more would allow construction of a tennis court, an amenity more popular in the between-war years than the swimming pools found in similar situations today. Since tennis courts, particularly hard courts, are not things of beauty, an architect would place them out of direct view from the house, carefully screened with trees and shrubs. A total area of some 30.48 by 15.24 metres was deemed desirable, with the longer axis aligned north and south so that the sun did not dazzle the players when it was low in the sky. A croquet lawn demanded even more space (32 by 25.6 metres) but with the Victorian popularity of this game waning fast, croquet lawns were seldom found in gardens designed after 1920. Summer houses remained popular because they allowed the garden to be enjoyed from mid-April to mid-October, whatever the weather. It was usual to position them close to the house to ease the task of bringing out refreshments. Southerly, south westerly or even westerly aspects each had advantages for this structure and some designs, necessarily small, could even be turned so that they faced the sun at any hour of the day.

# A Bungalow, A Piccolo and You

This popular song of 1933 highlighted the contemporary success of the single-storey home. The modern form of bungalow[23] had appeared in Britain towards the end of the 19th century but was at first principally used for seaside or rural residence. After World War 1, the detached bungalow was widely taken up for normal residential purposes and early in the twenties, it even enjoyed a brief popularity on parkland type estates in Surrey and elsewhere. In that decade and the following one, many thousands were erected, mostly by speculative builders. Offering one or two reception rooms and two or three bedrooms, they sold at £350–£400 upwards on suburban estates in places such as the metropolitan edges of Essex and west Middlesex as well as in holiday areas – in fact anywhere where the land was cheap enough for the bungalow's greater greed for space to be readily accommodated.

The detached bungalow was popular with the elderly retired, invalids and the partially-disabled; it also held a certain nostalgic appeal for those returning from colonial or Indian service, where they had been accustomed to an environment in which it was almost the only form of housing for Europeans.

But, for a variety of reasons, the bungalow was not universally regarded with approbation by the middle classes, especially in southern England. Fairly or unfairly, it started by acquiring an image of eccentricity and cheapness. Many were built in the 1920s on large plots of cheap land, from which the new owners, some of them bohemians or social drop-outs, sought to scratch a living or at any rate subsistence. In seaside, riverside and woodland locations, the bungalow was apt to acquire a slightly suspect social reputation, as the scene of illicit or promiscuous sexual behaviour, and worse, enough to make it less than respectable in some middle class eyes. This cachet tended to be confirmed by the British film industry, whose products, from *Bounding Bertie's Bungalow* of 1913 to *The Chinese Bungalow* of 1940 all seemed to portray the bungalow as background to crime or sexual high jinks. There was also its dubious social status, acquired once it became clear that this, in its cheapest form, was a house type not beyond the reach of at least some working class people. Lastly, detached bungalows of similar shape and size *en masse* without benefit of landscaping, were by no means pleasing to the eye and when in the 1920s they spread over high amenity value countryside in such places as the outskirts of Brighton, they aroused the anger of middle class proto-environmentalists and stimulated the formation of the Council for the Preservation of Rural England. The term 'bungaloid growth', coined by the clergyman/journalist Dean W. R. Inge in 1927, was much bandied about, and in his 1928 book *England and The Octupus*, the architect Clough Williams-Ellis talked of 'England's most disfiguring disease, having, from sporadic beginnings, now become our premier epidemic.' When the Surrey County Council purchased Norbury Park, north of Dorking in 1931, a middle class councillor described it as 'a headland rampant against the bungalow and other blights'.

The rapid spread of the detached bungalow in rural and seaside areas in the 1920s was associated with a demand from an increasing population of retired middle class (and to a lesser extent, retired working class), the availability of cheap land at a time of severe agricultural depression, and the improved accessibility to amenity areas which followed the expansion of rural bus services and wider motor cycle and car ownership. Bungalows continued to be built in large numbers through the 1930s in seaside and other retirement areas as well as being sprinkled about in suburban estates amongst other house types. But for the reasons given, irrational as it may seem, the middle classes as a whole never did quite take them to their hearts as part of their accepted lifestyle.

# Alternative Self-Containment: The Urban Flat

Before leaving the subject of middle class housing, some attention must be given to the privately-built urban flat, which although not detached was, in its most modern form, extremely well-insulated from its neighbours and almost invariably architect-designed. Indeed success with a large block of self-contained 'luxury' flats was a rigorous test of an architect's skill. Apart from the need to maximise the sense of separation and to achieve efficient handling of services and amenities, there were other demands. In 1907 W. Shaw Sparrow, in a book entitled *Flats, Urban Houses and Cottage Homes* remarked that

> members of the middle classes are called upon to keep up a position more or less beyond their means, because they can afford still less the danger either of living in a way that might stamp them as failures, or of dressing in a style that their clients or employers might regard as too negligent or too poor. This fact no architect should neglect when designing a block of flats for the middle classes. His building should have style. It must not be second-rate in workmanship; none who looks at it from the outside should be able to guess that the rents are low.

Middle class flats were not a 20th century innovation. When suburban residence became the norm for the middle classes fairly early in the Victorian era, there were always some who preferred to remain in the urban centres, at least for some of the year, whilst for others their occupation made an urban base necessary, perhaps only for part of the week. In London in particular, commercial pressures on desirable urban residential areas gradually depleted the number of middle class town houses available as well as removing the construction of new ones from the realms of practicality. Thus although it was possible to live for long periods in hotels, and many did this, there were always enough single people and childless couples and others needing a base in town to create a steady demand for the urban flats which were built from around 1870. And at major seaside resorts, especially in the south of England, a demand arose between the wars for similar accommodation as an alternative to hotel living, mainly from the rentier and retired middle class, and from singles and married couples with no children at home.

A minor flat-building boom in central London in the last quarter of the 19th century overflowed into the 1900s and 1910s, when large and often ornately-decorated blocks were erected, notably in the Mayfair, Marble Arch, St James', and Regent's Park districts, and along the Bayswater and Marylebone Roads. Some of these projects included restaurants for the convenience of those not wishing to keep servants. Rents, inclusive of rates and taxes, ranged widely, from £70 to £3,000 a year, according to the type of accommodation provided. Much of this provision was aimed at the upper rather than the middle class, since few of the latter could afford more than £150–£200 at this time, but by 1914 the needs of the very wealthy were very largely met.

Thus when the major boom in private urban flat construction came in the late twenties, lasting for almost a decade, it was mostly directed at the middle class market, until that too was almost saturated. The reasons for this surge of activity, which was almost entirely confined to London and the south east, can be traced to the shortage and high cost of suitable urban housing and the steeply increased cost of operating the old town houses, which needed large staffs of servants. At the same time, the real cost of building materials and labour fell sharply and money became cheap, a development which not only helped those financing flat-building but enhanced the attractiveness of this and other forms of residential construction as an investment. The huge amounts of capital required to build these extensive and complex blocks of flats were frequently obtained by raising low interest overdrafts at joint stock banks which were repaid on completion of the work by selling debentures, often to insurance companies looking for secure investments. The result of this activity was the appearance of many new blocks of 'luxury service flats' or 'self-contained flats', both in the centre of London, in the capital's inner and middle distance suburbs and to a smaller extent in the larger coastal resorts. To the disappointment of some architects and planners, who saw them as an alternative to suburban sprawl, they failed to attract families.

In London, the process began slowly in the mid-1920s with the construction of Devonshire House, Piccadilly (completed 1926), two blocks in Grosvenor Square (1927), Stratton House, Piccadilly (1927), Grosvenor House, Park Lane (1928–9), Berkeley Court, Marylebone Road (1929), Oakwood Court, Holland Park and Copthorne Court, Maida Vale (both 1929–30)[24]. But perhaps the most impressive product of this period was the Metropolitan Railway Company's Chiltern Court, completed above Baker Street station in 1929. This, with Grosvenor House, set the pattern of what was to follow. At Grosvenor House, residents could call upon a central pool of servants, whilst at Chiltern Court, which was operated as a subsidiary of the railway company, there was a liveried head porter, pill box-hatted and multi-buttoned lift boys and a large restaurant. Here central heating, constant hot water, rates and taxes were included in the rents for the 198 units, which ranged from three-bedroom 'bachelor flats' at £250 a year to ten-room 'mansion flats' at £1,000. There was no difficulty in filling all but the latter, and amongst the earliest tenants were H. G. Wells and Arnold Bennett[25].

During the peak of the London flat building boom in 1933–36, much attention and ingenuity were applied to refining the efficiency of noise insulation and to giving each flat and its balcony the maximum of privacy and daylight. These 1930s blocks provided a new level of luxury and amenities, including spacious underground garages; swimming pools and squash courts; gymnasia; cinemas; dance halls; restaurants; shops; servants' rooms; high speed lifts; and hairdressing and other services. Unless so inclined, the residents need not venture outside for days on end; their whole life could became as 'self-contained' as their flat. It was as if they were passengers on a great ocean liner, an image reinforced by the architectural style of some of the buildings. In several respects the lifestyle of those in the more expensive flats followed a pattern established in the USA some years earlier, one which was reflected, with only slight distortion, in the films of the period.

In central London, clusters of these new blocks appeared in the districts around Hyde Park/Marble Arch, the south end of Edgware Road, in St Johns Wood, around Marylebone Road and on the east side of Regent's Park. Among the most impressive were: Park West, Marble Arch (1936, with gymnasium, six squash courts, swimming pool, restaurant and residents' club and flats of one to five main rooms at £95–£320 a year); Lansdowne House, Berkeley Square (1934–5, with rents of £275–£1,118); Dorset House, Marylebone (1935, with underground garage for 200 cars, petrol station, sixteen shops and 185 flats at £165–£326 a year, ranging from one living room, kitchen and bathroom to two living rooms, four bedrooms and roof garden); Mount Royal, Marble Arch (1934, with 650 small service flats and restaurant); White House, Regent's Park (1936, with 758 flats at £70–142 a year, indoor swimming pool and refreshment lounge); Viceroy Court, Regent's Park (1937); and Barrie House, Lancaster Gate (1937, with its flats ranging from two bedrooms, two living rooms, bathroom and kitchen to seven bedrooms, two living rooms, three bathrooms, kitchen and pantry, at rents of £215–£1,000 a year). But quite the most ambitious project of this final phase in pre-war urban flat construction was Dolphin Court, Pimlico, overlooking the Thames. Completed in 1937, this complex of 1,310 flats covered 4¼ acres and boasted a sports centre with swimming pool, ballroom, several different types of garden, shops, services, a 300-car garage, nursery, children's centre and restaurant[26].

Rather less splendid were the blocks of middle class flats erected at the same time in the inner and middle-distance suburbs. Here rents tended to start at £75 a year or lower and rarely exceeded £275, many blocks having a maximum figure of £200. Although the accommodation was more limited, the cost of such flats compared favourably with the sum of mortgage repayments and heating bills for a small suburban house. Putney, Twickenham, Chiswick, Hampstead, Hendon, Streatham, Balham, Brixton and Finchley were favoured locations in the peak construction years 1933–37. Pullman Court, Streatham Hill, designed in the International Modern style by (Sir) Frederick Gibberd, consisted of three separate three- and seven- storey complexes totalling 220 flats, completed in 1935. Rents here were £68 for one-bedroom flats and £105 to £130 for three main rooms. At the nearby Du Cane Court, Streatham, (1937) there were 1,400 flats at rents of £60 a year for one main room 4.64 by 3.5 metres with tiny kitchen and bathroom, or £90 for two rooms and £115–£170 for three to five rooms. These amounts included central heating, constant softened hot water, and an electric radio and clock, but electricity and gas were extra. There was a large restaurant, a roof garden, a residents' club and shops. Many flats had private balconies and all had rubbish disposal chutes[27]. Greater luxury was available at Cholmeley Court, Highgate Hill (1933) where there were six floors of flats of three to five rooms, all with kitchen and bathroom, at £140–£255 a year. Some of the living rooms of the better flats here were quite spacious at six by 5.48 metres. More typical of the suburban provision was The Grove, St Margarets, Twickenham, which had Richmond Park, Kew Gardens and two golf courses 'at hand'. Only twenty five minutes by train from Waterloo, it was ready in 1937 to offer central heating, constant hot water, polished floors, and tiled bathrooms with heated towel rails. Its 'large airy rooms with big windows' and, 'for your convenience, luggage and pram stores' came for £90–£120 a year according to the size of the flat[28].

Brighton and other coastal resorts were quick to follow London. In 1935 on the seafront at the Brighton/Hove boundary there was completed a large concrete twelve-storey block of sixty-nine luxury flats of nine different types, designed by Wells Coates expressly 'for professional and business classes'. Every floor of Embassy Court had balconies overlooking the sea and the rents ranged from £160 (two main rooms) to £500 (four rooms). There were furnished guest rooms for those who wished to entertain friends to a seaside break. At the opposite end of Brighton was Marine Gate, a complex of 120 flats, each with balcony and sea view. Designed by Wimperis, Simpson & Guthrie, this was finished in 1939 and rents ranged from £140 a year for one-bedroom units to £450 for four bedrooms, two bathrooms and two living rooms. All had fitted kitchens which included a refrigerator.

By 1938 nearby Worthing boasted no less than eight blocks of luxury flats with accommodation of one to five main rooms, kitchen and bathroom at £90–£275, these rents including central heating, constant hot water, refrigerators and porters. Further east, at Hastings, the seafront Marine Court of 1937 was claimed as the highest residential building in Great Britain with its fourteen storeys 'in the latest fire-resisting materials' and its mysterious 'self-adjusting lifts'. Here there were 180 flats of one to six main rooms, each with bathroom and kitchen, at rents from £95. The fortunate occupants enjoyed such high technology as constant hot water, central heating, cookers, refrigerators, electric clocks, energised aerial radio and television reception and intercommunicating telephones. As well as a licensed restaurant and 'fully-equipped public rooms' there were twenty-five shops at street level and a private passage through to underground garages and promenade sun lounges[29].

# Not So Hot

Whilst all these new flats had central heating, the majority of both new and old middle class houses still lacked this basic amenity in the 1940s. Accustomed to wearing more and heavier clothing indoors than now, and still much imbued with the deeply-entrenched British attachment to fresh air, open windows in bedrooms and blazing but inefficient coal fires, many middle class people considered domestic central heating a namby-pamby American fad which produced an unpleasant and stuffy warmth. It was also expensive to install. In 1938, using the newly-introduced heavy cast iron flat panel radiators, the cost of fitting was given as £10 a room[30], a price which put this amenity out of reach of all but the affluent, since the total outlay could be as much as a tenth or more of the cost of a small house. At a time when domestic buildings leaked heat copiously, it was also an investment of dubious value.

As a result, middle class houses were damper and much colder than they are now. Although some of the more expensive semis and detached houses had what was optimistically labelled 'partial central heating' this consisted of nothing more than a single radiator in the hall, fed from the hot water supply, enough, it was claimed, to take the chill from the whole house. Until the end of the 1940s most middle class houses still relied on coal fires or the similarly highly-localised warmth of electric and gas fires. A 1939–40 study of middle class expenditure showed around six per cent of total outlay allocated to fuel and light, with coal burned on open fires alone accounting for nearly half of this, and coal and coke together over half[31].

Until the end of the 1940s, housecleaning and bedmaking in winter were indeed uncomfortable experiences for servants and housewives; once they left the living room with its blazing coal fire or the milder warmth of the kitchen with its coke-fired hot water boiler, they would find the rest of the house like an ice box, condensation frequently frozen hard on the insides of the single-glazed windows. At bedtime, bedsocks and stone hot water bottles (replaced by friendlier rubber ones in the 1930s) alleviated the discomfort of damp and cold sheets. Although the technology was available much earlier, electric blankets did not reach quantity production and sale until the 1950s. Surprisingly, all this winter hardship was cheerfully borne, perhaps because it had been taken for granted since early childhood and certainly many had known even more spartan conditions in private boarding schools.

## NOTES

1. In 1935 it was alleged that ninety-five per cent of the building work carried out in the United Kingdom was completed without the supervision of a qualified architect (letter from the Secretary of the Incorporated Association of Architects & Surveyors, *The Estates Gazette*, 10 August 1935). Matters were improving however if another estimate, made by S. C. Ramsey, FRIBA in 1938 was to be believed; he suggested that twenty per cent of the plans submitted to building societies in that year were drawn up by architects, compared with only five to ten per cent in 1928. In practice, builders of quite substantial houses would use plans executed by anyone with an acceptable qualification such as sanitary engineer or surveyor.
2. Advertisement, Watford Ideal Homes Ltd., in *Watford Homesteads Served By The Metro*, Metropolitan Railway, March 1926.
3. Among the best examples of International Modern Style applied to middle class speculatively-built houses were those by Herbert A. Welch for Messrs Haymills at Hanger Hill, Ealing, Middlesex, in 1935. Two years earlier, on speculatively built estates at Edgware, Middlesex, the same architect had produced toned-down versions, under pitched and tiled roofs, to appease local council objections. His modified style, with its plain, smooth light-washed walls and curved windows with horizontal Crittall glazing bars was widely copied as acceptable suburban 'modernity'. A very unusual departure was the employment of the Dutch architect V. Hamsdorff at the Coulsdon Vale estate, Surrey in 1933–6, where he provided distinctive and attractive three- and four-bedroom houses in the Dudok manner. (Information in this note is taken from sales brochures and contemporary advertising).
4. EN 2 May 1931.
5. The architects used by Laing were: Miss Frances Barker; D. A. Adam;

H. Clifford Hollis; Geddes Hyslop; and Arthur W. Kenyon. (Laing estate brochures 1937–8 and *The Builder,* 28 May 1937).

6. For a study of the development of a typical estate of this type, see the author's *The Residential Development of Deepdene Park, Dorking since 1920,* (1984).

7. Moor Park Estate brochure, nd but c 1925, at GLRO MET 10/153.

8. Noted by the Northwood (Middlesex) builder, Harold Neal, in *Housebuilding, 1934–35* (1934).

9. For a house costing less than £2,000 an architect was allowed to charge on a sliding scale diminishing from ten per cent to the standard six per cent on £2,000. In practice most charged six per cent, provided the final cost was only marginally below £1,000. (Briggs, Martin, S., FRIBA, *How To Plan Your House,* (1937). See also Wright, H. Myles, *Small Houses £500–£2,500,* (1937).

10. Barron, P. A., *The House Desirable,* (1929).

11. For plans and prices see Bateman, R. A., *How to Own and Equip a House,* (1926), Phillips, Randal, *The £1000 House,* (1928) and Wright, H. Myles, ARIBA, op cit (note 9).

12. Lewis, Leslie, *The Ideal Home* magazine, January 1929.

13. The concept of a large hall used as a 'living space' seems to have been revived for modern houses by the architect Mackay Hugh Baillie Scott (1865–1945), see his *A Country House* (1900). It was taken up enthusiastically by J. S. Brocklesby (1879–1955) and others of his generation.

14. Bateman, op cit (note 11).

15. Briggs, op cit (note 9).

16. Lewis, Leslie, *The Ideal Home* magazine, April 1929.

17. Briggs, op cit (note 9).

18. Lewis, op cit (note 16).

19. Lewis, *The Ideal Home* magazine, May, 1929.

20. Bateman, op cit (note 11).

21. This idea was used, perhaps for the first time in Britain, in 1904–14 at Letchworth Garden City in houses designed by Barry Parker and others. It was no doubt popular with those who had served in hot countries overseas.

22. Barron, op cit (note 10).

23. For a thorough study of the bungalow and its history see King, Anthony, *The Bungalow: The Production of a Global Culture,* (1984), on which this section is partly based.

24. Details and dates are taken from *The Builder* magazine, 1926–30, passim.

25. On Chiltern Court, see the author's *London's Metropolitan Railway* (1986).

26. Details and dates from *The Builder* magazine, 1933–38, passim, and contemporary advertising.

27. Details from advertising in Southern Railway Suburban Timetables, 1 January 1937 and 3 January 1939.
28. *The Builder* magazine, 19 October 1933, Briggs, Martin S, FRIBA, *Building Today* (1944), Anon, *Southern Homes, Surrey and Hants (Electrified)*, (1937).
29. Clunn, Harold P., *The Face of The Home Counties*, (nd), Anon. *Southern Homes in Sussex (Electrified)*, (1938).
30. Advertisement, Ideal Boilers & Radiators Ltd, in *The Ideal Home* magazine, September 1938.
31. Massey, Phillip, 'Expenditure of 1,360 British Middle Class Households in 1938–9', *Journal of The Royal Statistical Society,* cv part iii (1942).

# CHAPTER 5

# A COMFORTABLE LIFE

## The Keeping of Servants

Right through to the end of the 1930s, employment of living-in servants, almost invariably females, remained a lynchpin of the comfortable middle class life style. Providing an important status symbol, these were the people, who, in Lady Troubridge's phrase, 'live in our homes and labour for our comfort and happiness'.

The majority of domestic servants were to be found in middle rather than upper class houses and there were more in London and the south-east than other parts of the country. Defining 'standard of comfort' as the number of domestic servants employed for every hundred households, the 1901 census compilers found as many as eighty women in service per hundred in some districts of London, in comparison with around six in some quite large northern industrial centres.

In the first two decades of the century there were few middle class homes without the services of at least a 'maid of all work', this lowest grade of help being obtainable for the modest outlay of £12 to £16 a year[1], or as little as eight pounds if the girl were very young or otherwise inexperienced. Those lower middle class homes finding even this pittance beyond their means, or otherwise lacking suitable accommodation for a living-in maid, usually employed a daily or weekly outside helper for rough work or child-minding.

But change was already evident. As the size of middle class families began to shrink, the total number of servants working in each household in the 1900s and 1910s was showing signs of becoming smaller than it had been in Victorian times. (It should also be said that the corresponding reduction in working class family size was to have some effect on the supply, since parents were not subjected to such urgent pressure to farm out their older daughters as domestic servants at the point when they began exercise a strain on accommodation and on food and clothing costs.)

Wartime conditions and exigencies in 1914–18 also had an effect on servant-keeping, though not such a permanent one as many thought at the time. Some heads of household quickly seized the excuse to reduce expenditure, indulging a mean streak not uncommon in the middle classes. In the first month of war, one such drew up a 'war programme' of domestic economies in which the first item of several proposed measures was 'Servants must take 25 per cent less wages'[2]. This was a remarkably short-sighted move; as the demand for war factory and office labour mounted relentlessly some 400,000 women and girls (twenty three per cent of the total) eagerly exchanged the petty tyrannies of domestic service for the greater freedom, more amusing life (often hostel-based) and better pay offered by war jobs of all kinds[3].

Most of this loss was however recovered by the middle classes in the high unemployment of the early 1920s, since retailing or domestic service were almost the only employment for working class women and girls. This restoration of the pre-1915 position was aided by a wartime organisation, the Central Committee on Women's Training and Employment, revived in 1920 to struggle with the problem of female unemployment. It organised domestic service training for some 25,000 women, even supplying free maids' uniforms to those too poor to buy them. Later there were other state-aided or wholly private schemes which aimed to encourage girls from the depressed industrial areas of the north of England, Wales and Scotland to take up domestic service in middle class homes, mainly in the south, where most of the servant-keeping middle classes still lived*.

These initiatives were in part a response to strong middle class lobbying seeking an improved supply of good domestic servants to restore the situation to which many had been accustomed and indeed had accepted as the natural order of things. There was particular anger that girls were able to draw unemployment insurance payments if they had held any sort of job outside domestic service (which was not covered by the scheme). Also, from time to time between the wars, there were outbursts in the press and magazines which suggested a strong middle class resentment at an alleged lack of facilities and enthusiasm in schools in the matter of preparing girls for domestic service.

Even before 1914, something called 'the servant problem' had been a topic of conversation in middle class circles as well as being much discussed in newspapers and magazines read by them. After World War 1 it took on new urgency and emphasis. The 'problem' was an apparent decline both in the quantity and quality of the recruits coming forward, which was in reality simply a matter of demand outpacing supply. Whilst the number of women in England & Wales employed as living-in servants

---

* See Appendix B2.

fell only marginally in the first thirty years of the century, (census figures in 1931 revealed a figure of 1.14m against 1.29m in 1901), the steady rise in middle class prosperity and numbers meant these had to be spread over a rapidly increasing total of households of servant-employing status prepared to pay the going rate. By the mid-1920s, supply was well behind demand, particularly in prosperous southern England, and neither the break-up of many of the old upper class estates with their large domestic staffs after 1919 nor the general reduction in middle class family size did much to alleviate the shortage.

This new situation encouraged the more enterprising and intelligent women servants to assert greater independence and militancy in their relations with their middle class employers. There was much more moving around to improve conditions and pay, this having some effect on wages. The outcome was that from the end of the 1920s, with labour-saving domestic appliances, furnishings and decorations starting to appear on the market, new houses planned and equipped to make them easy to run and keep clean, and a widening sale of ready-prepared and processed foods, many middle class households, especially in southern England, began to reduce their living-in domestic staff to one or two at most whilst others, including most lower middle class families, managed with nothing more than an outsider coming in daily or two or three times a week to undertake the heavier tasks. In some suburban areas this 'extramural' domestic labour was a long-established feature; one variety, known as 'step-girls', operated in small gangs, from the late 19th century to the end of the 1930s, knocking on doors regularly and offering to clean the stones and tiles at front and back entrances. It was also possible to hire a girl to wait at table when guests were present, or as a morning housemaid. This had a strong appeal since these outsiders came complete with the usual uniforms and could be passed off as living-in servants to those not in the know.

The anonymous author of the post World War 1 edition of *Mrs Beeton's Household Management* recognised the importance of the 'servant problem' by referring to it on the very first page of this comprehensive and massive tome:

> The war and consequent heavy taxation brought about a social revolution . . . Good servants are hard to get, harder still, perhaps to keep, and even the wealthiest people prefer houses of manageable dimensions, with labour-saving fittings and appliances,[4]

By the 1930s, servant-keeping had largely become a matter of 'keeping up appearances', of following an outdated lifestyle with growing difficulty and expense at a time when domestic service as an occupation was increasingly despised by the peers of those who undertook it, offering little or no attraction in competition with the plenitude of office jobs, or work in the burgeoning retail, manufacturing, service and entertainment industries. Many of those servants still employed in the thirties and forties remained at their posts out of misguided loyalty, or were too old to consider a change of occupation, or stayed on simply because they were able to obtain an almost revolutionary easing of their working conditions. This last generation of indigenous domestics were mostly recruited from families suffering from the impact of economic depression in old industrial areas such as South Wales and the North East; others came from a poverty-stricken Irish background. They were increasingly helped in their daily tasks by their employers, most of whom learned domestic routines with remarkable rapidity. Much to general surprise, many more middle class households found they could adapt, with little difficulty, to managing without any living-in help at all.

Signs of this revolution in a way of life which had lasted over a hundred years were evident in those magazines aimed at the comfortable middle class family. Articles began to appear advising how to keep one's maids by making their rooms attractive and their chairs comfortable, on how to manage with only one servant, and, by 1930, how to cope with none at all[5]. Emphasis was placed on defining the maids' duties and on drawing up a comprehensive and detailed working timetable for each. The need to make these things clear was perhaps a reflection of the decline in the quality of the candidates coming forward.

Whilst the larger detached houses costing £2,000 or more often incorporated a maids' sitting room, in most middle class homes the servants would be expected to resort to their bedroom when not required, leaving at least one on duty in the kitchen with an eye on the bell indicator, ready to answer any ring. Space for sitting around comfortably in kitchens of the newer houses was limited and in the 1920s one magazine writer thought folding deck-chairs might be the answer to this problem[6]. A favourite occupation between duties, if there were no sewing or darning to be done, was the consumption of cheap romantic fiction, in magazines and paper-covered novels, though some mistresses would insist that the maid take an early afternoon walk.

A major problem for any employer was to ensure that servants were up promptly in the mornings; late rising could throw out everyone's timetable for the rest of the day. One suggestion of 1901, noting that 6 am was late enough to let a maid lie in bed, proposed a 'rising bell', operated from the employer's bedside, since 'it is unwise to rely on her to get herself up'[7]. Another writer, in 1929, commented that the furnishing of the maids' room should 'include a reliable clock with a clear face and alarum . . . personal responsibility for prompt rising should be enforced, as nothing can more disorganise a household than lateness with early morning work'[8].

Before World War 1, segregation, a basic tenet of the class system at its fullest vigour, was built into the larger middle class houses in the form of a separate servants' staircase (usually hidden, uncarpeted and with steeper treads) and a separate entrance for use by servants and tradesmen. As mentioned in Chapter 4, in the larger detached houses, servants were also given separate lavatories near the kitchen and there were problems about bathrooms.

Those working in the larger houses built before World War 1 normally slept in unheated attic rooms where they had to make do with secondhand or 'handed-down' furniture, few if any floor coverings and candles or oil lamps as lighting, the latter often continuing when the rest of the house was lit by gas or electricity. Until the mid or late 1920s, most middle class homes had no running hot water upstairs, little or no electricity, and coal fires in every occupied room in winter, depositing smuts and soot on the furnishings and entailing much laborious preparation, cleaning out, and lugging around of fuel and ashes. There were black-leaded fire places and cast iron cooking ranges, steel cutlery and many brass fittings, all of which required frequent, if not daily, cleaning and polishing. Washing clothes involved lighting a coal fire under a 'copper' to heat the necessary quantity of water, pummelling the clothes in hot soapy water in a 'dolly tub', lifting them out, rinsing and wringing, putting the larger items such as sheets through a large hand-turned mangle or wringer, drying outdoors (or, if the weather were unfavourable, on a kitchen airer-frame), ironing with flat irons heated on the cooking range, and finally, airing. This accumulation of work, together with preparing and cooking the numerous daily meals, waiting at table, answering bells, sewing and darning worn and damaged clothes and linen and general room cleaning, was considered in the first two and a half decades of the century to justify a staff of at least two and preferably three in the average household.

Each servant, in addition to wages, would cost around £26 a year to feed, rather more after 1915. The minimum establishment in all but the most modest middle class households at this period would be a 'cook-general' or 'general', obtainable for £20–£30 a year before 1914, a house parlourmaid at £15–£25, and an outsider calling in to do the rough work. The more comfortable households could afford a full time cook, who in the Edwardian period, might command £30 or more a year, according to her experience and ability and the number of staff employed. If she were the senior of several servants, she might receive £60–£80 or more, as 'cook/housekeeper'. Besides a cook and parlourmaid, such households would also have at least one general housemaid at £12–16 and perhaps a between-maid or 'tweeny' at £8–£10, the latter often recruited as young as thirteen or fourteen from a farm labourer's family or an orphanage.

Affluent middle class families would almost invariably employ a 'nanny' or childrens' nurse at £20–£40, the actual rate relating to her experience and the number of children in the family. As we shall see later, her relationship with the children was often closer than that they enjoyed with their parents. If no suitable schools were conveniently available for the younger children and girls, the wealthier families of the 1900s and 1910s might employ a governess at £30–£60. Since she was usually lower middle class, downwardly mobile upper middle class or a foreigner, the governess's status was indeterminate, although always somewhere above that of the normal servants. Governesses were a dying breed, even before 1914, as more and more middle class infants and girls were being sent to school from an early age.

Another species of indeterminate status somewhere above the ordinary servant was the lady's companion, employed by wealthy middle and upper class spinsters and widows to ease and lighten their otherwise lonely existence, arrange their social life, organise and share their holidays and so on. Such women, like governesses, were often upper middle class types who had come down in the world but some were intelligent lower middle class women who had acquired skill in the social graces, the manners and accents of their employers rubbing off on them to a remarkable degree. Other luxuries were coachmen and, from the middle 1900s, if the family were wealthy enough to afford one of the costly Edwardian hand-made motor cars, chauffeurs. Whilst these might be accommodated in a stable or garage loft, any gardeners or outside handymen employed would be most likely to come in to work on a daily, or part-daily basis, or if the property were extensive, they might live in a cottage or lodge in the grounds.

As mentioned earlier, at the bottom of the middle class pile in the Edwardian years only one woman or girl was affordable. This unfortunate and lonely drudge, confined to attic or smallest bedroom at night and for most of the day to the kitchen, with no other servants to keep her company or speak up for her, was all too often overworked by a mistress only just above her in social status and therefore all the more anxious to assert her position and authority. Not surprisingly, she was often known as 'the slavey'.

By the middle 1920s perhaps the most frequent combination of living-in servants was a cook-general at around £50 a year and a house parlourmaid at £26–£45. At the most basic level, only a cook-general would be employed. In both cases there would often be another woman coming into the house daily or less frequently to assist with rough work. Indeed it was difficult by then to recruit a good cook-general without the guarantee of such help. If there were two or more children in the family, a young girl might be employed, at £30 a year or less, as a nurse-housemaid or 'mother's help'; in some families she might be the only living-in servant.

Massey[9] found in 1938–9 that middle class heads of household with incomes of £250–£350 averaged an expenditure of just under £5 a year on domestic help, those with £350–£500 spent an average of £8.3s.6d, those with £500–£700, £16.17s and those at £700 and above, £38.10s. These figures were gathered from civil servants, local government officers and teachers and it is obvious that only those in the top income bracket were by that time able to employ even the most basic living-in domestic help.

Duties of servants varied considerably, but some indication of the usual pattern may be given. House parlourmaids were required to open and close blinds, curtains and windows, morning and evening; to empty night slops; to open the front door to visitors, showing them into the sitting room if the master or mistress indicated they were 'at home'; to lay the table for meals, wait at table and clear away; and to prepare and serve afternoon tea in the sitting room. They also saw to the valeting, mending clothes and linen, and to packing. They made and turned down beds; answered the telephone; prepared, lit and maintained coal fires in all rooms as required, and cleaned grates; they answered room bells by arrangement with the other servants; and dusted and cleaned all rooms. In the older houses, the house parlourmaid carried hot water upstairs in large brass, copper or white enamel cans for washing, shaving and bathing. She ran the baths, washed up crockery and cutlery and saw to the flowers in all rooms if this was not done by the mistress herself. Finally she acted as female butler, looking after the silver and plate, and seeing to the wines and spirits, cigars, cigarettes and newspapers under the direction of the master of the household. If a housemaid were employed as well, the post was known simply as parlourmaid, the duties restricted to the lighter and less menial of those named. As we shall see when we come to uniform, parlourmaids had a decorative function and a tall good looking girl always had an advantage in the competition for this rather better-paid position.

Although ladies' maids were rarely found in any but the most affluent middle class households, especially after 1920, something should be said about this 'educated, superior person', to use Lady Troubridge's description. A well-paid servant – the best were thought to be French girls – her sole duties were to dress and undress her mistress and look after her clothes, toilet and general comfort. She did no housework and wore no uniform, clothing herself quietly and neatly. She expected a workroom or bedroom and workroom combined and her accommodation would be kept clean and in order by other servants. Lower down the scale, a parlourmaid might have to take on at least some of these intimate tasks if one or more housemaids were employed to relieve her of the other chores. Both ladies' maids and parlourmaids enjoyed the special privilege of being addressed by their surname, prefaced by 'Miss' or 'Mrs' in the case of the other servants.

The cook was a key figure, preparing all meals except afternoon tea, including those for herself and other servants, also making bread, jams, cakes, pastries, wines and so on for the household's consumption. She was required to clean her kitchen; to light and maintain the fire in the kitchen range where this was the means of cooking and heating water; to attend to any separate water heater; to deal with tradesmen and answer all calls at the tradesmen's door; and if only a cook and housemaid were employed, the cook would also be expected to share in room and general house-cleaning duties. Should there be a kitchen or scullery maid, this girl would take over the more menial of these tasks.

In general the servants' day began at 6.30 am or earlier and lasted until around 10 pm. Although some enlightened employers allowed a weekly half day off even before 1914, for many in the first two decades or so of the century the only free time was an hour and a half or so in the early afternoon immediately after lunch, and perhaps an hour or a little longer in the evenings after dinner. One servant at least had to remain on call until the family bedtime or when told they were no longer required. In many households Sunday duties were lightened by the family taking the main meal at midday followed by a cold supper at night. This allowed at least one of the servants to attend church (usually with the family, but sitting apart) and perhaps also to visit relatives. Or, if only two servants were employed, the Sunday arrangements might be such that one was free after the midday meal on alternate weeks. In the north of England, where high tea replaced dinner, servants had a slightly easier regimen.

One day off a month was usual by the turn of the century, this gradually extended to at least half a day a week for almost all by 1930, in addition to the lighter Sunday routine. In these matters much depended on local custom; a mistress could not recruit servants easily if she were not prepared to give as much free time as that generally prevailing locally. Knowledge of this, and any trends, quickly spread through the network of small private domestic agencies which were the principal means of recruitment. Every household established its own routines but some idea of what was expected through the day can be gained from the 1920s and 1930s timetables reproduced at Appendix B1.

Servants were a mixed blessing in a household. They frequently caused problems and experienced emotional upsets which the mistress had to sort out. If she were young and just married, the handling of servants might be traumatic for her and it was not uncommon for novice mistresses to be frightened of experienced domestics. Relationships between the younger members of the family and the servants deserve a mention. Sharing as they did a common feeling of subordination to the master and mistress of the household, they often developed a close friendship. On occasion this could result in the undermining of parental discipline, for example when servants threw away uneaten food which children had been told they must consume at the following meal. As they grew up, children frequently learned the facts of life from servants, who might also be prepared to encourage illicit or forbidden relationships with the opposite sex by conveying messages or posting letters that parents would have stopped. Servants would also cover up by lying when parents enquired whether a teenage son or daughter was home or in bed. And they could be a source of forbidden reading matter for the curious adolescent.

Since servants were about the house, night and day, the family in one sense had always to be on their guard. The privacy so dear to the middle classes was difficult to maintain when they might come into a room at any time unannounced except by a quiet knock, and they had access to most drawers and cupboards, not to mention items inadvertently left lying around. Listening behind closed doors was a frequent amusement. Occasionally a master or mistress might become neurotic about the servants, suspecting them of plotting to allow burglars inside the house, perhaps in revenge for some reprimand or perceived slight. This fear was sometimes justified and police investigating robberies and burglaries would always initially focus their suspicion on the servants, who would be the first to be closely questioned.

Although it was the custom to stop talking about confidential or personal matters when they came into the room (in some households, conversation slipped into French, or more frequently, Franglais), servants inevitably overheard much and quickly picked up family disputes and scandal. What they learned, or manufactured from it, was passed on as gossip to servants of neighbouring households and to tradesmen. Loyalty and discretion among servants were less frequently found in middle class households than in upper class establishments, where employers were regarded with more respect and affection, partly because perquisites were much better and the servants, under the control of a competent butler or housekeeper, were left to run things on their own with the minimum of interference.

Whilst there were substantial compensations such as shelter from the rough and tumble of working class life, much better food than that enjoyed by the ordinary working class household and an enviable security of employment, from the servants' point of view it was a hard life for little reward, especially in the larger and older houses without central heating, running hot water and other modern improvements. Unprotected by any legislation similar to the Factory Acts, they worked a day of fourteen to sixteen hours that was physically exhausting, and often dispiriting, especially if alone or with only one other servant who was not necessarily a congenial companion. Master or mistress might be cruel, spiteful, inconsiderate or unduly demanding. Some middle class mistresses were mean enough to lock up their larders, doling out daily what the servants were to eat, a practice which tended to undermine one of the major perks of the job.

Mrs Beeton's somewhat perfectionist doctrine on servant-mistress relationships – that they should be based on a realisation of common humanity and mutual dependence and interest by each party[10] – was often remote from actual practice. The reality, virtually throughout the middle class, was closer to the perceptive 1925 assessment of Violet M. Firth:

> The middle class women are rigorous in their enforcement of caste reverence . . . they are so habituated to the presence of a being from another sphere who is credited with a blissful freedom from human feelings that it is a shock to them to find human nature akin to their own concealed by a servant's apron[11]

Mrs Peel, in her 1933 book, recounts her service on the post war committee mentioned earlier and wryly notes that the employers seemed to need training as much as the servants. It was certainly the case that in most households little or no thought was given to the comfort and attractiveness of the maids' rooms; door keys were often refused and mistresses considered themselves free to walk into their servants' rooms at will and go through their cupboards and drawers. Lewis and Maude suggest that these attitudes persisted right through to the late 1940s, playing some part in the steady decline of domestic service as a form of employment and its eventual almost complete extinction[12].

It is true that servants were free at any time to give in their notice, leaving then for another position, and could expect the necessary 'character' (reference), honestly written, if they did so; but they did not have the benefit of written contracts and their employers were not legally required to provide the reference that was essential to get another job. A fear of being dismissed without a reference or with an unsatisfactory one, kept many women at work in conditions they would rather have left. This situation was of course much less oppressive in the shortage conditions of the 1920s and 1930s.

Religion was often specifically mentioned in advertisements. Roman Catholic girls and women, though often forming a major element in the employment pool, frequently found their services unrequired since absence to attend early mass might disrupt household routines and a relaxed attitude to the Sabbath (for example, playing board games with the children) could cause offence in strict Protestant households.

Control was often close, extending even to censorship of all items of dress worn, outdoors as well as in. Uniform was important, especially for parlour and housemaids and nannies, and as we shall see in a moment, there were particular indignities and stresses associated with it. In the morning, a maid would normally wear a plain cotton print gown, simple white cap with white apron (a rough one if an assistant housemaid) and black cotton or woollen stockings. Until the early 1920s her footwear would be buttoned quarter-calf length boots, in later years replaced by flat-heeled, single-strapped rubber-soled and heeled indoor shoes. For lunch and remainder of the day, the parlourmaid (or sole maid) was normally required to retire to her room to tidy herself up and don black artificial silk stockings, a simple short black dress relieved by white lace collar and cuffs, a tiara-like cap held by a black velvet ribbon, a little white lace-trimmed apron and perhaps patent leather shoes. In the 1930s she might be seen wearing a brown dress with matching shoes and silk stockings. Servants had to supply their basic uniforms themselves, at a cost of around £5, before trying for any job at all. But once employed, master and mistress would customarily present lengths of uniform dress material, or give stockings at Christmas time. If special luxuries such as the afternoon parlourmaid's dress just described were required, these would be supplied by the employer.

Servants were very much regarded as a part of the image and display presented by their middle class employers to the outside world and this was sometimes carried to bizarre lengths. In the January 1930 edition of

*The Ideal Home* magazine it was announced that thanks to the ingenuity of Harrods, the famous Knightsbridge store, it was possible to have servants dressed to suit the architectural style of one's house, 'an effective finishing touch by choosing caps and aprons for your maids in harmony with the period'. A choice of Tudor, Cromwellian, Queen Anne/Georgian (a dainty mob cap with black velvet band and frilled apron 'faintly hinting at a pannier line') or Stuart cap and apron styles was available.

In the matter of uniform there were also dangers, and potential sources of family discord. It was not unknown for a jealous or narrow-minded mistress to forbid her prettier young servants to wear fancy underwear, sheer stockings or make-up, or to seek to subdue the impact of the parlourmaid's afternoon wear, on the grounds (not of course openly specified) that such things might prove unduly provocative for the male members of the household.

Plain uniforms and underwear and thick stockings notwithstanding, it was certainly the case that the presence of physically attractive young girls in the house at all times presented an often irresistible temptation for the men of the family, no matter how vigilant the mistress. The comic magazines, cinema films and picture postcards of 1900–20 testify to this in their frequent and varied presentations on the theme of master or young son dallying with a pretty parlourmaid, either undiscovered, or interrupted by the mistress of the house. Since most working class girls were brought up with a great fear of unwanted pregnancies, the experienced servant usually saw to it that such liaisons did not proceed beyond heavy petting, especially if the man or boy were younger and less mature. But should pregnancy ensue, it was the girl who had the rough deal.

Once an affair was discovered by the mistress, she would normally prefer to believe any denial by her husband, son or other middle class man living in the house, or at any rate pretend to believe it. The girl would be blamed. Dismissal without a 'character' would then follow, with the almost certain consequence that the unfortunate girl would be unable to secure a position in another household. Until the late 1910s, her only recourse might then be the workhouse or prostitution.

As part of their efforts to protect the virginity of their girl servants, and also as a precaution against burglars, mistresses usually forbade their domestics to entertain men friends (snobbishly designated 'followers') in and around the house, a condition frequently specified in advertisements for vacancies. But by the 1920s wiser counsels began to prevail, as we shall notice in a moment. Despite attempts at control, large numbers of girl servants did succeed in finding partners, most often amongst the tradesmen and errand boys who appeared daily at the kitchen door, an occasion which afforded much scope for flirting. Although it was for many years usual to seek the mistress's permission to go out, even to post a letter, this, liberally extended, together with afternoons and days off, gave ample opportunity to cement a relationship. Nor did the servant girls pay overmuch attention to their mistress's attempts to forbid visits to 'undesirable' locations such as a nearby army barracks or naval base, or fairs, since it was unlikely they would be detected in breaching such instructions. 'Mrs Beeton' was, of course, on top of all this sort of thing, advising readers:

> An hour should be fixed, usually about 10 pm before which every servant is expected to be in. To permit breaches of this rule, without good reason, is far from being a kindness to the servant concerned. The moral responsibility rests largely on the employer who permits late hours. Especial care is needed with young girls. They should be given opportunities of welcoming respectable friends at their employer's house, and not be forced to spend their time out of doors, often in driving rain, possibly in bad company, or at questionable entertainments[13].

A staple part of its lifestyle since the middle class first appeared on the British social scene, servant-keeping finally faded away from all but a tiny proportion of households in the 1940s, as more and more alternative employment opportunities of a more attractive kind opened up for girls and women, and as economic pressures on the working class over the whole country eased. In 1931 almost 500,000 households (4.8 per cent of the total) in England & Wales had at least one living-in servant and 41,000 (0.4 per cent) had three or more; twenty years later, only one per cent of households had a servant and a mere 3,000 (0.02 per cent) had three or more.

# At least Four Square Meals

The unnecessarily complicated daily ritual of meals in the English middle class household – breakfast, lunch, afternoon tea, dinner (and sometimes a late supper in addition) – was long an object of mild amusement to many foreigners. Like so much of middle class lifestyle, it derived from the customs of the upper class but whilst for the latter a multi-meal regime played an important part in relieving tedium, the fact that it became so rooted and widespread in the middle class, surviving more or less intact right through to the 1940s, perhaps reflects the role played by regular meals, evenly spaced through the day, as a means of keeping the servants of a small household busy when they might otherwise have had intervals of idleness. Set in their ways, generally conservative by nature, the middle classes wanted no variation when away, so their hotels and railway restaurant cars faithfully reflected the same regime, indeed continuing with it long after it had been abandoned in the home.

In the process of getting through these closely-spaced daily sittings, middle class people consumed much stodgy and starchy food as well as significant quantities of fat and sugar, which perhaps helped them to feel a little more comfortable in their inefficiently-heated and poorly-insulated houses. There was however a slow process of change in diet, beginning shortly after World War 1 and led by the women, as we shall see later.

The amounts of food consumed at each sitting were not usually prodigious; in many homes portions were quite small, even mean, and quality and imagination were often lacking. In the late 1930s the author's wife was invited to dinner with a very comfortable Surrey middle class family, where the main course, ostentatiously brought to the table in a silver salver by a manservant, consisted of nothing more than a single sausage per person, accompanied by a tiny dab of mashed potatoes and another of boiled cabbage, these served with equal flourish from silver plate.

In the more affluent middle class homes, the first refreshment was morning tea and biscuits brought into the bedrooms by the maid, although the eating day really began in earnest with breakfast, served at 8.30 to 9 am, (somewhat earlier for the lower middle class, whose breadwinners were to catch trains which would see them into their office desks by 9 or 9.30 am). 'The English breakfast,' observes the post World War 1 edition of *Mrs Beeton's Household Management*, 'even when taken at an early hour, is a substantial meal'. Indeed. Consumed in the breakfast room or dining room, it usually ran to at least three courses.

During the first two decades of the century this meal would begin with stewed fruit, or (more usually) hot porridge made with oats, but from the early 1920s, the first dish was increasingly a North American innovation, packaged factory-prepared breakfast cereals eaten with hot or cold milk. This was a brilliant commercial idea; it not only offered time and labour-saving advantages for the consumer but proved immensely profitable for the producer. Large sales were eventually generated for attractive cardboard boxes filled with miniscule densities of flavoured and toasted grain brought to suitable bulk with the help of generous amounts of air. The first of these newcomers, arriving in British shops in 1902, consisted of toasted wheat flakes flavoured with sugar, malt and salt. It was followed by many similar products. Initially the importers had a hard struggle to change middle class English breakfast habits but after the disruption of imports caused by World War 1, breakfast cereals returned in larger quantities and even greater variety, the North American manufacturers establishing their own factories in Britain from 1926 onwards. By about the middle of the 1930s, porridge had been all but replaced as a breakfast starter, except perhaps in Scotland, northern England and the armed services, where the old habits died hard.

Cereals consumed, there followed the traditional fried eggs and bacon, or other combinations of fried or grilled items such as kidneys, liver, chops, mushrooms, tomatoes and potatoes. Alternatively, for variety, a dish of ham and eggs, or perhaps fish such as haddock or kipper could be taken. Ladies and children and men with poor digestions might content themselves with one or two poached, scrambled or boiled eggs and children would dip fingers of buttered bread (known as 'soldiers') into the runny yolks of the latter. All this would be washed down with copious draughts of tea or milky coffee and the meal concluded with buttered toast and marmalade.

Since it was acceptable for the adult males of the family to begin to read their morning newspaper at breakfast, conversation was discouraged or restricted, a custom which suited temperaments not at their best at this hour of the day. However things might brighten up a little for the ladies and children when the maid brought in the morning post, which would be opened and discussed over toast and marmalade. Servants did the minimum of waiting at table for this meal, since most of the food would be placed beforehand on the sideboard or on a table laid the night before. A great boon to those households where arrivals at the breakfast table were well-spaced out was the spirit-lamp food-warmer, replaced by electrical devices in the 1920s affectionately known as 'The Sluggard's Delight'. Another innovation of the twenties, the electric toaster, enabled toast to be prepared in the breakfast room as required instead of being brought in from the kitchen to cool rapidly in silver-plated racks, a practice which generated an acceptance and eventually a taste for cold toast still persisting in some households today.

Lunch was a miniature dinner, with fewer courses, served in the dining room at 1 to 1.45 pm when, in the more comfortable homes, those at table would be waited upon by the parlourmaid in her afternoon finery. The meal would begin with a savoury such as sardines on toast, or with soup, normally followed by one main cooked meat dish (or cold meat left over from the previous day's dinner) served with boiled vegetables. Then came a boiled, steamed or baked pudding, perhaps followed by cheese and dry biscuits. Water was always on the table but wine or ale might also be served.

Afternoon tea at 4.30 to 5 pm was a ritual dear to the English and Scottish middle classes, largely confined to the ladies of the household and any afternoon visitors they might be entertaining during the usual hours for social calls (3.30–5.30 pm). In the more affluent homes, tea was brought into the sitting room by the parlourmaid, but if gentlemen were present it was customary for the maid to leave them to pass round the sandwich plates and cake-stands to the seated ladies whilst the hostess poured tea, assisted by her daughters or friends if the gathering was large. On fine summer days, the ritual was transferred to the garden. A choice of China or Indian teas was always available, dispensed from bone china or silver pots. Delicate sandwiches, small and crustless, of very thin soft white bread, buttered and filled with cress, cucumber or savoury items would be supplemented by buttered bread, preserves, biscuits, small fancy cakes, pastries and slices of various kinds of cake. Toast, muffins and or toasted tea cakes might replace the sandwiches in the cold weather. In the 1900s and 1910s, most if not all these items would have been made in the kitchen by the cook, including the bread and jam, but by the 1920s there was a growing choice of attractive teatime items available in shops, many of them distributed over wide areas by new large scale bakery enterprises such as that developed by the famous caterers, Messrs. J. Lyons & Co. In contrast to breakfast and the somewhat subdued lunch, teatime floated on lively conversation and gossip, which its arrival in the sitting room first interrupted, then accelerated. If there were no visitors, tea would be a less elaborate meal, taken on a tray or trolley in the sitting room, or at the dining room table with any children returned from day school.

In northern England and Scotland a 'high tea' often replaced afternoon tea and evening dinner. A somewhat moveable feast, shared with the working class, this was fitted into the activities of the household at any time between 5 and 7 pm. It consisted of one or two small hot meat, egg or fish dishes (except in summer), cold meats, salads, bread and butter and cakes, cold fruit tarts served with cream or custard, and fruit. Tea and sometimes coffee flowed throughout.

In all but the lowest echelons of the middle class, evening dinner was a formal daily ritual for which family and any guests changed into evening dress. 'The custom of dressing for dinner is generally observed amongst people of any means' noted Lady Troubridge in 1926. 'It is a cleanly, refreshing habit and economical, for street or afternoon dress soon becomes shabby if worn for hours at a time'. There had been some relaxation since the turn of the century: ladies dining at home appeared in *demi-toilette*, a simple kind of evening dress, not cut very low, or a tea-gown, but more formal dress was still adopted if guests were present.

Pre-dinner drinks were taken in the sitting-room or study, normally sherry for the ladies, whisky for the men. By the late 1920s, some of the more advanced southern English middles were experimenting with the cocktail habit, introduced from the USA and proselytized in Hollywood films.

At the summons of the gong, sounded in the hall by the parlourmaid at a fixed time between 7.45 and 8.30 pm, family and any guests would move into the dining room, where they would proceed to eat their way through hors d'oeuvres, soup, a fish course, a meat course (perhaps followed by poultry or game), pudding or sweet, cheese and celery, and finally fruit. Wine would be taken with the meal, whilst coffee and perhaps brandy and liqueurs would be available afterwards. An effort would be made to maintain a continuous flow of polite conversation at the well-decorated, softly-lit table. Opening gambits between strangers finding themselves together at the table tended to follow set patterns; in southern England one commonly employed was 'How far are you from Guildford?' and of course the ever-changing British weather was a safe topic. Although it was generally assumed (not always correctly) that everyone was a Conservative, politics were usually avoided, as was religion. The table itself would be covered with a stiffly-starched damask cloth which set off the silver or silver plate. And when guests were present, the decorations

The middle class dining at home, 1929

might be enhanced by artistically-folded linen table napkins which would be undone at the start of the meal and placed on the lap (some older men, caring less for appearances, stuffed one corner into their collars so that the napkin protected their tie and waistcoast). Napkins had class connotations. Since the average middle class household used their table napkins for several days at a time, between family meals they were rolled into a ring made of silver or some cheaper material, often engraved with the owner's initial. This contrasted with the upper classes, who were supposed to have the resources to afford a freshly-laundered napkin at every meal and therefore no need of rings. Since the working class did not use table napkins (which they and some in the lower middle class referred to as 'serviettes'), a neat if facetious definition of the English middle classes up to the 1940s might be that they were those members of the population using napkin rings at every meal.

If there were guests present, the ladies would retire to the drawing room after the coffee, cigarettes and cigars had been served, leaving the men to talk in a more relaxed way as they passed round the wine or brandy and smoked. After some ten or fifteen minutes the host would suggest 'Shall we join the ladies?' as he rang the bell for the servants to clear the table. Reunited, both sexes then chatted, listened to music or played cards for the rest of the evening.

Dinner was not necessarily the final meal of the day. An extended evening, perhaps spent at the theatre, or entertaining guests to a late hour, might conclude with a supper served between 11 pm and midnight or even later. This repast, perhaps laid out as a buffet so that the servants might be dispensed with, would consist of cold meats and other cold dishes or meat or fish pies, made up from the remains of the dinner together with selected sweets or fruit. Whisky and soda would be available in the hall as guests left.

This four or five meal routine was necessarily modified during World War 1 when many felt a moral pressure to make 'sacrifices' and everyone was affected by high prices and shortages of food. Breakfasts were simplified, the number of courses at lunch and dinner reduced, and in some families a light evening supper replaced the more formal dinner ritual altogether. Such modifications were perpetuated after the war in many households.

Between the wars, the lower middle class, in their new semis or Edwardian and Victorian terraces and mostly without servants, practised their own slightly different regimen. In many such homes the midday meal was the main one and known as 'dinner', although office-working fathers ate 'lunch' at or near their place of employment. On Mondays, when mother faced the heavy task of washing clothes, perhaps without assistance, this meal had to be simple in preparation, possibly a poached egg or cold meat with mashed potatoes followed by bananas sliced into custard. Tea in such families was an after-school refreshment, confined to bread and butter and jam (or Golden Syrup) and a piece of cake. At weekends however this meal was much-embellished, featuring such items as cold meats, shrimps, tinned fruits, jellies, trifles or blancmanges, as well as brown and white bread and many kinds of cakes, pastries and sponges, the variety to some extent depending on whether relatives or other guests were present. On weekdays, the evening meal was frequently known as 'supper' and featured a simple hot dish and hot sweet but on Sundays dinner was almost invariably taken at around 1 pm, its central item a roast joint of meat, served with several kinds of vegetables and only rarely preceded by soup. Within an hour or so of its completion, tea and biscuits would often follow, perhaps after the lady of the house had taken a short rest on her bed from her morning exertions. Sunday tea, as already mentioned, was enhanced above weekday standards, and taken very late in the afternoon, although in many households it had to be timed for a prompt arrival at 6.30 pm evening church service. The day would often conclude with a light snack such as biscuits or savoury sandwiches taken with Ovaltine or cocoa.

With their rising real incomes, the middle classes were able to enjoy to the full the greater variety of fresh and processed foods coming on to the market in the 1930s. As already noticed, the kitchen tasks were much lightened and reduced in this period, with the arrival in the shops of factory-made, packaged cakes, pies, tarts and puddings, and a great variety of convenience foods such as tinned fruit and fish, ice cream and packaged sponge, cake and custard mixes.

From about the middle of the 1920s, US influence, diffused through the women's magazines so widely read by middle class housewives, led to a gradual change in diet, with more emphasis on vitamins, fruit and salads and less on the traditional stodgy and starchy fare. In contrast to a general lack of change in working class diet over the half century, it seems probable that the middle classes were, from the 1920s onwards, consuming more fruit and vegetables, more dairy products and less bread and meat than their immediate predecessors. Such statistics as are available tend to confirm this. A 1926 analysis of expenditure in middle class households with incomes of £350–£575[14] reveals that thirty seven per cent of the total outlay on food went on meat, fish and meat and fish products, 12.7 per cent on bread and bakery products and 25.5 per cent on dairy products. Fruit absorbed only 7.5 per cent and vegetables

5.5. A similar survey just over ten years later[15] found that expenditure on meat and fish had declined to around twenty seven per cent, with more (twenty nine per cent) going into dairy products, fruit (around ten per cent) and vegetables (seven per cent). There was no change in the proportion spent on bread and bakery products. The effect of these slow changes on health, appearance and attitudes had hardly become significant by the end of our period.

# A Telephone at Home

Other comforts and conveniences associated with the middle class lifestyle call for review. By the time the Post Office took over control and responsibility for the national telephone service from private firms in 1912[16], the telephone was already installed in many middle class homes, particularly in urban and suburban areas, where local calls were free once the rental of eight pounds a year had been paid. Early telephone directories reveal that middle class domestic subscribers already tended to outnumber commercial, professional and other business users in areas outside city centres[17]. But there were many whose innate conservatism in the face of this innovation was reinforced by the brilliant efficiency of the contemporary letter service. In the 1900s and 1910s, the Post Office, able to call upon a vast pool of cheap and submissive labour, was providing same-day delivery in large cities and towns for items posted up to around teatime as well as collections and deliveries seven days a week. For even more urgent messages there was a telegram service.

By the mid 1920s, when there were well over a million subscribers of all types nationwide, most of the larger middle class houses had a telephone. This was usually placed in the hall, where it could be conveniently answered by a maid, although used at some risk to privacy. Throughout the three decades after 1920 the telephone was an important part of middle class daily life, regularly employed to call up local tradesmen, who would willingly arrange to have even the smallest orders for food and other items promptly delivered to the kitchen door. It was also the means of arranging social events, such as the afternoon 'at homes' and dinner and bridge parties. As the 1930s advanced, the lower middle class, in their semis, small bungalows and terrace blocks were also gradually becoming telephone subscribers but the spread here was slower since it was still very much regarded as marginal expenditure (in emergencies resort could be made to public call boxes, never then very far away in built-up areas, or to telegrams). Where it was installed, its use tended to be restricted to matters of urgency, in order to limit the expense. Indeed the extent to which telephones were used seems to have been very closely related to income; in the Massey 1938–39 survey of middle class expenditure[18], the highest income group (over £700 a year) recorded a weekly outlay on telephones and telegrams (the former would form the major element) of 5s 11½d compared with a mere 5½d by the salary group £250–350. These sums can be compared with the 5s 2½d and two shillings spent by these two groups on admissions to sports and games, cinemas, theatres and other forms of entertainment.

Some speculative builders advertised 'telephone recesses' under the stairs, whilst others offered free telephone installations to promote sales[19]. In the developing London middle class suburb of Edgware, the pressure on the 411 telephone lines at the manual exchange in 1927 was such that some local calls were taking twenty five minutes to connect; soon after this a new facility was provided and in 1929, with all equipment automatic, the number of Edgware subscribers had reached 1,300[20]. The uneven distribution of telephones between predominantly middle class and generally working class areas in the 1920s is well demonstrated by some statistics prepared in 1929[21]. Selecting a few examples, we find that in that year Bournemouth and Epsom had one telephone for every 3.5 households, Eastbourne one for every 3.9 and Guildford one to every four, but Merthyr Tydfil could muster only one to every forty seven, West Bromwich one to every 17.5, Barnsley one to every 16.9 and Whitehaven one to every ten.

## Easing The Pain

Amongst many other things, the middle classes used their telephones to talk to or summon the family doctor, who would readily attend his patients in their own houses, no matter how flimsy their reason for not going to him. No inquisition by female 'doctors' dragons' as to the urgency and nature of the problem greeted the anxious caller, merely the courteous acknowledgement of the maid, the doctor's wife, or the doctor himself. A reasonably prompt visit would follow, day or night. Such service was given for a fee well affordable by the better-off middle class and the rendering of the account might be long-postponed. Both doctors and dentists tended to graduate their fees with some regard to the type of house in which the patient lived. When visiting and treating his patients, the doctor was among social equals and behaved accordingly. For the well-to-do middle class, ill-health was made as comfortable as possible; if at all feasible, the patient remained in his own home, to the extent that minor operations were sometimes performed there, with a nurse living-in until recovery was complete. Otherwise, the sick person would be removed to a privately-run nursing home or the private ward of the local voluntary or cottage hospital. Such nursing homes were often organised and operated by consortia of private doctors, and in them the patients enjoyed the status of paying guests, surrounded as they were by many of their customary middle class home comforts.

The resources of most of the lower middle class were such that they were unable to share in all this, but by the 1920s and 1930s those earning less than £250 a year were protected from the full financial impact of private medical treatment by a compulsory statutory insurance scheme. This was funded by their own and their employers' weekly contributions and administered by private 'approved societies'. When ill, the subscriber received 'free' general medical practitioner services, undertaken by so-called 'panel' doctors, whose attitude to their patients was all too often far less caring and courteous than that of the fee-paid private doctor. For many there was the further indignity of an 'office doctor', whose loyalty was to the employers and whose chief task was to detect malingering by those drawing sick pay, ensuring that return to work was made as early as possible. If hospital treatment were necessary, the 'panel' patient usually paid nothing for it since most office workers also contributed to voluntary hospital insurance schemes such as the Hospital Savings Association. The families of the lower middle class were not covered by the compulsory medical insurance scheme and unless suitable contributions had been made by the head of household to voluntary schemes, the fees of the private doctor and the hospital charges had to be found.

Dental treatment followed similar lines. The lower middle class salary earner might have some assistance in return for his contributions to the voluntary insurance schemes mentioned (or in some cases through the approved society), although his choice of dentist would be limited. Free treatment of a rough and ready kind by students under supervision was available at dental hospitals. Unless he had made additional voluntary scheme contributions covering his wife and children, the impecunious lower middle class man would be obliged to find money for their treatment, or he might despatch his school-age offspring to the not so tender care of the stark and often traumatic low-budget school dental clinics operated by the local authorities. In contrast, the more affluent middle class visited a private practitioner, experiencing a soothing 'chair-side' manner and careful treatment in the dentist's own house, reassuringly like their own. If dissatisfied with either doctor or dentist they could turn to another ready to try to please them better. Awareness of this flexibility kept up the standard of private patient service.

# Private Wheels

One of the most prized aspects of the comfortable life throughout the first half of the twentieth century and one which remained virtually exclusive to the middle and upper classes, was the possession of private transport. In the 1900s and early 1910s those affluent middle class households which had customarily been able to operate their own horse and carriage were exchanging this luxury for a motor car. The hand-finished vehicles of this period were relatively expensive and their unreliability made it desirable to employ a chauffeur/mechanic to cosset and care for the beast. Since the open construction of most models made car travel a dirty and uncomfortable experience on the unsurfaced roads of the period, especially in bad weather, there was the further expense of special clothing. Women adopted dust cloaks, goggles, and motoring caps or bonnets, frequently wrapping their heads in fine gauze veils. Since there were often long sojourns at the roadside whilst the temperamental innards of the machine were restored to life, it was also wise for the car passenger to travel with knitting or books and some convenient form of snack such as biscuits or chocolate (a special brand known as Motoring Chocolate, fortified with raisins soon appeared).

With even the smallest models costing around £200 (a year's salary for a senior commerical or bank clerk) and no 'company car' perks, not to mention the need for special clothing and other extras, and with unreliability the norm, car ownership before the early 1920s was very much confined to the wealthier echelons of the middle class. Apart from a few doctors, most motorists used their vehicles solely for what were often laughingly described as pleasure jaunts. As no formal training or experienced supervision was deemed necessary by the authorities despite the highly lethal nature of the beast, there were frequent accidents, overturnings and collisions even on the lightly-used roads of the period.

The first mass-produced British car, the Morris Oxford 13.9 hp two-seater of 1923, was sold at £415 (a price reduced to £300 a year later) and the contemporary Wolseley 14 was £425. Even the low-taxed, underpowered 9–12 hp models of this period were £110–£175 and the cheapest Morris, the two-seater Cowley, was £198. These cheaper cars, taxed at £12 a year, produced around twenty five miles to the gallon and had an average speed of some twenty five mph, reaching forty to sixty at maximum. As the cost of even the smallest of the new cars was still equivalent to well over half a year's gross salary or more for the average clerk, private transport remained generally beyond the reach of the numerous lower middle class, especially of those who were married and committed to mortgages and hire purchase instalments on furniture (at that time it was of course highly exceptional for a wife to provide a second income to finance such luxuries). However a few lower middles did manage to scrape together the means to acquire a secondhand low h.p. car or were young enough or tough enough to face the rigours of using the cheaper motor cycle, with its pillion seat for the girl friend or possibly a weather-proof sidecar for wife and child. In the 1920s a 2¾ hp solo motor cycle sold at around £70, a combination at £95.

But to those with incomes of say £250 or more, the car, be it ever so small, was now affordable[22] and already becoming something they could not see themselves living without. Increasingly, from about 1923, it was driven by the owner or his wife rather than a chauffeur, and whilst not so fast as the train, was used for most types of short and medium length pleasure journeys, including visits to the London theatre, though parking was already causing problems in the centre of cities. The author of a 1929 book[23] directed at the comfortable middle class who might be looking for a detached house in a country or coastal setting, assumed that most of his readers were motorists and remarked how the 'weekend habit', followed by the purchase of a 'weekend cottage' and then perhaps a permanent country or seaside residence, had been fostered by the new adult toy. He also observed that the car 'frees us from the tyranny of railways', although he did go on to concede that trains were preferable for long-distance commuting and that good rail services had made it easy to live on the coast and work in town. 'The young wife of today', he suggested, 'has no desire for three acres and a cow; she would much prefer a quarter acre and a Cowley' (a reference to the classic bull-nose Morris Cowley 11.9 hp two-seater, whose price had come down to £175 in 1925).

Mrs Peel, writing in 1933, expressed the view that the cheap motor car had had a great effect on social life: 'Faced with the choice of a solid house, a nursery and children to put in it, or the possession of a car, the car wins the day and in order to afford it, the house becomes a bread and breakfast dwelling which may be run with little trouble and expense'. As a generalisation about the 1920s and 1930s this statement requires some qualification. The more affluent middle class could certainly afford a small family, a car *and* a 'solid house', taking great pride and joy in all these; but the lower middles in very large numbers gave priority to the house and a small family and then found they lacked the means to finance private motoring, any rate until the husband's working life was nearing its end, by which time most would consider it too late to take up driving.

Not surprisingly we find that private car ownership in the 1920s was very markedly concentrated in prosperous south-east England. In

June, 1938

The car comes almost within reach of the lower middles; the famous Ford 10 of 1938

1928 Surrey had one car for every 22.6 of its population, but in County Durham the equivalent figure was one to every 128.5 and in Glamorgan, South Wales, one for every 87.2[24].

Although cars above twelve hp were still quite costly in the 1930s (£235 for 13.9 hp models, £485 for a sixteen hp Humber Snipe and £695 for a twenty hp Daimler), rising real incomes brought the underpowered baby cars of eight to ten hp just within reach of lower middle class singles and those marrieds whose commitments and responsibilities allowed sufficient marginal income for saving the necessary capital or making the hire purchase payments. Fords' eight h.p. two-door Popular saloon, £120 ex-works in 1933, £100 in 1936 and £125 in 1939, was much appreciated by the lower middles. The tiny ('Baby') Austin Seven (seven h.p.), with its perambulator-like wheels and body, first introduced in 1922, was selling at £122 in 1938. Schoolteachers were numerous amongst its devotees. It was so small and light that it could be lifted without difficulty. One dark winter's afternoon in 1938 four homegoing older boys at the author's school provided a surprise for an unpopular teacher, who emerged some time later to find a treasured 'Baby' upended on its roof, its wheels impotently spinning in the air.

Since tax was related to horse power based on cylinder bore, manufacturers concentrated much of their output on the small underpowered cars and produced small bore engines with high piston speed which soon tore themselves to standstill. An eight hp car was taxed at eight pounds a year in 1933 but this was soon afterwards reduced to six. Comprehensive insurance cost about as much again, so with petrol at less than two shillings a gallon, running expenses were very low once the purchase hurdle had been cleared.

With this concentration on cheap, small models and an increasing number of secondhand cars coming on to the market in the 1930s, more of those lower middles whose incomes had previously restricted them to motor cycles were able to secure four wheels of a sort. This may have been a major factor in the decline in the number of motor cycles in use from a peak of over 724,300 in 1930 to a mere 418,000 or so by 1939. Car ownership in Great Britain, standing at around 132,000 in 1914, and almost 315,000 in 1922, rose to just over 778,000 in 1927 and exceeded a million for the first time in 1930. By 1938 there were 1,916,226 licence holders, the majority of them in the middle classes, although most lower middles lacked sufficient capital and marginal income to sustain the purchase and running of even the cheapest car. Right through to the end of the 1940s, this large group therefore continued to rely on public transport as much for pleasure journeys as for travel to work.

107

Even amongst those who owned cars, only a small minority used them for anything but short social and pleasure trips. On a road system still almost entirely that of the horse carriage and cart era, with the average car capable of only modest speeds, and a general lack of discipline amongst drivers, not to mention parking difficulties, and with urban main streets clogged with cyclists, slow moving horse drawn vans and carts, buses and electric tramcars, regular commuting by car was tiring, slow and often unpleasant. Added to this, most of the cheaper British cars built in the 1930s were badly-designed and prone to breakdown. They also had poor handling qualities that added to the other dangers of uncontrolled motoring, contributing to a road casualty figure that was very high in proportion to the number of cars in use.

Something has already been said in Chapter 4 about garages for the larger detached houses. As the incidence of car ownership rose in the higher income groups, most houses built for them after 1920 included motor car accommodation, but provision by the speculative builders, whose output was mainly directed at the lower middle class market, was much less consistent, reflecting the relatively slow growth of car ownership at that level.

As early as 1906, houses on the Hale Estate at Edgware in Middlesex were advertised as 'having room for motor' and 'motor houses' or 'motor sheds' were certainly included in a few speculatively-built houses erected around London from about 1912. But the great majority of such houses offered for sale in the 1920s lacked a garage or indeed even the space accommodate one at some future date. So low was car ownership amongst potential purchasers and so remote the assumed likelihood of it that estate developers found that a slightly higher-priced house with a garage sold much more slowly than those without.

From around 1924–6 what were sometimes advertised as 'car villas' (semi-detached houses with 'garage space') were increasingly seen. This new development necessitated a slight widening of the space between semi-detached pairs, but there were many examples in later years of such spacing being left too tight to comfortably accommodate adjacent car drives, or indeed any at all. Such lack of foresight was to be found even in prosperous south-east England as late as 1936 and 1937. Given that builders and developers generally kept a very sharp eye on the market, it provides evidence that few house purchasers at this level (ie for houses costing say £550–900) were expected to be car owners or even potential car owners. Below that price range, in the monotonous streets of £300–650 four and six-block terraces, only the end-of-terrace purchaser received minimal car space; as for the rest, the only resort for the then very rare car owner in this category of purchaser would be street parking or tortuous access via an unmade service road to a shack garage taking up as much as a third of his small back garden[25].

Where space was available, speculative builders in the 1930s would erect a brick garage for £30–£60, according to size and quality. In the last five years before World War 2, there was some recognition that the purchaser of houses priced at around £900 upwards might either have a car or eventually graduate to car ownership, and more and more speculatively-built large semis and detached houses were designed with integral garages. These created problems for their owners in the years after 1950 since they were often only just big enough to take the small eight to ten h.p. cars of the 1930s.

## NOTES

1. All figures for servants' wages given in this chapter are additional to the full board and lodging normally supplied by the employer. Servants also paid for their own laundry and any items broken or damaged. Wages rose after 1920 for skilled servants such as cooks and parlour-maids in short supply but in areas outside south-east England, where alternative employment opportunities for working class girls were scarce, those of inexperienced young girls remained much around pre-1914 levels.
2. Letter in *The Times*, 2 February 1916.
3. Report of the Committee on Women in Industry, 1919 (Cmd 135). The effect in south-east England was marked. Between the 1911 and 1921 censuses the number of servants for every hundred households in middle class areas around London dropped from 24.1 to 12.4.
4. Anon, *Mrs Beeton's Household Management*, New Edition, (n.d., but c 1921).
5. For example see *The Ideal Home* magazine, August 1929, January 1930 and February, 1930.
6. *The Ideal Home* magazine, article by Mary Gwynne Howell, August 1929.
7. EN 3 August 1901.
8. Howell, op cit (note 6).
9. Massey, Philip, 'The Expenditure of 1,360 British Middle Class Households in 1938–9', *Journal of The Royal Statistical Society*, Vol cv part iii. (1942).
10. Anon, op cit (note 4).
11. Firth, Violet M., *The Psychology of the Servant Problem*, (1925).
12. Lewis, Roy, and Maude, Angus, *The English Middle Classes*, (1925).
13. Anon, op cit, (note 4).
14. Jones, D. Caradgo, 'The Cost of Living of a Sample of Middle Class families', *Journal of The Royal Statistical Society*, xci, part iv (1928).
15. Massey, op cit (note 9).
16. Except in Hull and Portsmouth.

17. For example, see Perry, Douglas 'The Telephone in Pinner', *The Pinn* (Pinner Local History Society, x, 2, (1986).
18. Massey (op cit, note 9).
19. Telephone recesses were a feature of £795 semi-detached houses at New Eltham, London (Davis Estates publicity brochure, New Eltham Estate (nd but c1937). The same firm advertised 'free telephone installations' for the purchasers of their semis in 1936.
20. *Edgware Gazette* 18 November 1927, 9 December 1927, 9 March 1928 and 26 July 1929.
21. Anon, *Sell to Britain Through 'The Daily Mail'*, (nd.but c1929).
22. Anon, op cit (note 21).
23. Barron, P.A., *The House Desirable*, (1929).
24. Anon, op cit (note 21).
25. On a lower middle class estate of newly-built and occupied terrace blocks at Tolworth, Surrey, in 1937, in a road almost a quarter mile long, there was only one car owner. A civil service clerical officer with a salary averaging £260, he soon moved his family to a larger house.

# CHAPTER 6

# A WOMAN'S PLACE

Before we proceed further, let it be clearly understood that throughout the period which is our present concern, there were no *women* in the middle classes; only *ladies*. This was the accepted and expected verbal tribute to the gentility and respectability of all female middles, paid not only by their male peers (as in the toast, 'The Ladies, God Bless Them') but by all domestics, tradespeople and others serving them. When visiting shops, middle class women expected and received deference from shopowner, management and staff, happy to acknowledge their potential spending power.

The arrival of Gordon Selfridge with his American methods in 1909 led to the development of unhindered access within many department stores, and although this was accepted and indeed welcomed by the lower middles, who made up most of their custom, the better-off middle class often felt more comfortable with the old system of 'shopping through' which, with their support, persisted in some of the long-established stores until the late 1940s. Where this prevailed, a formally-dressed shopwalker would greet a lady customer at the shop entrance, summoning the appropriate assistant at her desired first point of call. She would be offered a chair at the counter whilst goods were displayed and discussed, then escorted to the next department required and finally to the street door and car or taxi. In smaller shops it was often the owner or the manager who supervised the purchases and conducted the polite ceremonies. All this nurtured class-conscious shopping. Whilst a salaried shopwalker, exercising his petty authority over the counter staff might be vaguely accepted as having a precarious foothold on the very lowest rung of the middle class ladder, a lady customer would tend to regard the shop assistants themselves as temporary personal domestics, treating them accordingly, using the same manner and tone of voice as she did at home. When trying on clothing a very high degree of privacy was *de rigueur* and woe betide any shopgirl in attendance behind the locked door of the fitting room who did not undo and do up every button and lace.

Since convention, and in some important areas, formal restriction, barred married women from most types of paid work except in the two world wars, the lifestyle of the typical middle class wife was predominantly home-centred and, for many years, totally leisured. The very clear separation of roles between husband-provider-head of family and wife-home maker-mother reinforced the class female sterotype, whose expected characteristics might be summarised as: often romantic when young; frequently impractical and helpless; emotionally unstable; and in all situations extremely modest. Whatever indiscretions might be practised in private, whatever poverty or scandal threatened, an outward impression of respectability and an assured position in society was to be maintained at all costs. Appearances were of the utmost importance.

In her teens and twenties, the middle class female was regarded as a decorative and amusing appendage to male existence. On reaching maturity, around the middle or late twenties, marriage was seen as her normal state. Her role thenceforward was very much to bear and rear children, play a part in conventional social life, be submissive to and supportive of her husband and run the family home within an allocated budget.

By the 1900s middle class women were not only having fewer children than their Victorian forebears but completing their childbearing phase earlier in married life. Thanks to a growing margin of disposable income arising partly from these developments, many families found they were able to send their children to private boarding schools from quite a tender age. Since there were adequate staffs of domestic servants in most middle class households there were fewer home tasks. Routine shopping would be undertaken by servants or orders placed by postcard or telephone would be willingly delivered to the kitchen door. (Before telephone became widespread in middle class homes in the 1910s and 1920s, grocers would send an assistant twice a week to the house to sit in the kitchen and take down orders).

Even during and after World War 1, when fewer households were able to maintain an adequate number of servants, most were able to avoid the heavier and rougher domestic tasks by employing a 'daily', a charwoman or a 'step-girl'. Furthermore, the whole trend of house and household equipment design, from the 1910s if not earlier, was directed towards reducing or eliminating the laborious duties undertaken up to that time by domestic servants. As servants became more difficult to obtain and this trend accelerated, many middle class women were able to buy all the labour-saving equipment they wanted.

## Edwardian Amusements

Within their home-centred, leisured lifestyle, aided by the rising prosperity of the middle class, the younger Edwardian married women

112

of the wealthier end of the spectrum pursued a largely decorative, status-supporting role, filling their hours with elaborate toilette and changes of dress, coiffured and beautified for an endless round of lunching, of taking tea and dining, of dancing, theatre-going, 'at-homes', country visits, city shopping and holidays.

From the beginning of the 1900s, bridge, played at private parties or at clubs, attained great popularity amongst middle class women, since it offered opportunities for conversation and the added excitement of gambling. Mrs Peel relates how in the 1910s 'bridge became an obsession with many women. By three o'clock they would be waiting impatiently to begin to play'. Lady Troubridge, writing in 1926, noted that with the exception of whist, bridge had taken 'a greater hold than any other card game . . . has now become universal and in many houses is now always played when guests are entertained'. She regarded it as something of a social litmus test, since in her view there was no game 'which proves good temper, tact and breeding more than bridge'. The stakes at auction bridge ran from sixpence to ten shillings a hundred (between the wars the norm was a shilling or 2s6d). Afternoon bridge parties in private houses usually lasted from 3.30–6.30 pm, with tea served at 4.30 or 4.45. Evening parties started about 9 pm, ending with refreshments at 11 or 11.30, usually soup and sandwiches, stuffed rolls, sweets, cakes and little pastries. At clubs, the vice was more generously indulged, starting in the afternoon, with tea taken at the card table. Interrupted by a light and hurried dinner, with conversation revolving around the game, it was then resumed, sometimes continuing far into the night. Rather less popular, but equally obsessive, was poker, which was played at some clubs until breakfast was taken at 6 or 7 am. Mrs Peel averred that card playing, above all bridge, had killed 'at-homes' and bridge partnerships offered an inexpensive way of entertaining friends.[1]

With almost unlimited leisure and insufficient outlets for their abundant energy, it is not surprising that many of the brighter and more spirited women of the upper middle class took up philanthropic or political activity of various kinds in the years up to 1914 (most of the suffragettes came from the middle classes). Others fell prey to sly indiscretions with presentable men of their own class and social circle. Further down the social scale, where such lax sexual behaviour tended to be rarer and moral codes stricter, middle class woman sublimated her urges and marital disappointments by reading romantic novels and indulging in afternoon visits to the theatre and cinema. She also entertained her neighbours to afternoon tea, visited the great new department stores, joined local operatic and dramatic societies, sung folk songs and madrigals, and played tennis or golf. Writing in 1909 of what he called 'The Suburbans', Masterman considered that 'The women, with their single domestic servants, . . . find time hang rather heavily on their hands. But there are excursions to shopping centres in the West End, and pious sociabilities, and occasional theatre visits, and the interests of home . . .'[2].

For those just clinging to a middle class foothold, life was not so leisured and 'the interests of home' involved hard work, although organisational change could ease matters. The wife of a junior bank clerk earning £150 a year described her weekends in the London *Evening News* of 28 August 1913. The family included two children and with this level of income and commitment, they were unable to afford a servant. Her husband arrived home from the bank about 3 pm on Saturdays to a 'scanty dinner or high tea'; the rest of that day was spent shopping and preparing for Sunday's 'big meal' whilst the husband pottered about in the garden or went to watch football or cricket. On the Sunday they rose about 9.30 am, the husband taking 'a depressing morning walk' (presumably with the children), returning before the midday dinner was ready. This meal completed, she did not finish washing up the dishes and smartening herself up until 3.30 pm, after which she rested before tea. Then came a walk or church. The purpose of the letter was to describe how she had changed this routine with good results. She now did her shopping on Fridays and gave her husband his 'big meal' on Saturday. This left Sundays free; they were getting up earlier and, in good weather, going out all day. This insight into Edwardian lower middle class life is interesting in several respects: it shows that Sunday churchgoing was apparently not as intensive as slightly higher up the scale; it indicates that the husband made no attempt to help his wife in any way with her domestic tasks; and we can perhaps surmise from the concept of the weekend 'big meal' that the couple had a working class upbringing.

## Wartime Ladies

By the beginning of 1915 the war was having an effect on the way of life that had been followed by most middle class women. For many the long days became more purposeful: formal entertaining almost ceased; there were fewer visits to town for theatre matinées; less leaving of visiting cards and dropping in to tea; and the over-extended afternoon and evening bridge games almost disappeared, although those women who had nothing else to do resorted to clubs to save scarce fuel and food. Many middle class women volunteered for nursing at war hospitals, other welfare work for the armed services, or for working parties making garments for refugees, soldiers and sailors. A journalist commented patronisingly: 'The truth is the War is doing the suburbs a lot of good'[3]. The eagerness of middle class women to become involved in the war effort was not immediately grasped by the authorities but after the middle of 1916, following the organisation of the Ministry of Munitions and universal male conscription, the situation quickly changed. There was something for everybody. A government propaganda film of 1917 depicted a very obviously middle class woman mooning around a large house with nothing to do. Looking idly out of the sitting room, she suddenly realised that if the spacious garden were turned over to vegetable and fruit production instead of grass, trees and flowers, the household could strike a blow against the wartime food shortage. A subsequent scene portrayed the now-fulfilled and purposeful housewife enthusiastically helping her husband achieve this objective.

Wartime demands and conditions brought some mixing of classes, helping to rationalise attitudes and increase social understanding. Sitting at a table to receive cash savings at a soldiers' and sailors' wives club, a middle class woman thought it wise to guard against the expected fleas and other unpleasant invaders brought in by these working class women by spreading round her little piles of insect-repellent powder[4]. No doubt she soon found this precaution was both unnecessary and ill-received. Mrs Peel records approvingly a great mingling of the classes in munitions factories, where 'munitionettes' ranged from 'girls of the very roughest type to young ladies well known in society'. But she also noted that only the working class girls had the energy to stay up half the night dancing after a full day's work[5]. Middle class girls were no doubt tired by the unaccustomed physical activity whilst their working class sisters were well used to a long and active day, having been called upon to help a harassed mother at home almost as soon as they could walk. And war brought not only social education and mixing to many hitherto blinkered and protected middle class women; a casualty rate amongst young army officers three times as high as that for those in the ranks meant that mothers, sisters, girl-friends and young wives suffered much emotional stress and trauma.

When peace returned, bringing a period of runaway inflation, some professional households experienced a financial stringency at first not recognised as temporary, so that the women in the more affluent families tended to continue with the quieter social life they had become accustomed to in the war years. Most of the women who had taken up paid or voluntary jobs during the war had lost these by 1919–20 but the many single middle class women in office work of various kinds did far better than most in holding on to regular paid employment.

## A Magazine Lifestyle

The growth in office employment and other middle class jobs for women after 1920 was largely confined to the unmarried. In all sections of the middle class, the between-war years were notable for the fact that wives, and particularly mothers, remained almost totally homebound. A new factor began to reinforce this: as servants became more difficult to obtain and more expensive to employ, many reasonably prosperous families began moving into new, smaller 'labour-saving' houses where they employed fewer servants (or none at all). Thus, by the 1930s, the woman of the house, increasingly involved in housework, was coming closer to the way of life of her lower middle class and working class sisters.

The rising prosperity of the middle class, the leisured and home-oriented way of life of most married women and, in a period when satisfactory domestic help was much more difficult to obtain, an increasing need to understand the technicalities of running a household efficiently, all combined to stimulate a boom in women's magazines. Although their circulations were small in comparison with what was to come later, these journals enjoyed a period of expansion and influence which lasted from the middle 1910s until it was much subdued by the shortages and rigours of the 1940s. It was an era in which women's periodicals and women's pages in newspapers consistently sought to reinforce the home concerns of their predominantly middle class readers and in collusion with their advertiser paymasters endeavoured to direct the expenditure of the rising level of disposable middle class income into everything associated with the home.

In seeking to stimulate in their readers an active discontent with their existing environment (and thus provoke them to expenditure on something new) the magazines promoted the latest ideas in house and garden design, the newest furniture and furnishing trends, the most modern items of bathroom and kitchen equipment, and innovations in other household labour-saving devices, mostly electrical. Side by side with this, from around 1930, came a new emphasis on fashion and cosmetics.

Typical of this new literature was *The Ideal Home*, which first appeared in 1920. Through the next two decades this lavishly-produced monthly concentrated on portraying quality middle class homes, their gardens and their furnishing. Supporting features dealt with pets (mainly dogs), cars, indoor and garden games, radios, gramophones, pianos and other music-making in the home, sea cruises and other holidays, parties and entertaining, and the organisation and handling of servants.

Other new arrivals included *Vogue* (1916, mainly fashion and directed at the upper as well as the middle classes and largely concerned with high fashion worn only by a few); *Homes & Gardens* (1919), *Good Housekeeping* (1922, a USA import) *Woman & Home* (1926), *Woman's Journal* (1927) and *Wife & Home* and *Harper's Bazaar* (both 1929). Whilst most of these monthlies mainly reflected the lives of the wealthier middle class reader, they were avidly read for vicarious enjoyment by almost all middle class women. In contrast, the significant newcomers of the next decade, *Woman's Own* (1932), *Woman's Illustrated* (1936) and *Woman* (1937) were directed at the lower middle class and the 'respectable working class', and concerned as much with the single girl as the married woman. Their promoters correctly discerned a gap in the market and *Woman* alone reached a circulation of around a quarter of a million in two years. These new weekly magazines of the thirties also devoted much space to home-making, attempting to raise the associated activities to the stature of fulfilling hobbies for the housebound middle class woman unaided by living-in servants. 'Housewife' now rather than mistress of the household, she was transformed into a species of home technician, wrapped in a new and powerful aura of homebound femininity. This was strongly portrayed as the ultimate achievement for woman. Advertising and fiction in these magazines were in agreement in assuming a ubiquitous and permanent stereotype life pattern in which a girl moved from school through a temporary phase of outside employment and heady romance with the man of her dreams into the role of contented married mother, happy and fulfilled as a home-maker, surrounded and enriched by a grateful husband and children. In support and encouragement of this role, the readers were treated to regular features on fashion, make-up, health and health problems and advice on relationships, the latter very much in line with conventional middle class Christian morality. Material on the development of intellectual, cultural and career interests was noticeably absent, as was any discussion of social or political issues such as the prevailing high level of unemployment and the threat of a new war.

## Around the House

The heavy and tedious physical work associated with Victorian and Edwardian middle class houses has already been noticed in Chapter 5. Whilst most women were happy and able to leave this entirely to their servants, changes were on the way even before 1914. From around 1910 houses began to be built to designs which avoided or lightened the traditional cleaning and servicing chores whilst new types of domestic equipment, mostly electrically-powered, were tentatively introduced with the same objective in view. This dual progress in design accelerated markedly in the 1920s and 1930s. The new houses of those decades all had running hot water upstairs and down; in all but the principal room in winter, coal fires gave way to more convenient and cleaner electric and gas heaters; gas and electric cookers with primitive heat controls replaced the messy and capricious solid-fuel kitchen range; gas and then electric light banished all the work associated with oil lamps and candles; kitchen units and fittings brought order and neatness to that important section of the house; and electric vacuum cleaners took over from brooms, brushes and dustpans. All this was nowhere more evident than in the middle class home.

By around 1930 in the majority of middle class houses the daily work routine had been reduced to less than a dozen core tasks: making beds; laying and attending to a single fireplace in winter; preparing and laying three main meals and washing up afterwards; tidying and straightening-up the rooms in daily use; and shopping for those few items which tradesmen did not deliver to the house. The outside help coming in for three or less days a week, would clean the bathroom, wash the kitchen floor and tables, clean the doorsteps, polish brass and silver, thoroughly clean one room or hall and stairs, and do the washing and ironing. Bed linen was often sent out to a commercial laundry.

A major agent in this revolution of labour-saving in the home was electricity, although its domestic advance was long delayed, and when it came, it benefited only the upper and middle classes. Electric irons, heaters, cookers, kettles, fans and other devices were available from the 1890s, but the abundance of servants and popularity of cheap coal fires, the unreliability and high cost of domestic electricity supplies and the fact that such supplies were mostly only suitable for lighting purposes, held back the full potential of electricity as a domestic labour-saver for another twenty to thirty years. The rationalisation and modernisation of electricity supply in Britain and its distribution through a new National Grid system, all of which followed the Conservative Government's Electricity Supply Act of 1926, was completed in 1935, neatly and happily coinciding with the middle class housebuilding boom of the early 1930s. This led to a rapid expansion in the domestic use of electricity and of those labour-saving appliances which so conveniently met the needs of the new one-servant or servantless middle class households. Production

119

of electricity, reflecting this demand, leapt from 11,413m kW/h in 1931 to 22,877m in 1937. Organisations such as the British Electrical Development Association (1919) and the Electrical Association for Women (1924) were largely concerned with promoting the use of electricity as a labour-saver in the home. Typical of this benign propaganda was an EDA silent film of the 1920s, *Edward and Edna*, which featured a young couple whose decision to marry came only when, having become convinced of its advantages Edna agreed to preside over an all-electric, servantless home.

A year after the foundation of EDA, only one house in seventeen in Britain was wired for electricity; in 1930 the spread was as great as one in three, and in 1939, one in two. The number of domestic electricity consumers rose from 730,000 in 1920 to 1.768 million in 1926 and almost nine million in 1938. That these were very definitely in the upper and middle classes is shown by the associated average annual incomes of the consumers in each of these three years: £1,212; £726; and £401 (at 1938 prices)[6].

Some of the equipment available to the middle class housewife by the 1930s should be briefly noticed. Electric fires were pioneered in Britain from 1912 by the Enfield firm of Belling. By the beginning of the 1920s a great variety of reflector and convector heaters were on sale, although a suitable fan for the latter was not developed until the 1950s[7].

Whilst the models available were adequate for most cooking tasks, the custom of hiring electric and gas cookers from the supply undertakings rather than purchasing them retarded development of these appliances before the 1930s. However by 1939 there were some improvements, such as acceleration of the heating-up and cooling-down of the solid electric hotplates on the hob and the wider introduction of frameless glass inner oven doors (first seen in 1927).

Vacuum cleaners appeared in Britain in 1912, under the US Hoover brand name. With a price tag of £25, almost twice the annual wage of the maid who might operate them, sales were slow. By 1915 there were about a dozen brands on the market and the price was down to around seven pounds, an opportune reduction as servants were deserting their posts in droves for war work. Quantity production did not begin until the 1920s. Hoover established a British production base in 1919, soon to face some serious competition. A Fulham firm founded by Hubert Cecil Booth (who had patented a vacuum cleaner as early as 1901) began to produce an upright bag model in 1921 and a cylinder cleaner quickly followed. Booth's used the Goblin trade name from 1926, moving to a new factory

120

at Leatherhead in 1938. From 1927 there were two more firms in this largely middle class market, English Electric and the Swedish Electrolux. Goblin and Electrolux concentrated on the cylinder type, with its variety of tools to suck dust, not just from the floor, but upholstery, furnishings and curtains, whilst Hoover favoured the upright loose-bag carpet cleaner and beater. Hoover, based at a fine new factory on Western Avenue, Perivale from 1932, tended to dominate the interwar scene, so much so that the verb 'to hoover' entered the middle class vocabulary. But in 1939, at £15–22, Hoover 'de luxe' models were still an expensive item for the mortgaged lower middles. This outlay represented more than a month's pay for the many clerical workers whose budgets allowed little margin for additional 'easy payments'.

Although domestic refrigerators appeared in the USA in 1913, few were sold in Britain until the arrival of the American Frigidaire ten years later. This found its way only into the wealthiest of homes since it was priced at £60, a sum which would pay the wages of a maid for three years or purchase a small secondhand car. Electrolux and English Electric refrigerators were in the shops by the late 1920s, still comparatively expensive items at around £50. Improvements in design and production techniques in the 1930s brought the price of the basic models down to about £20 but 0.17 to 0.23 cubic metre capacity models for family use continued to be comparatively costly items at £35–50 in 1939. Although the technology was available, domestic food freezers were not on general sale until the 1950s.

The washing machines of the 1920s and 1930s were so cumbersome, heavy and expensive that they did not sell widely to any but the most affluent middle class households. With the spin dryer not yet available, a wringer, which might be power-operated, was a necessary accessory. A full-size all-electric washing machine of 63.64 litres capacity, capable of taking three sheets at a time, sold at £30 in 1939, and could be used in conjunction with a 'family-size' gas or electric drying cabinet costing £15–18 and a £10 rotary ironer. Since the total outlay of over £60 was the equivalent of three months' salary for many clerks, most lower middle class housewives made do with electric or gas wash boilers costing about seven pounds, which they used with small rubber-rollered hand wringers selling at around two. The latter either folded out of use to form a small enamel-topped table or could be temporarily clamped on to the then usual wooden draining board.

Since electric dishwashers had only just begun to appear in British shops at the end of the 1930s the number in use in 1940s, with factories going over to war work, was minimal. Electric irons on the other hand were the most widely-sold appliance, available for as little as a pound as early as 1920. They received heavy use; in the absence of man-made materials, the ironing chore was heavier than it is today. To maintain the neat appearance so prized by most middle class people, it was necessary to iron some garments daily, between washes. Plugged into light fittings and lighting circuits, and without heat controls, electric irons were something of a safety hazard until the 1930s, when builders at last began to equip new houses with 'power' circuits capable of handling up to ten or fifteen amps. At the same time, the manufacturers were increasingly including thermostatic controls in their irons. Prices in 1936 were an affordable £1.12s–£2. By 1950 ninety per cent of wired homes had at least one electric iron.

Magazines of the late twenties were able to advertise almost the full range of the products surveyed above, together with novelties such as electric bedwarmers, heating pads, food mixers and beaters, milk warmers, shaving pots, clocks and toasters. Storage heaters were also available in the 1930s, but did not really become popular until promoted with cheap off-peak electricity some thirty years later. The relatively high cost of most electrical appliances in the between-war period is reflected in the average consumption of a wired home at the end of the 1930s – only about 500 units a year.

Until the 1950s it was mostly only the upper and middle class homes which were wired for electricity, so it was the latter which provided the bulk market for electrical appliances. A 1939 report revealed the following distribution[8]:

|  | No. per 1000 wired homes | No. in use |
|---|---|---|
| Irons | 800 | 6.5 million |
| Vacuum cleaners | 270 | 2.3 million |
| Cookers | 190 | 1.6 million |
| Water heaters | 56 | 0.5 million |
| Washing boilers | 42 | not available |
| Refrigerators | 23 | 200,000 |
| Washing machines | 17 | 150,000 |

Aided by positive sales promotion and the opening of showrooms offering advice and demonstrations, particularly of cookery, the domestic use of town gas and its appliances also prospered between 1920 and 1950. Gas cookers, generally more popular and widely used at this time than electric ones, were fitted with 'Regulo' thermostatic oven controls from 1923 onwards, and by 1934 were being sold in coloured enamel finishes with double glass oven doors. Many middle class homes had gas irons, self-lighting gas fires and water heaters and in more limited numbers, gas washing machines and refrigerators, the latter offering the advantage of noiseless operation. An advertisement of the British Commercial Gas Association in December 1935 claimed that the year had seen more gas fires, refrigerators, garage heaters, clothes dryers and water heaters sold than ever before.

## New Homes, New Problems

Trapped in their labour-saving homes, separated for ten or more hours each weekday from the companionship of their husbands and other adults (apart from tradespeople and any servant who might still be employed) and bored with their own company, the condition of many middle class housewives was by no means always as blissful and calm as that depicted in the women's magazines of the period. It was especially hard for those in a new house in a partially-developed or semi-rural area, well-distanced from relatives and friends. In such circumstances the pressures of loneliness and tedium could be strong, bearing most heavily perhaps on the lower middle class woman with limited mental resources who found herself surrounded by those she wished to emulate but whom she might consider (rightly or wrongly) looked down upon her social status. The reserved and essentially private nature of the contemporary middle class character, combined with the frequently total absence of community and social organisations in newly-developed areas often made it difficult for the newcomer to secure and cement new friendships, even in many cases to get beyond a passing daily nod to her immediate neighbours. Men did not suffer in the same way, enjoying the companionship of their peers at their workplace or striking up acquaintance with daily travelling companions of similar social standing in the train to town.

In this situation, some women developed minor indispositions such as headaches, depression and indigestion, the latter not improved by the excessive tea-drinking sometimes adopted as a diversion and comfort. Solace was also sought in romantic fiction, or in visiting the cinema once or twice a week. Others tried to drown their loneliness by having the radio on all day. Inevitably, this new, almost exclusively middle class, female condition came to the notice of the medical profession and received a label. The causes of 'suburban neurosis'[9] were said to be boredom through lack of friends; worries about money and the home; and a false set of values founded on books and films which suggested the existence of thrills unknown to the suburban existence[10]. Two years after the ailment was identified, another world war was to eradicate it completely, accelerating social changes which were to release many middle class married women from their domestic isolation.

# A Longer Leash for the Unmarried Woman

Whilst marriage remained the main lifetime vocation for middle class women, a widening range of employment opportunities opened up for the unmarried. No longer were they almost entirely restricted to such jobs as nursing the sick, school teaching and acting as governesses or nurses to children of the wealthy. From the 1890s lower middle class women had been recruited for Post Office Savings Bank and telegraph services and in the next decade they were in demand for the new telephone service, as well as for typing in many different kinds of offices. With the Liberal Government's limited venture into social insurance legislation, there were new opportunities in the civil service. Local government was also expanding its work force, taking some women into clerical work. At the Bank of England, women were recruited in small numbers from 1893 and about the same time clerical jobs were offered by the clearing banks and railways. In 1900 the presence of women in offices still occasioned somewhat surprised comment. Visiting a large railway freight depot in that year, a writer in *The Railway Magazine* found a 'mysterious room, which the "mere male" must not enter except "strictly on business", a section carried on by lady clerks.' He added coyly, 'we just peeped in, "as a guarantee of good faith, and not necessarily for publication" '[11]. At that large clerical barracks, The Railway Clearing House, twenty seven women, all relatives of the male clerks, started work in January, 1912; by 1914 their number had grown to almost 200[12].

This expansion in job opportunities for single middle class women, stimulated by the general boom in office jobs at this time, was very marked: between 1891 and 1911 the number of women in clerical type occupations leapt from just under 19,000 to almost 125,000[13] and by 1914 they comprised over a quarter of all clerks.

The war years 1914–18 saw an explosion in the market for female labour of all types, in which the middle classes participated. Frequently finding themselves away from home, many girls had to learn how to undertake domestic tasks formerly performed for them by servants. Although many of this new army of women workers were obliged to leave when the men returned after the war, the proportion of women at work, especially in the middle class salaried jobs, remained higher than before 1914. Census returns showed an increase of almost 1.4 million in salaried occupations between 1911 and 1931, of whom 650,000 were women. But it took another world war to effect a further significant increase in the number of middle class women in full time paid employment.

Although it was theoretically possible for women to be admitted to the legal profession after 1919 and to the top layer (Administrative Class) of the civil service after 1921, in practice so few had taken up these opportunities that they still remained something of a rarity as late as 1940. The medical and dental professions, opened up to them after 1908, were increasingly populated by women, although again the actual numbers remained tiny. By 1931 there were still only 1,245 women in the civil service top layer and the middle-level managerial Executive Class in England and Wales, most of them in the latter; twenty years later the same combined total was 14,103. Stimulated by the changes brought by World War 2, there were similar modest increases in the entry of women to such institutions as the major railway companies, although these remained more conservative in this respect than the civil service. Britain's second largest, the London & North Eastern Railway, employed 2,896 women officers and clerks in 1937 but ten years later there were 7,658; most of these, at both periods, would have been in fairly low grade jobs. In the period 1931–51 the number of women in professional and technical occupations increased by twenty five per cent; they were mainly to be found in nursing, industrial design and technical drawing, industrial chemistry, metallurgy, engineering, architecture and town planning, and the law and social work. Also in this period there were significant increases in the number of women running businesses, serving as company directors or working as bankers[14].

As has been suggested, many of the jobs before the 1940s were unskilled and routine; most were remunerated at lower rates than men received for equivalent tasks. After 1920 the brighter middle class girls leaving school still tended to take teaching, nursing or public sector office work, in all of which there were regulations requiring them to resign immediately they married. All had to strive against male prejudice. As Lady Troubridge observed sadly in 1926: 'years of blind adherence to what most of us now consider was false tradition have robbed women of their proper development in business and professional life, and in many cases woman is regarded as mentally inferior to man for the simple reason that she is a woman'. In the spirit of her time, she offered only quiet, non-controversial advice, suggesting that a woman should always be suitably dressed at her place of business and so well-mannered in all she did that no man could condemn her as 'unbalanced, tiresome or a mere slave to fashion.'

For those unable to find a marriage partner or not interested in marriage there were difficulties in making a reasonable career. Promotion in competition with men was never easy or straightforward, although clandestine affairs with married men in positions of influence sometimes helped. Career women in offices often found themselves locked into positions well below their capacity and intelligence. However with the increased employment opportunities available from the 1900s, unmarried middle class women did achieve a new self-confidence. It became possible for a single middle class woman to acquire a considerable measure of independence, living alone, or with a woman friend. Some made the most of this emancipation, flying aeroplanes and driving racing cars, and with it, reflecting it, came drastic changes in the way all middle class women dressed, as we shall see shortly. Not all approved. Speaking for the older generation, Lady Fortescue, in the October 1927 *Play Pictorial*, had worries about the eugenic aspects:

> Our Amazons of today play hockey, football, cricket and lawn tennis; they swim and dive, they hunt and fish and sometimes even shoot; they drive horses and cars equally well; some of them have taken up flying, and all physique has improved enormously, and although they may well have lost a certain dainty grace and charm, though they take larger sizes in shoes and gloves, one may say that they have sacrificed these things on the altar of health. Perhaps we overdo our sports a bit, here, in England. It seems unnecessary for women to imperil their lives or their health by dangerous aeroplane flights, car-racing adventurous tours to the ends of the earth, or attempts to swim the Channel. . . I am old-fashioned enough to believe the real pioneer work should be done by men. It cannot be good for the future of the race if women subject themselves to overstrain.

Unmarried middle class girls were also enjoying another kind of freedom. Chaperonage in the years between leaving school and engagement to marry was under attack by the popularity of the bicycle from around 1895, and a little later by the arrival of the motor car and motor cycle. The hothouse pressures and exigencies of World War 1 virtually completed this aspect of female emancipation. As Mrs Peel records, mothers and aunts, in canteens and workrooms all day, were reluctant to sit up half the night; taxis were hard to find and the cars owned by the more affluent families were laid up through shortage of petrol. All that could be done was to arrange that a daughter went to dances with known girl friends and did not walk or drive back home alone with a man. By 1919 most young middle class girls were free to visit cinemas and dance halls alone with their boy and girl friends, though many parents remained uneasy about this. Although she conceded 'the rules of chaperonage are now much relaxed', as late as 1926 Lady Troubridge considered there were then still many mothers who would be concerned at their daughters being asked to a party at a bachelor's house or rooms with no-one there to play chaperone. 'Many girls themselves' she added hopefully, 'still would resent it and consider it a lack of respect'. But she considered there was not the same objection for a theatre party, or a party at a restaurant, club or tea room. This cicerone to etiquette also noted the dangers inherent in taxi travel; she advised that no young lady of breeding should consider entering a taxi alone with a man who was not acting as her escort – 'all questions of convention apart, it is not prudent'. This was written against the background of largely unchanging standards of behaviour between the sexes; so far as the middle classes were concerned, it was remarkable that except during the emotionally-charged atmosphere of 1914–18, liberation from chaperonage did not lead to any widespread relaxation in this area.

There was however a more open attitude to such matters on the part of the many middle class women, accompanied by a very lively curiosity which was satiated for the most part vicariously, in gossip, in novel-reading, and in theatre- and cinema-going rather than practical experiment. When in the 1920s those writing for the West End stage began to use plays as vehicles for discussion and portrayal of a more relaxed approach to sexual behaviour, B. W. Findon, founder-editor of *The Play Pictorial*, and regular theatre-goer, writing in September 1927, suggested this new trend was frightening-off what he called 'the clean-minded women of the middle classes' and 'their sober-minded husbands', going on to comment that the audiences consisted mainly of:

> young women who singe their sick imaginations with sexual longings which they dare not gratify except in an unfruitful manner at the theatre. . . they will laugh unrestrainedly at the naughtiness (some of us call it nastiness) of the dialogue and revel in the barn door morality of the stuff provided by the dramatist.

Although he failed to see it, these 'vacuous females' as he contemptuously called them, 'septic carriers of a disease that is fatal to the constitution of dramatic art and death to wholesome managements' had to be mostly the daughters of his clean-minded middle class women and their sober-minded husbands. Three years later he concluded, probably with greater accuracy, that the new 'sex plays' were in large part sustained by the support of middle class women of all conditions and age groups. We look at this phenomenon in more detail in Chapter 9.

## Another War; Another Chance for Women

World War 2 once again saw women taking up without hesitation every type of non-combatant war activity. As in 1914–18, many middle class women undertook voluntary or paid work in public administration or in desk or other jobs in war industry, replacing enlisted men. The Women's Royal Voluntary Service for Civil Defence, a largely middle class-led uniformed organisation established in June 1938, did sterling work in Air Raid Precautions and in feeding and comforting the civilian victims of German air attacks. Later the WRVS also ran canteens and other welfare activities for the Armed Forces. Thousands of young middle class girls and women joined the Armed Services, most choosing the Women's Royal Naval Service and Women's Auxiliary Air Force because these offered sightly more attractive uniforms and marginally higher social status. They were given jobs as nurses, clerks, meterologists, radar, radio and telephone operators, aircraft plotters and a score of other occupations in which most worked alongside male officers. Some, notably in 1940–41 in the WRAF, were exposed to considerable danger from enemy attack or saw the worst effects of war. Others went into the Women's Land Army or the Air Transport Auxiliary, which ferried new fighter and bomber aircraft from the manufacturers. In all these war jobs they asserted themselves with vigour, demonstrating their sticking power, attention to detail and reliability in a manner which began to undermine the old male prejudices against equal pay and career jobs for women. There seems little doubt that in this matter, as with other things, war conditions accelerated a process which might otherwise have taken much longer.

As Britain entered the 1950s, middle class women were set firmly on the road towards equality of opportunity and reward in paid employment. Although there was still much to be achieved, cracks were beginning to open up in hitherto rigid male attitudes, even in the conservative professions of medicine, law and accountancy, where women still represented only a very tiny percentage of the whole.

## Dressing the Lady

There are several reasons why it is necessary to give extended consideration to the dress of the middle class woman. Feminine fashions of the period were very much a middle (and of course, upper) class phenomenon. Until the 1930s, when the mass retailing of cheap factory-made clothes began to get under way, it was the middle classes which formed the main market for new styles in feminine outer and underwear. A survey of middle class expenditure in 1938–9[15] showed that as much as forty to forty four per cent of total household outlay on all forms of clothing was being directed towards adult women's wear.

For almost the whole period with which we are concerned, a woman's dress and general adornment functioned as clear outward indicators of her class and social status. Also fashion's many changes can be seen as reflections and expressions of the evolving aspirations for the middle class woman and of her role in society. This last statement needs some qualification however, since cost sometimes precluded immediate and wholehearted adoption of the latest fashions by any but the more affluent, and from the early 1910s many of the new styles and fads did in any case only appeal to and suit the younger woman. Thus the assumption of new modes often happened only slowly and partially, with the older woman often reluctant to depart very far from the styles she had known in her youth.

Lastly there is evidence that the acquisition of expensive and elegant clothes was central to the life of many middle class women. That careful observer of late 19th and early 20th century manners and morals, Mrs C. S. Peel, remarked on the feminine passion for costly adornment, a passion which economic considerations limited to the upper and middle classes. She expressed the view that it ran strongly enough to be morally damaging, both to the customers and the tradespeople. Experience in operating a select West End millinery establishment in the 1910s showed her that many women 'were absolutely hypnotised by new clothes; have them they must'. Should the husband not be able or willing pay, then someone else would, or some stratagem would be evolved to secure the desired article. As for the salesgirls, they descended to 'all kinds of trickery and blandishment to sell their wares'[16].

In common with other comforts and pleasures of the more fortunate sections of society, the provision of quality middle class feminine wear relied heavily on the existence of a large and willing pool of cheap labour. This was available in the first four decades of the century, when most of the outer clothing of middle class women was custom-made by dressmakers or tailors, or cut out and sewn by hand in small workrooms to be sold through department and other large stores. The more expensive hats were likewise made in workrooms attached to or associated with millinery shops.

Finally, in introducing this survey, no apology is offered for the detailed consideration given to underwear. In the past, this subject has usually been treated facetiously or inadequately, quite often inaccurately. Yet it has a certain importance, not only because it formed the foundation for all else, an essential constituent of the total effect, but because its design, arrangement and display sometimes reflected contemporary middle class social attitudes and behaviour, or could provoke reactions which throw light on them. The annual changes in outer wear styles are not given much close attention since they have been well-documented in numerous published works, some of which are noted in the bibliography.

# Edwardian Mystery

Without doubt, the most extravagant modes of the century were those of the 1900s, although their high cost ensured that they were largely confined to the upper class and the more affluent sections of the middle classes. Both these social groups adopted the same styles, which evolved to a large extent from late Victorian dress. At this time there were special clothes for almost every activity and for morning, teatime and evening wear indoors: dresses for garden parties; for balls; for shopping in town; outfits for the seaside; for golf; and for cycling; motoring and rail and sea journeys.

Women in the more prosperous middle class families were dressed and undressed morning, afternoon and evening by their maids, without whom they would be virtually helpless in their daily quest to achieve an image of nature cunningly embellished by clever, frequently erotic, artificiality. Beneath long, floor-brushing dresses (with even longer trains in the evening) they wore numerous petticoats of embroidered silk, lace and fine cotton which created a *frou-frou* to excite the male ear and eye as the wearer moved slowly and elegantly across a room. A most important element in the final effect was their expensive and elaborate corsetry, into which they were very tightly laced through most of their waking hours. These concoctions of whalebone, coutil, silk and lace severely restrained and moulded the natural form, producing a pouter-pigeon effect at the bosom, a narrow waist, provocatively-rounded hips and out thrust buttocks. Corsets, known in polite society as 'stays', were always referred to in the plural although never mentioned in the presence of men, who were supposed to imagine the effect produced was entirely natural. Their relentless, multi-whaleboned embrace was a major factor in creating a potent vision of helplessness which constantly demanded the arm and attention of the male escort, symbolising the woman's

130

submission to and her dependence on her partner. This restriction of the wearer's mobility also underlined her exemption from physical work of any kind, an impression further advanced by tightly-buttoned gloves, which often extended the full length of the arm; by high-necked collars, laced and boned like miniature corsets, which raised her head and set off her ear-rings; and by tightly-laced or buttoned bots, cut high in the leg and sometimes perched on quite high heels.

In the manner of dressing and matters of dress, an air of mystery, unattainability and fussily fastidious propriety was also cultivated. To this end, little or no flesh was exposed and when in outdoor dress, even the face was concealed behind a fine veil. In the 1900s there was also another associated development; underwear began to be secretised and eroticised, much enhancing the sexual interest of the male and accordingly to endure for the whole fifty years. We shall return to this later.

Finally there was the question of displaying unequivocally the wearer's social standing and position. With her elaborate furs, stoles and wraps, her umbrellas with ornamental handles, her silk parasols, and her huge and dressy hats decorated with the plumage of exotic birds resting on coiffure built up with complicated arrangements of wires and pads, upper middle class woman of the 1900s was if nothing else a mobile exhibition of her husband's status and income.

On warm summer days, the younger women would loll in hammocks slung between trees in the spacious gardens of the larger suburban and country villas, affording favoured admirers glimpses of silk-hosed ankles and calves, and of the fine lace, complicated ruching and baby ribboning of their *frou-frou*, perhaps even allowing a teasing flash of a fancy garter, worn deliberately just below the knee for occasional privileged viewing. 'As I knew my frillies were allright, I hammocked, and it was lovely' wrote Elinor Glyn in her 1900 novel, *The Visits of Elizabeth*. Although the *décolletage* of Edwardian woman was less bold at the dinner table than that of her Victorian forebears, beneath her long skirts, her underwear, which she was beginning to call her *lingerie*, was rapidly assuming a less functional and much more erotic significance.

A fervent missionary for this new cause was Mrs Pritchard. Writing in 1902,[17] she proclaimed: 'Lingerie is by far the most important part of the wardrobe', and '. . . the cult of Chiffon has this in common with the Christian religion – it insists that the invisible is more important than the visible.' Mrs P. declared that a fifth of a woman's annual dress allowance should be put aside for underwear, which should include two new pairs of corsets a year. She wanted her readers to aim at possessing two dozen of each type of undergarment, though somewhat fewer petticoats would do (which was just as well, since the fancy type were outrageously expensive). A lady of limited means, she allowed, might have her lingerie 'made at some charitable institution or at her own home'. A prominent and perceptive theme in her book is that it would be wise for any woman to make her underwear alluring and interesting, and to cultivate a sense of mystery and beauty in this area if she wished to feel wanted and be loved.

Shopkeepers certainly did their best to maintain the mystery of what Mrs Pritchard called the 'things unseen' in their endeavour to pay proper homage to the feelings of those upon whom they relied for their livelihood. They readily grasped that respectability and modesty in these matters were prerequisites for the middle classes and although some garments were displayed in their windows, the modern practice of showing them in position on lifelike dummies would have horrified both them and their lady customers. Lingerie and corsetry departments were carefully located above the ground floor in positions which minimised the risk of male invasion. Some shops went further, protecting these departments behind lace-curtained doors, beyond which no man was normally expected to pass.

Only briefly, as its owner rested in her boudoir in the afternoon, or took tea with her guests, was the fashionable feminine waist released from the daytime restriction of tight-lacing. At this time of relaxation, before she was dressed again for dinner, she was helped into a loose-fitting diaphanous tea-gown, which, if at the upper end of the social scale, she slurringly called her 'teagie'. Beneath its all-concealing looseness, corset laces were discreetly slackened or the whalebone cage might be replaced by less restrictive 'ribbon' stays.

The order and arrangement of dressing was complicated, emphasising the total dependence on a maid. First came a chemise or shift, close-fitting, and of cambric, linen, muslin, or batiste. Trimmed with lace top and bottom, and dropping to just above the knee, it was tucked into knickers of similar materials, the latter a wide garment, finishing at the knee and divided vertically, for convenience, into two halves. Since their delicate ribbon and lace adornments could not be laundered too frequently without damage, knickers were often worn over a detachable washing silk or linen 'lining' of similar construction. As an alternative to chemise and knickers, there were silk, batiste or gauze combinations, ribboned over the shoulders, fitting closely to the body and with knee-length legs, also divided from the waist almost to the knees.

Next came the corsets, which since they were almost invariably back-laced, could not be put on without assistance. If well-made, and therefore expensive, they transformed even the more mature figures into eye-catching curves set above and below a tiny waist, prolonging physical attractiveness well into middle age. For the more generous forms, the corsetière Madame Voller of Portsmouth advised a model with 'extra heavy Spoon Busk, with the inward curve, the only Busk that suits the really stout figure'. This creation also featured a Top Belt Attachment which, as the catalogue caption noted, was easily adjusted to give 'a grateful feeling of support to the abdomen'.

Over the corsets, around the bosom, a *cache-corset*, or camisole was worn, and above this, two or more layers of petticoats. Stockings were short, reaching only to just above the knee and usually black. For those few inches around the ankle. which just might be seen, they were made of silk, and this section was often given some decoration. They were supported by long, decorated suspenders attached to the lower edge of the corsets or to a small belt worn over them. Of necessity, these straps passed outside the knickers, their rubber-buttoned stocking loops hidden in the complication of frills and flounces around the knee. By 1905 some women were beginning to wear knickers without the back opening; these went on over the corset and suspenders, an arrangement eventually to become universal as this new design was generally accepted.

Such extravagant and excessive prettiness in outer wear and lingerie was not obtained cheaply, especially if Mrs Pritchard's advice were followed[18]. Between 1900 and 1914 a good quality outdoor coat or tweed costume made to measure would cost between five and seven pounds, although coats were available from three. Whilst ready-made dresses could be bought at a pound or even less, a quality evening gown in satin, net and tulle was £8–£12 and an evening wrap might cost as much as £15. A muslin spring blouse could be had for 13s9d in 1905 but proper splendour, in delicate net and lace, required more than twice as much – 29s6d. Gloves, made by cheap female labour in crowded workrooms, were not unduly expensive: somewhat incredibly, three pairs, of real kid, twenty-button length, could be bought for a little over a pound. The large and elaborate hats were sold at £1.10s upwards, but individual afternoon models, crafted in a West End workroom by girls earning between eight and sixteen shillings a week cost from £8.8s to £10.10s[19].

Really well-made stays, important for comfort, effect, and wearing life, cost six pounds or more. However a great many corsets of seemingly acceptable quality were advertised at around £1–£3.10s. The small boneless 'ribbon' corsets, which had little or no effect on the figure, serving mainly to anchor the stocking suspenders, cost only two to ten shillings according to quality. In 1909, nainsook knickers with a Valenciennes lace trim and lace insertions, 'made by French peasants' were advertised at 2s6d but in milanese silk and other expensive materials, this garment would cost from one to two pounds. Most expensive of all were the fancy petticoats which were usually worn under evening dress. With their elaborate hand-sewn lace trimming, tucks and flounces, they were priced at £3.5s upwards or the equivalent of about three weeks' wages for an unskilled workman.

Down in the lower reaches of the middle classes, few could manage such luxuries. Younger women with passable figures economised by not wearing fully-boned and shaped corsets except perhaps on special occasions. A London typist earning a salary of £65 in 1910 recorded that she spent in that year just under one twelfth of her income on clothes. Her major purchases were: winter blouse material, and the cost of making-up, 7s5d: a coat, £1.1s; a felt hat, 5s6d; two flannel petticoats, 7s10d; ribbon corsets, two shillings; two pairs of knickers, 8s9d; two chemises, 8s9d; stockings, 2s1½d; one pair walking boots, 8s11d; one pair of shoes, five shillings; a pair of kid gloves, two shillings; and a pair of woollen gloves, one shilling[20]. This choice can be taken as typical for the lower middle class young, most of whom were unlikely to have heard of Mrs Pritchard.

## Fashion turns to Youth

Around 1908–9 the shape of fashionable woman began to undergo a considerable transformation. In part this arose from the influence of a young French designer, Paul Poiret, who later made the erroneous claim that he had freed women from what he called 'the tyranny of the corset'. Whilst the power of the corset industry and the long history of artificially shaping the female figure by tight-lacing militated against any sudden change, fashion did take a new direction at this point.

Out went the swan-like 'S' bend, with bust thrown forward and an overlap of blouse or dress falling above the straight-line front of the waist, a mode that had favoured the older woman and mature, full figure. In its place came a longer look, with a loosely-delineated, high waist and a slimmer, smoother hipline which hinted at the shape of the thighs. To achieve this effect, corsets came down much lower over the figure, reaching almost to mid-thigh. The tops of these new corsets finished just above the natural waist, thus removing the support formerly given to the breasts and creating a requirement for a separate bust-holding garment. One such, contoured and with separate cups, had been advertised in

France as early as 1903 under the name *soutien-gorge* and similar designs were sold in Britain as the *brassière* from around 1910. However, for the time being, many women preferred the less disciplined assistance and greater freedom of a shaped (sometimes boned) *cache-corset* also known as a bust-bodice or (wrongly) as a brassière. Others, having smaller breasts, managed with a tightly-stretched chemise[21].

Another feature of the 1909–10 fashion changes was the emergence into daylight of the feet, adorned in pointed toe shoes and lifted by curving Louis heels up to 7.5cm from the ground. Ankles generally remained concealed, though this was not always easy. Hats continued huge and wide, trimmed even more extravagantly, so that they produced a top-heavy effect above the new slim-hipped body shape.

Following the trend toward Poiret's altogether slighter, more willowy line, the new corsets of 1908–9 contained much less boning (some had none at all) and in most cases no busk now pushed in the abdomen. Some designs were made to come so low down the body, so restrictively, that it was difficult for the wearer to sit down. Clusters of up to eight powerful suspenders fulfilled the dual function of keeping stockings taut whilst preventing the corset from sliding upwards. Over their new shape, the fashionable wore a narrow and tight skirt which evolved into the 'hobble skirt' of 1910. This so restricted leg movement that walking became difficult and running virtually impossible. The shackling effect was further accentuated by the tying of large ornamental ribbons around the legs below the knees. Thus, although the waist-cinching bondage of the corset had been somewhat relaxed, a way had been found of perpetuating for a little longer the centuries-old corset-based symbolism of helplessness, inability to undertake physical work and subjugation and service to the male.

A radical transformation in dress was set off, not by Poiret, but by social changes of the 1910s. Young middle class women were beginning to enjoy a fuller life, working in offices, or taking part in voluntary social or political activities, not least the various branches of the suffragette movement. They needed greater freedom in movement than tight-lacing allowed, with simpler, easier-fitting clothes and more manageable hair styles. Fashion responded. By 1914 waists were in their natural position, corsets were less restrictive and hemlines had risen to just above the ankle.

Additional impetus came from the popularity amongst the middle and upper classes of new types of dance imported from the USA in the years 1910–14, many built upon the syncopated rhythms of ragtime and jazz music. These required greater agility than the old ballroom dances, movements impossible to achieve in the fashionable corsets and the new narrow skirt. To allow the legs some freedom, a side slit was introduced into the skirt but this very quickly aroused the condemnation of the ever-viligant middle class censors, churchmen and others, who saw the resultant exposure of silk-stockinged calves as sinfully provocative. Although the more modest 'harem' divided skirt solved the problem in 1911–12, this was never widely-adopted and was soon killed by ridicule and its impracticality for outdoor wear. More successful, but suiting only the tall, slim figure, was the peg-top skirt, narrow in the leg, but giving more freedom at the hips.

Arising from the same influences and much more lasting, was the trend towards shorter and lighter corsetry evident from 1911/1912. Advertised as suitable for tennis, golf, motoring and dancing, and made of vulcanised rubber with minimal boning, these new 'girdles' or 'belts', as they were soon to be called, adopting US terminology, extended only from waist to mid-hip level or slightly above. Sold at 14s to £1.1s they heralded the demise of their figure-shaping, severely-boned and laced forebears and in the next decade or so, the corsets worn by almost all women were to become shorter and less restrictive. Contemporary with their arrival was the abandonment of whalebone in the severer corsets in favour of more durable rubber-covered spiral-spring steels or celluloid strips.

The demand by the younger element for simplification and less restriction, the dancing craze, and the narrower skirts also saw the disappearance of flounced and multi-layered petticoats, bringing into the shops close-fitting 'Tango' or skirt-knickers. Although decorated around the leg openings, this garment lacked the former frills and flounces at the knee. Hair styles were also affected by the new influences. The American Irene Castle, who demonstrated the new dances in Britain with her husband, caused a 1913 sensation by having her hair cut short in a 'bob', presumably to avoid the problems rapid dance movements might cause to elaborately-stacked long hair. This shorter style was to become popular with the young in the years which followed, its wide acceptance further stimulated by the demands of wartime work routines.

Separate fashions for the younger, emancipated and more active woman, most of them middle class, were thus emerging even before 1914. And when the war brought an increase in job opportunities for middle class girls, those supplying their dress needs prospered even in the darkest years. Despite higher prices (just over two pounds for hand made crêpe de chine blouses and almost five for an 'inexpensive tea frock' of chiffon velvet in 1916) more girls were able to afford pretty things to brighten the grim sea of khaki uniforms seen everywhere, thus providing some welcome gaiety for men on leave from the muddy hell of Flanders. More than two and a half years into this dreadful war, with little hope of a conclusion in sight, a newspaper reported in March 1917 that low-priced luxuries such as ladies' lingerie 'continue in great demand. . .'[22] This situation is confirmed by the many advertisements for frivolous underwear in the illustrated magazines of 1917 and 1918, in which it is noticeable that the expressions 'undies' and 'nightie' were already in use. Mrs Peel, that reliable contemporary observer of social change[23], reported the 'silk stocking craze' as widespread in 1917. Skirts became shorter still during the war, rising to just below the calf, flared or fluted and bell-shaped from 1915, then narrower again in 1917–18. By 1921 they were just below the knee. Boots, reaching almost up to the hemline, laced or buttoned at the front and with high Louis heels, were also popular in wartime, although a leather shortage in 1917 temporarily reduced supplies. Blouses, which had been widely worn for almost ten years, took on a very soft and feminine look. Another wartime change was the adoption by many girls of the more practical male pyjamas as nightwear in place of the traditional full-length nightdress. Progress towards greater simplification of both outer and underwear and more functional, easier-fitting styles, already set off before 1914, was altogether greatly stimulated by wartime conditions and demands.

After a period of indeterminate fashions, the mode of the mid-1920s thoroughly revolutionised the appearance of the younger women, who demonstrated their emancipation by trying to deny their sex, making themselves look as much like a man as possible. James Laver has suggested that this major change in dress symbolised a subconscious rejection of the ultra-feminine mother-image after the carnage of war but the recent recurrence of this urge on the part of some young women to subdue their physical sexual characteristics, associated as it is with an uprising of active feminism, suggests it was then, as now, a reflection of aspirations for female emancipation and role-change. Curves were considered 'frumpy' and indeed a rounded figure was near-impossible to contain in the fashionable outer clothes of the day. The young and slim used no restraining underwear beyond a tricot belt around their hips but those with more mature figures or inconveniently large breasts were obliged to adopt ugly rubber, coutil or woven elastic corsets, firmly anchored by strong shoulder straps and suspenders, which diminished the bosom and struggled to subdue the natural curves of the hips and buttocks into a tube of equal girth. More extreme figures were the subject of further flattening pressure from a bandeau-type rubber brassière worn over the top of the corsets.

For outer wear the waistline dropped to what was a virtually nominal existence somewhere near the navel. Blouses and jumpers were pulled well down over the hips. Jumpers, seen everywhere being knitted in trains and buses, were favourite wear of the early and mid-1920s. Knitting was now a well-established middle class leisure activity. In wartime it had become very popular as a comforting, nerve-soothing occupation at periods of tension and strain. Otherwise idle middle class women, seeking some pleasant but purposeful task, had swamped the fighting men with an ever-mounting flow of woollen garments, most of them unwanted and immediately diverted to the cleaning of rifles and other gear.

Dresses of the mid and late 1920s, easy to make-up at home, were very plain and virtually shapeless, distinguished only by a strange uneven indentation at the hemline which was matched on the underwear. Skirts became shorter still: by 1926 they were above the knee, a year later they had risen another inch or two, reaching the limit of abbreviation tolerable at the time – it has to be remembered that only just over ten years earlier, legs had been completely covered. By 1927–29 long pendant extensions at the sides or at the back and front of the skirt were the only concession to evening dress, producing frocks ideally suited to the energetic popular dances of the period.

Despite the fact that it frequently aroused parental or husbandly anger, hair was cut short to reinforce the new boyish image, at first in a bob, a reversion to a style adopted by many in 1915–18 for practical reasons; then, in 1923–5, shingled: and finally, in 1926–7, even more drastically cut in a parted schoolboy style named 'Eton Crop'. As the so-called 'permanent waving' process introduced in the 1900s now took much less than the original eight to twelve hours to carry though, it became more popular especially as it enabled short hair to be given some style. It was however expensive, a whole-head treatment costing five pounds upwards in the 1920s, more than a week's earning for almost all office workers. By the late 1920s the minority of those women and girls still wearing their hair at full natural length often plaited and pinned it into circles over each ear in a style which looked curiously similar to the contemporary radio headphones. The new short hair styles saw off the last of the large and wide-brimmed hats, in their place came cloches, ugly and deep head-hugging helmets of felt or straw.

Underwear, in silk, crêpe de chine or artificial silk, was reduced dramatically in bulk and weight to suit the slim and abbreviated outer clothing of the 1920s. With pressure mounting to reduce the layers of undergarments worn, attempts were made to combine knickers with petticoats, knickers with camisoles (the 'cami-bocker'), and the bust-flattening brassières with suspender belts, as well as some other wilder flights of fancy, but the longest-lived of these combined garments (first appearing as early as 1916/1917 as 'specially designed for the war worker'), was the amalgamation of chemise and knickers, initially called 'chemi-knickers' then, more agreeably, 'cami-knickers', eventually abbreviated to 'camis'. Unlike the earlier 'combinations', camis were essentially loose-fitting, featuring wide and open ('French') legs, these covering about three-quarters of the thighs. An under-buttoning tab provided some highly tenuous protection for modesty and virtue as well as the necessary convenience, allowing the wearer to step into the garment (hence another name, 'step-ins'). In the 1920s the shape of the chemise itself changed to resemble a man's vest and the latter name was increasingly adopted. Like the original garment, these vests were worn *under* the brassière and girdle, a practice which endured until the late 1930s, when younger women gradually began to wear their figure control garments next to the skin. By 1926 the upheaval in underwear design had settled down, the typical middle class girl now wearing only a vest, brassière, girdle, cami-knickers and perhaps an underslip (the latter a new name for the petticoat, soon to be shortened to 'slip')[24].

Black silk or fine cotton stockings, virtually universal wear until this time, had of necessity to be made more interesting now that calves and even knees were on view. Early in the 1920s they began to be replaced by hosiery of lighter hues, the favourite shades gun-metal or 'flesh', the latter in reality a light tone of beige[25]. Almost invariably of silk or rayon (artificial silk), stockings became longer, finishing in a deep lisle welt at mid-thigh. The foot section was also often made in lisle to increase wear life. Garters, long since replaced by suspenders, enjoyed a revival amongst young women and girls in the 1920s, when their use enabled the wearer to further reduce the bulk of underwear by dispensing with the girdle. Amongst the middle classes, display of garters was regarded as rather less shocking than glimpses of suspendered thigh which would otherwise be a hazard of wearing short skirts and open-legged knickers. Most garters were now without the buckle and adjustment of Victorian and Edwardian designs, merely simple bands of elastic decorated with fancy trimming and ribbon bows. They were positioned just above the knees, where they were meant to be occasionally glimpsed, but sometimes two pairs were worn, one above and one below the knees. To afford the necessary protection to the suspended thigh as hemlines rose, much prettier and shorter 'directoire' or closed-leg knickers were widely adopted from around 1925. With decoration at their elasticated leg openings (eg the 'garter-knee' knickers of 1929) or, in the more expensive versions, panels and insertions of ecru lace, and sold in shades such as pink, peach and ivory, this garment now became something of which Mrs Pritchard would have approved, a far cry indeed from its dreary poor relation, the schoolgirl's 'regulation pattern' gym knickers. Directoires were studiously kept pulled down to conceal all but the lower edge of the stocking tops. It is interesting that they survived the demise of the short skirt and were still worn, especially by older women, under the much lower hemlines of the 1930s. Perhaps they provided slightly more comfort in cold weather, or was it that by hiding virtually all above the knees they gave a certain reassurance to the modesty and outward air of propriety so fondly nurtured by middle class woman?

Towards the end of the 1920s, it became general for younger women to adopt a separate brassière, worn with a small elastic and satin 'suspender belt'. The latter served primarily as a means of anchoring the stocking suspenders, usually four in number, fastened centrally at the front and side of each thigh. Those requiring some figure control chose a deeper belt with minimal boning. For still firmer restraint, there were 1920s versions of the corset: coutil and broché girdles of greater depth, usually fastened at the front or side with hooks and eyes rather than lacing and made up with elasticated sections, bones sewn in at strategic points. From about 1922, there were also corselettes, a US invention which combined girdle and brassière in a garment doing much to eliminate the ugly 'spare tyre' effect which tended to appear above the waist when the fleshier forms were encased in the separate 'foundation' garments. To prevent 'riding up', corselettes and 'firm control' girdles often had six or eight suspenders of stronger and wider pattern.

A word must be said about prices in the 1920s[26]. In 1929 a good quality suit of red and beige tweed together with a jumper in heavy beige crêpe de chine, a tie in two colours and a leather belt, was advertised at £12.12s. Other types of tweed costume were available at £9.9s upwards. A deep wrap-over travelling coat in reversible tweed (plain and tartan) with a sheared lamb collar was sold at £8.8s and three-piece knitted suits at just under five pounds. Hats and shoes could be obtained for one to three pounds. Slips in artificial silk were 16s, cami-knickers in crêpe de chine cost up to £2.10s, in satin just under three pounds, truly a luxury item, since for many young lower middles this was more than a weekly wage. Stockings in superior quality pure silk were £1.1s but spun silk and part-silk hosiery could be had at around five shillings a pair. Artificial silk stockings of high quality, with seams and 'fashioned marks', were available in 1926 at four shillings. Various types of light suspender belts and girdles were retailed in the price range 5s–£1.10s but a well-made firm-control girdle or corselette might cost as much as three pounds. To give some idea of relative values, we may note that the shop girls selling these items would be receiving between one and two pounds a week.

## Curves and Mystery Return

With the 1930s, there arrived a quieter, more serious fashion mood, bringing with it a resumption of groomed elegance, femininity, dignity and mystery. Hollywood, then approaching the peak of its power, proved a strong influence. Middle class clothes became very stylish, close-fitting and well cut. The curves of the buttocks were brought into prominence and so tight and smooth were the skirts at the hips and around the thighs in evening wear that the outlines of the suspenders became apparent through the dress. This feature provides an interesting example of how middle class sensitivities were respected; in an attempt to subdue the indiscretion of such a revelation, satin or velvet 'modesty' flashes were attached above the suspender loops and buttons of the more expensive corsetry from about 1932. Another problem was that the outline of the knickers also showed through, causing some women, when wearing their best, to omit this item of underwear.

This new figure-hugging fashion line was achieved with the aid of a dressmaking advance: bias-cut pieces made the fabrics shape to the figure, allowing sufficient stretch for the dress or skirt to be put on over the head or stepped into, thus eliminating the need for a side, front or back opening. Another new feature from about 1936 was the widespread use of zip fasteners in outer clothing and corsetry. This device also assisted the achievement of a smooth, close-fitting line. Day wear hemlines fell to a modest mid-calf length in 1930 and for evening, full length was ordained, although with a kind of reverse *décollettage* revealing large areas of the back and necessitating redesign of both the slip and the corsetry. Once again fashion allowed older women to participate in the wearing of the latest styles, even if some did have to slim to attain the requisite narrow hips and girlish buttocks. With evening dress still being worn for dinner in many homes as well as in smart restaurants, theatre stalls and boxes, the middle class woman needed to buy several evening dresses annually to avoid overmuch repetition. This was more difficult towards the end of the decade as evening gowns became more elaborate and expensive. Since even quite large middle class houses still frequently lacked central heating, an essential accessory was a small jacket with wide padded shoulders to give some warmth to arms, back and neckline.

Hair was now worn longer, often brushed back behind the ears, either curled loosely over the neck or rolled into a ribbon round the head. An upswept, so-called 'Edwardian' style arrived from the USA in 1938, surviving for around two years. Hollywood influences also stimulated the adoption of the 'page-boy' coiffure of 1938–9, straight flowing to shoulder length with the ends and fringe artistically rolled under, and also the long bob, kept in place behind hats with large-holed 'snood' nets. For these softer and fuller styles, milliners offered little confections of pillbox, flat beret and shallow-crowned shapes with small brims, worn at an angle or over one eye, but in 1937 hats moved off the face and became larger. A cute 'Tyrolean' hat with a little feather, widely seen from 1934 to 1939, inspired a popular song and headed a vogue for things Austrian.

Day dresses of georgette, crêpe de chine, artificial silk or flowered chiffon were sold in quantity in department stores and ready-to-wear shops at 15s to two pounds[27] but better-quality frocks in net and taffetta or in washing silk were £4–£4.10s. 'Washing frocks' in new fadeless and crease-resisting fabrics developed by such firms as Tootal and Horrockses, came on to the market in the mid 1930s, selling at around ten shillings. Full length evening dresses in georgette, silk chiffons, satins and crêpes were £3.10s–£12 but the lower middle classes made do with artificial silk jappe, art silk satin or taffeta versions at 12s 11d to £2.2s.9d. Lined coats in tweed mixtures or camel and wool blanket cloth could be had at two pounds upwards and a winter coat with collar and cuffs trimmed in sable coney at just over three (a week's salary for many clerks with up to ten years or more seniority). Although a 'man-tailored' camel coat could be bought in 1936 from £5.10s6d, a good hand-tailored and finished coat would cost seven to eight pounds or more. Only the upper middles could contemplate a white ermine hip length cape, offered in 1936 at 69 guineas (£72.9s), around a year's pay for a Lyon's teashop waitress. Rainwear in the form of Dunlop latex-proofed coats with inverted pleat and decoratively-stiched collar and belt in dark green, grey, navy or black cost £1.1s in the mid 1930s. Single and double-breasted costume suits, for morning and business wear, were obtainable for £2.10s to eight pounds, according to quality of cloth and tailoring. 'Two-piece suits' consisting of a long-sleeved dress with 'the new high bust-line' and three-quarter length lined coat trimmed with fur, to be worn over it, were popular in 1938; in soft bouclé cloth they sold at around five pounds or in soft woollen materials at £6.16s6d.

Although individual 'model' hats were five to ten pounds, the less prosperous could find plenty of felts, velours and straws for seven shillings to around four pounds. Berets, described as 'the latest craze'

(Greta Garbo had set the trend) in 1930, were two shillings to 12s 11d. As with hats, shoes were available in a wide range of styles and quality, from twelve shillings to £3.15s or more a pair.

Undies were now sometimes referred to as 'pretties' or 'frillies', an indication of their secondary role. Mrs Pritchard would have been well pleased. Washing silk 'Cami-bockers', in 1920s mode, with directoire style closed legs and lace bodice section (choice of ivory, beige, black, grey, parchment, peach, pink, sky or primrose) were still being advertised by Debenham & Freebody in 1936 at £1.19s6d, no doubt selling well to the more mature and conservative women. But for the younger set, from about 1931, there were knickers and cami-knickers with vestigial and very wide 'French' legs, much decorated with lace. Camis in 'silk satin' with a brassière top in fine lace, were available in 1933 for £1.10s but for lace and satin 'made in our own workrooms', Debenhams wanted as much as £2.9s6d in 1938. Such luxury for week or more's pay was obviously beyond the reach of the average lower middle class office girl, who, for special occasions, would probably select milanese or crêpe de chine alternatives, available at 10s–£1, making do for office wear with celanese (locknit) panties at around three shillings a pair, fairly close fitting, but still open at the legs. Just before the outbreak of World War 2, Kayser Bondor introduced a range of tailored slips in rayon crêpe and rayon satin in seven sizes with the slogan 'Modern fashion demands underwear that fits'. These had a high waist, brassière top and 'swinging hemline'. They continued to sell through the early 1940s at 8s7d to 11s2d according to size, and in 1943 there were matching French knickers at 5s9d and 7s6d and camis at 7s9d and 8s8d.

The reappearance of curves brought about a minor revival in corsetry, further encouraged by the arrival of new fabrics. From 1929 corsets were being made in lastex, a soft, thin elastic yarn which provided a 'two-way stretch' to hold the garment in position as it moved with the body. Controlling 'like cloth' it had 'the strength of human muscle and the soft, easy stretch of human skin' according to a Warner advertisement of 1937. Boning was virtually eliminated. Well-made girdles using this material were available at £1.10s–£4.4s in the mid-1930s and quality corselettes, now all fitted with zip ('lightning') fasteners, sold at up to seven pounds. A 'Corset Wardrobe' was suggested by Warners in 1936, a foundation garment appropriate 'for each and every occasion – sports, motoring, travel, Day and Evening wear etc. etc.' An advertisement of 1938 by the same firm proposed its 'Le Gant' lastex yarn corsetry as imperative for both mother and daughter, the former to preserve 'graceful lines' and give her 'complete control with an unbelievable comfort' and the latter 'because she knows she must discipline her figure to avoid the "spread" that inevitably overtakes the uncorseted.' In the accompanying photograph, 'mother' stands gracefully in a seamless hip corselette with satin front and back panels, 'ideal for evening and those special occasions', at £4.4s. 'Daughter' squats in the foreground, imperilling her tightly-suspendered silk stockings, in a belt with side panels of figured net, and satin back and front panels. This item, 'especially suitable for all sports and holiday wear' sold at £2.12s6d and was worn with backless satin bandeau brassière costing £1.1s. Both corsets featured a panel stretching up and down only, to give 'a flatter back and firmer hips'.

In May 1935, publicity in *The Tatler* told of another corsetry innovation, the pantie-girdle. This was a short pantie of lastex yarn, fitted with suspenders and without a single bone or seam, 'yet it moulds and holds the figure as firmly under control as any corset and is so supple and light that it will not show or wrinkle under a tight-fitting evening dress. It clings in fact like a second skin and weighs no more than a piece of lingerie'. It was claimed that this new treasure could be washed time and time again without losing its shape and was 'rolled on like a pair of stockings'.

Mature ladies, with 'difficult' figures, and others wishing to enjoy the reassurance and flattery of firm figure control, continued to patronise corsetières, who provided made to measure garments at three pounds upwards. These workers were still employing the old style bones and complicated lacing, buying in their 'parts' from firms such as Spirella of Letchworth Garden City. For the youthful figure, small silk or satin-faced lastex or elastic suspender belts were now available from three to ten shillings and if a modicum of control were required, there were many types of tea-rose or white lightweight wrap-around, hookside or 'roll-on' girdles in lastex and other materials at 10s to £1.10s.

Brassières, generally called 'bras' from the mid-thirties, added their contribution to the renewed emphasis on curves, designs from 1934 lifting the breasts from underneath in pre-shaped cups with and without boning, or by arrangements of bias cutting. Lastex yarn was widely employed in combination with satin and net. Lifting, shaping and wider separation tended to give more prominence to this part of the figure, heralding a trend to be much encouraged by Hollywood in the 1940s. Not all middle class figures could meet the new challenge: 'Many English women are too slim to wear the new fashions which accentuate the bust' proclaimed one advertisement of 1934, offering a discreetly-padded brassière at £1.1s and £1.5s. For evening wear with low shoulderless dresses or deep open backs, the 1930s produced first complicated arrangements of straps clipped to the top of the girdle, then strapless brassières, shaped and supported by light steel boning. Here again we encounter the concern for middle class respectability amongst those selling the more intimate garments. In March 1935 an advertisement proclaimed 'so that you may indulge your fancy for low-cut evening gowns without the haunting fear of "something showing", Kestos have designed this backless brassière'. At this time Kempat had begun to offer a special 'sports brassière' with shoulder straps that 'cannot slip and automatically adjust themselves during strenuous games'. Although not mentioned, this garment also served to control any unseemly joggling of the breasts during the same 'strenuous games' – yet another concession to contemporary middle class ideas of feminine propriety. According to the complication of its design and the quality of materials used, a brassière in the 1930s might cost anything from 2s11d to £1.10s.

Ever more glamorous and elegant, the best silk stockings were from about 1932 'fully fashioned' to the leg, with a prominent seam at the back and 'cuban spliced' or 'court' heels. Prices ranged from about five shillings to 10s6d a pair but cheaper and more durable designs with mercerised cotton or lisle welts and feet were available at four shillings or less. From 1937 stockings were sized to conform with the length of the wearer's legs, extending slightly beyond mid-thigh in response to the smaller dimensions of panties. Under Hollywood influences, other 1930s refinements included a picot edge to the tops and decoration at the shadow welt. There were new standards of sheerness: we read in *The Tatler* of 8 May 1935 that Kayser's 'Mir-o-Cleer' at seven shillings a pair were 'As transparent as a husband's excuses. . . never was silk so clear, so utterly free from every suspicion of shadow and ring. Never were stockings so flattering to the limbs inside them'. Popular shades were neutral grey-browns, cocoa browns, cinnamon, beige, black, and suntan. Silk stockings at four to ten shillings or more, according to sheerness and quality, were a frequent and regular item of expenditure since snags and runs were a common problem. An expensive pair could be ruined at first wearing. If the damage were above the knee, the poorer element of the middle class would repair it for further life, and so-called 'invisible mender' shops existed for those who did not wish or were not able to manage for themselves. To give additional emphasis to the leg-flattering back seams, young girls often wore their silk stockings inside out; the dress-conscious would be constantly checking through the day that seams were straight.

With the directoire knickers of the 1920s now yielding to the smaller and short-leg French or cami-knickers, there appeared a teasing little gap of bare flesh above the stockings, spanned by neater and narrower pale pink or white suspenders highlighted with dainty chromium-plated loops and slides. Such heady delights were kept strictly from view at all times and in the middle classes were generally regarded by 'nice' girls as properly available only to the intended marriage partner. When the Hays censorship code was revised in 1934, depiction of this stocking 'gap' was no longer possible in Hollywood films, a restriction which only furthered its erotic significance and mystery and led to such absurdities as the Can-Can dance performed in tights. The American fashion of rolling down the stocking top over a ring of elastic to a point just above or even just below the knees in warm weather, allowing the girdle to be discarded, was not widely copied by British middle class girls in the 1930s, perhaps because the British climate hardly encouraged it.

Pyjamas, first seen in fashionable bedrooms in the late 1910s, had become 'an increasingly popular form of nightwear', sold even at small country town outfitters by 1930. In nainsook, artificial silk, spun silk or celanese locknit, they cost up to £1.1s11d.

## Middle Class Make-Up

As early as 1902 Mrs Pritchard[28] had had much to say about the use of cosmetics in a chapter significantly headed 'Mysteries of the Toilet'. Twelve years later, a *Punch* cartoon had shown women making up their faces in an hotel lounge. By the 1920s more and more young middle class women were using powder, rouge and lipstick in public, applied from a vanity case carried in their handbags. Lipstick in particular was frequently renewed and its marks were seen everywhere on cups and handkerchieves, providing a tell-tale which called for much male alertness. A Hollywood-inspired fashion in the mid-1920s reduced the size of the natural mouth by emphasising a small rosebud, 'bee-sting' or 'Cupid's Bow' shape with dark lipstick. In the next decade, when make-up generally was less heavily applied and less garish, and magazines constantly instructed their readers on its use, Hollywood decreed a large full mouth and this was widely copied in Britain. Indelible, so-called 'kissproof' materials became available in the late 1930s: Guitare Cyclamen lipsticks, 'indelible-natural-traceless' were advertised in 1939 as 'thanks to the "Kissfix" base. . . proof against smoking, eating, drinking and even kissing.'

Use of nail varnish became general in the 1930s but coloured varnishes and the painting of toenails were generally thought by the

146

middle class to be in poor taste. Indeed many restricted their attentions to careful manicure, finished off by polishing with a pink powder and a chamois leather pad.

Women first smoked cigarettes in public around 1899 but few would be seen to light one, even in the privacy of their own houses, and if a girl smoked in a restaurant, she was laughed at or despised as having made herself conspicuous by 'an act of bravado and bad taste'[29]. It took World War 1 to change this, the habit spreading only very slowly through the 1920s, when the younger element used long holders as display-objects, toying with the cigarette rather than smoking it seriously. Advertising began to show middle class women enjoying cigarettes, sometimes cleverly appealing to their physical anxieties, as in the 1929 Kensitas suggestion that women should smoke between meals to avoid 'harmful overweight'. Despite the now frequent appearance of women smokers on the stage and in films and the employment of smartly-dressed models in cigarette advertising, as late as 1939 smoking was still thought not quite the thing by many middle class women, particularly in public. Smoking in the street, like eating in the street, was much frowned upon by the middle classes. This was soon to change: the 1940s brought pressures, social mixing and tensions which increased the smoking habit amongst women of all backgrounds.

## Sportswear and Spectacles

Sportswear underwent drastic change between the wars, mostly reflecting everyday fashion. Until the last few years of the 1920s, tennis was played in generous skirts and white or cream tennis stockings. A Lux soap flakes advertisement as late as 1926 listed tennis underwear as: 'pale pink vest-corselette, white cami-knickers, white underslip and cream artificial silk stockings'[30]. But suspendered silk stockings laddered quickly under the strains of tennis and, when hemlines rose in the mid-1920s, with risks of 'improper' displays, out they went. By 1932 most played in white socks and divided skirts. Shorts were an acceptable alternative to the latter from about 1934.

Swimwear also became briefer and lighter in the 1930s, mainly as a result of the new sunbathing cult. The short sleeves and legs, shoulder straps and modesty skirts of the costumes used since the beginning of the century gave way around 1935 to much briefer two-piece designs or one-piece backless styles in elasticated material, with and without a minimal skirt to conceal the contours of the *mons Veneris*. A close-fitting all-wool bathing suit (sic) with low back was available in saxe, brown, wine or black and contrasting stripes for 8s11d in 1932, or for another shilling, with skirt. The black or white cotton or wool stockings worn with the bathing costume since the turn of the century were not generally seen after the mid-1920s, and by the beginning of the 1930s, costumes were less frequently covered with beach wraps when the wearer was not bathing, although if required, wraps were still available at 3s3d to 6s11d. White rubber bathing helmets appeared around 1924. As the sun-worshipping cult grew in strength from the mid twenties, beach pyjamas appeared. Sun dresses, with short shoulder straps and mid-thigh length skirts (or shorts) followed about ten years later.

Tailored slacks were increasingly worn in the thirties for informal occasions and for golf, mostly by younger women; older golfers preferred the traditional deep-pleated skirt, usually in tweed. Most lady golfers favoured a masculine showerproof jacket, sometimes made in leather. One mid 1930s style seems to have inspired the World War 2 army battle dress jacket.

Pleasure cycling over considerable distances, organised and otherwise, was predominantly a lower middle class activity but there was no snobbery about this form of mobility and even the upper middles used bicycles for short trips in the country and town. Whilst skirts remained long and full, skirt guards had to be provided over the back wheels of ladies' machines, which were also fitted with chain guards to keep stockings and shoes clean. Reductions in skirt length presented problems of modesty for the silk-stockinged middle class girl or lady cyclist, especially on windy days, and accessory manufacturers came to their rescue with elastic cords which looped around the shoes and clipped on to the hem of the skirt at the upper ends, keeping it pulled down whilst the legs were in motion. Although this device continued to be sold until the 1940s, most lady cyclists had by then adopted divided skirts, slacks, shorts or a form of plus fours. Zip-up cycling jackets, similar in style to those worn by men, on the same lines as golf jackets, were worn for pleasure trips, often with a beret or bandeau.

For women unfortunate enough to require spectacles, almost the only design available was the circular-lensed horn-rimmed type, similar to those worn by men. These were distinctly unflattering, no doubt inspiring Dorothy Parker's cruel comment 'Men seldom make passes at girls who wear glasses'. Perhaps in retribution, a film cliché was evolved in the 1930s and 1940s in which 'nice' middle class office girls were seen to assume a new and kissable beauty as a male admirer removed the glasses in what proved to be an initial step towards a properly-censored seduction.

# The 1940s: Class Distinction in Dress Disappears

By 1940, with the rising prosperity of the employed working class, and the arrival of mass-produced clothing in shops all over the country, the dress of the younger middle class woman was already starting to become almost indistinguishable from that of her sisters in the 'respectable' working class. It was only in details, such as the use of gloves, well-made hats, good shoes, tidy and expensively-sheer stockings, subdued, skilfully-applied make-up and clean well-cared for teeth and nails that she could be recognised before her speech was heard. In the 1930s, but decreasingly so in the wartime conditions of the 1940s, middle class women still did not consider themselves properly dressed outdoors without gloves, hat and stockings, whatever the season of the year. Stockings were worn at all times, winter and summer, even under slacks, except perhaps on the beach. Hats were kept on in restaurants and when making brief social calls in private houses. A Surrey doctor's wife, reminiscing about the 1930s, told the author that whilst she might not bother with them for a quick shopping expedition by cycle in her own town (where her face and status were of course well-known), she always wore both hat and gloves when shopping in neighbouring Reigate.

As the war grew more serious in the summer and autumn of 1940, women of all classes relaxed into ugly hair-concealing turbans or head scarves tied beneath the chin, these worn with padded-shoulder jackets and coats over jumpers, and with slacks and flat-heeled shoes. Utterly depressing and drab, but eminently practical, this outfit was so popular that it outlasted the war by several years – the head scarf was even taken up by the royal family. Office girls, constrained by male-inspired rules that forbade such transvestite eccentricities as trouser wearing, retained some prettiness by appearing in jumpers, blouses and knee length skirts, but the wearing of trousers spread rapidly elsewhere as good stockings disappeared from the shops. In the first half of the 1940s, dresses and coats featured ugly militaristic tones, with squared shoulders and large, prominent belts, as if the women were demonstrating their adherence to the common cause by adopting features of the male fighting uniform. In fine warm weather young middle class girls now started to go out without hats, perhaps wearing a head scarf around the neck ready for use if required.

Prices did not rise very sharply in the 1940s. A 'utility' (wartime economy) suit in check or plain colours was offered at £3.13s7d in 1942, with better quality models at up to £7.10s. Purchase tax (October 1940) and clothes rationing (June 1941) added further to the general classless dowdiness and lack of style. By 1944 a tailor-made herringbone tweed suit was eight pounds, absorbing eighteen of the precious twenty-four clothing coupons which were made available every six months. A brushed wool coat at £13.9s9d required an equal number.

In this final decade of our period, most new fashion developments were shared by all social classes. Nylon, which has been called the 'invention of the Devil and the Du Pont Company', arrived in Britain in 1942, via US servicemen, who, for sexual favours received or anticipated, dispensed to all and sundry of suitable age the very sheer and yet durable nylon stockings then only being made in their homeland. With production of silk hosiery banned in 1941, these goodies assumed a powerful attraction; it was not until early 1947 that British output reached the market in any quantity. Nylon parachutes were also adapted to make underwear during the war years, anticipating the way in which this immensely versatile and glamorous man-made fabric would replace silk and artificial silk for that purpose in the late 1940s and early 1950s.

Christian Dior's full skirted 'New Look' of 1947, heralding a return to feminity with its emphasis on breasts, small waist, and hips, did not become fully established in Britain until 1949, when the eight-year period of clothes rationing at last ended. Since the elaborate tailoring and generous use of material of the New Look made it rather costly, the suits, coats and dresses of this style were mostly seen on middle class women. Pretty lingerie and corsetry were also reappearing in 1949, although the latter long remained in short supply. As the 1940s drew to a close, that favourite and typical middle class wear, botany wool 'twin sets' (long-sleeved cardigan and jumper) were seen in the shops in beige, dusk, pink, ice blue, flannel grey or white at £2–£2.10s[31].

By that time, apart from quality and cut, and sometimes a more successful display of good taste, the dress and outward appearance of the younger women of the upper and middle classes no longer stood out from that adopted in their leisure hours by their now more affluent 'respectable working class' sisters.

# NOTES

1. Peel, Mrs C. S., *Life's Enchanted Cup: An Autobiography (1872–1933)*. (1933). Details of bridge parties from Troubridge, Lady, *The Book of Etiquette*, (1926).
2. Masterman, C. F. G., *The Condition of England*, (1909).
3. 'England in Time of War', *The Times*, December 1914–February 1915.
4. Peel, Mrs C. S., op cit (note 1).
5. Peel, Mrs C. S., op cit (note 1)
6. Figures supplied by the Electricity Council.
7. Information in this and subsequent paragraphs on the development of electrical appliances is mainly based on Byers, Anthony, *Centenary of Service*, (1981).
8. Anon, *PEP Report on Household Appliances*, (1939).
9. The term was coined by Taylor, Dr Stephen (later Lord Stephen), see *The Lancet*, vol. ccxxxiv, January–June 1938, p.759.
10. *Hendon Times & Borough Guardian*, 24 June 1938.
11. Metcalf, J., 'Railway Goods Depots: IV: King's Cross Goods Station', *The Railway Magazine*, April 1900.
12. Bagwell, Philip, *The Railway Clearing House in the British Economy, 1842–1922*, (1968).
13. Holcombe, L., *Victorian Ladies at Work*, (1973).
14. Marsh, David C., *The Changing Social Structure of England & Wales 1871–1961*, (1965).
15. Massey, Philip, 'The Expenditure of 1,360 British Middle Class Households in 1938–9'. *Journal of the Royal Statistical Society*, vol cv part iii (1942).
16. Peel, Mrs C. S., op cit (note 1).
17. Pritchard, Mrs Eric. *The Cult of Chiffon*, (1902).
18. Prices and details in this and the following paragraph are taken from contemporary advertisements.
19. Peel, Mrs C. S., op cit (note 1).
20. Anon, *Accounts of Expenditure of Wage Earning Women & Girls*, Board of Trade, (Cd 5963), (1911).
21. Changes in corset and underwear design had much increased the use of the brassière by 1915–16. *The Lady* of March 1915 noted: 'A pretty bust-bodice now counts quite as much an essential as the corset, so fine now and extremely devoid of superfluous folds and insertion and ribbon adornment is the lingerie, and so low-cut the corset. . . even with the camisole, the addition of a dainty bust-bodice is more often than not regarded as necessary to the equipment. On the other hand the brassière usually supersedes the camisole and is therefore greatly in demand among women who are other than slim, as, while dispensing with the extra garment, it also moulds the figure gracefully'.
22. *The Times*, 13 March 1917.

23. Peel, Mrs C. S., *How We Lived Then, 1914–18; A Sketch of Social and Domestic Life in England During the War*, (1929).

24. Advertisement for Lux Soap Flakes, EN 11 August 1926.

25. Beige stockings had appeared in London's West End as early as 1921, challenging the hitherto near-universal black. Beige was a widely used shade for clothes and home decoration throughout the 1920s. James Laver makes the plausible suggestion that its ubiquity was due to a large surplus of wartime khaki dye, from which it was obtained by dilution.

26. Prices and details are taken from contemporary advertisements.

27. Prices and details in this and following paragraphs are taken from contemporary advertisements.

28. Pritchard, op cit (note 17).

29. Fortescue, The Hon. Lady, *The Play Pictorial*, 308 (11.1927).

30. EN, 1 July 1926.

31. 1940s details and prices are taken from contemporary advertising.

# CHAPTER 7

# MIDDLE CLASS MAN

Much of what needs to be said about the middle class male falls conveniently into other parts of this book. Here we look first at his general lifestyle, concluding with some account of his dress.

Many, especially the lower middles, were under continuous pressure to maintain appearances considered appropriate to their station in life, both as regards themselves, their homes and their families. To sustain status, they faced visible display expenditure on house, dress of all family members and, where possible, on living-in domestic servants, which could impose crippling strains on incomes often little above those of the better-paid workers, who had no such concerns. Middles on relatively low pay would have a substantial portion locked into rent or mortgage repayments, insurance, hire purchase instalments and perhaps school fees. Compared with the working class, they spent significant amounts on clothes worn at work since they were expected to attend in 'decent professional garb' – suits, collars and ties, and the accompanying formal headwear. The National Union of Clerks, demanding a minimum salary of £91 a year in 1909, based their claim not only on a perceived differential between the clerk and the manual worker but also on the necessity for the clerk 'to appear like a gentleman and pretend to live like a gentleman, and to have the manners of a gentleman'[1].

Quite apart from the expectations of their employers that they would lead blameless and respectable lives and be worthy of trust, the heavy financial commitments entailed in keeping up appearances tended to inhibit many lower middle class men from any behaviour which might prejudice the security and progress of their salaried employment, with its opportunities of promotion and perhaps a pension at age sixty or sixty-five. In this respect their fate was usually at the whim of employers or senior managers, since the white collar classes had traditionally regarded employee organisations as ungentlemanly and inconsistent with their perceived status. Apart from civil servants, local authority officials, railway clerks and school teachers, few middle class males were organised for negotiation with employers and most had no effective means of securing redress when there were genuine grievances. It followed that many were exploited and much outrageous and unthinking behaviour by employers and managers had to be faced. This situation was usually tolerated with resigned cheerfulness, or at any rate mute submissiveness, in an effort to retain a hold on a position which provided regular income and some hope of eventual advancement, however distant. Security of tenure and the mistiest of promotion prospects weighed more heavily than the size of the immediate salary. When many junior clerks lost their jobs during the depression years of the early thirties without compensation of any kind this often started off downward mobility because alternative employment of comparable quality to the lost position was hard to find in a decade in which competition for middle class jobs remained keen.

# An Unchanging Lifestyle

Edwardian middle class men, accustomed to doing little or nothing to help in the domestic routine, were often only tenuously associated with the homes they provided. The outward movement of the middle class from the centres of the cities and towns, already well established at the beginning of the century and continuing through the next four decades, required the male to spend most of his waking hours either at work or travelling to and from it. It was a life pattern which encouraged him to pursue leisure interests in the company of office colleagues or other friends in town, circles quite distinct from those in which his wife and family moved. Apart from the one and a half day weekend, only a few brief evening hours were available for family and home life, and Saturday afternoons would often be devoted to either playing or watching ball games. This increased the father's separation from his children, who, unless they were very young, or the family had a low income, would generally be away at boarding school for much of the year. And, as we shall see later, the family often spent long summer holidays by the sea during most of which the father was absent for rather more than 5½ days each week.

Influences working in the opposite direction, towards a greater domestication and more home-centred life, remained weak throughout most of the period with which we are concerned. They were most apparent in the lower middle class, where there were no domestic servants and children were living at home rather than boarding school. Whilst it is true that the servant shortage may have tended to increase sharing of domestic duties and responsibilities with the wife and any older daughters through a wider sector of the middle classes after 1914, this seems unlikely to have been either permanent or important, given the counterbalancing labour-saving benefits available from new house

154

designs and new types of domestic equipment. In households where absence of paid help was a more or less permanent feature (a situation most likely to be found amongst the lower middles from that time) some men may have been moved towards greater domestic participation in the early years of establishing the marital home and whilst the children were very young. That they should help would not have been obvious to them, and even if they did participate, it would not have been easy to adapt, since their upbringing would not have prepared them. The lifestyle of their peers and accepted role patterns would also have discouraged any thought of it as a normal situation. Thus any such phase would have been temporary, brought to a conclusion as early as possible. In many homes any necessary help at times of stress for the young wife would more likely be given by women; her mother, or mother-in-law, or her sisters, or by somehow finding the money for outside help. In mixed communities of lower middles and 'respectable working class' there were many active widows in reduced circumstances to whom even a modest pittance for such temporary domestic work was welcome.

It has been suggested[2] that even as early as the 1930s, the extension of the years of married life in which the couple had no young children to look after (following the decrease in family size) may have contributed to a greater domestication and home-orientation of the husband, leading, as is nowadays often the case, to sharing of leisure time with the wife and more involvement in such activities as shopping and home improvement. To support this, the existence of new supercinemas and larger 'road house' style licensed premises has been cited as possible evidence. It is doubtful whether this can be applied to the between-wars middle classes. Whilst it is true that the lower middle and the 'respectable working class' husbands usually shared all cinema visits with their wives, there was nothing new about that and it had always been possible for them to find child-minders. As for the 'improved' public houses of the late twenties and early thirties, their clientele consisted mainly of young single people and married men unaccompanied by their wives rather than the married couples, at any rate middle class marrieds. The almost simultaneous arrival of the supercinemas and the superpubs on the early 1930s scene owed more to economic and technical developments than a new social demand.

It seems likely that most middle class men, finding themselves with more free time as their children grew up, simply devoted more energy to their personal leisure interests and were content to see their wives doing the same. Apart from the construction and planting of a garden for the new house, often a solitary male occupation in this period (and certainly left to professionals by all who could afford the then much lower real

155

costs of labour), the new owner-occupiers of the 1920s and 1930s were not much concerned with 'do-it-yourself' work inside or outside the house. The phrase was unknown to the contemporary vocabulary and the lack of such activity is confirmed by the virtual non-existence of any marketing and retail organisation to service it. New houses needed very little maintenance and any work that was necessary, including redecoration, would be readily done at low cost thanks to the existence of a vast pool of willing and cheap labour.

If we disregard a modest expansion and development of his personal and leisure interests, it would seem that there was very little change in the basic lifestyle of the middle class male until the 1940s. There were however changes in attitude, notably a gradual easing of formality in his relationships with his children. The hard Victorian middle class father was certainly still easily found, but he was slowly on the way out.

Increased male attention to leisure activities in the years between the wars faithfully followed the already established trend of 'suburban values', tending towards play and hobbies rather than intellectual or cultural pursuits. This development was quickly reflected in what was almost the only significant change in male costume in the half century.

# Dressing the Man

As with that of their women, the dress of middle class men continued to function as an outward expression of status, aspirations and class. Appearance distinguished even the most humble members of the middle classes from the workers. Photographs of construction projects reveal the important part played by headgear in this respect: even as late as the early 1940s we see workmen in cloth caps whilst the heads of the engineers and technicians are adorned in soft trilbies. On the railways, locomotive shedmasters, inspectors and other minor officials not put into uniform were immediately recognisable by their hard bowler hats[3], a form of headgear which, with rolled-up umbrella, also remained obligatory until the 1960s for army officers attending workplaces in civilian clothes.

Middle class males were essentially conformist in matters of dress, rarely diverging from the accepted norm, which copied upper class styles and practices as far as possible. It was regarded as good form not to dress in a conspicuous manner, avoiding loud patterns and clothes in the extreme height of fashion. Except among the lower echelons, who had to make do with the best they could afford, middle class man was always dressed for the occasion. There was a constant striving for correctness and for the toning of accessories such as gloves and ties. Quality in materials,

A lower middle class commuter leaves suburbia for the office, 1901. Status symbols include the morning coat, silk hat, newspaper, rolled umbrella, gloves, spats and Gladstone bag.

tailoring and craftsmanship was much sought after – it was correctly said that you could judge a man's social status by studying his shoes. The cut of his suit also indicated not only whether he could afford bespoke tailoring but the sort of tailor he patronised.

Another notable feature was a tendency, especially amongst professional men, to adhere to outdated styles until they became a kind of uniform. For middle class man, appearance was everything; he must dress as his employers or as his clients expected and his approach to his appearance would be taken as reflecting his attitude to his work. No lawyer, doctor, banker or school teacher could expect to begin to earn respect, attention and confidence unless dressed neatly and smartly in the customary style of his profession.

Thus for everyday business wear many middle class men of the 1900s and 1910s continued to be seen in the knee-length cut-away or double-breasted frock coat, or the less dressy morning coat. Both were worn with a waistcoat, a stiff and high-winged collar decorated with silk stock or tie, and narrow trousers of matching or lighter hue, often striped. Outdoors, a top hat and leather gloves were essential and a silver-topped walking stick or well-made umbrella completed the accessories. The waistcoat was important, not only because it hid the ugly braces supporting the trousers; it assumed special emphasis at middle age and after, when it overlaid the broad belly or 'corporation' which indicated good living and prosperity. Across this inflated expanse was displayed the principal item of male jewellery, the heavy gold watch chain with its ornament or personal seal.

The more up to date office workers, and the younger clerks, wore short black jackets and waistcoats with matching or pinstripe trousers, the latter of lighter hue. This uniform also included a white shirt with separate rounded or winged collar high enough to conceal most of the neck; both items were stiffly starched, and the tie was sober and dark. Outdoors, all heads would be covered with bowler or trilby hats but many older office workers continued to wear top hats until the end of the 1910s. Straw boaters were a summer indulgence for some. Most would carry a tightly-rolled umbrella, whatever the season or weather, and perhaps a small leather or imitation-leather suitcase, an accessory which by the 1920s had all but replaced the earlier Gladstone bag. In winter a dark calf length melton overcoat would be worn. On Sundays, since most middle class families attended church, it was customary to wear a suit all day, usually one kept for the Sabbath and special events.

For less formal town occasions, there were single and double-breasted lounge suits, always worn with waistcoat, stiff collar and tie, the jackets long in the skirts and split up the back, the trousers narrow in the leg. Whilst jackets and trousers were of the same material, waistcoats could be white or white with coloured ribbing. Outdoors this garb would be accompanied by a soft trilby or homburg hat, or perhaps a bowler, and in summer a straw boater or panama. More affluent heads might wear a deer-stalker or tweed trilby or cap in the country. By the 1910s trilby, homburg and bowler were increasingly seen in place of the top hat for town wear[4] on all but the most formal occasions and winged collars were giving way to a design which was still stiff but had turned-down points or rounded corners covering all but the knot of the tie at the front.

Although not tight-fitting generally, all trousers in the first quarter of the century were cut narrow in the leg. A front crease down each leg appeared from the 1910s, accompanied by turn-ups. Boots continued to be widely worn for some years but shoes were increasingly seen from the 1910s. Both were frequently covered, especially in winter, with light grey, cream or yellow cloth spats, buttoned over. Some boots were made with cloth tops to resemble spats but none but the sloppy and impecunious lower middles would resort to such a lazy subterfuge. However when royal feet were seen without spats in the 1920s the middle classes as usual quickly followed their example, even if a few isolated eccentrics could occasionally be seen in them in London as late as the 1960s.

In the country, for golf or cycling, or at the seaside, Norfolk jackets were worn with a tweed cap, knickerbockers, and long woollen socks, the latter more easily cleaned than trouser bottoms. Occasionally in summer on the river or beach, panama hats, alpaca jackets, off-white flannel trousers and open-necked cricket shirts were seen. Otherwise leisure and casual wear were virtually unknown in the 1900s and 1910s and even in the hottest weather, many middle class men out of town retained their formal dark suits, stiff collars and ties.

Hair was arranged short and flat with a centre parting (later moved to the left side). Brushing the hair straight back from the forehead and smarming it down with oil or brilliantine became popular from about 1910. Although some young men sported small moustaches, the general fashion of the middle classes was to be clean-shaven. Beards and whiskers were largely confined to the elderly or naval persons.

Prices asked for these clothes were generally low, resting as they did on a basis of very cheap and often sweated labour. A mediocre suit or overcoat could be bought for around two pounds, rather more than a week's income for most clerks, although twice that or more would be asked for skilled tailoring and the best quality cloth. In 1904 Chas. Baker & Co. of London advertised frock coats and vests from £1.19s6d to £3.4s.6d, tweed and serge three-piece suits at £1.15s.6d to £3.9s.6d and Chesterfield overcoats, summer or winter weight, at £1.9s.6d to £2.19s.6d, all these made to measure and alleged to be 'at least 25% under usual West End charges'. This firm's business was largely founded on the custom of office workers and their families. An Acquascutum quality waterproof raincoat, advertised in the 1905 *Play Pictorial* at £3.3s would not be seen on the backs of many lower middles.

Styles changed little in World War 1, a period when large numbers of the middle class put on the uniform of an army officer. An incongruous feature of this was the widespread adoption of equestrian trimmings, wide-top breeches, long leather gaiters, boots, and spurs, despite the fact that most of the wearers never had the occasion, or even the ability to mount a horse. The military jacket and breeches were protected by a good quality belted gabardine raincoat with double-yoked shoulders and epaulettes, known as a trench coat, or trench warm, introduced by the firm of Burberry with War Office approval in 1914. This garment was soon widely adopted for middle class civilian wear, and eponymous versions of it were to remain popular for decades. Under military influence, hair became even shorter and very small moustaches were frequently worn.

By far the most important event of the 1920s in the male fashion world, and arguably the only important one of the whole period, was the trend towards more comfortable and less formal leisure wear. Trend-setter for this was Edward, Prince of Wales, whose style many middle class young men avidly tried to emulate. Tweed suits were soon followed by close-fitting 'sporting' (later 'sports') jackets, sold at three to five pounds[5]. These, with two buttons, of which only the top one was normally fastened, entirely replaced the Norfolk coat, and were worn with wider, more loosely-cut and turned-up grey flannel trousers costing £1.12s to £2.5s. But perhaps the most characteristic of all middle class styles of the 1920s was the general adoption by young men of the special type of knickerbockers known as 'plus-fours', formerly virtually confined to the golf course. Worn with long check or jazzy-patterned woollen socks and brown lace-up shoes, these first came into general use around 1921, soon becoming almost a uniform for the younger middles. With other casual wear, they were particularly prominent in and around university and college towns and amongst those 'helping out' in the General Strike of 1926.

Another very middle class leisure garment was the blazer or reefer jacket, a short double-breasted affair in navy blue, adorned with club, school or regimental badge over the breast pocket and on its three brass buttons. Dating from the mid-19th century, this had its origins in a naval uniform. Uppers and upper middles also applied the label to boating coats in college or club colours which they wore at summer events on the river with boaters and light-coloured trousers.

Almost all the casual wear trousers of the 1920s were designed to be held up with belts, an accessory first seen in the early 1910s. For the new leisure wear, fancy-patterned pullovers were knitted in Fair Isle or check patterns to replace the waistcoat. Sleeveless or long-sleeved styles were popularised by Edward, Prince of Wales from 1922 and they endured until the 1940s. Casual outfits were completed with soft cotton 'cricket' shirts with attached pointed collars and a soft trilby hat with wide brim, often worn at the rakish angle made fashionable in World War 1 by Admiral Earl Beatty when appearing in a peaked naval cap. Some, schoolteachers in particular, favoured a trilby with very wide brim which they turned down at the back as well as the front. In summer the knitted pullovers were often worn without a jacket and the soft shirts, normally white, were left open at the neck. Many of those dressed in the clothes just described would be seen with a pipe in their mouths (often unlit) for much of the day. Umbrellas were not carried with leisure wear, but a raincoat was commonly held folded over the arm. Young lower middle class men also adopted this habit with office wear, spurning the traditional rolled brolly as rather stuffy. Bathing costumes of this period had shoulder straps and brief legs. Their ugliness was accentuated when the dark coloured wool of which most were made hung down in folds when wet.

Hair remained short between the wars and was kept right off the neck. Solid brilliantine and later, oil-based perfumed creams, kept it well under control at all times. Brylcreem, one of the latter, was widely used by lower middle class youths and when these entered the Royal Air Force in considerable numbers in 1939–45 to take air crew and technical posts they became known as 'The Brylcreem Boys'[6]. During the 1920s and 1930s, facial hair came under wider and daily assault from the increasingly popular safety razor, although miniature ('natty') moustaches were the pride of many younger men. Shoes, were now virtually universal amongst the middle classes – the continued association of boots with the working class and memories of World War 1 discomforts no doubt helped to kill the popularity of that form of footwear. Greater use of shoes brought brighter socks, many with clocks and other patterns at the ankle.

From the early 1920s the jackets of lounge suits were cut shorter in the skirt whilst the associated trousers became wider a little later (the ridiculously-wide 'Oxford Bags' were a transient undergraduate fad of the middle 1920s, their popularity wildly exaggerated by journalists). Creases down the centre of each trouser leg became the norm in the 1920s, especially amongst the younger element. With this development, trouser presses achieved a wide sale and before each weekend, the steam presses in dry cleaner's shops would be seen working furiously in the same cause.

From the end of the 1920s a suitably sober dark lounge suit gradually became acceptable for business and office wear, though the waistcoat and separate stiff or semi-stiff collar with its studs back and front, and white shirt with cuffs fastened with links were retained. As early as 1922, Summit 'soft' collars, with eyelet holes to take a collar pin inserted under the knot of the tie to keep the collar points in position could be had at six shillings for a box of six, but these would raise frowns in the more formal offices. Impecunious clerks would try to keep cuffs clean for at least two days by wearing elastic or metal link sleeve bands halfway up the arm. Older office workers continued to wear black jackets and pinstripe trousers and these were still to be seen into the 1940s alongside the lounge suits and the new white collar-attached shirts worn by the younger men. Whilst at their desks, if out of public view and under a tolerant management, clerks seeking to lengthen the lives of their suits would sometimes don 'office jackets', taken from suits too threadbare and shabby for normal wear.

For the great majority of office workers, the hat remained very much a badge of status, together with the rolled umbrella, carried in all weathers. By the 1930s bowlers, dark homburgs and (for the more youthful), trilbies, were the usual headwear to and from the workplace. Even when in casual clothes, few middle class heads were seen without some form of covering. The low round-crown 'pork pie' felt hat, which had originated as women's wear in the nineteenth century and was still occasionally seen as such well into the twentieth, was adopted by men in the mid 1930s.

Again taking a cue from royalty, the middle classes abandoned the frock coat from around 1925 and apart from very formal occasions, such as royal garden parties, investitures, weddings, Royal Ascot, and Eton v. Harrow matches, and on stationmasters at principal stations, the top hat and morning coat had virtually disappeared by 1930. Even here there was some relaxation, and grey morning dress became accepted at all but the most formal and solemn events from the mid 1930s.

As the thirties came to an end, many younger middle class men were abandoning any form of headwear, even when dressed in sober lounge suits, whilst others carried their hats in their hands. What started this retreat from head covering is unclear, but it seems to have been a mixture of a reluctance to disturb carefully-combed hair and a subconscious revulsion against the studied formality of elders. Enforced wearing of caps and steel helmets during the war years strengthened the desire to leave the head unencumbered and many of the hats issued with demobilisation suits were immediately discarded. Later, the low roofs of modern cars may have been a factor in accelerating this development. By the 1950s the 'no hat' movement was spreading from the young to the middle-aged and the men's hat industry was in sharp decline. With the disappearance of the hat went the long-established ritual of hat-raising when greeting or offering a civility to a lady, or as an act of deference by a young man to an elderly one.

Prices were substantially higher than before 1914[7]. A good quality suit or overcoat could not be obtained for less than about six to nine pounds in the 1920s; a shirt then cost twelve shillings to one pound; and shoes were £1.10s upwards according to quality. A full evening dress suit could be had for around nine to twelve guineas, a dinner suit at eight to ten guineas but for the best material and tailoring, the purchaser would have to find at least fourteen guineas for the first and sixteen for the second.

Dressed for the evening at home, in restaurants and at the theatre, or in men's clubs and night clubs, middle class men now wore a black tie with dress shirt, black waistcoat and a single or double-breasted short 'dinner jacket', called by the Americans (who invented it) a tuxedo. Once again royalty (this time Edward VII) had started the trend. Double-breasted dinner jackets were worn in the 1930s after Edward, Prince of Wales had been seen in one. A little earlier he had also introduced a soft pleated-front dinner shirt with a turn down collar.

For all formal occasions the full evening dress of cut-away black tailcoat and trousers, white waistcoat, stiff-fronted white shirt, white tie, stiffly-starched wing collar, white gloves and top hat remained the required wear. However by 1920 the old rule of white tie, tail-coat and white waistcoat at all dinners where ladies were present and black tie when dining in all male company no longer prevailed.

As already noticed, the trend towards greater informality grew even stronger in the 1930s. Following the general adoption of the Saturday half-day in offices, it was convenient for men to attend dressed ready for the afternoon's activities (often at the office's own sports ground) and before long, sports jackets, white collar-attached shirt and tie and grey flannel trousers became tolerated on that morning alone. The same garb was widely adopted (often without the tie) as summer holiday and weekend wear. Polo-necked sweaters worn without jackets and self-supporting trousers with integral waist straps were 1930s innovations, as were corduroy trousers. Working men's wear for many decades, adopted by bohemians in the 1920s, corduroys were now taken up more widely by the middle classes as leisure dress and were popular for their durability and lack of fussy creases. Some academics wore them most of the time. With the arrival of the sun cult about 1932, bathing costumes were soon abbreviated to legless trunks, belted around a low waist.

Wrist-watches, available in the 1900s but first made popular by their practicality for trench life in World War 1, were almost universal by 1930.

Prices ranged from eight to ten pounds for models in 18 carat gold cases to as little as five to ten shillings but the cheaper models tended to be very unreliable. By that time the watch chain across the waistcoat had been replaced by a new form of middle class male jewellery, the gold-banded, gold-nibbed self-filling fountain pen and matching propelling pencil, worn in the top pocket of the waistcoat. A serviceable Waterman's self-filling pen could be purchased for under one pound by the 1920s but much higher prices were asked for luxury models with gold fittings.

Suits and coats in the 1930s exhibited a broader and fuller look, with wide shoulders on overcoats and raincoats and square shoulders and big lapels on jackets. Trousers remained wide in the leg, hanging baggily from pleated waists; only the odd eccentric now wore them without turn ups over the shoes. The new look was widely adopted for the ready-made or stamp-cut mass production suits and coats increasingly seen at low prices in the flashy shops being opened all over the country by Burton and similar firms. However the bespoke tailors remained wary of these new trends, modifying them so that their customers were not introduced to them too suddenly. This was of course a recognition of the strong conservatism that middle class man had about this appearance. Tailors' pattern books remained full of the older styles well into the 1940s. Following the introduction of the lightning or zip fastener in ladies' wear in the mid 1930s, some attempts were made to persuade men to use a zip fly in place of buttons in trousers, but this device was long attended with mistrust and suspicion, not becoming universal for another two decades or so.

White shirts, a powerful symbol of class, since they were readily spoiled by any form of manual work, remained unchallenged for office and other formal wear throughout the 1930s and 1940s, but the old pull-over-the-head design was gradually ousted by the coat shirt, with button cuffs replacing slots for cufflinks and tails becoming ever more skimpy, especially during the textile shortages of wartime (those shortages also started to kill off the waistcoat for everyday wear, a process accelerated in the 1950s by better heating of offices). The 1930s saw the turn-down collar adopted by all except the older professional men and a few very conservative office workers. The appearance of this type of collar also improved with the contemporary introduction of the better-fitting Van Heusen brand, incorporating fabric woven on the curve and a fold line woven into the collar. Collar-attached shirts for town day wear were beginning to become popular by the late 1940s, the points of their collars braced stiff by slip-in-strips of plastic. Before leaving the shirt, it may be noted that the English middle classes were long reluctant to remove their jackets in public, since the shirt was regarded as an undergarment which it was improper to display. There was a similar sense of discomfort and disquiet about opening the neck of the shirt and discarding the tie, even in very warm weather, except when wearing casual clothes (and even then the inhibition often persisted). Today it is with a sense of considerable shock that the older middle class generations view younger men, many of them newly-arrived middles, sitting down to eat in hotels and restaurants without coats or ties, although some establishments do still try to maintain the traditional standards.

As late as the 1930s and 1940s older men continued to buy generously-cut sleeved- and neck-buttoned vests of wool or cotton complimented by ankle-length or short leg pants of the same materials, buttoned at the fly. These pants were held in position by cotton tapes at the top edge through which the leather button-holed straps of the trouser braces were threaded. Both undergarments had remained virtually unchanged in design since before 1914. However from about 1934, briefs with elasticated waists, some wholly of elastic fibre, arrived from the United States. These were worn with sleeveless vests or singlets and the young were quickly converted to both, duly noting they were worn by their favourite American film stars. US influences, primarily exercised through Hollywood films, also introduced brighter patterns for pyjamas, which appeared with elasticated-waists, lapels and cuffs, in cottons, rayons and silks, designs which were then to remain static for several decades. As they were consider 'pansified' (mildly effiminate), such innovations were ignored by the working classes, even if they could afford them.

Since elasticated or other self-supporting tops were still uncommon in the 1930s and 1940s, socks soon crumpled round the ankles unless taken in charge by the calf-encircling elastic sock suspenders or 'Boston Garters', first available in the early 1900s at one and two shillings a pair. Another refinement scorned by the working class, these were fitted with loops and buttons similar in design to those of ladies' stocking suspenders but much more robust in appearance. They had a comic rather than erotic aura; always appearing mildly ridiculous on the hairy male leg, they were invariably good for a laugh when deliberately revealed on the stage.

The appearance of the younger, less affluent middle class male was much smartened up with the advent of 'made-to-measure' mass-produced men's clothing in the 1930s. Perhaps the best-known of the firms involved in this new phenomenon of combined manufacturing, distribution and retailing of clothing was the Leeds-based Montague Burton, whose slogan was 'Let Burton the Tailor of Taste Dress You'. Burtons opened shops in almost every British High Street during the decade, selling

165

suits and overcoats at just over two pounds. An advertisement of 1935[8] offered suits at £2.5s in a choice of 500 patterns, 'in Yorkshire tweeds, smooth-draping serges, new worsteds and Scottish and Irish tweeds . . . to personal measurements cut and designed for you alone'. Overcoats of 'Five Guinea Value' were sold at £2.5s in the mid 1930s. With their competitors, The Fifty Shilling Tailors, Jacksons and Weaver to Wearer, Burtons introduced a version of made to measure tailoring to many lower middle class men for the first time as well as offering a whole range of ready-made suits and coats. The quality and finish were very close to that offered by firms such as Austin Reed, who catered almost exclusively for the mainstream middle class, offering both ready-to-wear and the full trimmings of a traditional tailoring service. Many of the newly-arrived lower middles of the 1930s and 1940s would hesitate to enter the latter's premises, fearing they might find the experience too intimidating.

The influence of Burtons and the other stamp-cut, mass production firms was not confined to the middle class man; by the 1940s they had ensured that his appearance was less easily distinguished from the 'Sunday Best' of the 'respectable working class', just as that of the lower middles was by then not too different from that of the rest of the middle classes. As with women, before speech and attitudes were revealed, a man's social class was now displayed only in details, such as the design of the tie, the quality and cut of his shirt and suit and the type and quality of shoe. Then, in 1945–7, as if in a state-funded attempt to put a seal on the steady trend towards the standardisation of male dress irrespective of social class, every demobilised officer and serviceman was given a Burton/Fifty Shilling ready-made suit and raincoat. At that point one might say the division between the classes fell fairly neatly between those who were seen wearing these parting free gifts from a grateful government and those who immediately gave them away to the deserving poor or put them at the back of the wardrobe as a treat for the moth.

## NOTES

1. *The Clerk* (organ of the National Union of Clerks), January 1909.
2. For example, Stevenson, John, in his *British Society 1914–45* (1984).
3. 'The entire executive staff who work underground at night wear black bowler hats and smoke large briar pipes' (article on the London Underground Railways in *The Star* newspaper, 1 March 1938).
4. In his *LNER* (1986), Geoffrey Hughes tells of a formal afternoon visit by one railway officer to another's home in the early 1920s at which the visitor, then in his sixties, was wearing a top hat. But this was in Doncaster, not London!

5. Prices and details are taken from contemporary magazine and newspaper advertising.

6. From its formation in 1918 the nature of many of its functions and activities tended to shape the Royal Air Force into a largely middle class institution. The upper classes remained faithful to the army and navy and the working class populated their other ranks. It is perhaps significant that Colonel T. E. Lawrence, seeking a refuge from fame, chose to serve as a ranker in the RAF. Most young aircrew came from a middle class background and the introduction of the then highly-secret radar in the late 1930s and early 1940s, for which recruitment of operators and mechanics was initially confined to secondary school leavers with General School Certificate or better, added to this leavening. It may be noted that in 1939–45, the RAF, alone among the three services, issued its non-commissioned men with ties, collars and shoes, and overseas, pyjamas and sheets.

7. Prices and details are taken from contemporary newspaper and magazine advertising.

8. *News-Chronicle*, 3 May 1935.

CHAPTER 8

# GROWING UP MIDDLE

## Bringing up Baby

One consequence of the middle class trend towards smaller families was to secure most children a greater share of attention, energy and expenditure. The consumer and service industries, notably private education, responded enthusiastically to this challenge.

Although the middle class child started life with considerable advantages, in the early decades of the century even the best doctors were powerless to protect it from many common bacterial hazards. Childbearing and childbirth were also still attended with much risk for both mother and baby. Confinement took place either in a comfortable private nursing home, where the mother stayed for two weeks or more under the care of her own doctor, or in the family home, in which case a living-in maternity nurse would be engaged for several weeks before and after the event. Even the lower middle class would usually manage to employ a daily nurse for a short period.

As early as the 1900s, new parents did not lack medical guidance as to the child's physical health and welfare. Contemporary advice placed great emphasis on fresh air; on bedroom windows open all night in the coldest weather; on giving baby a daily 'airing'; and on ensuring small children were taken out for a walk every day, playing in the open air whenever possible. In part, this fresh air cult arose from a potent fear of pulmonary tuberculosis, a disease which haunted many families, remaining a killer until the 1940s. Another fetish, worshipped with equal fervour at home and at boarding schools, was the regular daily bowel movement. Firm and direct questioning on results was routine and any signs of hesitation or shy head-wagging were met with doses of evil-tasting 'fruit' laxatives or syrup of figs. Lasting damage was often wrought by such well-intended nagging and over-medication. In a world which knew nothing of antibiotics and little of inoculation, children were at risk from pneumonia, rheumatic fever, scarlet fever, measles, diphtheria and whooping cough, none of them respecters of middle class hygiene and all not infrequently fatal, or at any rate liable to leave lifelong problems. In the absence of other remedies, mothers and children's nurses resorted, especially in

168

winter, to 'building up' their infants with cod liver oil and malt, Virol, Scott's Emulsion, Parrish's Patent Chemical Food and other proprietary mixtures, hopefully trying to ward off infection by rubbing juvenile chests with warm camphorated oil or by hanging camphor blocks over them from a string around the neck. Anxieties and precautions of this type were particularly rife amongst the lower middles, whose children were often obliged to rub shoulders at school with those of the lower orders, automatically assumed to be a constant and potent source of all kinds of infection, mental as well as physical.

It was not until the late 1920s and the 1930s, and then largely by American influence, that middle class parents received any sustained advice on the emotional and social needs of children. Much of this filtered out through the columns of the new women's magazines. But there was someone who had known about such things much earlier, even if she was not able to express her advice so readily on paper. She also had remedies for health problems, even if these were not always in line with the latest medical theories. That someone was of course nanny.

## Nanny knows Best

In the more affluent middle class households the organisation of the care and upbringing of the younger children revolved around the day nursery. This large room was usually at the top of the house, well-separated from the accommodation used by the adult members of the family, often insulated by a green baize door. It either adjoined, or was combined with the night nursery (the children's sleeping quarters). A comfortable place in which a child would feel very safe, the nursery was normally out of bounds to older brothers and sisters. It was the undisputed domain of the children's nurse or 'nanny', a devoted soul, usually without children of her own, who, before 1915 for around £16–35 a year and perhaps up to three times as much between the wars (the precise amount depending on her experience and the number of children to be cared for), would give up almost the whole of her life to looking after other people's children. Nanny, once installed, became the centre of the child's existence, a focus of stability, trust and love, the sole mentor and arbiter of blame as well as licensed dispenser of punishment. The system insured that she normally enjoyed a far closer relationship with the children than the mother. Her Edwardian uniform of high stiff collar and cuffs, leather-belted gown and spotless starched white apron (over which she wore a cape and bonnet outside the house) changed somewhat in the 1920s and 1930s. By then

169

the much rarer nannies were seen in soft felt hats or even berets and grey capes, with light-toned sheer lisle or artificial silk stockings instead of the drab Edwardian black wool or cotton.

Most nannies had a working class background and were self-taught, usually undergoing an apprenticeship as nursery maid, but as with other superior servants, middle class habits, accents, attitudes and manners rubbed off. By the 1900s professionalism was entering this very special little world and the more comfortable middle class families were able to employ a Norland Nurse, thus acquiring a fine new badge of class status. Norland Nurses sometimes came from the middle classes themselves and all had benefited from special tuition at the Norland Institute, established in Notting Hill Gate, London by Mrs Emily J. Ward in 1892. Encouraged in their training to think of themselves as rather superior persons, they were advised to take discreet steps to emphasise their special position in their employer's establishment, for example by taking along the silver-backed hairbrush they were expected to have and placing it where it would be seen. Their standing was emphasised by a distinctive uniform and high wages. Mrs Peel, who had one for her children in the 1900s and 1910s, comments that they were an expensive proposition at £40 a year, plus the cost of their keep. Others followed in Norland's footsteps: the Princess Christian College, starting in Manchester in 1901 and the London Wellgarth College in 1911, each with its distinctive style and uniform. Affluent middle class families employing independent nannies increasingly made sure theirs was fitted out in a smart uniform so that she appeared to be college-trained, even if not. This practice ran to such lengths that hospital nurses became concerned about the copying of their cloaks, belts and bonnets, securing a special act of parliament in 1925 to protect them from such snobbish acts of piracy.

Although this specialised training for children's nurses did much to underline it, nannies had never regarded themselves as ordinary servants. It was customary for them to be allocated the services of a maid, at least part-time, to relieve them of menial tasks such as carrying hot water from below for the children's bath before the nursery fire, attending to that fire, cleaning the nursery and washing and mending the children's clothes. Nannies took their meals with the children and again expected these to be brought up and cleared away.

The nursery, quite simply furnished, was often painted white. Essentials were a large fireplace with deep brass fender and tall brass-railed fireguard (which doubled as clothes warmer and airer), a good solid table and chairs for meals and games, an armchair in which nanny rested or read to her charges, a bookcase, and cupboards and drawers for the children's toys and clothes.

In nannied families, it was customary for mothers and even more so, fathers, to distance themselves from their offspring, seeing them perhaps only once or twice on a normal day. The system allowed this, and indeed it was usually difficult for any mother who might feel so moved to interfere with or participate in any activities the nanny regarded as her department. The usual routine was for the nurse to dress and tidy up the children after nursery tea, after which they would be taken downstairs for perhaps half an hour to play with their parents in the sitting room, perhaps going into the garden together for games in fine weather. Many fathers were not yet home and had only a brief contact just before the children's bedtime.

In some families, young children left the nursery to eat with their parents on Sundays, the nanny taking her day off. Children were also often allowed to participate in their mother's afternoon 'At Homes', when they would be paraded before the guests in their very best clothes for appreciative comment and to demonstrate how well they were absorbing the good manners and social graces that it was nanny's task to instil during these early years. If their parents were entertaining guests in the evening, it was a special treat for the children to stand on the stairs, peeping at the arrivals passing through the hall, or listening briefly to the distant tones of the piano and the singing.

Apart from these occasions, and family holidays, intervention of the younger children in their parents' lives was minimal. Not surprisingly this process of separation, which was continued, at any rate for the boys, when the time came to go away to boarding school, made parents, and fathers in particular, aloof and stilted in their relationship with their young, who were apt to see them as formidable, even intimidating, half-strangers. It followed that a child looked to nanny, rather than its mother, for emotional support and friendship. There were, as might be expected, some cruel nannies, dispensing an excess of physical punishment and firmness, but this kind of behaviour was usually discovered before too much damage had been done.

Except on her day off, a nanny rarely left the house unaccompanied by her charges. Going out with her usually involved a visit to the local park, where the local nannies would gather, with their perambulators and push chairs, to discuss their charges. For the boys, as soon as they could sit up, a favourite objective was a convenient railway bridge or station where they could watch the passage of trains. Just after World War 1, a journalist commented on this aspect of the education of the middle class male infant:

The 'iron horse', despite modern competitors, such as the motor and aeroplane, appears to have as much fascination for the very young fry of 1920, as it did for those of 1840s. On fine afternoons there can be seen at the far end of no. 1 platform at Paddington, amongst the milk churns, nursemaids in charge of perambulators, in which are ensconced small boys who evince the liveliest interest in the passing of 'Saints', 'Stars', 'Kings' and other specimens of the Great Western Railway's locomotive stud.[1]

Thus were lifelong interests implanted. In the big cities, nannies would also introduce their charges to the delights of zoos and cinemas or give them a breezy and exciting ride in the front seat on the open top of a bus or tram, though these were treats rather than regular daily pleasures.

Children's parties were defined in 1926 by Lady Troubridge as 'a pleasant way of inculcating a feeling of hospitality in the child and improving his manners. They teach him to consider others rather than himself and when the child is no longer young, he may learn a valuable lesson when he perceives that without order and method not even a party can be a success'. Since order and method were the very bread and butter of nannies it was natural for them to organise such parties, the mother only entering the scene once all the hard work had been done. A party was an occasion for dressing the girls in their finest clothes in a highly-competitive way, each mother trying hard to make her child the most attractive and eye-catching in the room. Manners too were again on display, with the little boys carefully attending to the needs of their female peers. For children aged below ten, the usual duration of a party was 3.30 to 6 or 6.30pm. The meal, served at a decorated table, would consist of milk and weak tea, bread and butter, ices, cakes, sponge and jellies and blancmanges, concluding with the pulling of crackers. Then came an entertainment and games.

Over the age of ten, children generally partied between 4 or 5pm and 7 or 8pm (later for those over fourteen). Here the refreshments and games were rather more sophisticated, the former usually taken as a sit-down supper or substantial buffet. For those between twelve and eighteen, dancing at parties was popular in houses with large sitting rooms, furniture being moved out and carpets rolled up to allow the guests to enjoy the veleta, waltzes and other classic dances to gramophone, piano or other instruments. The first stirrings of interest in the opposite sex were often experienced on such occasions, either during dances, or when playing such games as 'Murder', 'Winkie', 'Sardines' or 'Postman's Knock'. However the participants were always under the alert eyes of mothers, aunts and other adults, whose vigilant presence was in high profile at all stages of the proceedings. Those disposed to enjoy themselves merely by

172

sitting in a quiet corner holding hands, looking into each other's eyes and perhaps even kissing or petting, would usually find themselves being disturbed and gently encouraged to join in the organised entertainment.

In the better-off middle class families, a boy reaching the age of eight or so would be sent off to boarding school, his only contact with home a weekly letter, parental visits on sports days and holidays once a quarter. At the same age, a girl would probably start attending a local private day school, but some would be boarded, when, as was often the case, there was no suitable private school nearby. If there were then no younger children left in the nursery, this was time for nanny to leave for another post, though many kept in regular contact with each of their former charges. Once out of the nursery stage, older children were encouraged to mix more with the adults in the house and by their early teens, when at home, they would be expected to contribute to adult conversation and demonstrate their good manners by making guests feel comfortable. Staying at home as they often did when boys went away to school, daughters developed close relationships with their mothers, and as they became older, would be encouraged to help in suitable home tasks and with the entertainment of guests.

By the mid 1900s there were progressive mothers in all sections of the middle classes, who, seeing the dangers of too much nannying, were beginning to encourage the younger children to roam the house and garden at all times. Such mothers would actively participate in their children's daily outings and excursions, although this might require some tact and diplomacy if there were a nanny on the books.

Of course, even in the advantageous years before 1915 there were many middle class families unable to afford the nanny regime, especially since this almost invariably brought with it the expense of a further maid for the additional nursery work. In such households, children tended to have a less formal relationship with both parents but equally parental attitudes and paternal disciplines and punishments could often be harsh and hard to endure without a comforting presence in the nursery.

Although nannies were beyond the financial resources of most middle class households after World War 1, as we have seen, some sort of outside help with child-minding remained a priority throughout the period for middle class women, at least so far as the baby and infant years were concerned. These outside helpers, and of course the spinster aunts so often found in between-wars middle class families, did

173

provide another shoulder or lap to cry on when times were hard for the younger child.

# Education: the Key to it All

Education and the English class system were, and to a large extent still are, independent and inseparable. Writing in 1929, the Conservative Prime Minister, Stanley Baldwin observed that the classification of English schools was on the lines 'of social rather than educational distinction: a youth's school badge has been his social label'. Not surprisingly, despite an implication in this that change must come, neither Baldwin nor any other Conservative politician of the period ever took any steps to alter this situation. It is hardly possible to lay too much emphasis on the part played by schools and education in supporting and enlarging the middle classes, sustaining their ethos. Most middle class parents awarded very high priority to private, fully-segregated education for their children and were prepared to make almost any financial sacrifice to achieve it, although many had to compromise. It was not simply a matter of protecting and nurturing the middle class way of speaking and manners, or of avoiding nits, fleas, bedbugs and other unfortunate consequences of contact with the rough proletariat, real and imagined, though these were in mind. It was above all else a desire to confirm the child in the parent's culture, ensuring that it was instilled and handed on. Insofar as this was prompted by a sense of insecurity, the motivation was of course at its strongest amongst the newly-arrived. Middle class parents were also anxious for their boys to have 'character' and 'manliness', believing that such assets could be induced if they had not come with the genes, and this aspect assumed a major role in middle class private education, much more so than in the council schools. These qualities, sometimes collectively known as 'moral fibre', were seen as an essential element, never more so than in a nation feeling itself and its influence threatened by war in the years up to 1914 and to a lesser extent, for the same reason, in the 1930s.

For those able to afford private education there was an incidental benefit. Such schools, unlike the secondary schools maintained by public funds, placed no bar on children of limited intelligence or retarded intellectual development. Ability to pay was virtually the only criterion for entry, and once in the school, pupils were able to linger until seventeen or eighteen, receiving the benefits of tuition under a regime in which the ratio of teachers to pupils was substantially more favourable than at the best of the local authority schools.

In addition to all this, the subject of education deserves special attention here because the way in which the independent grammar and local authority secondary schools developed and operated in the first half of the century gave them a positive role in shaping the class structure. The existence of separate, well-patronised independent schools alongside an expanding but sometimes inferior publicly-financed statutory system served to reinforce and perpetuate class inequalities as one generation succeeded another. But equally significant was the fact that the publicly-financed secondary schools of England and Wales, predominantly middle class in tone and outlook, also worked to expand and sustain the lower middle class. Their product was designed to fill middle class jobs, particularly office jobs. Their method of selecting potential entrants at age eleven and their general regime from eleven to sixteen and beyond, at a stage in the child's development when the advantages of their home background and supportive parents were critical, tended to favour the progeny of the lower middle class rather than those of the working class and the very poor. And it was of course the case that economic pressures usually forced the poorer parents to direct all but their most gifted male children into paid employment at the earliest possible age. Thus it was that right through to the 1940s, access to anything other than the most rudimentary education facilities was virtually confined to the middle and upper classes.

Rising real incomes for the between-wars middle classes stimulated a significant expansion in the private education sector, especially up to the early thirties. Three new boys' public schools were opened: Stowe and Canford in 1923 and Bryanston in 1928. In 1914 there were 22,000 independent schools classified as efficient by government inspectors, in 1930, 82,000. At the same time many of the existing schools, enjoying unprecedented financial prosperity, were able to expand their accommodation and facilities.

Such was the breadth of choice available to middle class parents that each could provide according to his means[2]. Many made considerable sacrifices to attain their objective. Ideally, the child would be placed in a local private day school or kindergarten at five or six years of age (in the 1900s and 1910s, in the more affluent middle class families, some children still continued to receive their first lessons at home from a governess, though this was dying out as other job opportunities for such women developed). These private primary schools, taking in both boys and girls from age five up to eight or nine charged from five to twenty pounds a year for tuition before World War 1, and upwards of twelve later.

Having completed this initiation, boys following the accepted preferred path would enrol as boarders at a private preparatory school, paying around ninety pounds a year in the 1910s, £110 or more between the wars. This institution, having developed the right contacts or patronage, would have no difficulty in securing places for its pupils at one of the privately-financed 'public' schools. The move would be made at age thirteen, the child again boarding in most cases. Beforehand a so-called 'Common Entrance' examination was taken, more to determine the child's level of academic attainment for placement in the new school rather than as a hurdle before acceptance. The preparatory school child had a virtual passport to the public school.

The new arrival would often find himself mixing with the sons of the upper class, especially if his parents were wealthy enough to afford one of the leading schools. The fact that a father or brother had been a pupil was of great assistance in placement. At eighteen, some went up from public school to college or university whilst others passed directly into suitable mainstream middle class occupations at home and overseas, finding no great difficulty in securing good positions by virtue of old school tie alone. Public schools played a much less important role in the education of middle class girls, since there were far fewer for them, either single-sex or co-educational. Moreover, when there were boys as well as girls in the family, the former would have prior claim on such money as was available for this purpose.

The day school/preparatory/public school/university route, paying all the way, was rigidly exclusive, since its cost and its selection processes virtually eliminated any entrants from the lower middle or working class. Successfully achieved, an education of this kind more or less guaranteed access to any of the major professions and the top jobs in the civil service and elsewhere. A good income was certainly essential for any parent considering it; boarding fees at the better public schools in the 1930s ranged from £145 to £245 a year[3] exclusive of the cost of special tuition, uniforms, sports and other equipment. Whilst it is true that some of the public schools did admit day pupils at lower fees, such attendance was usually difficult and inconvenient to arrange.

Another possibility, open to those with sufficient means, was to pay for a boarding or day place in a private school which provided an alternative to the publicly-financed elementary and secondary schools by offering a similar education from ages four to six right through to School Certificate standard at sixteen or beyond, after which the pupil might go on to university or some other form of higher education. This was a favoured course for girls, who, as already mentioned, had less opportunity of gaining a public school place. Before World War 1, the fees of these second-tier private schools ranged from around £7.7s a year upwards with an additional fifty pounds or more for board. Some of them also admitted boys, although usually only up to the preparatory school age, since co-education after puberty was still widely regarded as a dangerous American idea.

With pupils with names like Felicity, Minette, Millicent and Roma, one such 'all ages' private school between the wars aimed 'to help the children to develop their characters on the highest lines and to teach them the value of self-control and consideration for others'. To this end, facilities for tennis, rounders, eurhythmics, Brownies, Girl Guides, drama, drawing, netball and hockey appeared to receive as much, if not more emphasis as the academic side, though some of the sixteen-year old girls did apparently conclude their stay by obtaining an Oxford Board School Certificate. The total of day pupils and boarders at this school ranged from fifty to seventy and the average number in each form was only eight. Boarders under ten years old paid £42 a term, those over that age £47.5s. Day pupils were charged £14.14s a term. In addition £2.2s a term was required if the school's bed linen was used, £3.3s a term for piano or violin lessons, £2.2s for dancing or ballet and £4.4s for riding instruction (presumably it was thought genteel to quote most of these items in guineas). The daily timetable of this school, described as 'flexible', is reproduced in detail at Appendix C.

Another alternative for girls from age four through to nineteen were the privately-funded independent day schools. Here the regime was more rigorously academic in tone, culminating in the School Certificate and Higher Schools examinations or university scholarships and entrance. Among the best-known of these were the twenty five establishments operated by the Girls' Public Day School Trust, founded in 1872 to offer an education 'such as is provided for boys by the great public schools'. Mainly for fee-payers (typical day fees were £4.5s to £10.10s a term in the 1930s, according to age), the GPDS schools did however offer some free places to bright children from low-income families. Boys were also accepted but only from four to eight or nine, when they went on to a preparatory school.

However for the majority with average middle class incomes, the usual course if funds were tight was to send the child to a small local private day school from which a fee-paying place at an independent grammar school[4] or even at a local authority secondary school would be sought, though the latter type of school tended to be less socially acceptable, especially if its catchment area was not predominantly middle class[5].

Many lower middle class children started their education in church infant schools, going on to the local authority elementary (primary) schools, where they could be identified by their neater and more formal clothes. In the playground they mixed freely, blissfully innocent of social constraints in the absence of parental supervision. For them, class segregation of a sort would come with the arrival of secondary education at around age eleven.

## The Examination Factories

Throughout the period, day school secondary education was very largely the prerogative of the middle and lower middle classes. At the independent grammar schools, most of the children came from fairly comfortable middle class families able to afford fees, the only barrier being a fairly mild entrance test. Such schools usually offered a limited number of free scholarships to those children of poorer parents who were bright enough to pass a more challenging entrance examination, probing their grasp of English, arithmetic and general knowledge; an oral interview or test often followed.

The local authority secondary schools, established by legislation of 1902 and 1903, were maintained by the county councils and, in the larger urban areas, by the county borough councils (in the capital, the London County Council was the well-respected authority). They soon gained a good reputation. Writing in 1909, Masterman considered these new schools provided 'the best education which England is giving today'[6], though that was not perhaps claiming overmuch. In contrast to many in the small private schools, all the teaching staff except those solely concerned with art, crafts, commercial studies and physical education would have university degrees, and this also applied in the independent grammar schools. Tuition fees at local authority secondary schools were relatively low (£2.6s to ten pounds a year in the 1900s and 1910s and £15 to £30 a year between the wars are typical London examples). From 1907, a limited number of free scholarships were available for places in all these new schools (for all places in County Durham). These were open to children of low income families able to pass a fairly stiff written test in English, arithmetic and general knowledge followed by an oral interview at which the class prejudices of teachers might well come into play. Parental encouragement and a suitable home atmosphere generally were important in that prospects of success in the examination might well depend on careful practice and preparation. These factors tended to favour the child from the lower middle class household. This was the route followed at age eleven by the more able children of the lower echelons of the middle classes and, to a lesser extent, those of the 'respectable working class'. It was an important move which tended to confirm and reinforce future class status.

Opportunities for this form of education increased slowly: the number of council secondary schools in England & Wales grew from 1,205 in 1920 to 1,307 in 1931; by 1938 the population of such schools was 470,000. In England and Wales in 1914 only around one child in forty went forward from free elementary to free secondary education at age eleven, but this figure rose to one in twenty by 1920 and by the end of the 1930s to one in thirteen[7].

A crucial question was whether the parents of such children could afford to maintain the child at school beyond the normal elementary school leaving age of twelve (raised to fourteen after 1918). Some parents at the bottom of the middle classes and most in the working class simply could not face the financial sacrifice involved in continuing to support the child, paying for his or her special needs at the school whilst foregoing the earning capacity until age sixteen or more. Thus secondary and higher education opportunities were frequently relinquished or at any rate curtailed for children of such families, no matter how intelligent they might be, whilst boys would be given priority over girls, whatever their respective levels of intelligence and intellectual potential. Many other lower middle class parents, exhausted by the effort of keeping the child at school to complete a secondary education up to age sixteen or seventeen were unable to face the financial sacrifices involved in allowing continuance into higher education.

What were these council secondary (and independent grammar) schools about? In the 1930s a typical prospectus claimed the school provided 'a sound liberal Secondary Education which shall be an excellent preparation for professional, scientific, technical, mercantile and administrative careers'[8]. Fine words, but in practice the major aim of such schools was to get as many pupils as possible through the Oxford or Cambridge General Schools Examination (School Certificate) at age sixteen, preferably with a result which secured exemption from matriculation (the university entrance examination)[9]. 'Matriculation standard' was achieved if the pupil attained marks of at least fifty per cent in mathematics, English language and literature, Latin or science, a modern foreign language and two other subjects, all for papers *taken at the same time* – failure in any one meant retaking the whole examination. The education given in all the publicly-financed secondary schools was with few exceptions primarily academic, in essence a five-year preparation for this examination, the passing of which was treated as an end in itself. Given the marginal differences between the various types of School Certificate examination used in different areas, the curriculum throughout England and Wales varied little between one secondary school and another.

If after passing the General Schools Examination, the pupil's parents could afford another year or two's education, he or she might enter a sixth form where, in separate small units, copying public school practice, individual attention was provided (at any rate in theory) whilst preparing for civil service Clerical and Executive grade examinations, Higher School Examination, the Intermediate Arts, Science and Commerce Examinations of universities, or whilst awaiting entry to teacher training colleges or training as a hospital nurse, the last two options much favoured for girls. In practice staffing constraints often meant that this final period of formal education took the form of fairly ineffective private study with inadequate supervision, during which youthful high spirits were often more in evidence than hard work. Again success much depended on parental support and encouragement and opportunities for study at home, assets most likely to be forthcoming in the middle class household. Although all council and independent secondary schools were able to offer a tiny number of scholarships and grants covering all or part of the cost of higher education, and some could offer grants to cover staying on up to two years in the sixth form, many lower middle class parents could not face the financial consequences involved in such a commitment, even with such help. Thus, along with inadequate teaching resources and facilities for sixth forms, it is not surprising that only five to seven per cent of English council secondary school leavers in the 1920s and 1930s managed to reach a university. (The independent grammar schools, with their higher proportion of fee-paying students from more comfortably-off middle class families, gave better service at this final stage, achieving a rather more impressive proportion of higher education student output). Thus whilst the more intelligent children of lower middle class background in the fifty years or so up to the late 1940s had reasonable opportunities for an academic type secondary education to university entry standard, all but a tiny minority were denied higher education beyond age sixteen or seventeen.

Despite this there were important social effects. The ability of an independent grammar school or a good council secondary school during the five to six year course to induce and reinforce middle class manners, attitudes and behaviour in children from lower middle class or 'respectable working class' backgrounds was considerable. Girls, in particular, responded readily, gradually modifying their speech

180

inflexions, appearance and manners until by the time they were ready to leave school, interviewers would often find it difficult to guess their family and home background[10]. More subtle indications of class such as the correct way to hold a knife and fork and other acceptable patterns of social behaviour, if not inculcated at home, were quickly acquired by such school leavers in their early years of adulthood as they mixed with those who would soon accept them as social equals.

The vast majority of pupils leaving local authority secondary schools up to the 1940s flowed into clerical and other white collar jobs which rarely made best use of their potential, especially in the early years. Despite this, most tended to achieve moderately-rewarding and sometimes very successful careers, becoming increasingly secure in their middle class status. But frequently they were obliged to endure years of dull and often humiliating work before opportunities equal to their abilities finally appeared.

## The Rod, Fagging, and Playing The Game

As we have seen, the privately-financed public schools, especially the leading ones, were the virtually exclusive preserve of the children of the upper classes and the more affluent middles. With rare exceptions such as Bedales and Dartington Hall, they were also single-sex establishments.

Traditionally the formal education at public schools was academic, placing emphasis on the classics, rather than English, modern languages, and science, but a predominant and widespread characteristic of these schools was the excessive, even obsessive, attention given to fostering team spirit and character-building through athletics, rowing and above all, organised ball games, which were raised to an absurd level of importance, unmatched in the education of children outside Britain and its Empire. It has been suggested that this almost religious devotion to team sports developed out of the need to find a release from the sheer drudgery and dullness of a teaching regime dominated by Latin and Greek. Whatever the explanation, there can be no doubt that academic prowess took second place as the successful manipulators of bats, balls and oars were raised to the level of minor deities, held in awe by their juniors. Those good at games received privileges denied to all others, including distinctive features in the uniform. It was not unusual for the achievers in sport and athletics to be virtually the only pupils rewarded with any personal interest or goodwill from the teaching staff. Boys not endowed with the necessary skills or without interest in sport were ill-regarded by peers and masters alike, derided as 'cissies' or 'swots'.

181

At Lancing College, the contempt was manifest in the label 'wrecks' for such misfits, who were usually thoroughly miserable in the public school environment. One such was Sir John Betjeman, the late Poet Laureate, who in his *Summoned By Bells* (1960), recalls 'the wonderful release from games' at Marlborough.

The importance given to team ball games, principally rugby and cricket, was rationalised by regarding them as a major factor in shaping the desired and instantly recognisable product, teaching as nothing else could the qualities of leadership, motivation, 'manliness', self-control and working with others towards a common goal. Such character formation was the principal concern of these schools. In 1909 Masterman talked of the public schools professing 'to teach "character" rather than to stimulate intelligence'[11]. Using raw material increasingly provided by moderately-affluent middle rather than upper class families, the essential objective was to turn out recognisable products, capable of shaping readily into leaders of men, builders and defenders of Empire. Public schoolboys tended to become army and navy officers, civil administrators, doctors and lawyers, rather than captains of industry and commerce, scientists, engineers, and technicians. For such careers, sport and athletics, combined with rather less glamorous features to be mentioned in a moment, were thought to be thoroughly effective preparation. Set in their ways, these schools continued doggedly along the same path through to the middle of the century, ignoring the fact that Britain's needs and circumstances were changing faster after World War 1.

Public school conditioning sometimes led those who had experienced it to attempt to impose it on the less fortunate. An example of this was Robert Baden-Powell, who on becoming an army officer after an education at Charterhouse found that his rank-and-file soldiery ('lads from the Board Schools'), whilst proficient enough at arithmetic, reading and writing, were 'without any manliness, self-reliance or resourcefulness' (*Indian Memories*, (1915)). This discovery led him to institute scout training in the British Army and later to establish the Boy Scout and Girl Guide movements, a selfless attempt to instil 'character' in those sections of the nation's youth lacking the benefit of a good middle class private education. We shall return to this.

Behind the manly games and athletics were less attractive aspects of 'character-building'. At these schools, living conditions and diet for boarders were often spartan. Most pupils accepted this as normal having endured a similar regime in their preparatory boarding school. This feature also possessed advantages for the school management in that it kept costs down.

Discipline was strict. In the boys' schools, corporal punishment was widely practised, both by teachers and senior pupils, those so-inclined savouring the opportunities to flirt with sadism. There is ample evidence of this dark side, for example in Betjeman's account of Marlborough in Chapter VII of his *Summoned By Bells* and in Roald Dahl's autobiographical *Boy: Tales of Childhood* (1984). Dahl vividly describes severe canings suffered at his preparatory and public schools in the 1920s and early 1930s, noting how puzzled his Norwegian mother was by this strange British practice. He tells of boys being cruelly caned in their pyjamas by masters and prefects and how the Headmaster of Repton (a future Archbishop of Canterbury) administered severe beatings on bared buttocks, pausing between strokes to light and then puff at his pipe whilst lecturing the young victim on his misdeeds. This carefully-structured ceremony, by no means untypical, was completed with a suitable gesture of Christian charity – the offer of basin of cold water and a towel for the boy to use on his afflicted flesh.

Partly as an economy and partly as a precaution against homosexual temptations, privacy for the public school child was usually at a premium, Eton almost alone in giving each boy his own room. Snobbishness was virtually unknown, since it was accepted that all came from the same background; indeed it was thought desirable to provide practical experience of taking and obeying all sorts of orders. To this end, at most public schools, junior boys were obliged to serve as 'fags', in which capacity they acted as the minions, some would say slaves, of the senior pupils, who were given a surprisingly important role in the day-to-day running of the school and the maintenance of good discipline. Younger boys were expected to receive uncomplainingly the bullying, humiliation and ill-treatment that inevitably accompanied this arrangement and indeed did so readily, secure in the knowledge that in a few years their turn would come. Fagging was frequently developed to a high degree of refinement: Dahl's book mentions that at Repton, in cold weather, the duties of fags extended to sitting on the wooden lavatory seats in the early morning to warm them up for prefects' use.

Lacking the physical punishments and the worst rigours of the fagging system, the small number of girls' public schools were nevertheless capable of imposing subtle mental and emotional cruelties on their youthful inmates. Most of these schools were imbued with a fierce spirit of competitiveness in academic and sporting achievements, an attitude urged on the girls by spinster teachers who were often proto-feminists, anxious to prove that 'equality' of the sexes might be a reality. Alongside this, the same staff took elaborate measures to protect their charges from all contamination by the male, not least those of the same age and social class.

It is interesting that many features of boys' public school practice and organisation, such as house competitions, house colours, trophies, prefects, school and house captains, school songs, sixth forms, speech days, compulsory cricket and rugby, unusual ball games (such as 'fives'), and sports days were slavishly copied by the independent grammar schools and the county secondary schools, whose staff and governors (together with many parents) were often uncritical admirers of the public school ethos, even if many of them had no personal experience of such establishments. The pupils were generally less enthusiastic, enjoying reading about public school life in annuals, books and magazines like *The Magnet* but not really envying those subjected to its rigours and disciplines.

## Other Private Schools

The great public schools represented the elite tier of private education. They obtained the best teaching staff by paying more than the going rate in publicly-financed schools, although able women teachers often preferred the less restrictive regime of the latter. Elsewhere, the standards of private schools varied widely. Many were staffed by teachers with clouded pasts and dubious or meaningless qualifications; background and family were the usual keys to appointment rather than academic attainment and teaching skills.

Anyone able to accumulate or borrow the necessary capital could start a private school and many were operated by married couples in unsuitable premises such as converted private houses with small rooms and inadequate outdoor play space. These schools, day and boarding, proliferated and prospered simply because so many middle class parents were prepared to pay to have their children segregated from the perceived tainting of the social mix in the council schools. By ensuring that their children associated exclusively with their own kind, they hoped they would at least remain clean and well-mannered and protected from undesirable speech inflexions and behaviour. With luck, they might also acquire some middle class 'polish' where this was lacking. Such schools were of course also an essential route to the better private establishments, and in some cases, the boarding type were a useful convenience when parents spent much time abroad, or were separated. But the majority of children boarded-out in private schools were sent away to them simply because it was a tribal custom of the British upper and middle classes, a feature which never ceased to astonish foreigners, who considered the system if not barbarous, neither necessary nor beneficial.

Other advantages were seen in the private school alternative, even if a good public school was beyond the parents' reach as the ultimate objective. Classes were very small (rarely more than eight to ten, compared with forty to fifty at council elementary schools and twenty to thirty at council secondaries) and children, especially the duller ones, were likely to receive much more personal attention, even if the teaching standards were suspect. Finally parents would be able to find out much more about their children's education and progress than they would at the local authority school, where, until the second half of the twentieth century, parental presence and participation were often actively discouraged, especially at the infant and elementary levels.

## The Middle Class at University

There was some expansion in British higher education in the forty years before World War 2 but nothing to match that which came in the 1960s. In England & Wales one new university was established between the wars (Reading) and university colleges were opened at Swansea, Leicester and Hull, but these and the other so-called provincial universities lacked the social prestige, community spirit and college rivalries and loyalties of Oxford & Cambridge.

The 25,000 post-school leaver students of 1900–01 in England and Wales had grown to 69,000 by 1939. These figures included an increase in the number of university students from 20,000 in 1900–01 to 29,275 in 1925–6 and 48,000 in 1938–9. At the very end of our period (1952–3) there were over 81,000. Even the highest of these totals represented only a tiny proportion of the population of student age in all social classes; almost all students were drawn from the upper class and the more affluent middles. In 1938 only two per cent of nineteen year olds were undergoing any full time education, an improvement of a mere one per cent over 1900–01. Another inequality lay in the uneven regional distribution of university places available to the school leaver; the number per 1,000 of population at the end of the 1920s was only 7.8 in England, compared with twelve in Wales and 21.1 in Scotland. This situation barely improved in the next two decades.

For those coming up from privately-financed schools, the process of higher education was reasonably painless and usually very enjoyable, since their parents could normally provide adequate living allowances in addition to the fees. Entry to Oxford and Cambridge was not difficult for those who could afford to pay; if without the necessary School Certificate passes, they had only to pass the 'Responsions' (Oxford) or 'Previous Examination' (Cambridge), generally assessed as a less formidable barrier than the matriculation hurdle set before the local authority secondary school leaver. Once admitted, many privately-educated students were content to idle away their new-found freedom pleasurably, aiming only at an 'ordinary' degree, an attainment which required neither undue effort or great ability. Writing of the period just before World War 1 (and change thereafter was only very gradual), Masterman, in his usual incisive style, described the English universities as 'encouraging

VARSITY TYPES, No. II.—THE SCHOLAR.

University student, 1904

large expenditure on comfort, limitless bodily exercise and an exiguous standard of intellectual effort'[12].

Those few lower middle class students who did manage to get to university frequently had a difficult time. Although often at least equal in ability and intelligence to many of their privately-educated contemporaries, they lacked the self-assured, gentlemanly bearing and broad cultural background of the average public school product and in particular had not learned to be good losers. Few of them shared the public school man's passion for playing team games and his aptitude for skylarking, practical jokes and excessive drinking. Often enough emerging with a good degree since they were generally more studious as well as sensitive to the tenuous and sometimes sacrificial nature of their financial backing, they found the lack of a public school background and polish could operate against them, inhibiting access to positions commensurate with their academic qualifications and ability.

## Signs of Change

As the mid century point approached, the pattern of middle class education described above was beginning to change. Reform of secondary education had been under consideration between the wars but financial restrictions and then the outbreak of war had prevented any implementation. An important Education Act, passed in 1944, was largely directed at providing some form of secondary education for all children and from 1 April 1947 the school leaving age was raised to a minimum of fifteen, a move proposed (by a 1936 Act) to start in 1939 but postponed by the outbreak of war. When the necessary buildings and teachers had been provided, most of the older children found themselves in 'secondary modern' schools which were little more than stretched versions of the old council elementary schools. A process of selection by testing at around age eleven filtered the more able children of both middle and working classes into the former grammar and county secondary schools, to which all fee entry was abolished.

The social repercussions were not insignificant. Since they were likely to have a home background more conducive to coaching and preparation for the test and parents who would encourage and motivate them, middle class children continued to have a slightly better chance of entry. However, as the now more prosperous working classes were better able to face the prospect of their children remaining in full time education to age sixteen or later, significant numbers of their brighter offspring flowed into these schools. The less bright middle class children, unable to pass entry examination to the grammar schools, whose parents could not face the social stigma and other disadvantages of attendance at the predominantly working class 'secondary modern' schools, pushed up the demand for private school places.

Another factor was contributing to the vitality of private education. Foreseeing postwar pressures for change and concerned about their deteriorating financial position, the public schools had agreed to a fundamental review during the war years, and the Fleming Report of 1944 had recommended they reserve a quarter of their admissions to children coming up through local authority-funded scholarships. This move, eagerly adopted, held a threefold attraction: it not only appeared as a substantial gesture towards egalitarianism; it provided a guaranteed source of regular income and brought in a valuable injection of high flyers, thus raising the general academic standard of these schools.

It may have had a further advantage in taking some of the steam out of the political pressure to rid Britain of this 'elite' tier of education which contributed so much to the perpetuation of class differences. Certainly there seems to have been insufficient political will, even in the reforming Labour Government of 1945, to do anything about dismantling the public schools. Perhaps it was that there were even more serious problems to tackle but a significant proportion of the more prominent influential Labour politicians had attended these schools and maybe they lacked the heart to attack them. Thus, somewhat unexpectedly, at the end of the 1940s, with a strong spirit of idealistic socialism alive in Britain, cutting across the classes, the public schools found themselves facing the future with considerable confidence.

As for the universities, in the five years after the end of World War 2 there was a modest expansion; but only one (Keele) was added to the seventeen existing in 1945. Even as late as 1962, the proportion of nineteen year olds undergoing higher education was still only seven per cent although it was soon to grow dramatically. A generous injection of public money produced a total of twenty six new universities by the end of the 1960s, populated by 211,000 students, almost five times the 1939 total. University education at least had become classless, even if, to quote Kingsley Amis, more meant worse. . .

# Children's Pleasures

A visit to the house of any reasonably well-provided middle class family around the turn of the century would reveal that the children's toys were still relatively unsophisticated: wooden railway engines, tops and hoops;

lead soldiers and farm animals; wooden forts; doll's houses; a rocking horse; gollywogs,[13] (teddy bears were as yet unborn); and dolls with adult faces and hand-made clothes. But the scene was already changing as an expanding toy industry geared itself to soak up the growing amounts of disposable income that were becoming available to spend on the middle class child.

Humphrey Household[14] has noted that scale model railways were beginning to appear around 1900 and a few years later accurate models of the locomotives and carriages in use by the leading British railway companies were 'within the reach of middle class pockets'. Pockets that is, that could afford in 1909 £1.10s.6d for an 'O' gauge clockwork Great Northern Atlantic, three or four coaches at 5s6d each and half a dozen goods wagons at 1s10d, together with several more pounds for track, stations and so on. By 1913 A. W. Gamage Ltd of Holborn[15], whose store represented a very close approximation to heaven on earth for children, in that a large proportion of it was given up to toys, games and models of every kind, were selling the same locomotive at £1.2s.6d. They could also offer even more impressive scale model clockwork-powered gauge 'O' engines at up to £2.15s. Like much of the new toy output of the period, many of these models were made in Germany. If real steam propulsion were desired on the same track gauge, the prices were £1.12s.6d to £4.4s, the latter representing about eleven ten-hour days' pay for a contemporary railway engine driver. The same catalogue featured electrically-driven scale models and a variety of track, stations and other accessories.

For those seeking other types of toy at Christmas 1913, Gamages offered a wide range of sophisticated items including electric cranes complete with 4-Volt accumulator (£1.5s.6d), stationary steam engines (up to £4.4s), constructional outfits and building bricks (up to £1.1s), chemistry sets (from seven shillings to several pounds) and cinematograph projectors (from £2.10s to £17). Girls had a wide choice of dolls at prices from sixpence to £3.3s (the latter 'handsomely dressed in the latest London and Parisian styles'), as well as trunks of dolls' clothes, dolls' cots, prams and baby baskets, dolls' houses, and Wendy Houses. Costumes for dressing up, at parties and at home, were available for both boys and girls; Red Indians, Cowboys, pierrots, pierrettes and fairy queens were among the most popular.

Meccano, a clever metal parts construction system invented and perfected in 1901–8 by a Liverpudlian clerk, Frank Hornby, encouraged children to develop and stretch their mechanical and engineering skills by completing elaborate models of bridges, cranes, vehicles, cableways and many other structures and devices. Early publicity played cleverly on the motivation of middle class parents: 'Every boy should have the opportunity to learn (while playing) how to do things that will help him to be successful when he becomes a man'. In October 1916, from a base at Binns Road, Liverpool, Meccano Ltd. began to publish a fine monthly magazine which not only showed what could be made with the firm's products but also reported on the latest developments in railway, marine, aviation and general engineering.

The 1920s brought further refinements in toys, including Lott's bricks, whose smooth, round-edge real stone was strangely satisfying to handle. There were exciting new products from Frank Hornby's Liverpool factory, including perfected Meccano engineering construction sets with coloured parts instead of dreary nickel plate (1926), and the famous Hornby gauge 'O' clockwork and electric train sets and accessories (1920). In 1938, some years later than the Germans, Hornby produced smaller ('00' gauge) model trains, even more refined Meccano outfits, with a further change of colour, and also a whole range of die-cast model figures, railway platform and lineside features and vehicles known as Dinky Toys. It seems likely that the progressive narrowing of model railway track from the Edwardian gauge 1 (44.45 mm) through 0 gauge to the 00 gauge (16mm) of the 1920s and 1930s was in part a reflection of the reduction in size of the average middle class house over the period.

War toys and model soldiers were less popular after 1918. Toy aircraft, motor vehicles and ships made from tinplate and realistically painted, did not sell well, probably because they were less satisfying to play with. The author recalls a large tinplate reproduction of a airliner, coveted and finally bought in the early 1930s for five shillings, then an enormous sum in his eyes. It proved an immense disappointment, soon relegated to the innermost recesses to the toy cupboard since its awkward bulk not only quickly suffered some irrepairable damage, but could not produce the lasting satisfaction and fulfilment so readily obtainable from the complicated and infinitely varied manipulations and manoeuvres possible with Meccano and Hornby Train.

Few girls showed interest in military, constructional and railway toys, indeed the manufacturers would have been surprised had it been otherwise. For the vast majority, although their dolls and dolls' houses and associated equipment kept up with the latest fashions, little variety and innovation in their toys was offered, except in the field of board games, which they shared with boys.

Children's books, magazines and comics were produced for a largely middle class readership. Proletarian youngsters did enjoy what was available if they could get to it, but for them periodicals, let alone books, were usually seen as a luxury purchase which could well be omitted from a restricted household budget. They also had less leisure time since most were obliged to help at home or earn extra money by taking errand-boy or other part time jobs. Most council schools lacked libraries of their own until the late 1940s whilst the children's sections of public libraries were not fully developed until the 1930s or even later in many areas. Unaffected by these limitations, middle class children spent many hours reading.

There was a prolific flow of children's fiction, supplemented each Christmas by annuals such as *Chatterbox, Blackie's Children's Annual, Cassell's Annual* and *Father Tuck's Annual*, each crammed with short stories, features and illustrations. Reinforcing and reflecting the imperialistic, militaristic outlook of the period, much of the boys' fiction of 1900–1920 had a military or naval theme, or dealt with the adventures of plucky, patriotic Britishers at home and abroad. John Bull's sons and (less often) daughters were depicted as upholding justice and fairness, always in the right. Frequently they were shown overcoming the plotting and wiles of sinister foreigners (those not fortunate enough to be born British were always either sinister or comic)[16]. Boarding school life was another favourite topic, both for boys and girls. A sample of titles advertised in the Gamage 1913 catalogue gives a taste of the diet offered:- *Sultan Jim –Empire Builder; Through Veld & Forest; When East meets West; John Graham, Sub-Lieutenant RN – A Tale of the Atlantic Fleet on Foreign Service; The Stolen Cruiser; The Rival Submarines; With Axe and Rifle; For School and Country; Rosaly's New School; The Chesterton Girl Graduates; Derrick Orme's Schooldays; and The Leader of the Lower School.* For boys there was also a good deal of informative non-fiction, mainly about railways, aircraft, ships and engineering generally, whilst girls could share with their brothers books about dogs, horses and other animals.

Joanna Smith has identified another characteristic of children's literature of the Edwardian era, noticing that whilst taking for granted loving care and kindness to dogs, cats and horses, writers usually applauded the often cruel hunting of wild animals, describing it in detail[17]. She illustrates this by quoting a passage from Arthur Mee's very middle class *Children's Encyclopedia*, first published in 1908. Mee suggested to his young readers that the fashionable lady's love of fine furs had beneficial effects on world exploration, employment and city-building. He depicts a little girl admiring and stroking a lady's furs, saying 'And this beautiful soft fur coat . . . once had a great beast inside it; and now it has got an angel!'

191

The girls' school stories of Angela Brazil (who between 1900 and 1939 produced over fifty titles), the charming little books written and illustrated by Beatrix Potter, first published by Frederick Warne in 1902–13, and such works as Kenneth Grahame's 1908 *Wind in the Willows*, Arthur Ransome's 1931 *Swallows & Amazons* and its later companion volumes, J. M. Barrie's 1904 *Peter Pan* and the 1920s output of A. A. Milne on the adventures of Christopher Robin and his friends quickly found a place in middle class homes alongside such classics as Lewis Carroll's *Alice's Adventures in Wonderland* and *Alice Through the Looking Glass*, all of them faithfully reflecting the shared manners and attitudes of authors and readers. Below this level of quality were the fictional works of scores of lesser writers, all projecting similar attitudes and mores to willing purchasers for an enthusiastic readership – no parent or relative need have cause to worry about content unsuitable for consumption by a middle class child. Of course not all authors were popular, and fashions changed. An example of this were the eighty or so adventure stories for boys by G. A. Henty (1832–1902), an author who interweaved historical incident with his fiction, producing somewhat indigestible books much favoured by adults for their patriotic tone and instructional value. A doctor treating the author for mumps in 1929 scanned the bedroom bookshelves, expressing great surprise that no Henty was to be seen. Subsequently one was obtained experimentally but interest waned after only a few pages. Much more enjoyable and still fondly remembered after almost sixty years was a cousin's copy of the first English translation (1931) of Eric Kaestner's *Emil and The Detectives*. This had two special qualities: it not only offered a fascinating glimpse of contemporary life in another country (pre-Nazi Germany) but exploited a completely fresh theme for the juvenile reader.

Arthur Mee (1875–1943), mentioned earlier, was a prolific, somewhat pompous writer for children, apt to talk down to them, but his work was popular with middle class parents for its educational value and widely bought for their offspring. His *Children's Newspaper and Children's Pictorial* first appeared in March 1919, to tell 'The story of the world today for the men and women of tomorrow'. At 1½d and later twopence a week, the middle classes would order it from their newsagent to be delivered with other newspapers and periodicals, but a working class child, obliged to finance such an item himself from his few pence a week pocket money, would tend to decide there were more urgent priorities. From 1908 to 1933 Mee edited *The Children's Encyclopedia*, whose volumes were to be found in many middle class homes, parents considering them a useful supplement to the formal education of their offspring. Plunging into

1. 'Tunnel–Back' terrace housing for the Edwardian lower middle class. Outram Road, Wood Green, c1908. Thousands of such houses, built in depressing uniformity around the fringes of London in the 1990s, sold at around £350 leasehold, £450 freehold.

2. Between–wars speculative builder semi–detached 'chalets' for the lower middle classes: Bradstock Road, Stoneleigh Park, Surrey, soon after completion in 1933. These houses originally sold at £775–795.

Heath Drive, Walton on the Hill.

Published by Roberts Burgh Heath.

3. Decent separation for the more fortunate middle class: large detached houses at Heath Drive, Walton-on-the-Hill, Surrey, about 1908. Some have an attic storey above the first floor to accommodate servants' bedrooms.

4. Fourteen storeys of service flats at the seaside in ocean liner style: Marine Court, Hastings, Sussex, soon after completion in 1937. A typical example of flats construction in London and coastal resorts during the 1930s.

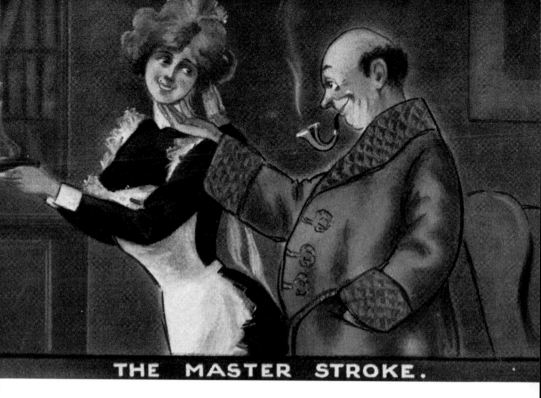

## THE MASTER STROKE.

5. Dalliance with the parlourmaid. An Edwardian comic postcard which delicately hints at a not uncommon feature of middle class home life.

6. A prosperous middle class family proudly pose with their capacious motor car at Birchington-on-Sea, Kent, in September 1930. Whilst the parents favour formal dress for a day's motoring, son and daughters exhibit typical leisure wear of the period.

7. Expensively–adorned upper middle class women window-shopping in London's Bond Street about 1904. Note that the only flesh shown is the face, and in one case even this is discreetly veiled.

8. New technology brings employment opportunities for middle class women: a central London telephone exchange in 1908.

9. Office wear and office furniture in May 1914: the Fidelity Department of the Guardian Assurance Co Ltd at 11, Lombard Street, City. Electric light has been installed but no telephone is visible.

10. A nanny and her charge at Bournemouth c1928.

11. Interior of Surrey preparatory school about 1935. The boy boarders of this small private establishment appear to enjoy every middle class amenity, including Lloyd Loom chairs, superhet radio and the game of 'bagatelle'; indeed this interior is not unlike the sitting room of their own homes.

12. Gym slips, pigtails, straw bretons and black stockings. A private boarding school (Stonar House, Sandwich, Kent) about 1928. For cycling the girls on the left wear a variation of the uniform – a close-fitting cap.

The Mid-day Meal     Boy Scouts Series

13. Boy Scouts at 'the Mid-day Meal' during camp c1912. Note the military style uniforms of the Scoutmaster and his lieutenant and the 'macho' attitudes they strike for the photographer.

14. Girl Guides demonstrating their cycling skills. One of a series of official postcards published in 1932.

15. This illustration of about 1935 not only depicts an indisputably middle class family enjoying an outing by train, perhaps going on holiday, but it is of interest because as a school teaching aid, it demonstrates the strong middle class bias of primary education at the time.

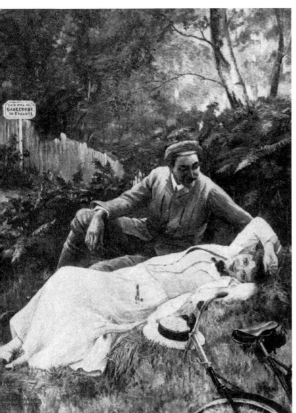

RIGHT   THIS HILL IS DANGEROUS TO CYCLISTS

16. The perils of unchaperoned Cycling. This mildly erotic postcard of about 1905 illustrates the greater freedom the bicycle allowed to young middle class couples. Perhaps we are meant to assume that the Norfolk–jacketed man and the rather relaxed young lady are engaged to be married.

'' What could be nicer ? ''

17. The cinema also provided new opportunities for middle class youth to taste the joys of physical proximity well away from parental interference. A comic postcard of about 1911.

18. This advertising postcard issued by a Sussex (Eastbourne and Heathfield) outfitter in about 1928 bears the message on the back 'New Styles for Gentlemen and Their Sons'. Despite the assertion of innovation, there is as yet little evidence of informality in out-of-school wear.

P. J. MARSHALL
Terminus Road an
Crown St., EASTBOURN
High St., HEATHFIEL

(606)

BELLE'S OF THE BEACH

19. An attractive trio of middle class eleven or twelve year-olds with buckets and fishnet on Selsey West Beach, Sussex, in about 1910.

20. Middle class commuters return to the new London suburb of Edgware around lunchtime on a July Saturday in 1926. Hats are worn almost without exception and all but three are men. Some are being met by their wives and children.

21. Elaborately dressed middle class women receive attention on a one-to-one basis in a show room of the Peter Robinson Oxford Street department store about 1911. Two of the three women carry parasols. A bombazine-swathed supervisor looks on to ensure that service is flawless. All are severely corseted.

22. Fashionably-dressed middle class ladies (and a few men) take tea after shopping in John Barker's new restaurant, 1914. Barker's, Derry & Toms' and Ponting's department stores, all in close proximity in High Street, Kensington, attracted a middle rather than upper–class clientele.

"Mountview Café"
**LYONS' OXFORD CORNER HOUSE**
*Oxford Street & Tottenham Court Road, London, W.1.*

23. In the affordable luxury of the Lyons' Corner House, all sections of the middle classes rubbed shoulders but lower middles tended to predominate. This is the Mountview Café at the 1928 Oxford Corner House, with internal décor by Oliver P. Bernard. The proud boast at the time was 'open 24 hours, for ever'.

24. Women and men in full evening dress leaving a London theatre after the show, about 1906. The original caption of this postcard reads '… as 11o'clock comes and passes, the theatres disgorge their immense crowd of pleasure seekers and hurry and bustle are rife; cab whistles and shouts disturb the former stillness, while beautiful figures and dainty toillettes lend their charm to the midnight hour'.

25. Dance hall scene about 1926. All are in evening dress and artificial silk stockings shimmer in the light of the cameraman's flashgun. There was still a great shortage of eligible young men in the aftermath of World War I and the sight of two women dancing together, as seen here, was not unusual.

26. In southern England, golf clubhouses were veritable temples of the old middle class, wherein only the carefully-selected few might enter, after their social status had been thoroughly vetted. This example is at Aldeburgh, Suffolk, photographed about 1938.

27. Tennis Club tea at Dorking, Surrey, 1926; a picture which successfully captures the very essence of between-wars middle class England – and middle middles at that.

28. The first Dip of the Holiday: Rosemarkie, Ross & Cromarty, Scotland, July 1919. Although the bathing costumes provide cover adequately satisfying the requirements of middle class respectability they could cling revealingly when wet.

29. The 'Fathers' Boat'. Still in their City business clothes, lightened in some cases by summer boaters, fathers and elder sons return to join their holidaying families on the East Anglian or Kent Coast, c1910.

30. Some very middle class hikers and cyclists leaving the new Youth Hostel at Holmbury St Mary, Surrey, after a night's rest, 1937

31. The middle classes take to the air. Passengers joining a Swiss Air Lines Douglas DC2 for a Croydon–Zurich flight about 1936. Note the general formality of the attire of these holidaymakers, especially that of the man on the left, whose outfit, with its lingering signs of Edwardian fashion, forms a piquant contrast to the modernity of the aircraft.

32. Careful class distinction is evident in the draughtmanship of this 1915 poster, which seeks to encourage the idea that women of all classes should unite in urging their menfolk to go off to fight the Germans.

them for material to use in school tasks, children obtained early training in research skills.

For younger children, a school teacher named Enid Blyton was beavering away with her twopenny illustrated weekly *Sunny Stories for Little Folks*. First published in 1926, these each had a satisfactorily happy ending but left very little to the young imagination. Her output, quintessentially middle class in tone, and mainly aimed at those under ten, continued through to and beyond 1950 in magazine and book form, subsequently arousing much controversy amongst librarians and educationalists. In practice it was in general much enjoyed by children, producing excitement which stimulated them to read more widely.

Weekly comics which might be safely consumed by the middle-class child of primary school age included *Chicks' Own, Rainbow* and *Tiger Tim's Weekly*. There were others, regarded as more dubious in tone and content, such as *Comic Cuts* and *Chips*, and from 1938, *Dandy* and *Beano*. A magazine popular with middle class parents, who approved of its high moral tone and its patriotic, 'manly', true-blue approach, was *The Boy's Own Paper*. It enjoyed a long run (1879–1946). With its strong bias towards 'healthy' articles and fiction about football and cricket, athletics, overseas adventure, scouting and the open air life generally, BOP never strayed from its original Victorian ethic. During World War 1 its militaristic, almost jingoist tone ensured continuing parental approval. Scattered with such expressions as 'jolly good show', 'playing fair', 'beastly good of you', and cricketing imagery such as 'playing a straight bat', the language used by its writers was impeccably upper middle class. Particularly revealing were the answers given to readers, whose full names and letters were tactfully omitted. Over the years anonymous editorial staff curtly and dogmatically dispensed practical advice and very occasionally moral guidance, the latter always in guarded terms. Much of this magazine seems as it if were written by clean-living, cricket and football-playing Anglican clergymen educated at public schools. BOP's adventure tales also appealed to some girls but there was a similar *Girl's Own Paper* from the same publishers. Not so successful, it later tried to widen its circulation by including features for adults.

So popular was the public school theme with girls as well as boys that several magazines and annuals were given over entirely to it. The best known writer in this genre was Charles Hamilton (1875–1961), who used the pseuydonyms Frank Richards and Martin Clifford. His stories, mainly based on the imaginary Greyfriars and St. James's Schools, appeared respectively over several decades in weekly magazines called *The Magnet* (1908–40) and *The Gem* (1907–39). In a typically pretentious piece published in 1940 after their disappearance under war conditions, George Orwell interpreted these magazines as social conditioning which engendered in the lower middles and working class a deferential respect for their 'betters'. This questionable theory still enjoys a certain respectability in some quarters. Although these stories and their equivalents in *Schoolgirls' Weekly, Schoolgirls' Own* and *Schoolgirl*, were certainly read avidly by lower middle class children, to whom such institutions might just as well have been in a foreign land, they were consumed for amusement only, and there is little evidence to show that the perceived indoctrination (surely not consciously exercised by Hamilton) was absorbed by the average reader to the extent of colouring his attitude to the public school product.

On the radio, from the early 1920s, 'Children's Hour', broadcast daily after tea, was distinctly middle class in tone, with its 'uncles' and 'aunts' and its genial establishment-oriented comments on current affairs by Stephen King-Hall, a retired naval Commander. Announcements, plays, poems, and stories were all spoken in reassuringly middle class accents. The whole thing ran well into the 1950s, with little or no change in style, exercising the childish imagination as no television broadcast could. Apart from this programme, the rather stuffy BBC output held little interest for the unmusical child. The late 1930s however brought the brief novelty of commercial Long Wave broadcasts in English from France and Luxembourg which included the famous 'Ovaltineys'. Adolescents received lasting impressions from the immediacy of radio reporting of current events such as the abdication of Edward VIII and the portentous activities in and around Germany.

Before television took its relentless hold on the attention of the young in the 1950s, reading had few serious rivals as an indoor pastime. Indeed it was so avidly indulged that many middle class parents, becoming alarmed at what their children might absorb from the printed page, attempted to exercise censorship. Whilst no objection was taken to periodicals such as *The Modern Boy, The Gem, The Magnet* and *The Meccano Magazine*, the appearance of two new boys' story weeklies in the 1930s, *The Hotspur* and *The Wizard*, caused some parental disquiet. For one thing the monopoly of middle class tone was well and truly dispelled; there was for example much mention of Association Football. Even worse, their contents often included wildly imaginative and sensational war and science fiction with illustrations to match.

Newspapers, even the more 'serious' ones, were not thought to be good for middle class children. Efforts were made to keep them out of sight and reading was actively discouraged, although it was difficult to enforce a total ban. Many wet afternoons were spent greedily absorbing the more sensational and intriguing contents of a pile of old papers found in the garden sheds of grandparents' houses, or in other households where the approach was more relaxed. Not everything of course was understood and questioning of adults seldom produced satisfactory explanations.

Unexpurgated versions of the fairy tales of the Brothers Grimm and Hans Andersen were placed out of reach on high shelves by the author's mother; Andersen longer than Grimm, since for some unfathomable reason it was judged the more harmful. Other children, finding bookcases locked against them, were tantalised by the forbidden titles and there were awkward occasions when forced locks would not re-seat properly, making discovery inevitable. Religious publications were of course freely available, but surprisingly sometimes contained provocative illustrations and descriptions of pagan images and practices not always suitable for consumption by juveniles blessed with the over-active imagination of early puberty.

# The Great Outdoors

Middle class children had more leisure time than the working class young, who were frequently made to help out at home or earn a few shillings for the family coffers by taking odd jobs outside school hours. Much of this free time was spent outdoors, where the social conditions and climate of the period allowed a great deal of safe freedom. Since parents were not burdened with worry about possible risks once children were old enough to go out with others of their own age, boys and girls wandered freely about towns and countryside, exploring the land and streetscapes, fascinated by the great variety of public transport and absorbing other sights and experiences. One dark cloud was slowly moving into this idyllic picture. From around 1930, the growth of motor traffic, accompanied by a general lack of discipline on the part of drivers, increasingly exposed untutored children to injury or death on the roads. Apart from this, the streets, parks and countryside held no threat. On several occasions the author and a friend, both in their early teens, walked some two miles through the streets of North London before dawn, and at least once the same journey was made alone. The objective was the main line into Kings Cross, with a prospect of unfamiliar locomotives bringing Cup Final Excursion trains from the north.

There was no concern on anyone's part, that there was any danger in this; nor was there.

## Boy Scouts, Girl Guides and Youth Hostellers

Juvenile fondness for exploration and activity outdoors in 'gangs' and 'camps' was exploited from 1908–9 by two successful and influential movements which provided opportunities to exercise it in a purposeful and structured manner. Both sprang from the ideas and initiatives of Lt. Gen. (later Lord) Robert Baden-Powell (1857–1941), son of an admiral's daughter and an Oxford professor, pupil of Charterhouse School and recipient of an immediate commission on joining the army, – an impeccable middle class background indeed. Concerned by what he saw as the lack of 'character' in the youth of his time, and profiting from the friendship and support of William Alexander Smith, founder of the Boys' Brigade, Baden-Powell developed the idea of scouting for boys out of a training system he had devised for the British Army. Initially he wanted to weld it on to the largely working class Boys' Brigade and other existing church youth organisations, but it soon evolved into a separate and independent institution, with, as we shall see, a distinctive and largely middle class character and tone. Forming into 'Troops' named after their district or local founder from early 1908 onwards, Baden-Powell's Boy Scouts were aged eleven to eighteen. Eight years later, the Wolf Cubs were set up for the eight to elevens, with activities and nomenclature based on Rudyard Kipling's *Jungle Books*.

For the boys' uniform, Baden-Powell suggested the khaki shorts, short-sleeved shirt, scarf and broad-brimmed hat of the South African Constabulary, a force he had raised after the end of the Boer War. A stave was substituted for the SAC rifle. This outfit was adopted and remained in use through to the 1940s with only minor modifications.

In the first year or so, Baden-Powell was greatly assisted by financial appeals organised by the Conservative and middle class *Daily Telegraph* and by the Conservative newspaper proprietor and publisher C. Arthur Pearson (later Sir Arthur), who provided finance and publicity, placed an office at BP's disposal and issued a penny weekly paper, *The Scout* from 14 April 1908. This 'official organ of The Boy Scouts', which achieved a weekly sale of around 110,000 in its first year, was similar in content and tone to *The Boys' Own Paper*, each page carrying three closely-printed columns, illustrated with line blocks (photographs were added in 1910). The stories had a scouting, public school, marine or overseas background, the latter featuring the adventures of 'plucky Britishers'. There were also 'yarns' by Baden-Powell, nature notes, 'Tricks and Teasers', and 'Things All Scouts Should Know' (such as how to climb over high walls, and how to protect your ribs in a crowd). A column headed 'Boy Scouts' Official Notes & News' covered the activities of troops and individual scouts throughout the country. All this was laced with occasional articles by clergymen and others, imparting light moral instruction. The Movement also received useful propaganda support from the infant British film industry, which between 1909 and 1913 provided no less than eighteen films featuring Scouts. Only three were comedies; the rest showed the new force of junior middle class heroes vanquishing evil-doers in the form of burglars, gipsies and tramps. As a topic for cinema entertainment, Scouts were somewhat eclipsed after 1918; there were only five more films, the last Ralph Reader's *Gang Show* of 1937.

By the end of 1909, Baden-Powell, flushed with the success of the Boy Scouts, was preparing a scheme for Girl Guides which would have the same overtones and pursue similar activities. He was at pains to stress it would be a separate and distinctive organisation, unlike the Girl Scouts, who were already causing some embarrassment by trying to infiltrate that movement on equal terms. E. K. Wade's 1929 book mentions that the use of the word 'scout' for girls was seen as not only alienating parents but also as deterring boys 'from what they had hitherto regarded as a manly pursuit'. In practice, the more determined of the early Girl Scouts proved awkward to suppress and the new Guide Movement suffered a slow and difficult start because many active girls found it insufficiently scout-like. Middle class parents of potential Guides considered the concept, watered down though it was from scouting, both unladylike and tomboyish.

Although always anxious to emphasise that both Scouts and Guides crossed all class barriers (his 1907 experimental camp on Brownsea Island, Poole Harbour had included both public school boys and members of the proletarian and lower middle class Boys' Brigade), Baden-Powell seemed to want them led and organised by the middle class, and consciously or not, his ideas set out in large part to impose middle class value systems and philosophy. In the elaboration of the 'Scout Law' which he included in his 1908 handbook *Scouting For Boys*, Baden-Powell required a Boy Scout to promise not only to be loyal to his Sovereign, his officers, his parents, his country, his employers, employees and his comrades (sticking to them 'through thick and thin against anyone who is their enemy or who even talks badly of them'), but to obey the orders given by his officers and parents without question, carrying them out 'cheerfully and readily and not in a slow, hang-dog sort of way', even if he did not like them or agree with them. It was made plain that a Scout was expected to smile and whistle under all difficulties, never to grouse at hardships, nor whine or swear. Another middle class virtue appeared in Item no 9, which decreed that a Scout is thrifty. 'That is', explained Baden-Powell, 'he saves every penny he can and puts it into the bank, so that he may have money to keep himself when out of work, and thus not make himself a burden on others. . .' Middle class sexual morality came into the tenth and final law, which he added in 1909. In this, the Scout was directed to be clean in thought, word and deed, '. . . he must not let himself give way to temptation, either to talk it or to think or do anything dirty. A Scout is pure and clean-minded and manly'.

Baden-Powell's Scheme for Girl Guides, first published in the November 1909 issue of *Boy Scout Headquarters Gazette*, also reverberates with his middle class attitudes and intentions. He begins by pointing out what he sees as a need for 'character' in the nation, suggesting that the future manhood of the country should be 'men of character', since this would be 'the only guarantee for safety of the nation'. Here we discern the shade of the contemporary middle class bogey of moral degeneration, leading to decline of the Empire and the possibility of invasion and defeat in a German-generated European war, which we shall look at later in this book. BP then goes on to explain that this noble objective can only be achieved if the mothers and the future wives, 'the guides of those men', are 'women of character'. Whilst not wishing to 'make tomboys of refined girls' he considers the new movement should attract 'and thus raise, the slum-girl from the gutter'. He shows himself much concerned with subject of national decadence, both moral and physical, which he sees as in process, and blames this squarely on 'the ignorance or supiness of mothers', who he suggests are prepared to leave the moral education of their children 'pretty much to the school masters'. Girls must be 'partners and comrades rather than dolls'. Their subsequent influence on the actions and quality of men he assesses as very great; they will 'become their "Guides" ', which means they need character training just as much as boys. Hence the Girl *Guides*.

Both at this time and later, Baden-Powell was much exercised by the dangers of idleness amongst young people and comments here on the 'over-dressed and idling' girls to be seen in the streets in the evenings and at seaside resorts, 'learning to live aimless and profitless lives'. His introductory sermon ends with a little homily on the state of the masses, clearly lacking middle class virtues and 'character' which should have been instilled when they were young: 'loafing, trusting to luck, want of thrift, unstableness' are listed as increasing defects amongst 'our men' (and women); 'good servants are hard to get', he continues, 'homes are badly kept, children are badly brought up'.

In time, it would seem, his Girl Guides would put all this right. Meanwhile they must be organised. BP describes how this should be in the hands of committees of 'ladies' who would 'then get hold of the right kind of young ladies to act as Captains' (the latter were to be over twenty one years of age). In passing he notes that the Boy Scouts had got 'gentlemen to take command as officers'. The terminology is significant.

Although it was claimed from the start that scouting and guiding were essentially a form of character and general training for good citizenship, patriotism and the threat of foreign invasion were also stressed and there was an unmistakable military flavour about both movements in their first two decades[18]. It was not only that the Scouts were largely governed and directed by retired army officers and used military titles and arm stripes. An impartial observer might assume that it was surely less an accident than an intentional convenience that the skills taught had an undeniable military application, or would at any rate be useful in wartime: Guides, for example, were trained in 'finding and treating the wounded'. On Empire Day 1914, the 1st Alderley Edge Company of Girl Guides (middle class to a lass?), participating in a rally at Heaton Park, Manchester, are typically recorded as having given an 'interesting display of bridge-building and ambulance'. From 1908 until 1910 Baden-Powell was also active as a Territorial Army Divisional Commander and his Boy Scouts were seen by many as a recruiting agency for that force. Those in high places certainly appreciated this military-imperialistic bias. Field Marshal Lord Roberts, advocate of conscription in Britain, had written to Baden-Powell in 1908 expressing the hope that his new Boy Scouts would be training themselves in their youth 'to be ready to defend their country when they arrive at man's estate, should the need of their services ever arise' (*The Scout*, April 1908). In a message to the 1909 rally of Scouts at the Crystal Palace, London, King Edward VII expressed a similar sentiment: '. . . the sense of patriotic responsibility and happy discipline which they are now acquiring as boys will enable them to do their duty as men, should any danger threaten the Empire'. And the cartoonist Bernard Partridge epitomised the widespread assumption in a 1909 *Punch* drawing entitled 'Our Youngest Line of Defence' which depicted a small Boy Scout assuring 'Gran'ma Britannia' that no danger could befall her now. Lord Haldane, Secretary of State for War, was among the first to commend Baden-Powell's scheme, whilst Lord Roberts joined the Advisory Council in 1909 and Field Marshal Lord Kitchener ran his own Scout Troop in north London.

Not surprisingly, when war broke out in August 1914, both Scouts and Guides were expecting to be used in an active sense to support and further the nation's war effort. And many were. At any one time between 5 August 1914 and 7 March 1920, some 1,500–2,000 Sea Scouts were on duty as coastguards, releasing men for the Navy and receiving financial support from the Admiralty. Done at the specific request of Kitchener, it was described by Baden-Powell as 'an integral part of the machinery of national defence'. Scouts and Guides undertook many and varied tasks on the Home Front. Typical in their expression of contemporary middle class enthusiasm for the quasi-military role taken up by the Scouts are the 1914 reports to Headquarters from Scout officers quoted in E. K. Wade's 1929 book:

> On August 2nd I rushed about in my car . . . and had the railway line between Hayward's Heath and Lewes allocated to us, to guard against German spies blowing up railway bridges etc. Within twelve hours we had 500 Scouts on the line, and within thirty-six hours 1500 were in position. The Scouts were very energetic, and in one case rushed a protesting entomologist off to the nearest police station – he was removing a chrysalis or some other harmless affair from the brickwork under a railway bridge.

The Kenty County Commissioner proudly recorded of his Scouts:

> . . . they have watched all main telegraph and telephone lines which pass through Kent from London to Paris and Brussels, they have watched many bridges, tunnels, culverts etc. They have stimulated recruiting for the Army, hunted out Germans, manned several coastguard stations, accounted for a good many spies. . .

A 'Scouts' Defence Corps' was later raised to give those approaching military age training in drill, rifle firing and other military arts. On joining the Army, it was noticeable that most ex-Scouts quickly gained commissions. The twelve wartime films about Scouts reflected all this, showing them capturing and frustrating German spies, even taking 'despatches' to the French front at risk of capture.

It was not only a question of the Scouts and Guides having a middle class tone and fulfilling a role in the middle and upper class view of society and the threats it faced. Despite Baden-Powell's good intentions of establishing classless organisations, it was the middle classes that had flocked to join these new movements as well as to organise them. As early as 1910 he had confessed to a meeting of the National Defence Association that scouting appealed more to the lower middle than the working class, although there had been some success amongst the largely proletarian Glasgow Boys' Brigade. The reason for this was of course that only the middle class children had the leisure time and money for the uniforms, equipment and the open air camps which were a central feature of the activities. And the associations with organised religion and militarism were assured of a much more enthusiastic reception from middle class parents; the attitude of the proletariat and the very poor towards these ranged from negative to hostile. Membership was high in the prosperous London and south east region. J. O. Springhall's statistical sampling shows that in the 1920s, the density of recruitment amongst the potentially eligible was greatest in the more prosperous areas. He notes, 'a middle class boy of fourteen living in the South East of England was far more likely to join the Boy Scouts than his working class equivalent in the North of England or Scotland'[19]. That this continued into the next two decades tends to be proved by a 1966 Mass Observation survey of adults which found that forty four per cent of the sample categorised as middle class had been Boy Scouts against only twenty five per cent of the working class men interviewed. This survey also established that the middle class element had remained longer in the Scouts and that membership was most popular in the south of England.

Public schools enthusiastically encouraged their pupils to participate in their own Scouts' and Guides' organisations and cadet units were formed to train the 'officers' (later known as 'Scouters'). Leading girls' schools such as Roedean and St James' West Malvern were pioneers in this respect. Eton accepted a Scout Troop in its lower school in 1921, an example soon followed by most public schools, where Scouts found themselves competing with the openly military activities of the longer-established Officers' Training Corps. The Rover Scouts, formed in 1919 to enable 'old Scouts' over eighteen to follow what Baden-Powell called 'Life-Sport' (others called it 'institutionalised adolescence'), appeared in most universities and these establishments also sheltered facilities for training Scouters.

For the middle class child the attractions of the Scout and Guide movements centred upon their predominantly open air activities, the peaceful break they provided from the constant checking of parents, the comradeship so sedulously fostered, and the encouragement of self-reliance and self-respect. Right from the start, once they had grasped what it was all about, enthusiasm for Scouting genuinely bubbled up from the children themselves and this continued. The association of many Scout and Guide troops with churches also aided recruitment, especially as boys and girls found themselves with young adult leaders they knew already. Equally the formation of independent troops gave non-Christians and non-churchgoers the opportunity to participate for although stressing the importance of 'doing duty to God', Baden-Powell wisely recognised no difference of creed or country as well as of class, an aspect increasingly important as church attendance declined after World War 1.

Popular as these movements were, many other middle class children, lacking a strong herd instinct, or simply resenting the idea of adult-organised leisure, continued to remain aloof, preferring to find their amusements alone or with a select few of their peers. And, except perhaps during both wars, those that did join tended to default at the time they left school and interest in the opposite sex flowered. The wastage after age fourteen became a growing problem, causing increasing concern to the leaders of both Scouts and Guides.

In the political and social atmosphere of the 1910s, middle class parents had warmed to the quasi-military and highly patriotic tone of the Scout and Guide movements, which seem to have appealed particularly to the lower middles[20]. The sentiment of bettering the quality and efficiency of the nation through improvement of its youth was especially acceptable to the middle classes of the time. But as World War 1 lingered on and the young were slaughtered on the battlefields of Flanders, a reaction set in. As early as 1917 some of the military titles were abolished. Then, as military preparedness became unfashionable in the aftermath of a terrible conflict, a positive redirection of incentive and tone was required.

The answer was found in the encouragement of the noble but seemingly impracticable quest for 'international comradeship'. To this end, an International Council was set up, with an invitation for all nations to affiliate to it following the first World Jamboree held at London's Olympia in 1920. A quarterly international scout journal, *Jamboree*, was published from 1921. Alas, the seeds of a new World War had been sown, and no amount of international comradeship through Scouting and Guiding could prevent it, or indeed any smaller armed conflict. In the meantime both Scouts and Guides in the UK continued to prosper. Between the wars, middle class parents remained supportive, seeing these organisations as a valuable means of implanting or reinforcing self-reliance and a generally conservative and conformist conditioning. The great expansion of purposeful activity in aid of the civil and military power in World War 1 had boosted the number of UK Scouts from 152,000 in 1913 to over 200,000 in 1920. Hard work and undiluted enthusiasm within the movement, the arrival of Wolf Cubs and Rovers, and the increased prosperity of the middle classes which formed its backbone and main support, all helped to almost double the numbers by the end of the 1930s. In 1939 there were also some 40,000 adult-trainers, all dedicated volunteers and almost all recruited from the middle classes. After marriage in 1912, Olave, Lady Baden-Powell had injected new life into the flagging Girl Guide movement, which increased from 8,000 British members in 1910 to over 38,000 by 1915. Younger girls, brought in as 'Rosebuds' in 1914 were more felicitously known as Brownies from the following year, and senior Guides became Rangers in 1920. Sea Guides (later Sea Rangers) appeared in 1920 as a result of an infiltration by ladies who had served in the wartime Women's Royal Naval Service – their uniform had similarities to the WRNS outfit. Finally Air Rangers appeared in 1943, resplendent in RAF blue. Both sub-groups were officially recognised by the parent armed forces. Benefiting from the same wartime and other influences affecting the Scouts, the Girl Guides continued to expand between the wars, although failing to attract such a high proportion of the total in the age band as their brother movement. In World War 2, Scouts and Guides again contributed strongly to the national effort at home, with rather less emphasis on quasi-military activities and military preparation.

In the 1920s and 1930s increasing numbers of young people went off into the countryside at weekends and holidays on foot or cycle, both independently and in organised groups, many of them with an affection for the open air life first developed as Scouts or Guides. The Youth Hostels Association for England & Wales was formed in 1930 to lead the young to a 'greater knowledge, care and love of the countryside'. Scotland followed a year later. Patterned on the long-established German *Jugendherbergen*, it coordinated local organisations of a similar nature. It provided facilities for the hitherto largely unorganised ramblers and cyclists, offering simple and clean accommodation for which those aged fourteen to eighteen paid only sixpence a night. Alcohol was not permitted, the sexes were properly segregated, and all guests were expected to reach the hostel by foot or bicycle. By 1939 the YHA, with 297 hostels containing almost 11,000 beds, had acquired 83,418 members, the majority of whom probably came from the middle classes.

## Accepted Discipline

Perhaps the main behaviour characteristic of middle class children and youth over the period was a negative one. The great majority accepted and followed the culture and moral standards handed down to them by parents, teachers, priests. Scoutmasters, Guide Captains and others in a position to influence them, taking it all virtually without question, evincing only occasional rudeness or revolt. Their conditioning, generally successful, tended to suppress individuality and self-expression whilst promoting deference to all adults in the middle and upper classes. Social environment played an important role: such factors as the strong and often harsh discipline prevailing at both the private and the council schools, the very low percentage of young people enjoying the relative freedom of university and college life, and last, but by no means least, the complete absence of anything remotely resembling the hedonistic youth culture so strongly and ceaselessly promoted and sustained by today's media, advertising, clothing and entertainment industries.

Since Victorian beliefs and behaviour persisted in many middle class homes for a decade or more after 1900, the child's life was often hard, even austere. Careful study of contemporary photographs of children will sometimes reveal strained, cowed features that suggest harsh suppression of the spirit. Received wisdom suggested to parents and guardians that all children had innate tendencies towards sin, eradicable only by firm guidance, backed up by sharp and regular physical punishment. Gradually this inheritance from the previous century was blown away by more liberal and humane attitudes until, by the late 1920s, although by no means dead, the old ways were far less evident.

At home, most middle class children were accustomed to order and regularity and were obliged to conform from an early age to a prescribed routine of discipline which included such things as personal cleanliness, punctuality, tidiness, obedience, 'eating up', 'sitting up straight', not sitting at table till all others were in place, staying at table till all had finished the meal, not speaking until spoken to, and not interrupting anyone else's conversation. Great importance was attached to etiquette and good manners, including such things as making people feel comfortable, closing the door after passing out of the room, opening and closing doors for others, and so on. Bedtime was strictly enforced at the same hour each day, irrespective of whether the child was ready to sleep, and children as old as ten or eleven were sent upstairs by 8.30 or 9 p.m. Much of this domestic and social training would have been instilled by the time a child first went to school, a circumstance which greatly helped in acceptance of that institution's additional disciplines, which were usually complicated and often more rigorous.

We have earlier stressed the more generous leisure time available to the middle class child but one qualification should be entered. During school terms, from the age of eleven upwards, spare time was increasingly restricted. Children attending day schools, especially those residing in thinly-populated areas, could spend up to two hours a day travelling by bicycle, train or bus to the more widely-separated secondary schools, and in addition, the rigid demands of an academic curriculum linked to the School Certificate Examination meant that at first 1½ hours' and later as much as three hours' homework had to be done each evening in addition to the school day of seven forty-minute periods between 9am and 4pm. Leather or canvas satchels bulging with books were carried home at teatime and back again next morning, the tasks completed, often with parental or peer assistance. This onerous homework regime could impose quite a strain on the adolescent child, particularly girls. At the private boarding schools, older children were similarly kept at set desk work ('preparation') or other supervised activities in the early evening after formal lessons had ceased and often before breakfast as well. There were also formidable academic tasks to be completed during the long holidays.

Middle class children were constantly checked and corrected by both parents and teachers and frequently obliged to suffer verbal abuse and corporal punishment, the latter often thoughtlessly and coldly given for quite minor faults and omissions. At home and at school, boys received cuffs around the ears, canings across the hands or, for what were deemed the most serious offences, on the buttocks. Girls were by no means always exempted from slapping and caning and in the home children of both sexes were frequently put across a parent's lap and spanked. Although parental and pedagogic authority might be resented, they were rarely challenged. Shutting children away in dark cupboards or locking them in their bedrooms was another common form of punishment. All this was not without its long term effects; many middle class Englishmen brought up in the early decades of the 20th century apparently found solace in what the French delicately referred to as *le roman anglais*, to an extent that it became a minor branch of Parisian publishing.

Outbreaks of wilful naughtiness and insolence at home and school were by no means rare but very few middle class children behaved badly enough outside the house to incur the attention of the police, and in this respect they conformed with the generally law-abiding attitudes of the middle classes as a whole. Policemen regularly patrolled the streets on foot and were to be found directing traffic at all busy road intersections. This high profile was sufficient in itself to deter most middle class children from any misbehaviour. It also contributed to parental confidence in the safety of the streets, as did the extreme rarity of reported physical and sexual assaults on children.

The conformism and unquestioning acceptance of what was handed down was continued into early adulthood. For the reasons touched on earlier in this chapter, many in the lower middle class were employed in jobs well below their intelligence and ability. In the 1930s those leaving school faced what was predominantly an employers' market, so much so

221

that even the smallest of commercial enterprises, when filling vacancies for the humblest office jobs, could demand, and get, young people educated to university entrance ('matriculation') standard. Through their late teens and much of their twenties middle class school leavers all too often had to be content to stay in dull second-rate jobs with poor working conditions, low pay, and harsh discipline. Petty tyranny from immediate superiors who took the attitude 'At his age, I suffered it, so shall he. . .' had to be tolerated in a working environment in which the norm was to perform as hard and as well as possible. For many there was no alternative between this and the degrading unemployment that pride and self-respect would not allow them or their parents to contemplate. They soldiered on, making the best of it. This pattern was especially prevalent in small towns and cities where there was little choice of middle class jobs, though of course many did make the sometimes difficult decision to uproot themselves and take up posts in London. Civil service offices in and around Whitehall in the 1930s and 1940s were full of bright young expatriate middle class Scots, Welsh, Mancunians, Liverpudlians and other provincials living a somewhat lonely life in suburban lodgings or inner city hostels.

## Youthful Morals

Conformism was also evident in sexual morality during adolescence and in the long period between school and marriage, at any rate for the majority. In basic knowledge of sexual matters, both physical and psychological, the generations up to and even beyond 1950 entered adulthood remarkably ill-equipped, and were often repressed and shy in their attitudes to the opposite sex. Only a minority of middle class parents provided even the simplest sexual instruction; for the rest it came by word of mouth from around age ten or eleven at school (sometimes from school friends who had received it from progressive parents or helpful older siblings). This was filled out in more detail later when sufficient money and daring were accumulated to send for sexual manuals, discreetly despatched in plain wrappers. From around 1930, the bare clinical facts were made known to the secondary schoolchild in a very cold and formal way in biology lessons, leaving much unanswered. Earlier, knowledge had been even more sketchy: as late as the 1920s it was not uncommon for middle class married women to reach their first pregnancy still uncertain as to what exactly would happen to them when their baby was born.

There was a good deal more clarity and certainty about the moral issues associated with sexual behaviour. Adolescents were left in no doubt as to the dangers and sinfulness of what religious and other manuals usually termed without elaboration as 'self-abuse', 'unclean thoughts' and 'unsuitable' or 'unwholesome' literature. From time to time, in veiled terms, adults hinted at such matters to those in their charge. Throughout the half century, the middle classes in general remained reticent in their attitude towards sexual behaviour and sexuality, regarding lifelong marriage if not as a sacrament, as a sacred obligation with divorce as the last resort of the desperate and truly forlorn. Pre-marital and extra-marital sexual intercourse were acts no respectable middle class woman should permit to happen. In the middle classes, at least until the 1940s, it was generally accepted that any unmarried girl who gave in to male sexual demands and acquired a reputation for being 'easy' would soon lose the respect of eligible young men to an extent which would seriously reduce her all-important chances of making a good marriage. Most middle class girls were left in little doubt that they were expected to preserve their virginity for their eventual marriage partner, nor would they encounter too much difficulty from their male peers in attaining this objective. Indeed many young men were more shy of making physical advances than their partners – the girl often gently took the initiative and controlled the pace. Although he thought that about sixty per cent of unmarried men had tried sexual intercourse 'at least once, probably with a prostitute or some girl of easy virtue', Rennie Macandrew, a widely-read and wise writer on sexual relationships in the 1930s[21] maintained 'there is not more than one unmarried middle-class girl in a dozen who has given up her maidenhood' and explained that very few men would react violently if refused intercourse 'because of their inherent courtesy to the opposite sex, or fear of the consequences'. Moreover, he added, 'a girl can practically always command the situation'. Strange as it may seem today, it was still not unusual in the 1930s, as it had been for earlier generations, for a young middle class boy and girl to enjoy a day alone together in the country without anything more than the mildest of physical contact, yet return home in the evening full of sexual exhilaration, quite drunk with the experience of each other's company.

In such circumstances venereal disease was relatively uncommon and Macandrew was able to reassure his readers, in a phrase that reveals who he was writing for, that 'fortunately there is very little syphilis among clean-living middle class people'. Indeed even discussion of this subject was taboo in middle class circles. When Eugène Brieux' play *Damaged Goods (les Avariés)* was first given a private performance at London's Little Theatre in 1914, the very middle class *Play Pictorial* thought its subject matter 'so gruesome and repugnant that its details cannot be discussed here'.

Great care was taken to protect adolescents from undue stimulation of their burgeoning sexual feelings. The organisers of the Boy Scout and Girl Guide movements in the 1910s were strict in not allowing the two to mix, also ensuring that Guides in their care were not out after dark. Even marching and training together were forbidden, although combined inspections were not ruled out when these were organisationally convenient. On the outbreak of war in 1914, Girl Guide Captains were warned in a Headquarters circular, 'Every safeguard must be given to girls, even more now than in time of peace'. Parental permission in writing was required for each Girl Guide undertaking war duties and each carried a card with her name and address, the exact nature of the task and the hours she was to work.

Middle class social and religious pressures against pre-marital sexual intercourse remained strong right through to World War 2. They were reinforced by shyness and uncertainty and often, when all else was overcome, by difficulties in obtaining the necessary privacy. Although opportunities were increased as young men began to purchase cheap second hand cars in the 1930s, the whole period (with the temporary exception of World War 1) was remarkable for a considerable amount of restraint in physical lovemaking amongst the young unmarried middle class during what was then the ten or more years between the attainment of full puberty and marriage (which had to be postponed until the male, as the sole breadwinner, was earning enough to set up a household). Before the wedding day, heavy petting was the limit for most middle class couples and Macandrew provided advice on how this might be pursued to mutual satisfaction. Most middle class girls would make it clear, even when marriage was firmly on the horizon, that 'going all the way' must await the wedding night and this was usually respected. In her thoughtful account of her middle class upbringing in between-wars Surrey, Eileen Whiteing[22] comments that in what she calls 'our circle', abortions and illegitimate babies were unknown, 'our sex life was expected to be (and generally was) almost non-existent before marriage'. She adds 'Girls and boys alike seemed to know by instinct the limits to be imposed in any love-making, even during the longish engagements which were normal.'

It should also be said that so strong was the instilled middle class moral code, the feeling of guilt associated with sexual fulfilment outside marriage, especially amongst women, that adulterous liaisons were often abandoned before consummation. In this respect David Lean's beautifully-observed 1946 film, *Brief Encounter*, (based on the 1936 Noël

Coward one-act play *Still Life*), with its faithful reflection of several facets of middle class manners and behaviour, was absolutely true to its time.

# Courting

In their attempts to select and obtain partners, most middle class Edwardian boys and girls faced serious impediments. Into their late teens and early twenties many continued to accept home disciplines. Girls were not expected to go out alone with men until they were engaged to be married and both girls and boys observed a parental curfew (usually no later than 10.30 p.m.) for returning home. Parents sought opportunities to appraise any potential marriage partners and would not hesitate to make their frequently irrational disapproval known.

In towns the younger element in the lower middle class often joined in the working class courting or flirtation ritual known as 'The Monkeys' Parade'. This was the Saturday and Sunday evening custom in which groups of both sexes walked up and down in their smartest clothes in parks or at other recognised rallying points until two girls paired up with two boys thus providing a measure of mutual support and observing the letter of the chaperonage rule. As dusk descended, the couples might separate, especially when they were already known to each other, the two girls making sure they remained in calling distance.

But the great majority of the middle class first met partners of similar status and background after Sunday church services, at church social functions, at dances, in their office workplaces, or at tennis and golf clubs. Very occasionally serious courtship was manouevred into being by prior arrangement between the respective parents and received their subsequent encouragement. Opportunities slowly widened; there were more eligible young single girls entering office employment and by the mid 1920s parental control was becoming sufficiently relaxed to allow girls to go out, if not alone, at any rate with known friends or sisters. But the manner and means of making the initial contacts remained very much the same.

# Wartime Lapses

Both world wars saw a temporary breakdown in the generally tight observances of the middle class code of sexual morality. Mrs Peel notes that 'as the casualty lists lengthened' in World War 1, many marriages were made after 'a few days' acquaintance', or there were what she coyly refers to as 'temporary connections'. In the same passage she speaks of an increase in drinking, gambling, drug abuse, dancing and 'an utter breakdown of what people of my generation considered to be sexual morality'[23]. It did not last. In less than a decade, even for the advanced minority, and despite the efforts of some dramatists writing for the West End theatre, the pendulum was swinging back again, with young people finding out the eternal truth that, to use Mrs Peel's words, 'a union which is merely physical is of little value'.

The release from social and parental restraints and the widening of social opportunities provided by World War 2 brought a repetition of what had happened a quarter of a century earlier, even though the element of emotional stress associated with incessant and horrendous slaughter was not so pronounced for the majority. A new factor was the presence in Britain of many thousands of uninhibited American, Polish and other Allied servicemen, who, far from the restraints of their home environment, bearing gifts unavailable in the shops, easier than British men in their relationships with the opposite sex, and exploiting the charm and attraction of the new and unknown, often found the young British middle class woman no more difficult to seduce than her working class sister. For British middle class males, many forcibly exiled overseas for several years, the opportunities for sexual adventure were frequently limited to those readily dispensing their favours, with whom consort was, as the authorities ceaselessly pointed out, physically dangerous. At home, middle class men remaining in civilian life by reason of age or 'reserved occupation', with Home Guard, firewatching or other wartime posts that took them away from home and wives for long and uncertain hours, had a wide range of opportunities for sexual laxity in an atmosphere which encouraged abandonment of the old restraints. Many yielded to temptation. Middle class girls, who had joined the women's services in very large numbers, or had been moved away as civilians from their normal environment by evacuation or other exigencies of war, saw no reason for not having the 'good time' so frequently offered to them by compatriots in and out of uniform as well as the many foreign servicemen. Then, once the war ended, middle class sexual morality and behaviour along the lines already described again returned to majority acceptance, just as it had done after World War 1, nothing very much changing in the remaining years of the half century.

# Dressing the Child[24]

For the middle classes, the appearance of children, (and also their behaviour and speech), was just as much part of the display necessary to establish status and social standing as it was with adults. Great importance was therefore placed on dressing them in conformist style as smartly as could be afforded. Middle class children were also the main wearers of school uniforms but since these had special connotations which merit separate consideration, they will be examined at the end of this chapter.

One rather curious aspect of children's wear which survived into the mid-1910s or even later must have left a permanent mark on many a psyche. This was the custom of dressing little boys as girls. Until the age of five or six, boys were attired in various types of frock, some extremely feminine in design, adorned with quantities of lace and ribbons, whilst others were of plainer style, with wide collars. This offered a certain convenience at the napkin stage but there was more to it than that since it was continued well beyond. Hair was also worn a girlish length, tied with ribbon bows, and if straight, was artificially curled. The final result made it difficult to distinguish the sex of an infant when dressed. One can only speculate as to the origins and hidden meanings of this strange ritual. Perhaps the mothers, aware that boy babies were more delicate and vulnerable than girls, were hoping to deceive the Grim Reaper, or were they compensating for not having the girl they had really desired?

In violent contrast, from the time of first attending school, most boys in the 1900s and 1910s were dressed with full masculine severity, reflecting the formal styles of fathers and adult brothers. They were given dark-hued jackets and waistcoats, the latter duly adorned with watch chain across the pockets. Neckties were arranged round very large high stiff collars which projected awkwardly and uncomfortably over the top of the jacket. Instead of trousers, there were knickerbockers, closed with a buttoned strap or elastic at the knee. Long black or dark brown woollen socks disappeared into these. From around 1910, shoes began to replace boots on the feet of middle class boys. Caps, and in summer, straw boaters, completed an all the year round outfit which was torture to wear in hot weather. Junior-sized walking sticks were available for country excursions.

Following a trend established by British and European royal families, white sailor suits and round sailor caps became very popular for younger boys, remaining so until around 1915. The strange maternal desire to feminise the male child was also evident in the fashion for soft velvet suits and silk shirts or blouses on small boys, which persisted well into the 1920s.

Around 1905 Chas. Baker & Company's best quality boys' Eton Jackets and Vests were available in four sizes at 18s11d, £1.5s9d, £1.11s6d and £1.19s6d, an outfit completed with striped long trousers at 6s11d, 8s11d,

10s9d and 12s11d. From the same firm, a 'Howe Overcoat' in blue serge and plain blue cloth, with four pairs of buttons was available in six sizes from 6s11d for the smallest to £1.4s6d. In the years up to 1915 or so, serge or tweed suits could be had for one to three pounds according to size and quality and a small boy's sailor suit in white drill for fifteen shillings to a pound. The infants' frocks referred to above, in muslin, trimmed with embroidery, flouncing, lace and ribbon, were sold at eight to twelve shillings.

Edwardian girls wore frocks which came to or just below the knee and in contrast to those of the 1890s, these were made up with lighter materials, in pastel colours. Styles differed little from those of the previous decade, and large collars and short sleeves were fashionable features. Hair was often centre-parted and tied in bows at each side of the head. Sailor collars and blouses were also popular, again following royal fashion. By the middle 1900s, small girls were beginning to appear in knee-length socks but summer and winter, the legs of their older sisters were usually clothed in long woollen or lisle stockings, almost invariably black. Until the mid 1910s, lower middle class girls were often seen outdoors and in schoolrooms wearing white lace-edged aprons or smocks to protect their frocks from too much soiling. This reflected financial constraints – the dresses were difficult to wash and iron frequently and in the absence of an extensive wardrobe and adequate domestic help, laundering was postponed as long as possible. Many girls still wore boots to ankle or mid-calf length but by the middle 1900s more shoes were appearing in their place. With them came gaiters, which were to prove an enduring method of protecting girls' legs and stockings. Made of felt, stockinet or leather, and side-buttoning, they covered the shoes, calves and knees and were held by elastics over the instep. For winter wear they were fur-lined.

Following the adult trend, the early 1910s saw the introduction of loose-cut, easier-fitting girls' clothes in brighter colours. Wool and cotton began to replace the earlier muslins and serges. At this time a medium-quality girl's coat and three-quarter length skirt in serge sold at 12s11d for size four to 19s2d for size nine. 'Maids' (a trade term for teenagers which remained in use until at least the 1940s) could be dressed in wool serge costumes from 18s11d to £1.5s.9d according to size. From around 1912 smart little girls were seen in dresses gathered into a belt or wide ribbon with large bow at the back, placing the waist around hip level. Skirts were now just above the knees, the reduction in length continuing until by 1916 they barely covered the thighs of the younger ones. Curiously, both hip level 'waist' and short skirt anticipated the adult fashions of ten years later. In 1917 the natural waist was restored and skirts became wider. At this time although good quality girls' clothes were expensive, they were, despite wartime conditions, by no means difficult to find. A coat dress in heavy crêpe de chine with collar and cuffs of fine net-edged filet lace available in 'saxe, rose, sky, recida or ivory shades' and suitable for a girl of four was advertised in that year at £3.5s.9d. The accompanying wide-brimmed hat in black, trimmed with black lace and a wreath of small flowers, cost £1.9s.6d. A year later Harrods' announced a new trend in girls' wear: 'the dress needs of young girls are studied. The new Spring Models, whilst offering a very definite degree of "style", in no way imply a dressiness beyond the years of the intended wearers'. But the price of this advance was high – around five pounds for the navy and purple gabardine frock illustrated alongside. Those that could afford such prices (they came down a little in the 1920s and 1930s) could from this time readily find stylish, well-cut and well-made dresses, coats and hats for girls from three to sixteen.

Until the late 1910s, head hair was allowed to grow naturally, reaching waist length or just above as a girl entered her teens. It was worn either loose or plaited, and if loose, was normally tied at the nape of the neck with a large (usually black) silk taffeta wing-bow. This mass of tied-up hair flapped against the girl's back as she walked, hence the term *flapper*, coined in the late 19th century to describe a girl teenager, a description enduring until the mid or late 1920s. On leaving school at sixteen to eighteen a girl would 'put her hair up' on top of her head. At the same time, her skirt length descended to the ankles (later, as adult skirts shortened, to mid-calf). These changes signalled her entry into womanhood and invitations to adult social functions would follow, but the process of growing up, for both boys and girls, was not regarded as complete until the twenty-first birthday, marked by a special celebration.

Until the late 1900s middle class girls up to about eleven years old wore miniature versions of adult corsets in dove sateen, reinforced with cording. From eleven or twelve, to give fashionable shape to the maturing figure, more sophisticated boned and laced styles were adopted. Vollers' catalogues of the 1900s show seven shilling 'maids' corsets' in French grey single coutil, shaped with whalebone and featuring a medium low bust, deep hips and just two front suspenders.

Then, around 1908 there appeared pliable 'corset bodices', of which the best known was the Liberty Bodice[25]. Both this and the Peter Pan bodice (named after Barrie's 1904 play) were close-fitting, easily-washable garments in dove coutil or knitted fabric, worn over the chemise or vest. They were designed, as the Liberty advertisements noted, 'to assist the graceful development of the body', though it is not clear how they achieved this. Early styles were buttoned down the front but around 1930 a slip-on version appeared. The bodice extended to just below waist level with complicated arrangements of buttons in sets above the hem, each having a designated purpose: one group for attaching stocking suspenders, another to hold up knickers and yet another to anchor the petticoat. In the quest to keep the Liberty Bodice soft and manageable for its young wearer, the tension of the suspenders worn with it was adjusted by a series of button positions instead of the usual metal slide. The whole concept proved a great success, remaining in general use for young girls until the late 1940s, although from the mid twenties it was increasingly seen as frumpish and old-fashioned by older girls. Around fourteen or so, from the 1930s onwards, these would demand the more up to date adult-style suspender belts with a suitable brassière, pointing out that friends had already made this advance towards maturity. Prices of Liberty Bodices 'in white and normal shades' ranged from about two shillings for the infants' size to four to five shillings for girls aged nine to seventeen, not increasing significantly between the 1900s and the late 1920s. Both Liberty and Peter Pan Bodices were made in adult sizes and were popular with those older women who, feeling no compulsion to follow fashion or consider the preferences of the male eye, happily reverted to the familiar and comfortable garment they had known in childhood.

Other underwear for girls tended to follow adult styles and arrangement although there was usually slightly less decoration. By the end of the 1920s unless school uniform was being worn, girls' legs were increasingly seen in ankle and three-quarter length socks instead of black lisle or silk stockings. However from around the age of twelve or thirteen, most girls were very eager to get into 'grown-up' stockings so that they could compete with their older sisters in the display of long shiny-silked legs.

Although the practice of allowing the hair to grow was still followed by some girls well into the 1930s, from the late 1910s many wore their hair quite short, often leaving it straight, perhaps with a forehead-concealing fringe. Hair thus 'bobbed' would be home-curled at the ends or 'Marcel' waved at the hairdressers for parties and other special occasions.

At the end of the 1920s young girls' dresses became less fussy, though the best quality ones showed distinctive style. In the middle of that decade little girls were offered smaller versions of the close-fitting adult cloche hats and one such in best velour, trimmed with ribbon, sold for three pounds in 1929, though there were cheaper versions at around one pound. Good quality tweed coats for girls were advertised in 1929 at six pounds, which, it should be remembered, was rather more than a week's pay for many senior office workers.

During the 1930s girls' dresses continued to display simple, easy-fitting lines but became more shapely, with a defined waist and full length skirts. Amongst the new designs of the period was a long button-through shirt-style dress which became so popular that it was to endure into the 1940s and 1950s. Top coats were also shaped to the figure in this decade, fastening high-up. They were trimmed with braid or had velvet collars and cuffs. As late as the 1940s there were no special teenage styles. At sixteen and even seventeen, larger versions of little girls' dresses with puff sleeves and bows, were normal wear, although for casual occasions, older girls were increasingly seen in jumpers and skirts. The transition in appearance on leaving school was more abrupt than now, bringing with it freedom to wear adult clothes other than jumpers and skirts, to use make-up and jewellery and choose hair styles. As with adults, middle class girls, from infant to school leaver, continued to wear gloves and hats outdoors. Many of the younger girls were still seen in soft leather gaiters coming well above the knee, especially in winter. During the 1930s and 1940s girls' hair styles were still short and straight, often with a forehead fringe, and as in the twenties, for those unblessed with natural curls, hair was only seen curled or waved on special occasions. Small round-crown hats with brims upturned, or turned down over the eyes, and berets were the most popular headwear in the 1930s and 1940s.

From the 1920s almost all middle class boys were seen in double-breasted jackets and all year round, wore matching short serge or flannel trousers which left knees bare above woollen socks patterned around their turned-down tops. Socks were kept up by garters of plain white or black elastic concealed under the turn-down. Outdoors, cricket-style peaked caps or soft grey dome-crowned felts with front brim turned down were usual, the former not often seen above the lower middles. It was not until the 1930s that middle class boys began to appear hatless and then as a rule only when on holiday or otherwise in casual clothes. At around age fourteen there was a long-awaited transition to long trousers, although white flannel versions were worn for cricket from eleven upwards. Some day school boys were so eager to display this new glory for admiration that they travelled to and from the sports fields in their new long whites rather than change in the pavilion. By the 1930s boys' shirts were invariably soft-collared although still frequently worn with ties, even when out of school uniform. Patterned long-sleeved wool pullovers (sometimes with a wool collar) covered shirts in all but the hottest weather and when

231

jackets were discarded, were retained to hide the ugly braces which were still necessary – trouser tops shaped to a boy's waist were not widely available, even in the 1930s. Itchy woollen vests with buttoned-necks and short-legged pants of the same material were the usual underwear, though exchanged for cotton garments of similar pattern in the warmest weather. In summer, both boys and girls wore openwork strapped leather sandals or light canvas and rubber lace-up plimsolls, sometimes without socks.

# School Uniform[26]

Great stress was laid by the middle class private schools on the finest details of uniform, especially those for girls, which offered more opportunities for complication. The county secondary schools followed eagerly in the rear and although many low-income parents of children at such schools found it hard to pay for it, they welcomed the effect uniform had of making all the children at a school look the same, disguising parents' financial status. For the school authorities and teachers, there were other considerations: a private school, by insisting on very expensive and elaborate uniforms purchased from a designated shop, could reinforce its exclusivity. And the wearing of uniform was also seen as a symbol of conformity, suppression of individuality and subservience to the school regime. Obliged to continue dressing in the same standard way right up to age eighteen or so, the older boys and girls were constantly reminded they were still *children*. The wearing of the uniform at all times had other advantages: it conveniently identified pupils when outside school premises, restraining any tendency to unbecoming or unruly behaviour; and finally, for girls, who were not normally subjected to the same degree of corporal punishment as boys, the complications of uniform and adherence to fussy uniform regulations provided a useful alternative means of chastisement and humiliation.

The privations of World War 2 brought no relaxation in the uniform cult. At a St. Albans secondary school, following the introduction of clothes rationing in 1941, the headmistress promptly addressed the girls, telling them they should be proud of their uniforms, which ought to have the first call on the precious coupons. Only when these had received their due, might they consider the purchase of other such items of clothing as the residue allowed. However wartime shortages did bring about one change for girls, forcing most schools to agree to the substitution of white socks for the hitherto almost universal black or brown full-length stockings. Contrary to general expectation, this became a permanent feature at most schools after the war.

232

Except at those more eminent and ancient public schools (such as Christ's Hospital) which treasured eccentric traditional dress requirements, boys' uniforms, which did not change greatly between the 1900s and 1940s, usually consisted of a serge or flannel jacket or badged blazer (sometimes edged with coloured piping) and short trousers (longs for older boys), with tie in school colours and peaked cap with school badge. Grey was quite the most popular hue for shirts, socks, suiting and caps, especially from the 1920s on. The pattern and type of the shirt would frequently be prescribed and for the privately-financed public and preparatory schools there would be lengthy lists of specified underwear and footwear. At some schools, boys wore straw boaters all year round, at others only in summer. In summer, a blazer, with school badge, would be worn over a white open neck shirt, with white trousers, for cricket, rowing or other sports. Special types of shirts and shorts would usually be required for gymnastics and football. Underwear followed the general pattern already described.

As with boys, there were a few long-established girls' schools with a traditional uniform, but for the majority of schools, the concept of a uniform for girls arose from the simple need to find something more flexible than the tight-fitting, elaborate and corseted fashions of the late 19th and early 20th century for gymnastics and organised games. In a curious way schoolgirls thus became pioneers of 'rational dress' for women. By the early 1900s the pupils of the largely middle class North London Collegiate School for Ladies were wearing regulation white blouses, mid-calf length skirts, ties, belts and shoes for lessons as well as games and gym. Other schools adopted tunics of knee length worn over knickers or knickerbockers and tam o' shanters or straw boaters as headgear worn with cloaks for outdoors. At Roedean, the girls were equipped with sailor-neck blouses and skirts with a wide braid trim, later replaced with a standard dress and enveloping cloak. But the most widely-adopted uniform was the mid-calf or even three-quarter length drill or gymnasium tunic or slip, in dark blue or grey, worn over a white shirt or blouse and long-legged baggy navy blue knickers. The latter had handkerchief pockets and finished at the knee in elasticated or button-tab cuffs which concealed the tops of drab black wool or lisle stockings. Introduced around 1890 and at first confined to drill, gymnastics and games, this outfit had by the 1910s become the standard all-day uniform at many middle class girls' schools. When at drill or gymnastics, the girls discarded the slip, tucking their shirts into the knickers, thus achieving even greater freedom of movement. Gym-slip and shirt were to endure as a widely-used uniform style for fifty years, virtually universal in council secondaries, although some private schools retained simple belted tunic frocks of various kinds.

From the 1910s, the gym (or drill) slip, now usually in box-pleated serge, was most often navy blue in colour, but by the 1930s bottle green, grey, maroon or brown were introduced by some private schools. Displaying the school or house badge just below the neck, the slip or tunic (both words were used) fell straight down from the yoke without shape until held at the waist by a tied braid sash. But not always at the waist; in an interesting variation which reflected contemporary middle class attitudes to sexuality, many schools insisted the sash be tied at hip level, thus partly concealing the curves of the growing girl in the baggy upper folds. Prefects wore a striped sash in house colours and were also often identified by a special badge. Since they were invariably obliged to wear the standard uniform, the older girls, apart from their height, and pleats of the slip forced slightly open by maturing breasts, looked no different from the juniors. Hems rose above the knee in the mid twenties, reflecting contemporary adult styles. This required the knickers to be redesigned with shorter, closer-cut legs and the stockings to be made longer. A 1925 advertisement refers to the 'long gym stockings now being worn', offering these in black at mid-thigh length for 3s10½d a pair. It is interesting that the new shorter skirt length (the largest size generally available measured only 39 inches (99 cm) from shoulders to hem) was still maintained for school uniforms after women's hemlines dropped to mid-calf around 1930. Whether this was because the short skirt was seen as more practical for school life or whether it was considered too much trouble for all concerned to make further changes is not clear. In these matters as in others, the private schools set the trend and the rest followed.

Beneath her gym slip, the schoolgirl wore a long-sleeved white poplin or wincyette shirt-blouse with a square neck or turn down collar, the latter held at the neck by a tie in the school colours. Her underwear consisted of regulation vest, Liberty or Peter Pan bodice and regulation pattern interlock gym knickers of the same hue as the slip, these covering stocking tops and suspenders. Inside them were flimsy white cotton 'linings', worn for reasons of hygiene. Handkerchieves were kept in a pocket in the knickers but any inadvertent display of bare thigh above the stocking induced when seeking them, or in some other way, was regarded as mildly improper and castigated by mistresses and other schoolgirls as 'showing a smile'. At some schools, to avoid such embarrassment on special occasions like gymnastic displays, the tops of the stockings were sewn to the knickers, thus anticipating modern tights. Stockings were black, grey or brown lisle or cashmere, to match the uniform, wool in winter, lisle in summer, and until around 1930 were worn at all times, even for physical training and organised games. They were held up by the button-adjusted suspenders of the Liberty Bodice although, from the late 1920s, older girls would wear the more stylish adult satin-elastic suspenderbelts, should school discipline permit such outrageous liberties.

A cardigan and serge or reefer overcoat or cloak covered this uniform in winter, a flannel blazer, single or double breasted, with school badge, in summer. Shoes were flat-heeled lace-ups, usually at least three pairs, one for walking out, 'house shoes' for wear inside the school buildings and soft shoes for gymnastics. Another item insisted upon by most schools was a raincoat and hood or sou'wester. In the more exclusive establishments, girls also had blazers, white gloves and tan silk stockings for special occasions and Sunday walking-out. The hat, in the same shade as the gymslip, was most usually a round-topped felt with brim turned up all round breton style, or pressed down in front. It carried a band in the school colours, perhaps showing the school badge at the front. In summer term girls often wore a panama or straw boater with ribbon in school colours. Berets or gabardine storm caps were decreed for cycling, the latter also for wet weather wear. In addition to the normal uniform, there would be dresses for Greek dancing, tennis skirts, and special items for other games and activities. On average in the 1920s and 1930s it would cost two to three weeks' salary for a senior clerk – ten to fifteen pounds – to fully kit out a girl in all the items described, rather more at the most exclusive schools. After that there followed regular outlay on renewals and the inevitable progress through ever larger (and more expensive) sizes. Often no economies were possible by buying lower-quality items, since most schools insisted on parents using an approved, and usually expensive, firm of outfitters. A typical clothing list for a small private girls' boarding school in Surrey is given at Appendix C; as well as providing some impression of the cost involved, this affords some clues as to the exclusively middle class nature of such establishments, and their privations.

Uniform regulations were often very strictly enforced, both for boys and girls. At boys' schools, minor infringements could stimulate bullying and sometimes sadistic punishment from older boys invested with a measure of authority. Schools, even the most humble county secondaries, would insist that headwear be worn out of doors at all times and there existed such pettiness as not showing hair below the cap peak (vide John Betjeman on Marlborough in his *Summoned by Bells*).

Girls were required to wear their hair either in plaits or (in the 1920s) 'earphones' if long, otherwise it had to be cut short above the collar. Braid girdles around gymslips sometimes had to be knotted in a special way so that the ends hung from the same place to exactly equal length. Any form of make-up, lipstick or jewellery was strictly forbidden, inside and outside school premises. Pupils at a Hertfordshire County Council secondary school were told in 1940 by their headmistress that she would refuse to speak ever again to 'any of my girls seen wearing lipstick in the street'. Eating in the street was also treated as a serious offence. Hem levels of gym tunic were the subject of particular attention; they frequently had to be a set distance from the floor when kneeling, usually four inches (10cm) after the shorter skirts were introduced in the mid-twenties. Regular uniform inspections were held at many schools, especially at the start of term. During these a mistress or prefect would check the skirt lengths of the kneeling girls with a ruler. At one convent school in South London in the 1920s a pair of scissors was also carried and if any skirt were found too short, the stitching of the hem would be ripped out there and then and the material tugged down in a ragged array to render the culprit what the nuns called 'decent'. Big girls, growing fast out of their uniforms, would understandably be reduced to blushing and even tears by such deliberate public humiliation. At other private schools, girls were made to stand on their desks whilst a mistress or the matron walked round checking their skirt length and peering up at their underwear to make sure all was neat and conforming to regulations.

By the early 1930s there were some concessions. Many schools began to allow a simple standard pattern button-through gingham dress instead of the gym slip in summer term. With this went lighter and briefer open-leg panties and tan lisle, rayon or pure silk stockings but the old style knickers and the white shirt were retained for physical training. Sometimes the younger girls were allowed to wear white socks with such summer dresses, or even with the winter gymslips, but at one Surrey independent secondary school, when this concession was sought by junior girls, the reply was, 'willingly; if you are prepared to wear your dresses down to your shoes'.

So were the young subdued.

## NOTES

1. *Transport & Travel Monthly*, April, 1920.
2. On what could be afforded at various income levels, see Chapter 2.
3. In 1938, annual boarders' fees at some of the more eminent public

schools were (day pupils' fees in brackets where applicable): Eton £245, Harrow £216 (£90), Repton (£177, Cheltenham £174 (£66), Westminster £160 (£75), King's Canterbury £150 (£60), St. Paul's £144 (£45), Merchant Taylor's £135 (£45).

4. In 1926 a Conservative Government provided Exchequer grants for certain independent secondary schools, effectively providing a state subsidy to schools which catered almost exclusively for the middle class and which continued to enjoy the social cachet of not being operated by local authorities. Such schools, which included the GPDS, then became known as 'direct grant' schools.

5. The situation described in this paragraph was slightly different in Scotland where, until the early 1920s, the publicly-financed system produced a high percentage of secondary school places and it was much easier than in England & Wales for a bright child from a low income household to obtain secondary education. However after 1923 there was a division into junior and senior secondary schools for all children at and over age twelve, the senior schools concentrating on academic education. This created a sharper social segregation, with the latter type of secondary school largely filled with middle class and lower middle class children.

6. Masterman, C. F. G., *The Condition of England*, (1909).

7. Lowndes, G. A. N., *The Silent Social Revolution: An Account of the Expansion of Public Education in England & Wales 1895–1965*, (1969).

8. Prospectus of a Middlesex County Council Secondary School, 1935.

9. The dominance of the General Schools/matriculation objective compared with other types of examination success is demonstrated by the results of this school over the twenty six years 1910–35, printed in the same prospectus:

| | |
|---|---|
| University Scholarships | |
| (Oxford 2, Cambridge 6, London 28, Durham 1) | 37 |
| State Scholarships | 10 |
| Royal Scholarships | 7 |
| Royal Exhibitions | 2 |
| Higher School Examination (University of London) | 95 |
| Intermediate Science " " | 70 |
| Intermediate Engineering " " | 5 |
| Intermediate Arts " " | 45 |
| Intermediate Commerce " " | 8 |
| Matriculation " " | 704 |
| General Schools " " | 551 |

10. For some interesting views on the education of middle class girls in the inter-war period, including this comment, see Newsom, John, *The Education of Girls*, (1948).

11. Masterman, op cit (note 6).

12. Masterman, op cit, (note 6).
13. This black-faced doll was invented by Florence K.Upton, whose first Gollywog book appeared in 1895. Teddy Bears, named after the USA president Theodore Roosevelt (not King Edward VII as some English children thought), first appeared in 1907 and quickly became popular in middle class homes.
14. Household, Humphrey, *With the LNER in The Twenties*, (1985).
15. *Gamages' Christmas Bazaar, 1913*, facsimile reprint of catalogue, with introduction by Aldburgham, Alison, (1974).
16. For a discussion of the social roots of lower middle class patriotism and jingoism in the early years of the twentieth century, see Price, Richard N., in Crossick, Geoffrey (ed.) *The Lower Middle Class in Britain 1870–1914*, (1977).
17. Smith, Joanna, *Edwardian Children*, (1983).
18. The militaristic aspects and background of the Scout Movement are considered by Springhall, J. O., in 'The Boy Scouts, Class and Militarism in Relation to British Youth Movements 1908–1930', *International Review of Social History* XVI, 1971, Part 2.
19. Springhall, op cit, (note 18).
20. See note 16.
21. Macandrew, Rennie, *Friendship, Love Affairs and Marriage* (nd but c1938).
22. Whiteing, Eileen, *Anyone for Tennis?*, 1979.
23. Peel, Mrs, C. S., *Life's Enchanted Cup: An Autobiography 1872–1933*, (1933).
24. Most of the detail in this section is taken from contemporary newspaper and magazine advertisements and photographs.
25. The Liberty Bodice was invented by F. Cox of R. & W. H. Symington & Co., Market Harborough, in 1908. See Page, Christopher, *Foundations of Fashion*, (1981), from which some of the information in this paragraph is taken.
26. The author is indebted to his wife and two other ladies who provided the details of school uniform and uniform discipline in the 1920s and 1930s used in this section. Prices and other information are taken from contemporary advertising and illustrations.

CHAPTER 9

# UP TO TOWN

By 1900 the homes and workplaces of most urban middle class breadwinners were well-separated, requiring daily outward and return journeys sometimes of considerable length, mostly by train. Travel along the same axis by other members of the household, normally for pleasure purposes, was also frequent. This large scale suburban and extra-urban settlement of the middle class was further facilitated by the very rapid development in public transport which took place in the first two decades of the present century, a period which saw the electrification of street tramways and some urban railways, the construction of new electrically-worked underground railways in London and the arrival of the motor bus. At the same time, in an attempt to compensate for loss of inner area revenue to these new modes, the railway companies sought to extend and improve their steam-hauled outer suburban and extra-urban commuter services.

In the years immediately before 1914 it was thus becoming easier for the wealthier middle class business or professional man to choose a very attractive rural or seaside home, since many such locations were now within an hour or so by train of the urban workplace. This process was greatly accelerated between the wars by further railway improvements, notably the electrification of the Southern Railway in Surrey, West Kent, East Hampshire and much of Sussex. By this time the more fortunate members of the middle class were able to live deep in the country or at almost any point on a suitable stretch of coast, perhaps at some distance from their commuting railway station, which they could reach quickly in their private car. Season ticket rates for long distance commuters were low; a pound a week would cover the cost of First Class travel between London and the south coast, a rate which for six return journeys a week came out as three miles for one penny (1d), at a time when the normal standard or Third Class ordinary ticket rate was over a penny a mile. Even at this period, when the roads were relatively lightly-used, it was wearisome to drive a car twice daily over such distances, ending or beginning with a long and dreary crawl through London and its suburbs. First Class rail travel was a much more attractive alternative. To a lesser extent railway electrification north of the Thames and in the outskirts of Liverpool, Manchester and Newcastle had a similar effect but more important, so far as areas north of London and around the great provincial cities were concerned were the improvements made to steam railway services, often with new and more comfortable rolling stock, serving places far from the urban centres.

Even before 1914 the more prosperous London businessmen were buying houses at locations over ten miles from the centre such as Surbiton, Guildford, Haslemere, Epsom, Ashtead, Purley, Chislehurst, Caterham, Bromley, Pinner, Harpenden, Gerrards Cross, Chorley Wood, Bushey and Gidea Park, all of which had excellent rail services. Seaside resorts like Southend, Herne Bay and Brighton also housed some London commuters by this time. After 1920, as just mentioned, the more affluent middle class scattered their homes far and wide around south east England whilst most of the rest settled in the new suburbs being built at a rapid rate in outer London itself.

Thanks to the rail services offered, comfortably-off middle class Manchester men were able to set up homes at Alderley Edge, Didsbury and Wilmslow, or even further afield, at Southport, Lytham St. Annes, Blackpool, the North Wales seaside and Windermere, leaving the villas of Cheetham Hill, Whalley Range, Chorlton-cum-Hardy, Fallowfield and Withington to the less prosperous. Middle class Liverpool dwelt pleasantly enough at Ainsdale, Formby, Southport and West Derby, whilst others chose the Wirral Peninsula, or the North Wales resorts. Their Leeds and Woollen Towns peers were found in Headingley, Harrogate, Ilkley or Wetherby. Birmingham's middle class settled in Stratford-upon-Avon, Solihull, Sutton Coldfield, Lichfield, Knowle or Edgbaston, according to their means. Between the wars, this city developed a small reflection of London's semi-detached suburbia along the Great Western Railway to the south as far as Shirley and Dorridge. Middle class Newcastle bought salubrious homes to the north of the city and at Whitley Bay; Hull's businessmen dwelt at Filey, Withernsea, Hornsea, Beverley and Cottingham, Nottingham's at Wollaton, West Bridgford and Mapperley Park, Bristol's at Clifton, Cotham, Redland and Bath. Alsager was a favourite refuge for the Potteries middle class. From most of the places mentioned, the breadwinners travelled daily to work by rail but a few of the wealthiest began using motor cars from the mid 1920s.

In practice, even in the congested London area, middle class rail commuting was by no means always the 'cattle truck' ordeal so fondly nurtured by hack journalists, whilst peak hour journeys in and out of the provincial cities and towns were normally accomplished without difficulty or stress. Although commuting could hardly be regarded as the most comfortable hour or so in the daily round of the London office junior or typist, most of these had robust spirits and constitutions which allowed them to treat its trials and crushes lightly. Those with seniority and position were usually not required to attend before 9.30 am or later, by which time the worst of the crowding was over (in the 1900s and 1910s, the Waterloo & City Tube railway carried most of its passengers to the City between 9.20 and 10.00 am). Experienced commuters unable to avoid the peak times learned to ease their journey by using the less crowded rear of the trains, or, as their income rose, bought space with a Second or First Class ticket. Train time would then be occupied with the newspaper or a book, completing a crossword, or in convivial conversation with regular and chosen travelling companions. Thus we read in *The Ilford Recorder* of 6 March 1903 of 'The 8.52 Social', a group of a dozen men travelling to London daily on this train in the same compartment and meeting regularly for supper and entertainment in a local public house. As at the middle class breakfast table, talking in the morning train was sometimes discouraged. Between Harrogate and Leeds, a group of regular rail travellers in the 1910s imposed a fine of a half-a-crown (2s6d) on the first to speak each day, financing an excellent annual dinner from the proceeds. On the Brighton to London line in the 1910s and 1920s, eight daily users of the all-First Class 8.45am *City Limited* (non stop to London Bridge), sitting in the same compartment each day, followed an accepted procedure: after an initial 'Good Morning' no conversation was allowed for the first part of the journey so that newspapers and stock market reports could be adequately absorbed. At Earlswood, approximately halfway, where the windows of the compartment could be opened if the weather permited, social contact was re-established. *The City Limited*, the prestige commuter train out of Brighton, was exclusively First Class until 1926, when a new train offering a high ratio of First Class seats (312:192) was introduced. In the spring of that year one of the First Class coaches was replaced by a First Class Pullman car, *Princess Patricia*, in which breakfasts were served. Tea could be had on the corresponding Down train, the 5pm from London Bridge. With electrification in 1933, special stock was again provided for this train, still with a very high portion of First Class seats (276:244). Departures from Brighton earlier in the day had nicknames which reflected social graduation: the 7.35am was known as the *Office Boys'* and the 8.05 *The Managing Clerks'*.

For those with sufficient income to live some distance out from the large cities, life could be pleasant indeed. Barron, no friend of the railways, wrote in 1929, 'An hour, or perhaps one hour and twenty minutes, in a corridor express with buffet car attached may be a restful pause between business cares of the day and the healthful outdoor recreations of summer evenings spent by the sea or in the country'[1]. Such longer-distance trains were not overcrowded, especially in the First Class accommodation, and travel on them to and from town was civilised and relaxing compared with the stressful motorway commuting practised by many coast and country-dwelling businessmen today.

Some middle class rail commuters were especially pampered. Between 1910 and 1939, residents along the Metropolitan Railway between Aylesbury and the City of London not needing to be in their offices until around 10 a.m. were able to make use of a Pullman car right into the very centre of the City. For a supplementary fare of one shilling (sixpence inwards from Rickmansworth) they enjoyed comfortably-upholstered individual armchairs, most of them at glass-topped tables, in a saloon panelled in oak or mahogany, bathed in soft light from 'electric lamps of chased design'. Indolent pressure on a finely-chased ormolu bell-push brought to their side an attendant ready to serve a full breakfast, alcoholic refreshment, a light snack, or a hot drink. A coupé compartment fitted with 'specially-woven green damask blinds' secured extra privacy for confidential business conversations or discreet entertainment of lady friends[2]. From the 1920s, similar Pullman cars were attached to business hour trains operating between London and the Sussex or Kent coast, again enabling breakfast to be taken on the journey to town.

Pioneer long distance commuters often enjoyed special facilities. Some 200 Second Class season ticket holders from stations between Ramsgate and Faversham, paying £6.16s5d a quarter for this long journey, organised themselves as early as 1911 into 'The Association of Regular Kent Coasters', persuading the South Eastern & Chatham Railway to reserve them special compartments on the 7.55 am Up and 5.10 pm Down daily. By 1914 they were enjoying reserved saloon coaches on three principal Up trains and two Down trains together with some reserved compartments. Their special coaches were fitted with tables used for the card games which were a regular feature of the daily journeys. The Association arranged sports and inter-town billiards tournaments as well as an annual dinner presided over by its barrister chairman. After deductions for expenses, the surplus arising from the annual subscription of five shillings was distributed in gratuities to the train crews and donations to the Railwaymen's Convalescent Home at Herne Bay. By pitching the subscription at a comparatively high level, it was possible to exclude from membership fellow members of the middle class, described contemptuously as 'the casual summer passenger who takes out a monthly season ticket'.

Reviewing this development in *The Railway Magazine* of July 1914, one of the members confessed he had been concerned as to whether travelling 1,068 miles a week by train imposed a nervous strain which more than neutralised the undoubted advantages 'gained by residence in the free air of the open coast'. However his doctor had advised him he had nothing to fear and he was able to conclude, 'Thanks to the Association, the four hours spent daily on the train have become not the least pleasurable part of the daily routine, and occupied as they are in comfort and companionship, seem no longer than the lonely minutes of pariah-like isolation from some dingy suburb.'

But perhaps the ultimate in rail commuting comfort, were the businessmen's Club Cars[3]. In 1895, partly because they wished to segregate themselves from largely working class holiday trippers on the eighty minute journey between Manchester and the Fylde Coast towns, commuters formed the Lytham St Annes and Blackpool Travelling Club (the order of words in the title is not without significance). Guaranteeing a minimum membership of forty (later raised to fifty), who would be willing to pay a premium above the £31.12s annual First Class season ticket rate, they persuaded the Lancashire & Yorkshire Railway Company to provide three special saloons for their use. One of these was placed in each of the three morning business trains from Blackpool to Manchester and in the return runs each evening. A janitor employed by the Club made sure that no strangers boarded the cars (even members' guests were barred) and that all windows were kept firmly closed against the chill northern air. Refreshments were served by a railway company steward and there was a barber on board to shave the members' overnight stubble and trim their hair, a useful time saver. Each member had his personal padded armchair and spittoon, the latter a feature which tended to give the lie to the famous notice in Paisley tramcars: *Gentlemen will not spit; others must not*. Smokers, not universally popular in all-male circles even at this time, were confined to a separate closed section of the cars. This Club was still thriving in 1935 when the London Midland & Scottish Railway Company built it a new car, a luxurious vehicle fitted with armchair seating, tables, and a small kitchen for the service of refreshments.

There were similar facilities elsewhere. From 1 November 1907, the London & North Western Railway provided two saloons for the Travelling Club operating between Llandudno, Colwyn Bay, Rhyl, Prestatyn and Manchester. Members paid two guineas (£2.10s) above the quarterly First Class season ticket rate in return for travel in electrically-lit, steam-heated cars panelled in mahogany with tulip wood inlays and furnished with wicker and divan easy chairs, tables and upholstered armchairs. A uniformed attendant served light refreshments and kept out strangers. Club members were given keys to a personal locker on the car. In 1910 two of this Club's cars, connected by a central gangway, were included in the 8.10 am from Llandudno, which reached Manchester two hours later. In the evening, the return train, the 4.55 pm, arrived at Llandudno at 6.42. A similar Club Car train ran between Windermere and Manchester, another journey of two hours or so, and from 1919 there was one between Llandudno and Liverpool. Club cars were also operated for commuters between Filey, Withernsea and Hull and between Southport and Manchester at various periods. Southport was an important source of valuable middle class commuter traffic for the railways right through to the 1940s; in the 1930s the 8.30 am departure from that town to Manchester consisted of nine First Class cars, with a mere two Third Class coaches, one at each end[4].

Wartime travelling constraints caused the withdrawal of all the Club Car facilities. Although some were revived with the return of peace, all had disappeared by 1966, by which time road improvements at the taxpayers' expense and the new subsidised perk of 'company cars' were beginning to tempt at least some of these prosperous commuters to a much more stressful, if more convenient alternative.

Except where they ran for some distance through middle class areas (as did the London United in metropolitan Surrey), electric street tramways did not prove very attractive to the white collar worker and his family. In most cities anyone venturing on to a tramcar would most likely find themselves, at least for part of the journey, rubbing shoulders with the Great Unwashed, many smoking strong shag and spitting freely, or if not, the aftermath of such patronage. One tramway authority, seeking to maximise its revenue, decided to meet this problem by providing First Class cars. In Liverpool up to sixty eight such cars were operated, each finished in two shades of cream with elaborate gold, red and blue lining-out, and furnished with blue plush seating, coir carpets, curtains and cut glass lamp bowls. Introduced in 1908, they survived until 1923 when they succumbed to economic pressure for more intensive fleet utilisation and the competition of the more comfortable motor buses which by then served those middle class suburbs without convenient rail access to the city centre.

## Town Treats for Ladies

A middle class lady suffering from depression was once advised by her somewhat desperate doctor to make regular rail journeys, each time to

244

a different town, where she was directed to spend the time agreeably, looking at the shops, taking a meal or two and crowning the day by the purchase of a new hat or some other luxury item. This she did, with apparent benefit. From the 1910s onwards such morale-raising expeditions were certainly a feature of the life of the ladies of the middle class suburban or extra-urban families, although their destination was normally confined to the nearest large city or town, where they would indulge in some shopping, visit the cinema, change books at Boots' Library and take afternoon tea. Some railway companies set out to encourage this business by arranging special facilities. In June 1912, *The Railway Magazine* reported that 'so many ladies are now regularly in the habit of going from the suburbs to "shop" in town' that the London Brighton & South Coast Railway had offered a fifty per cent reduction on season tickets taken out by the wives of season ticket holders. The Metropolitan and Great Eastern Railways followed with a similar concession later in 1912, stipulating that travel should not start before the end of the morning rush period. The Metropolitan Railway also issued day shopping tickets at reduced First Class fares between 10.30 a.m. and 4 p.m. Later, in the 1920s and 1930s, there were many examples of cheap day return facilities in the off-peak period, both First and Third Class, to stimulate this type of travel. These were so inexpensive that on the Southern Railway, during Ascot Week, lower middle class suburban ladies would journey up to Waterloo simply to stand and stare at the fine dresses and hats of the wealthy as they took trains to the race course.

The trend observed by *The Railway Magazine* in the summer of 1912 was a clear response to the efforts of the burgeoning service sector to attract the middle classes. Although department stores had their origins in the mid-19th century, expanding rapidly in the final three decades, their development did not reach its peak until the early 20th century, a period when much rebuilding took place and which saw a most impressive and influential newcomer.

The great Selfridge store, with its 1,800 staff and eye-catching window displays brilliantly lit until midnight, graced London's Oxford Street from March 1909. This stone-faced, steel-framed building in extrovert North American neo-classical style, with its vast interior spaces was something new for Britain. Selfridge aimed to attract the women of the middle classes and one of the early advertisements dedicated the new store to 'the Service of Women'. He spoke of his enterprise as a social centre rather than a shop. It included an information bureau, writing, reading and rest rooms, a restaurant and even a post office, but efforts to secure a special Selfridge's tube station and public telephone exchange failed. In accordance with the US practice in which its owner was well-experienced, initial publicity expenditure reached more than one third of the value of the opening stock. The venture proved a success, so much so that within a few years of World War 1 the store, which was imitated elsewhere in London and in the provincial cities, was much enlarged. 'Why not spend a day at Selfridge's?' suggested the advertisements, and although few were likely to go so far, it is certain that the majority of middle class women on a shopping trip to town would ensure they gave it at least a couple of hours.

Selfridge did not have the field to himself in developing middle class retailing techniques and facilities. When Debenham & Freebody rebuilt their nearby Wigmore Street premises in 1908–09 to the designs of the architects James Gibson and William Wallace, the result was a vast baroque palace faced externally in creamy Doulton tiles. Within, amenities included a 'quiet, elegant restaurant' which had a smoking room and gentleman's cloakroom attached. For the middle class lady visitor, there was a 'luxuriously-appointed suite of Ladies' Dressing and Retiring Rooms' which must surely have appealed to that special liking for privacy at more intimate moments. Here was a set of completely private individual retreats each one equipped with individual dressing table and mirror, marble wash basin and mahogany-seated 'Cavendish' w.c. pan[5], altogether a most agreeable alternative to the spartan public lavatory with its imagined perils.

During 1911 Harrods completed the rebuilding of their enlarged Knightsbridge store in pinky-buff terracotta. The interior featured such delights as an Arts & Crafts style Meat Hall decorated with hunting scenes and a 'Ladies Club' where the pampered female middle class clientele might meet friends and take tea. This 'Club' was furnished in Adam style with figured satinwood, its chairs upholstered in green corded silk, taste-fully decorated with appliqué embroidery. Sensitive to their customers' preferences and needs, the designers included Ladies' Retiring Rooms of some luxury: 'nicely fitted out, the effect in marble being admirable. The windows are of stained cathedral glass while the walls are covered throughout with panelled Brecchi Sanguine Parannazi Levantine marble and onyx panels. . .'[6]. Although few approached the West End standards of sumptuous luxury and layout, most new and rebuilt department stores in suburban London and the provinces after 1905 featured capacious restaurants serving dainty meals, and well-appointed powder and rest rooms all designed to restore the energies of their lady visitors for a second bout of shopping before returning home.

These magnificent early twentieth century department stores with their bright, exciting atmosphere, through which the shopper could roam freely, unmolested by the traditional British shopwalker or over-eager assistants, were a major objective of the middle class lady spending a day 'in town'. She had no problems about carrying purchases, since anything bought, large or small, would be delivered without charge, distance no object. If unable to make a personal visit, she had only to consult the free and bulky catalogues regularly despatched to her home and the goods required would be sent in response to a telephone call. The cost of all these services was of course built into the prices charged, but this was tolerable in an era of very cheap labour.

To ensure that middle and upper class customers received the most courteous treatment, these stores took great care in recruiting sales staff. Should any employee upset a customer, the result might well be instant dismissal without a reference. As late as the 1940s, Harrods confined recruitment of sales girls to lower middle class candidates by insisting on a good secondary school education up to Matriculation standard. There was no shortage of suitable girls, attracted as they were by promises of future training for management or as a buyer. By adopting this policy, the administration secured considerable assurance that customers would be handled tactfully, sympathetically and intelligently.

Whilst Selfridges, Harrods and the other large West End stores and their opposite numbers in the large provincial centres were very largely middle class in tone and clientele, the upper and working classes having their own retail facilities, the main stores in smaller towns had of course to cater for all social classes if they were to remain profitable. Thus in the 1930s, W. E. White, drapers, milliners and outfitters of Guildford, would dress their windows twice on Saturdays; in the morning to attract the middle class trade, and in the afternoon and evening for their working class customers.[7] At nearby Kingston-on-Thames, however, the expensively-rebuilt Bentall store of 1935 had a catchment area which supplied a predominantly middle class clientele drawn from the newly-built suburbs of north east Surrey. Here, at the afternoon tea hour, wives of mortgage-payers were entertained in the Tudor Restaurant by Albert Sandler's BBC orchestra.

Another feature of middle class urban social life, in this case shared with the upper class, was the club. Men's clubs offering facilities for members of the same profession, interests, or political beliefs to gather for relaxation, conversation or refreshment and often equipped with bedrooms and serving as a convenient *pied à terre*, were of course a long-established upper and middle class institution, principally found in London's West End. Much more novel were the similar clubs catering exclusively for women, of which some twenty had been established in central London by 1914, many new since 1901. About the same number survived to the 1940s. Opinions on this innovation differed: in her *Manners For Women*, published when these clubs were first appearing, Mrs Humphry recommended joining one, since it provided opportunities to converse with other ladies of 'culture and distinction', but Queen Victoria apparently considered them hotbeds of idleness and mischief. If playing cards is idleness, then the royal view was fair comment, since, as we have already noted, bridge was a favourite pastime within their walls.

## A Great Middle Class Institution

Unescorted visits 'to town' were further encouraged by teashops and restaurants which offered secure and respectable sanctuary for the middle class woman. These spread very rapidly in the first two decades of the century, notably in London. Messrs. Fuller, the Aërated Bread Company (ABC) and later the Express Dairy established many branches and were among the most enduring. In 1911, between midday and 3 pm, the Cottage Tea Rooms in London's Piccadilly, Regent Street, the Strand, the Old Jewry would provide a 1s6d luncheon consisting of soup, lobster mayonnaise or mutton cutlet or Madras curry or roast beef (all with two vegetables); French pancakes or apple pudding or Welsh rarebit; and cheese. Later in the afternoon, tea could be had for sixpence or a shilling. The usual charge for a table d'hôte dinner at a middle-grade West End restaurant at this time was 2s6d or three shillings.

But the real leader in popular middle class catering was undisputedly, J. Lyons & Co., founded by Joseph Lyons and Montagu Gluckstein in the late 1880s and registered as a public company in 1894. Their first teashop, opened in September that year on the south side of Piccadilly, near Piccadilly Circus, was followed by many more, in London and in towns and cities all over England, each readily recognisable by its fascia of raised gold lettering on a white ground. Popular with lower middle class office workers at lunchtimes and before and after the cinema or theatre, these shops, which served light refreshments and meals from early morning until late in the evening, could always be relied upon to provide a cup of tea of consistently high quality, properly and freshly brewed, together with many other beverages, such as hot milk with a 'dash' of coffee, a firm favourite with older children. Often on two, sometimes three floors, frontages were sometimes very narrow to reduce rents in expensive locations. Customers sat at marble-topped tables where they were courteously served by waitresses officially designated 'Nippies' from

January 1925 after a competition to suggest a name. These girls wore a smart derivation of the parlourmaid's afternoon uniform described earlier; a black and white headband or cap, front-buttoned black dress with white collar and cuffs, a white apron, black lisle or rayon stockings and black low-heeled shoes. A bill-pad and pencil dropped on a chain from the waist belt. Strict supervision was exercised by Lyons' manageresses, who evinced the special enthusiasm of those promoted from the ranks; any serious complaint by a customer or a manageress could result in a Nippy losing a job which could be filled without difficulty.

It was not long before Lyons were looking to further fields of development. In October 1904 the firm inaugurated a 'Popular Café' at the Church Place corner on the south side of Piccadilly. Designed by C. W. Oakley, this represented a new departure in catering, described by contemporary publicity as 'luxury for the million at popular prices' and providing a *table d'hôte* dinner to the music of a live orchestra for half a crown (2s6d). In 1916 a similar establishment was opened in Oxford Street as 'Maison Lyons', this time designed by Lewis Salomons & Sons. It boasted four large public rooms, one at each level from basement to second floor. With its Dixieland Band, London's 'Maison Lyons' was well-timed to profit from the West End's wartime retail and entertainment boom. It lasted until 22 October 1933 when the site was redeveloped for the Lilley & Skinner shoe store. By that time Lyons had something bigger and better just up the street at Marble Arch.

These two restaurants were the prototypes of a new venture, the Lyons' Corner Houses, establishments described by one 1920s writer as:

> . . . an elaborate and sumptuous development of the tea-shop, enhanced by the attraction of music and with an atmosphere that is peculiarly their own. . . Not even New York has anything that is comparable with the Corner House, which is the Café Royal of the great English middle class. Here one can obtain anything from a cup of tea and a bun, or a bottle of beer and a sandwich to an epicurean repast of several courses, all at remarkably reasonable prices and in the cheerfullest of environment.[8]

Open throughout the twenty four hours, the Corner Houses[9] were sustained by the huge pool of willing and cheap service labour then available. Each included several large and stylish restaurants in which Nippies and (in their basement *brasseries*) aproned male waiters served a vast range of inexpensive food and drink in a pleasant and informal environment against the background of virtually continuous live music. Until 1939 a Corner House three-course lunch could be had for as little as 1s6d, to which the customer might add a generous twopenny tip for the

249

service. Much of the ground floor area was taken up with retail counters selling confectionery, bread, cakes, pastries, biscuits and delicatessen, most of it coming from Lyon's own Hammersmith and Greenford factories or food preparation rooms in the Corner House itself. Flowers and fruit were also sold and there was a telephone bureau with girls waiting to obtain any number required. Customers could book theatre seats or secure a District Messenger to carry a parcel or note.

Several generations of middle class parents, grandparents, aunts and uncles took children to the Corner Houses for their first experience of eating-out. Between 1929 and 1937, a visit to one was an essential element in the author's annual pantomime and Bertram Mills' Circus excursions in the company of an aunt and several of her friends with their nieces and nephews; they made a lasting impression. The reaction of a child was well expressed in a broadcast by Rabbi Lionel Blue when he recalled, with enthusiasm, that 'Going into them was for me like going into the Gates of Paradise'[10]. Certainly at busy times one often had to queue for Paradise but it was always worth the wait; the crowds were invariably patient and good-humoured, with unquestioning faith in the fairness of the marshalling porters and busy little men at the restaurant doors whose task it was to direct them to vacated tables. For the lower middle class youth treating a girlfriend to an evening 'Up West', Corner Houses were a godsend. Their affordable luxury and efficient service generated a immediate enhancement of mood, contrasting greatly with the drab surroundings and dull routine of their daily toil. We can see this in Alfred Hitchcock's 1929 film, *Blackmail*, in which the young Scotland Yard detective takes his girl into a bustling Corner House; it is significant that the establishment is also patronised by an artist who is clearly rather higher up the social scale, with whom the girl flirts.

An important contributor to the Corner House atmosphere was the luxurious and imposing décor, featuring compositions of marble and glass and cleverly-arranged subdued lighting. Informality was achieved by placing the small tables diagonally rather than at right angles to the plan. Although maximum usage of commercial space was carefully studied, there was never any sense of overcrowding.

On arrival, customers passed under the surveillance of brown-uniformed porters six or more feet tall, normally gentle giants but alert for rowdies and other undesirables, especially during the night hours. After visiting the luxuriously-appointed cloakroom to deposit outer clothing and wash, customers approached the restaurants by wide marble staircases or attendant-operated lifts. On reaching one of the main floors, they found seats in comfortable basket-backed chairs at tables

250

covered with neat linen cloths. If tea were required, it would quickly be brought in silvery hotel ware, accompanied by bread and butter and jam, huge chocolate éclairs and other cakes and pastries. Those with large appetites might order such extra items as a poached egg on toast or a welsh rarebit, whilst others would select a Knickerbocker Glory or Peach Melba in a tall glass. For a full breakfast, lunch or dinner, a wide choice of dishes was available.

In the restaurants themselves the atmosphere was redolent of comfort, order, relaxation and security. Footfalls were quietened by thick carpets, the ear receiving only the music floating up from the band as it mixed with the background buzz of conversation and the tinkle of porcelain and cutlery. Lyons' themselves modestly summed it all up as 'luxury without ostentation at popular prices'.

The first Corner House was opened at Coventry Street/Rupert Street, halfway between Piccadilly Circus and Leicester Square, on 4 January 1909. Designed by W. J. Ancell, it had 2,000 seats and in 1920–24 was greatly extended westwards with elevations in white glazed terracotta by F. J. Wills. It then offered 4,500 seats in nine separate restaurants. On the ground floor were extensive retail food counters and a hairdressing salon. *The Architects' Journal* enthused on the sheer grandeur of it: each floor 'half the size of a football pitch'; the striking marble work in the interior ('a fortune must have been spent on this alone'); the profusion of costly and beautiful woods, mahogany and walnut for the most part; and lastly, the riot of other decorative features, modelled plaster work, glazed screens, colourful friezes and shining glass, cartouches, raised and sunk panels, architraves, pediments complete and pediments broken, scrolls, swags, consoles, dentils, keystones, aprons, columns, pilasters and sunbursts. Styles of the various public rooms ranged ambitiously through Louis XIV, Empire and Adam to Louis XVI, each with its electroliers carefully matched. There were four Weygood-Otis passenger lifts, rising at 300ft a minute, their bronze-finished cars fitted with glazed panels. Air was changed fifteen times an hour, filtered, purified and heated or cooled as necessary. Between the wars, this flagship among the Corner Houses employed forty-six porters to keep out unwanted customers and marshal the queues. In its restaurants, eighty-four full time musicians in seven twelve-piece bands played non stop from noon till midnight. Fresh bread rolls arrived every two hours from Lyons' bakeries at Cadby Hall, Hammersmith, but all other food preparation, even the manufacture of confectionery, was carried out on the premises by a staff of 200 cooks and chefs. The total number employed here in the 1930s exceeded 1,400.

Coventry Street was followed by Strand Corner House near Charing

Cross station, also by Ancell, and opened in 1915 with 2,500 seats. Then came the Oxford Corner House (2,500 seats) designed by F. J. Wills, with a stunning interior décor by Oliver P. Bernard and ready for customers on 3 May 1928. In what now seems a poignant burst of optimism and confidence, The Oxford was announced as 'Open for 24 hours, For Ever'. It had a 10,000 ft super (over 930 square metres) floor area comprising three restaurants, each with its own kitchen and servery, a total of 2,500 seats, and retail and cloakroom space. The walls and floors were covered with over 550 tons of marble and the wall decorations and murals, in fifteen different kinds of marble, 6.1 metres high and many metres long, depicted water, rocks, snow clad mountains and cascades (first floor) and a panorama of waterfalls, scenery and forests torn by blizzards (ground floor). The lighting struck an entirely new note for restaurants. Isolated marble pylons supported lotus flower units 2.44 metres in diameter, each with twenty four 100W pearl lamps. Major and minor wall fittings of similar design were lit by flame-tinted colour-sprayed lamps. All fittings were glazed with a special form of diamond raindrop glass with flesh colour relief and metal work in gold or silver gilt. Writing in *The Builder* in January 1929, the architect Howard Robertson enthused:

> The interiors, with their magnificent spaces, their clean, marbled gaiety, their soft and brilliant lighting, cannot but have a good effect upon the taste of their enormous clientèle. In comparing the decorations of this building, so carefully studied and finely executed, with those of other recent Corner Houses, one feels that the improvement is as enormous as it is significant in its promise.

The last of the Corner Houses was Marble Arch, within Lyons' new Cumberland Hotel. This was opened on 23 October 1933, its designers again Wills and Bernard. One of its restaurants alone, the basement Quebec café, had 1,200 seats. Here Bernard made use of the newly-developed neon strip lighting arranged at ceiling height along the tops of the walls and around massive upwardly curving 'coal shoot' pillars. In contrast to all earlier Corner House décor, a striking simplicity was everywhere apparent: lighting and ventilation and heating features formed the main details of design, applied decoration being almost entirely absent.

By the late 1960s, with sharp increases in the real pay rates in the catering industry undermining their whole financial structure and their site values attaining levels offering almost irresistible temptations to sell-off, the Corner Houses were doomed. The last, the Strand, then a

252

mere shadow of its former self, succumbed in 1977. The tea shops went the same way, for the same reasons.

Lyons were also involved in the hotel business, again principally directed towards a middle class clientele, and offering in the 1930s bed, bathroom and full breakfast for as little as ten shillings. Their three establishments were the Strand Palace (opened 1909, and greatly extended in 1930 with an eye-catching art-deco entrance and ground floor by Bernard), the Regent Palace, Piccadilly Circus, (opened June 1915, enlarged in 1934 and given a new and typically stunning Bernard decor) and the Cumberland, Marble Arch (1933, interior by Bernard). All three survive today, under new ownership[11].

As in London, shopping in the large stores of the provincial cities would be pleasantly interrupted or concluded by lunch or afternoon tea. At the latter meal, toasted teacakes or buttered crumpets were much in demand, served by waitresses dressed as parlourmaids, often to a background of chirpy music from a quartette or trio. By the late 1920s, Lyons had their Popular Café in Manchester and State Café in Liverpool, offering rather more refinement than their usual tea shops. Amongst the many other pleasant middle class haunts of similar type in the provinical centres, were the Kardomah, Fuller's and Ridgeway's cafés, and at York, Harrogate and Bradford, the much-loved Betty's.

## A Mostly Middle Class Theatre

When she had finished window-gazing and swanning through the department stores, 'retiring' in their elegant facilities and refreshing herself in their restaurants or at other suitable establishments, our lady of the suburbs might well join husband or friend for a theatre matinée or evening show, a diversion not usually available nearer home. The middle classes in town for pleasure demanded escapist entertainment, comedies, revues, musicals, society and costume dramas. They liked plays to have well-rounded plots which were easy to follow, preferably with a happy ending.

Since virtually all first performances of new work were staged there, sometimes after a trial run in the suburbs or provinces, London tended to dominate the theatre world. In the 1900s and 1910s, with the middle classes forming the major element of their audiences, managers of commercial theatres knew there would be little profit in mounting Shakespeare and other classics or adventurous new serious drama and poetic plays. Such fare was rarely given more than ten performances, mostly patronised by the urban or visiting intellectual and by earnest youth. This category never amounted to more than ten per cent (usually much less) of the annual total of new productions in London's commercial theatres. Noble attempts by J. E. Vedrenne and Harley Granville-Barker to mount 'seasons' of quality drama in London in 1904–07, 1908, 1910 and 1913 proved difficult to sustain, often leading to financial failure. Mainstream opera and ballet formed an even smaller percentage of the annual presentations, restricted as they were to a limited clientele and here again runs were very short. World War 1 saw something of a minor boom for London's commercial theatre but with sharply increased production costs and wider audiences, managements tended to concentrate on musicals, revues, farces and revivals of popular plays, seeing these as offering the least degree of risk.

Middle class taste continued to dominate the theatre between 1920 and 1950 with much the same results as in the two earlier decades, although, as we shall see, the nature of that taste did change somewhat. Writing in January 1920, B. W. Findon, the editor and founder of *The Play Pictorial*, a close observer of the theatre world since the late 1880s, noted 'there is little or no sign of any strong desire for the poetical drama, or plays that are not obviously intended for entertainment'. And in July 1922, commenting on the failure of 'Grand Guignol' at the Little Theatre, he observed that the prosperity of the London West End theatre rested on the tastes of 'the home-loving Englishwoman'. He thought a lesson should be drawn from the fact that the biggest successes of Irving, Bancroft, Wyndham, Tree and other famous names in the modern theatre were 'in plays that appealed to the great middle class and it was mainly to that class that they played'. During the 1920s Findon became convinced that the London West End theatre rested mainly on the support of middle class women, returning to this thesis again and again. Men, it would seem, went to most theatre performances mainly to please their ladies. In his 1942 book *Theatrical Cavalcade*, Ernest Short also mentions the 'dominance of women in theatrical audiences' between the wars, suggesting that the boyish feminine fashions of the twenties 'alone unfitted many actresses for roles which were regarded as classical in Victorian times and thus contributed to a new type of drama in which feminine interests were dominant instead of secondary'. We shall return to this new trend in a moment.

The commercial theatre of the first half of the twentieth century was without doubt very much a middle class institution, relying upon the steady patronage of this section of the community for its sustenance. It was of course also supported by the upper classes, but within the total audience, their numbers were tiny. As for the manual workers and the poor, even if they could exceptionally afford a visit to a theatre, the fare offered was in general not to their taste, since it was almost entirely attuned to middle class culture. Only a very few houses, mostly to be found in inner south and east London, periodically offered their lower middle class and plebeian clientele 'legitimate' theatre, as distinct from the traditional diet of 'variety' or low melodrama. Here, and in the provinces, any remaining tenuous allegiance to the theatre on the part of the working class was destroyed by the increasing success of the cinema. In 1935 *The New Survey of London Life and Labour* (H. Llewellyn Smith etc, vol. 9,) noted, with excessive caution, that the theatre 'has only a limited appeal to the working classes today'.

Apart from all else, cost was an efficient guardian of class barriers. With all the incidentals, an evening for two at a West End theatre in the 1900s and 1910s would leave little change from a week's pay for a junior clerk or a London postman. Admission prices ranged from around one to four guineas or more for a private box, 7s6d and 10s6d for the stalls, five shillings to 7s6d for the dress circle and three shillings to five shillings for the upper circle. By paying a small premium, what were often the best seats could be purchased more conveniently through agencies. It is true that a few unreserved pit seats were available at two shillings or 2s6d and that there were gallery seats for as little as a shilling but these last were hard wooden benches offering a vertiginous and very distant prospect of the stage. Increasingly the unreserved 'drop-in at whim' nature of pit and gallery, traditional resorts of the enthusiastic but impecunious theatregoer, became eroded by the introduction of a queueing system. This was impracticable for most manual workers since they would not be able to leave their employment early to stand in a queue and securing a place beforehand required a visit during the day to pay a nominal sum for a wooden stool which could be left unoccupied until the last moment. The middle class theatregoer could find time to buy a stool or afford to pay a District Messenger to stand in the queue until the last moment. Once the ticket was bought, the theatregoer faced further demands on his pocket. What Baedeker called 'the objectionable custom of charging for programmes' meant parting with a further sixpence and other extras were cloakroom charges, drinks in the interval, hiring of opera glasses, a box of chocolates to be enjoyed during he performance and some refreshment taken in a café or restaurant.

Except for the addition of entertainment tax, introduced as a wartime expedient in 1916 but continued between the wars, ticket prices did not increase significantly in those two decades. Indeed in the 1930s, under the stress of competition from the cinema, some managements reduced prices for long running shows or popular light entertainment. But this was the exception rather than the rule and at the end of the 1930s the standard prices for stalls were 12s6d, for the dress circle, eight shillings and ten shillings, and for the upper circle five shillings and six shillings. Pit seats were 3s6d and gallery benches two shillings. In general provincial theatres charged rather less but everywhere, by the end of the 1920s, the cinema was offering the better bargain in comfort and convenience.

Most theatres mounted matinée performances on two (sometimes three) days a week, usually Wednesday and Saturday, at 2.00, 2.15 or 2.30 pm, during which teas on trays would be served to the audience in their seats at the interval. To allow dinner to be taken beforehand, the main evening shows started between 8 and 8.40 pm, lasting until around 11pm. Audiences then stood for the playing of the National Anthem before emerging to seek a late supper in town and their last trains home. Between the wars those fortunate enough to live on the Metropolitan or Southern Railways would find trains at Baker Street, Charing Cross and Victoria on which they could enjoy the luxury of a light 'theatre supper' served whilst on their homeward way. London theatregoers from further afield would have no difficulty in securing comfortable hotel accommodation in the years up to World War 1 at five shillings or 7s6d for room, bed and full breakfast, or ten shillings to a pound between the wars.

By 1910 evening dress was no longer compulsory in the bookable seats at theatres but it was still customary for those sitting in the stalls and dress circle and very much *de rigueur* in most parts of the house at the opera. Even as late as 1930, the Whitehall Theatre, newly-opened that year, included facilities in its Ladies' Room for changing into evening wear.

With the great majority of new plays depicting the manners and customs of upper and middle class society, the working class only intruding as easily recognisable and often comic stereotypes, the audiences of the 1900s and 1910s were comfortable in a familiar and predictable environment. The Lord Chamberlain, a court official, exercising statutory authority, employed two readers to censor all commercial stage scripts, paying them two guineas a time. Although their main task was to prevent the depiction on the stage of the Deity, the modern royal family and other public figures, these officials also helpfully used their blue pencils to delete from scripts all items regarded by them as unacceptably obscene and salacious, including any suggestion of nudity. If the theme was unacceptable, the whole play would be banned. In short, they sought to ensure that nothing offensive to the establishment and middle class respectability and susceptibilities appeared on the so-called 'legitimate' stage (music hall and ballet were outside their remit) and the vigour and vitality of the drama was not unaffected by their activities. Whilst their work was not always fully effective because performers could transform seemingly innocent passages by gestures, inflections and expression, there was a long-stop. Should the 'undesirable' emerge, self-appointed censors would usually move into action; the Lord Chamberlain's officials might then attend a performance and such initiatives could cause a show to be stopped or modified.

Even before 1914 there were signs that some of those writing for middle class audiences were beginning to reflect social changes and 'modern' attitudes likely to shock the older generation. Casting a retrospective glance at the 1900s, Somerset Maugham, in his 1931 preface to his *Collected Plays* noted, 'it was the middle class, with its smug respectablity and shameful secrets, that offered us our best chances to be grim, ironical, sordid and tragic. . . we went the whole hog.' In Allen Monkhouse's 1911 play *Mary Broome*, the eldest son of a respectable middle class family typically enjoys an affair with the housemaid but when his irate father insists on its legitimisation by marriage, he is greatly shocked because the girl summarily rejects his son as a suitable husband. Stanley Houghton's 1912 *Hindle Wakes* depicts a young middle class couple indulging in a secret weekend together, the man having already promised to marry another girl. Again marriage is proposed to restore respectability and again the girl is shown as rejecting the offer. In this play she goes further, exhibiting an attitude hitherto considered solely a male preserve by telling the man he has merely been 'her little fancy', someone with whom she has had a bit of fun. Much upset, he castigates her attitude as 'so jolly immoral'.

As we shall see in a moment, this new spirit of revolt and desire to question established middle class values and attitudes, initiated in the early 1910s, was to be taken up with great enthusiasm by dramatists in the following decade, but for the time being, such 'modern' themes remained the exception rather than the rule. Until the 1920s most dramatists, coming from the middle class themselves, and therefore sensitive to the tastes and attitudes of the majority of the audiences, exercised a considerable degree of self-censorship with regard to sexual matters. In the April 1921 *Play Pictorial*, we find the editor, B. W. Findon, pronouncing that it was seldom 'a really "naughty" play has a long run in London. Immorality is not a popular card to play to middle class England. . .' But he then went on to state that 'salacious provender is consumed mainly by the stranger within our gates, the temporary denizens of hotels, who like to see the "smartest" thing in town and who return to their provincial homes to resume the snug propriety of their native surroundings.' Seeming to overlook that the 'strangers' were also from the same social grouping, this statement is a revealing insight into the contemporary middle class hypocrisy regarding such matters.

As the 1920s progressed, the Lord Chamberlain's office was under insidious and relentless pressure from dramatists, most of them young, who were now more than ever determined to be 'modern' and reflect in plays the changing outlook of the age. This led to a more relaxed censorship of sexual themes. Findon became increasingly exercised at what he interpreted as a downward slide in the standards of contemporary writers, including in his condemnation Sir Patrick Hastings and the youthful Noël Coward. He considered this perceived decline was frightening away the more solid middle class support which had for many years regularly occupied dress and upper circle seats once a month or once a fortnight. By 1925 he was recording regretfully, 'Today, a play, broadly speaking, must be socially salacious or it draws no money' and in July of the following year he wrote, 'Unquestioningly the drama, through the medium of certain authors, is depraved to an extent that has not been in evidence since the worst days of the Restoration writers.'

This new trend worrying Findon was expressing itself in plays tame enough by the theatrical standards of the 1960s and later. For example, Miles Malleson's *The Fanatics*, staged in 1927, had what Findon called 'an unclean theme' which upset him considerably. Against the background of a typical middle class home, this play features the young daughter discussing with her brother her desire for a trial marriage accompanied by birth control measures. This and similar topics are then argued between son and father, the latter concluding the first act with the shattering line: 'Just one thing. Not a word of this business to your sister!' Jon van Druten's *Young Woodley*, which ran for 425 performances at The Savoy in 1928–9, also disturbed Findon (and the censors) because it dealt with the love of a seventeen year-old public schoolboy for his housemaster's wife. By this time Findon had concluded that what he had described as the 'sexual offensiveness' of the contemporary stage was being supported by the 'bright young things' of the day, the emancipated single women (also principally from the middle classes, although he did not say so). It seems likely that many middle class husbands of the period would have found these interminable discussions of sexual mores and scenes of emotional sexuality somewhat tedious. Their attention would revive when the stage was enlivened (as it was ever more frequently from around 1927–9) by the appearance of decorative actresses clothed only in their lingerie or pyjamas. More important, most middle class married couples of the period were still sufficiently repressed to find such performances embarrassing to watch in each other's company. Although Findon at first supposed that 'Our clean-minded women of the middle classes' were staying away from these so-called 'sex plays', he eventually realised, as we shall see, that many were in fact going to see them at matinées, on their own, or with women friends.

In the 1900s and 1910s, Findon's 'clean-minded' middle class ladies would certainly have felt uncomfortable at the average music hall. With their general vulgarity, coarse humour and audience participation (in the theatre, the middle classes clapped but rarely laughed), music halls were very much a part of plebeian culture. However by 1911 *Baedeker's Guide to London and its Environs* felt able to concede 'the entertainments offered by the music halls have certainly improved in tone during the last ten or fifteen years, and ladies may visit the better class establishments without fear, though they should of course eschew the cheaper seats'. Further respectability was endowed in 1912 when the first Royal Command variety performance was held at London's Palace Theatre. With the middle classes very much in mind, Mrs Peel, looking back to the early years of the century, wrote 'Young girls did not go to music halls; but married women might go to a box or to the stalls at certain houses'[12]. All this reflects a new trend which had started early in the 1900s when music hall began to evolve into 'variety' or 'vaudeville', a programme made up from a selection of entertainments of different types, usually acceptable for general middle class consumption. To accommodate this slightly refined format, a number of grandiose 'variety theatres' were built. Notable examples in London were The Gaiety (1903), the Coliseum (1904) and the Victoria Palace (1911). At such theatres, the audiences were always 'respectable' and predominantly middle class, the vulgarity pretty well under control. From the early 1910s this new trend was further stimulated by the competition of the cinema and variety programmes began to include one-act plays designed as publicity vehicles for well-known actors and actresses.

Whilst some central and inner London music halls turned over to 'legitimate' theatre in the 1920s, and the West End Variety theatres remained 'respectable', in the inner London suburbs and in provincial cities and towns a form of music hall or 'variety' lacking in sophistication, with humour closer to the traditional plebeian coarseness persisted into the 1930s. Attracting a mixture of working and lower middle class patronage, its comedians and acts were increasingly drawn into sexual innuendo and titillation as the cinema, followed closely by a selection of other rival attractions, relentlessly eroded audiences.

There were other new forms of stage presentation. Revue, a type of fast-paced and highly ephemeral light entertainment copied from France, its content frequently topical and laced with song and dance, offered an alternative form of show very much to the taste of many middle class people, especially men. Introduced to London's 'legitimate' theatres in the 1900s and 1910s by Harry Pelissier, Albert de Courville, Charles B. Cochran and others, it took firm root in World War 1, remaining well-patronised right through to the 1940s. Gradually, from the late 1910s onwards, the emphasis in revue shifted from wit and dialogue to sexual titillation and spectacle.

Cabaret was another new form of stage presentation principally designed for middle class consumption. From the early 1920s, large hotels and restaurants, mainly in London's West End, organised this light entertainment to amuse their customers whilst they ate and drank. Singing and dancing were interspersed with brisk performances by 'near the knuckle' comedians. Scantily-dressed girls were a regular ingredient, with breasts exposed by the late 1930s. At London's Hotel Metropole in 1925, with alcoholic refreshment available until 2am, entertainment, dinner, dancing and supper could be had for £1.11s6d inclusive. In 1938 there were about a dozen hotels and restaurants in the West End offering cabaret, whilst from 1936 onwards The London Casino, 'the only theatre-restaurant in Britain' staged its Clifford C. Fischer revues and presented the leading dance bands for the amusement of diners.

Central London had fifty theatres in the mid-1910s, forty in the West End. There were some forty more in the suburbs, although most of these were in the inner districts and older suburbs, often presenting a mixed diet of straight plays and variety through the year. Besides these were the many music halls, usually to be found at the fringes of the central area or in the older suburbs. At this time the annual output of the central London 'legitimate stage' averaged around 120 or more new productions, excluding one-act 'curtain-raisers'. The first three and a half decades of the century saw the final expansive phase of new building for London's commercial live stage. Between 1900 and 1919 thirty-three additional theatres were opened, almost all in the West End, this figure including those establishments devoted almost entirely to variety. With the cinema taking hold as a formidable rival and other attractions sapping the allegiance of the largely middle class audience, the pace of new construction slowed significantly after 1920. Between the wars London gained only eighteen entirely new theatres, mostly in the West End, the last to open there being the 1,200-seat Saville, in Shaftesbury Avenue, in 1931. By this time, some theatres were also showing films, or going over to them entirely. Two notable conversions to the silver screen very soon after opening were the 1927 Carlton and the 1929 Dominion.

Despite this fall in new investment, there were still around 120 new full-length productions annually in the London theatres in the twenties[13], many of them 'sex plays' of the sort castigated by Findon, who by 1930 had concluded these were mainly watched and enjoyed by middle class women of all ages, married and single[14]. This emphasis on the erotic and loosening standards of sexual morality at the expense of strong drama arose not only from a desire to exploit and encourage what were perceived by the new generation of dramatists as changes in middle class outlook and behaviour. It must also be borne in mind that playwriting which pushed to the limits of the censor's tolerance in these matters filled seats at a time when the cinema, revitalised by the arrival of the talking picture in 1928–29, was growing daily more competitive for the same middle class patronage[15]. By the end of the 1920s the prospect for the commercial theatre looked gloomy indeed, and whilst competently-crafted plays, well-staged musicals and themes of sexual morality generally ensured a measure of profitability, there were many failures, surviving for less than the hundred or more performances necessary to cover costs. Theatre managements began to exercise economies such as the abandonment of 'curtain raiser' one-acters and the introduction of tinny amplification of gramophone recordings instead of live music.

The rapid turnover of new productions which had been a feature of the mid and late 1920s, when many plays had failed to achieve fifty performances, slowed down somewhat in the next decade and despite prophecies of gloom and despair after the arrival of talking pictures, the London commercial live theatre did not sink into the decay and oblivion expected by many, including those in the 'profession'. Thanks to the buoyant prosperity of the London region and a general recovery of spending power by most middle class victims of the depression, the West End theatre kept going much as before. There were in fact more theatres in central London in 1931 than twenty years earlier, a total of fifty nine (fifty of them in the West End), though it was rare for all to be open to the public at the same time. Actors and actresses found new income and greater fame by exploiting their talents in the film studios, bringing their middle class accents and manners before a much wider audience but always carefully maintaining their links with the live theatre, where their new screen fame served to enliven interest. Well-crafted plays by J. B. Priestley, John van Druten, Emlyn Williams and others continued to come forward whilst farces, musicals and the new 'non-stop' revues supplied the frothy light entertainment which satisfied the majority of the still largely middle class patrons. Continuous revues featuring displays of half-dressed girls, singing and dancing, and comedy routines were a response to the very real competition now being experienced from the cinema. At the Prince of Wales' Theatre, revues with French titles, copying the Folies Bergères, were staged continuously from 2–11.30pm with seats selling at West End cinema prices. This was what *The Daily Mail* called in 1936 '*The* show for tired businessmen', a place where middle class philistines were to be found in large numbers watching the dancing and posturing of the 'Fifty Petulant Pretties' and enjoying saucy humour. There was a similar programme at The Windmill, which from 1932 introduced its continuous 'revuedeville', a judicious mix of promising young comedians and long-legged show-girls. When in a state of near-nudity, the girls were kept motionless to avoid incurring the Lord Chamberiain's displeasure.

On the 'straight' commercial stage after World War 1, the tone of the staple diet of plays and farces remained much as before, generally projecting the comfortable middle class or so-called 'smart' society, which, in its top layer, merged with the upper class. They were shown at home in southern England, or perhaps on holiday on the French Riviera, in Scotland, or at some other suitable location. In faithful reproductions of their bedrooms and sitting rooms, furnished by Maples, Hamptons or Waring & Gillow, attractive young actresses in expensive negligée or the latest thing in cami-knickers, paraded, lounged, and embraced presentable young men, taking care to display their silk-stockinged legs to advantage. Servants entered, left, and lively youngsters, tennis racquets or Abdulla cigarettes in hand, leapt through French doors opening on to imaginary gardens of sumptuous dimensions. By the late 1920s, against these backgrounds, dialogue exhibiting a loose attitude to sexual morality in and out of marriage became so normal as to no longer excite comment. Sometimes it was all done rather well, with wit and precision, particularly so by Noël Coward, a leading exemplar of the genre. Occasionally something exceptional surfaced, its quality overcoming any reluctance by promoters to depart from the norm. Plays such as R. C. Sherriff's *Journey's End* (1929–30 and 1934) and Walter Greenwood's *Love on the Dole* (1935–36) brought a rare glimpse of other worlds to the West End stage, as had the earlier (1923) Charles McEvoy drama of slum life, *The Likes of Her*.

Few questioned what the combination of middle class patronage and commercial management was doing to the British theatre but now and again a note of discontent erupted in the theatrical periodicals. Thus in November 1936 we find Fred Majdalany grumbling in *Theatre World* that the typical young West End actress was 'an upper middle class young Englishwoman giving a graceful impersonation of an upper middle class young Englishwoman. Exhilarating no doubt, to mothers of public schoolgirls; unsatisfying if you expect a little vitality in the theatre'. He suggested this situation was partly due to the 'now standardised RADA/Old Vic stage education, but chiefly to the young ladies, who will be such confounded ladies. . .' All he could suggest was that they should try harder to emulate the great actresses of the past.

Some published estimates, admittedly broad-brush, indicate that the decline in middle class London theatre-going in the first four decades of the century was substantial. Charles Eyre Pascoe, in his 1901 book *London of Today* suggested 'on a modest computation' that at least 60,000 attended the theatre nightly. If something is added for the twice or thrice-weekly matinée audiences, this produces a weekly total of almost half a million. In contrast, a March 1937 *Theatre World* editorial article estimated, perhaps with some optimism, that 'more than a quarter of a million tickets' were then being sold each week for London theatre seats.

The end of the 1930s brought further depression to the West End. In 1938 the mounting international crisis was seriously affecting attendances. A third of the thirty six houses shown in the London 'Theatre Guide' were shown as 'closed' in August 1938 and the first weeks of the war in 1939 saw the majority shut. But this proved to be a temporary setback. Still opting in the main for safe fare that promised long runs rather than the classics or pioneering new drama, the commercial theatre continued to thrive during World War 2 and the late 1940s, sustained by servicemen and women from all the allied nations. It was in this period that it began to draw the educated working class not only into its audiences but into its pool of writers. By the mid-century, the London commercial theatre was still very much alive but there were signs of change in the predominant tone. The long period of pandering to largely middle class audiences was coming to an end.

Outside London, the decline of the middle class commercial theatre between the wars was even more evident, since it had a far less substantial base. Here, apart from occasional pre-West End trials, audiences were in general given only inferior re-runs of the more successful London productions, in theatres much more thinly scattered. Compared with London's total of over ninety houses presenting straight plays, revues, musicals, opera and ballet, Manchester could only muster nine 'legitimate' theatres in 1915, whilst Birmingham, Glasgow and Liverpool had about half a dozen each, Edinburgh, Leeds, Sheffield, Belfast, Newcastle and Cardiff no more than some three apiece. Unless they were holiday resorts attracting a seasonal audience from outside, many of the smaller towns had no theatres at all, or at best made do with their Corn Exchange or Town Hall for the occasional production.

The modern repertory movement, which began at Manchester in 1907, worked hard to sustain an interest in the live theatre outside London. Glasgow followed Manchester's lead in 1909, Liverpool in 1911 (with around 1,300 shareholders), and Birmingham in 1913 (the first to have its own custom-built theatre). Manchester's enterprise succumbed in 1917 but the other struggled on after 1920, joined by new ones, such as Bristol rep. in 1923, Northampton in 1927 and Coventry in 1931. After only four years, Coventry had accumulated 1,100 members and after eight years Northampton could boast 1,300, some regularly chartering special trains to travel in from Bedford and Peterborough. But to achieve even such modest progress was uphill work. Lack of a strong middle class base made the continuing existence of most forms of live theatre the more precarious in an age of increasing counter attractions. Thus in the 1930s, Birmingham, with a population of over a million, remained largely indifferent to live theatre, mustering only a mere 2,500 seat holders for its repertory theatre, and supporting only three 'legitimate' commercial theatres. In contrast this large city could boast over 100 cinemas.

September 1935 found the editor of *Theatre World* lamenting the fact that 'Only in the biggest cities is it possible to enjoy really first class acting and production and the state of the smaller towns is deplorable.' Two months later in the same magazine, Robb Lawson noted that out of 450 UK theatres listed in the *Era* annual twenty years earlier, there were but 130 left, depending on a mere ninety-six companies and twenty-seven stock or repertory companies producing straight plays. He estimated the national audience for live theatre had declined since 1915 from three to only about one million weekly, a figure which compared with the weekly attendance of twenty million claimed by the cinemas. As we have seen, at least a quarter of the audience was in London, which now possessed more than half the much-reduced total of theatres. Lawson's article refers to economies made by the provincial theatre managements and touring companies in the face of competition from the cinema and other attractions: reductions in front of house lighting; cheaper scenery and costumes; neglect of seats; dowdy decorations; grubby carpets; poor ventilation; grimy dressing rooms; and cuts in salaries which caused the 'stars' to leave provincial productions to inferior performers. Theatres had been converted to cinemas or sold to cinema circuit owners and about half the theatrical undertakings of the mid 1910s had gone out of business.

But it was not all gloom and decay outside London. Amateur dramatic societies and clubs, putting on two or three public performances a year, often in conditions of great discomfort and adversity in unsuitable halls, thrived amongst the suburban and provincial middle classes, their numbers in the UK totalling 1,250 in 1935, with perhaps some 13,000 members in all. Southampton was an exceptional case of a major centre acquiring a large new commercial theatre as late as 1928, making a total of two in that relatively small city. It may have been that the potential audience was judged higher than normal, partly owing to a prosperous middle class hinterland but also to the transit population of passengers and ships' officers at a time when the city was at the peak of is maritime prosperity. Lavishly equipped, The Empire was one of the finest of modern provincial theatres, where a box seating a small party of people could be obtained for £1.3s and a seat in the orchestra stalls cost 6s6d. Such commercial enterprises had become rare indeed. One of the very last was a bravely optimistic venture at Brighton, the Imperial Theatre, designed by Samuel Beverley, with a stunning 2,000-seat auditorium in vermillion, pale jade green and gold. Launched at a most unpropitious time, it was not ready until 1940 and closed for regular stage performances after only one show. Later it became a cinema, with very occasional stage productions.

## The Cinema becomes Acceptable

As an alternative, an afternoon or day in town might be crowned by a visit to the cinema. By the late 1910s this form of entertainment was becoming an acceptable option for the middle classes. Acceptable that is in a qualified sense, for the building itself had to possess a certain status and enjoy a regular and substantial middle class patronage. Thus middle class cinema-going was for many years largely confined to London's West End and leading houses in the provincial towns and cities. Then, with the suburban building boom of the interwar years virtually coinciding with the arrival of the sound film and the 'super-cinema', the new suburbs around London and the larger cities attracted cinema construction. There followed a substantial expansion in middle class patronage and the Odeon circuit formed in 1933 in particular set out to project an image of luxury and respectablility to cater for this new market.

Middle class attitudes to the cinema were for many years ambivalent. There existed a great deal of prejudice against what was seen as its pernicious and unhealthy influence on the plebeian masses, prejudice expressed by teachers, educationalists, conservative politicians, magistrates and other guardians of public morality and British standards of civilisation. And, when it threatened competition on Sundays, the cinema was also attacked by many churchgoers and churchmen.[16]

Socially, until the mid 1910s, visiting the cinema was considered not quite respectable in middle class eyes, since it had still to disassociate itself from its early 'flea-pit' origins in converted shops and other unsavoury environments such as fairgrounds and music halls. Also for a decade or so, many middle class people, set in their ways, remained loyal to the live theatre. Few cinemas were built in middle class suburbs before 1914; when they were, it was very necessary to reassure the potential customers and provide an attractive environment. Thus when the Crofton Park Picture Palace was opened in a predominantly middle class area of south east London in July 1913, with admission prices of threepence, sixpence and a shilling, the management made sure its policy was promulgated in *The Brockley News*:

> A special effort is being made to cater for the residents in the vicinity of the hall and it will be found that in framing the programme this end has been kept in view and the merely sensational, with the vulgar or the questionable has been scrupulously avoided. The orchestrina will provide musical selections.[17]

Middle class cinemas arrived in London's West End in the late 1900s[18]. Complete with dainty Japanese tea garden in the basement, the first had opened in Piccadilly as early as 1907. Perhaps the most impressive of this pioneer group were the New Gallery (January 1913) with some 800 seats and 'the largest cinema orchestra in London'; the West End Cinema, Coventry Street (March 1913) with 684 seats; and The Marble Arch Pavilion (March 1914) with 1,189 seats, six private boxes and a tea lounge. Eyles and Skone, in their valuable survey of West End cinema history, note that patronage of the Marble Arch Pavilion in 1924 and 1926 by King George V and Queen Mary 'did much to enhance the reputation of the cinema as a whole'[19].

World War 1 powerfully stimulated the popularity of the cinema, not least amongst the middle classes. Like the live theatre, the cinema, dominated then and later by US output, offered them much-needed escapism from the grim realities of trench warfare, the tedium of UK camp life and the restrictions, food rationing and casualty lists of civilian existence.

No doubt concerned by the rapid growth of this lusty child, *The*

*Play Pictorial* published some articles on the subject in December 1919, attempting to belittle this new threat to the live theatre. After visits to 'four leading cinemas', the editor tried to make the best of it:

> I found the audiences at the respective theatres average specimens of middle class life. Presumably they are intelligent beings, though how any intelligent person can become cinema *habitués* (sic) I fail to understand.

In similar vein, in the same issue, Charles Frederick Higham MP dismissed it as a temporary phenomenon: 'It is a poor business at its best, and already the intelligent public are tired of it'.

But they were spitting against the wind; the strength of the new middle class demand was to be confirmed by the construction and success of many imposing cinema buildings in central London in the following two decades, all of them able to attract large audiences week after week[20]. Even Findon, the conservative editor of *The Play Pictorial*, had to give way. He was expressing concern as early as July 1923 that three shillings for an unreserved theatre pit seat was not competitive with better accommodation in a nearby cinema and just over a year later was gazing in wonderment from his Strand office window at the 'costly automobiles' bringing upper middle class patrons every afternoon to the newly-opened Tivoli cinema opposite. 'The cinemas in the West End are attracting crowded audiences', he conceded in January 1925. Bowing to the inevitable, he announced in the next breath that a Cinema Supplement would be included from the following month's issue.

Until the arrival of the suburban 'super-cinemas' in the 1930s, the new central London cinemas and those in the centres of other large cities tended to be rather more sumptuous and luxurious than those elsewhere. Their carpets were thicker, the seats, plushier and roomier, the staff more plentiful and attentive, the ladies' rooms better-appointed. A feature which made London's West End cinemas special was that they alone showed the very latest releases. To meet the extra costs, admission prices to these superior houses were set a little above the usual ninepence, 1s3d, 1s6d and 2s4d charged elsewhere between the wars. At the London Tivoli, with a programme changed twice weekly and performances at 2.30, 5.30 and 8.30pm (6 and 8.30 pm on Sundays), tickets in the 1920s were 3s6d, 5s9d and 8s6d for reserved seats and 1s3d and 2s4d for unreserved. In 1926 at the Regent Street New Gallery, films were shown continuously from 2 until 11pm with seats priced at 1s6d to 5s9d. And when the Odeon, Leicester Square, one of the last luxury super-cinemas to be built in central London, opened in 1937, admission prices were 2s6d, 3s6d, six shillings and 8s6d, although some seats were sold at 1s6d for the first performance, a concession the author well recalls exploiting during school holidays.

For the lower middle classes in particular, these palatial cinemas provided affordable luxury for evenings out, generating temporary illusions of grandeur similar to those experienced when patronising Lyons' Corner Houses. Indeed to maximise the effect, the two pleasures were often combined in one evening. Contemporary with the new West End cinemas were many more, often of equal or larger size and near-equal luxury, in the new middle class suburbs around London and the larger urban centres outside. Others, somewhat less splendid, appeared in even the smallest towns[21].

Class discrimination in cinema patronage did not entirely die out between the wars. Some middle class parents, remembering their own upbringing, would endeavour to forbid their children entrance to the humbler 'flea-pit' dating from the early 1910s, although their audiences were no longer sprayed with disinfectant. But both these parents and their offspring were only too eager and content to visit the modern cinemas, generally separating themselves from the masses by paying a little more for the better seats. They were reassured, no doubt, by the sight of the cinema manager, himself solidly lower middle class, standing in the foyer resplendent in evening dress to welcome his 'patrons'. This token obeisance to the middle class traditions of the live theatre, could be witnessed in even the humblest small town and suburban cinemas as late as the early 1950s.

Around 1930 the cinema was beginning to acquire more prestige as an entertainment medium and art form, even generating its own literature. No longer was it held it contempt by middle class intellectuals, nor was there any shame for a member of the educated classes in being seen to enter a picture house. However it should be said that the more intellectual middle class filmgoers did much of their viewing at film society showings.

Not a great deal needs to be said here about the content of the films shown since this has been exhaustively examined elsewhere[22]. Under government protection, the British film industry began to flower in the 1930s, developing further in the next decade or so, when it produced many fine films, confirming the emergence of a valid national cinema soon to gain world-wide acclaim. The best of the home output received support mainly from the middle classes, the working classes on the whole continuing to prefer the Hollywood product. It is hardly surprising that this should be so since British films, still very closely associated in the 1930s and 1940s with the West End stage and its players, and permeated with middle class attitudes and accents, rarely portrayed British life in a form recognisable to the masses. In contrast, the well-made American talkies were much less stage-bound, quite classless, had universal entertainment appeal, and hardly ever depicted manual workers as comic stereotypes or halfwits.

The major proportion of films seen in Britain after 1914 came from the USA and the ways in which these influenced British middle class home environment and fashions have been touched upon elsewhere in this book. Where American middle class life was depicted, this was reassuringly seen by the middle class British cinema-goer as similar to his own, after making allowance for the differences in culture and the usually rather better US standards of living and domestic equipment. Indeed the general ethos of American films was exactly right for the British middle class. In his *The Hollywood Story* (1988), Joel W. Fowler notes that from the early 1910s, anxious to overcome the dubious origins of cinema entertainment, US film-makers adopted 'the middle class values of the period, which stressed the sanctity of home and family, embraced Christian values and were strongly anti-union and heavily patriotic'.

It is true that the 1920s and early 1930s saw some sexual licence creeping into Hollywood films, but much of this was trimmed by the British censors and after 1934 when the revised Hays Office code took a firm grip on Hollywood's public sexual morality and prissily confined provocative female display, British middle class audiences had no fear of being corrupted, or even mildly sexually excited, by what was seen on the screen. The Hays Office, whose edicts were strictly observed by Hollywood, made it almost impossible for normal sexual behaviour between men and women to be depicted, laying down rules in absurd detail about such matters as the number of inches of breast 'cleavage' which could be shown and the number of seconds a kiss should last without a break (eight). After 1934 Hollywood could be relied upon to see to it that those who did right trimphed in the end, in this as in other areas. If anything, conventional North American middle class sexual morality and social attitudes as enshrined in the Hays' edicts were every bit as inhibited, if not more so, than the British equivalents.

British film censorship, established in 1912 by the industry itself, was firmly in the hands of the upper and middle classes from the start[23]. At first the censors were much concerned with 'morality' (by which they usually meant nudity), 'the exhibition of female underclothing', sexual licence, and anything which brought into contempt the institution of marriage and the 'sacredness of family ties'. In these matters the 1934 Hays Code considerably eased their task because the majority of the films presented for exhibition then needed no further scrutiny of that type. As regards the home product, the censors continued to keep a close eye on the 'undesirable' without laying down the rigid detail of Hays.

The British censors also strove to uphold the established institutions and removed anything which seemed to them likely to arouse religious or political controversy. In general they seem to have been frightened into timidity by the sheer size and the nature of the national cinema audience, by the fact that cinema-going had become a habit with patrons mostly thought to have little or no power of judgement or discrimination, and by the great power of film as propaganda. It is interesting that, faced with plays which had been allowed for performance before middle and upper class audiences in the live theatre, they insisted on mutilation almost beyond recognition or banned them altogether. And when exercising their special powers over film performances, the local authorities sometimes behaved in a similar way to the Board; thus great Soviet films such as *Battleship Potemkin* and *Mother* (banned in uncut versions as 'controversial' by the Board) would be passed by the LCC for exhibition to a middle class film society but not to a workers' film guild. The Board was also very protective of middle class interests, much concerned to eliminate anything which reflected badly on the competence of the governing and professional classes. Amazingly, even Shaw's play *The Doctor's Dilemma*, which had at least four separate runs in London commercial theatres between 1906 and 1939, was considered 'absolutely unsuitable for exhibition as a film'. There is no doubt that the censors were always aware of another factor which in a sense lightened their task in that it virtually removed one type of film from the realms of practical possibility. Unlike the theatre, where they were rarely seen except at shows designed for them, children had formed a substantial element in cinema audiences from the earliest years. There were almost always some present at any public film performance, although latterly they were not admitted to see horror films. Very occasionally a local authority might license a film for exhibition to adults only. Apart from these comparatively rare exceptions, there was until 1951 no effective means of showing a film in public nationwide to a wholly adult audience. This came about because there were (apart from the 'H' (horror) not introduced until 1933) only two forms of certificate for public exhibition: 'U' (universal) and 'A' (adult). Although unaccompanied children were not supposed to see films in the latter category unless accompanied by an adult who in theory took the responsibility seriously, in practice the thing rapidly became a nonsense, far more dangerous in another sense. When programmes included 'A' films, children simply stood in the foyer, or on the entrance steps, ticket money in hand, until an adult responded to their plea: 'please take me in'.

All these restrictions and inhibitions combined to produce a generally innocuous diet, almost entirely oriented to entertainment. Both the US and the native production offered far less of a threat to traditional middle class sexual standards and attitudes than that of the much less influential live theatre, which, as we have seen, was from the 1910s increasingly challenging these conventions.

British films of the 1930s and 1940s worked to confirm and reinforce existing attitudes to both social class distinctions and behaviour and national pride and prestige. Documentaries, particularly newsreels, also contributed not insubstantially in the same directions. As for the overwhelmingly preponderant US film output, this could be relied upon to propagate not only middle class values but the normality of the profit motive and of private ownership of property. It was usual for Hollywood to portray woman as at her finest in the role of wife and mother and to demonstrate that crime was invariably and inevitably both unfruitful and suitably punished. Thus it was that right to the end of the 1940s, the middle classes, along with the rest of the nation, saw their social norms, patterns of behaviour and general expectations from life faithfully reflected and confirmed each time they visited the cinema.

It can also be said that the film, even much of the supposedly classless Hollywood product, encouraged and supported a general tendency, noticed elsewhere in this book, for middle class culture and individuality to be seen by those washing up against its lower slopes as the desirable, attainable ideal. There is plenty of contemporary evidence that film stars (the Americans being far more numerous and influential than British) operated as role models. Their activities, their clothes, their appearance, their manners, their lovemaking, their homes and general lifestyle all went to structure the dreams and even the behaviour of the upwardly mobile young.

Some statistical information is available on middle class theatre and cinema expenditure at the end of the 1930s. A sample of middle class households showed spending of between £2.12s and £4.5s.7d annually on cinema admissions, the higher figure associated with incomes over £700 and the lower with those over £250 and up to £350. Taking 1s6d as a reasonable average ticket price paid by a middle class adult in the lower band and assuming the wealthier ones bought the best seats at say 2s4d, this suggests about 34–38 seat purchases a year and of course a lower number of actual attendances, given that many would be of husband and wife together, perhaps accompanied by one or more children. In

271

contrast, the combined expenditure on theatres, concerts, music halls and dances is given as £1.14s.8d for the £250–350 band but £4.18s.7d for the £500–£700 band and £7.14s.11d for those earning over £700. Assuming all the expenditure to be couples taking theatre stalls, this suggests a visit about once every two months in the wealthiest band. As well as confirming the decline in theatre patronage amongst what were formerly the commercial theatre's main supporters, from the smallness of the amount shown for the lowest band we may deduce that until the 1940s serious regular theatre-going continued to be largely confined to the higher income groups.[24]

## NOTES

1. Barron, P. A., *The House Desirable*, (1929).
2. For details of the Metropolitan Railway Pullman operation see author's *London's Metropolitan Railway*, (1986).
3. Information on Club cars in this and subsequent paragraphs from *The Railway Magazine*, June 1898, March 1901 and November 1910, *The Railway and Travel Monthly*, February 1911, *Transport & Travel Monthly*, January 1920 and *The Railway Gazette*, 26 April 1935, 9 January 1942 and 30 January 1942.
4. Priestley, Henry B., 'The Tramways of Southport', *The Tramway Review*, vol. 16 no. 124.
5. Adburgham, Alison, *Shops and Shopping*, 2nd edition, (1981).
6. Harrod's Diamond Jubilee brochure (1909).
7. Surrey Record Office, Guildford, caption to photograph of White's shop.
8. Anon (White, Charles), *London Town & Country, A Guide for the Visitor*, (1928).
9. Information on Lyons' Corner Houses in this and subsequent paragraphs from the author's personal recollections and: *Evening Standard*, 9 April 1970, *The Sunday Telegraph*, 14 June 1970, *The Builder*, 16 April 1915, 11 May 1928 and 4 January 1929, *The Architects' Journal and Architectural Engineer*, 4 October 1922, 13 June 1923, 25 July 1923, 2 January 1924, and 2 April 1924, *The Architect & Building News*, 27 October 1933, and contemporary advertising.
10. Rabbi Lionel Blue, in a broadcast on LBC radio (London), 6 October 1986.
11. For descriptions of these three hotels as built, see *The Architect and Contract Register*, 17 September 1909, *Architects' and Builders' Journal*, 30 June 1915, 29 December 1915, *The Builder*, 22 December 1933, *The Architect & Building News*, 29 December 1933.
12. Peel, Mrs, C. S., *Life's Enchanted Cup; An Autobiography 1872–1933*, (1933).
13. The total annual output is misleading in that many more plays were now

being withdrawn after very short runs. In the first half of 1927, thirty-four plays were produced and withdrawn, an average of fifty-four performances each (five had less than twenty performances). Although the talking picture had yet to make its impact, in the first six months of 1928 forty plays had less than 100 performances, eight of these less than twenty. (*The Play Pictorial*, 306,316).

14. '. . . would authors devote their brains to the composition of sex plays if it were not for the women? I think we may venture to say they would not. . . the drama would be dead if woman were to turn her back on the stage. Women are the biggest factor in keeping alive the contemporary drama.' (B. W. Findon, *The Play Pictorial*, 342, September 1930).

15. The decline in support for the London West End Theatre can be attributed to a combination of factors: the revulsion of many older and staider middle class people against the so-called 'sex plays' and the sparsity of what they regarded as acceptable theatrical entertainment; some loss of real income amongst the professional classes in the 1920s which made it necessary to cut back on luxuries; and the emergence of rival attractions, chiefly the cinema (especially after the introduction of sound films at the end of the 1920s), but also dance halls and motoring.

16. These middle class anxieties are carefully examined in Richards, Jeffrey, *The Age of the Dream Palace: Cinema and Society in Britain 1930–39*, (1984), p 48 et seq.

17. George, Ken, *Two Sixpennies Please: Lewisham's Early Cinemas* (1987).

18. For historical and other details of all West End cinemas see Eyles, Allan, and Skone, Keith, *London's West End Cinemas*, (1984) from which much of the information given in this chapter about buildings is taken.

19. Eyles and Skone op cit (note 18).

20. Notable additions included: The Tivoli, Strand, 1923, 2,115 seats; The Capitol, Haymarket, 1925, 1,700; The Plaza, Lower Regent Street, 1926, 1,896; The Astoria, Charing Cross Road, 1927, 1,650; The Carlton, Haymarket, 1928, 1,159; The Empire, Leicester Square, 1928, over 3,000; The Regal, Marble Arch, 1928, 2,400; New Victoria, Vauxhall Bridge Road, 1930, 2,600; The Leicester Square Theatre, 1930, 1,760; The Curzon, Curzon Street, 1934, 492; Odeon, Leicester Square, 1937, 2,116; and The Warner, Leicester Square, 1938, 1,789.

21. For cinema history generally in London and elsewhere, see Sharp, Dennis, *The Picture Palace*, (1969) and Atwell, David, *Cathedrals of The Movies*, (1980).

22. See for example, Richards, op cit (note 16) and his excellent bibliography.

23. What is said here about British film censorship is partly based on Richards, op cit (note 16).

24. Massey, Philip, 'The Expenditure of 1,360 British Middle Class Households in 1938–9'. *Journal of The Royal Statistical Society*, vol cv part III (1942).

# CHAPTER 10

# MIDDLES AT LEISURE

## Sitting Room Pleasures

Unlike the working class, whose overcrowded and uninviting homes prompted them to resort to the convivial and lively warmth of public houses and music halls, the less gregarious and more home-centred middle classes preferred a quieter setting for most of their indoor entertainments. Card-playing was popular and the avid feminine interest in bridge, by no means confined to the ladies' clubs, has been mentioned earlier. Card games enlivened the long dark winter weekend evenings at home and were made more exciting by a cash 'kitty' placed alongside the bowls of fruit and sweets on the table. This diversion was particularly popular at Christmastime, when children, allowed to stay up late, would join in, savouring a mild sense of sin.

Whist was a great favourite of the lower middles and whist drives, to raise funds for various causes, or simply to provide pleasure, were a popular suburban amusement from around 1908. Held in church halls and similar buildings, they offered a respectable environment in which single men and women not given to dancing or tennis might meet new partners. For a child they provided opportunities to undertake important-seeming jobs such as changing the sign which indicated the trump suit, presenting the prizes, or helping with raffles. There were occasional exceptions to the general tone of respectability. A cinema in Holloway, north London, converted to a whist drive centre in the 1920s, was closed in 1930 when the patrons resorted to blows in squabbles over the prizes. This was surprising and untypical behaviour indeed for the lower middle class, the exception which proves the rule[1].

Other table amusements nurtured by the middle class domestic lifestyle included jigsaw puzzles, a pastime invented at the end of the 19th century. During the 1900s and 1910s these sold with up to 1,000 plywood pieces but in the following decades completion became more difficult and time-consuming when they appeared in 2,000 or more fiddly cardboard sections of irregular shape. Another domestic diversion was ping pong, later dignified as table tennis. This was played from around 1902 either on the dining room table or a special folding table. For quieter moments, most families possessed sets of dominoes, draughts and numerous dice-throw board games, ranging from the traditional Snakes and Ladders to the usually short-lived novelty of the year.

In the larger houses, a special room was sometimes to be found on the ground floor, perhaps as a single storey extension of the main building, expressly provided for a billiard table, cue racks and score board. Although some Edwardian speculative builders in the more affluent new suburbs had offered this facility, it was rarely encountered after 1920 in new houses except when specified in an architect's plan. With full size tables costing as much as £75 to £100 in the 1920s, cues at around £1.10s each and ivory balls at around five pounds for a set of three, and the demand on space, this tended to be a pastime found only in the more prosperous households[2].

In contrast, during the first three decades of the century the possession of some sort of piano was virtually universal amongst all sections of the middle class. Dominating most sitting rooms and a focal point for home-made entertainment, its popularity endured until the end of the 1920s when it gradually gave way to radio and gramophone. In 1928, with a decline beginning to set in, total sales were still as high as some 100,000 a year[3]. Always an expensive item, the piano was nevertheless very much seen as a status symbol amongst the lower middle class, justifying sacrifices elsewhere, ('Pride, Poverty and a Piano') and only the very badly-off resorted to secondhand ones. Cheaper upright or 'cottage' models, which had sold at between £16 and £42 before 1914 were £48–£100 between the wars. A baby grand, a suitable cachet for the more comfortable middle class home, would cost upwards of £72 before World War 1 and £136 to £302 afterwards. With the piano in so many homes, sheet music sales thrived and music stools were packed with popular vocal pieces such as *Devon, Glorious Devon; The Holy City; On the Road to Mandalay; Indian Love Lyrics;* and *Drake's Drum* along with tunes of the war years, songs from the theatre musical shows and, after the mid-1920s, the hits of the radio dance bands and the cinema.

In middle class suburbs children were encouraged to develop even the slightest musical talent and were to be seen carrying music cases through the streets on their way to and from pianoforte or violin lessons in the teacher's private house, whilst piano tuners made their regular calls along suburban roads and avenues. Winter weekend evenings and Christmas gatherings saw groups forming around the piano to render popular pieces, but in the 1900s and 1910s, when the enthusiasm was at its height, there was more to it than that. A resident of a lower middle class estate in south east London reported in 1902 that on walking home from the railway station each evening he heard the sound of vocal and piano practice from 'practically every other house'[4]. Sometimes, for variety, the singing around the piano would be interrupted by a monologue or a poem or two. By 1929, Harrods catalogue was offering a noisier alternative form of home music-making; a jazz set with twelve and twenty-inch drums and accessories, complete with waterproof canvas cover, for £4.15s.

A potential competitor to home music-making first becoming generally available in the 1900s was the gramophone. Early models were operated by a clockwork motor wound by a handle at one side, the sound emerging with metallic tones through a large amplifying horn. Wide sales followed the establishment of EMI Ltd. in 1898 and the opening of The Gramophone & Typewriter Company's ('His Master's Voice') 18-acre works at Hayes, Middlesex, in 1907. Portable gramophones, which could be taken into the garden, on to a punt on the river, or to a picnic, were in the shops by the mid 1910s, ready to provide much-needed relaxation in officers' quarters on the Western Front in 1914–18, a period when sales of records boomed. No doubt owing to the steady growth in demand and improved efficiency in production, gramophone prices remained remarkably stable over the years at three to eight pounds for a small portable, £12 to 16 for a table model and £22 to £60 for an upright freestanding cabinet, the higher prices for the latter related to the quality of wood and craftsmanship. According to length of play, records ranged from 1s3d to 12s6d (the best double-sided twelve-inch discs were 12s6d and ten-inch three shillings in the 1920s). Around 1930, Woolworth's managed to offer a playable product carrying popular songs and dance music at their then maximum price of sixpence. By 1928 some 500,000 gramophones were being sold annually, together with around 30 million records[5].

Electrical recording and reproduction, available from the mid 1920s, vastly improved the quality of gramophones. The era of the radiogram dated from this time. Very much a sitting room piece, it incorporated an electrically-operated record player (often fitted with automatic record changers) with a radio in one freestanding upright cabinet. At first the newcomer sold at £52.10s upwards but later in the thirties prices varied from just over £25 to as much as £63 for more powerful models with well-made cabinets. New recordings were publicised and reviewed in a magazine called *The Gramophone*, which was found in many middle class homes but they were also played on BBC radio by Christopher Stone, who carefully read out the producing company and number of each one; although logical enough, this was a blatant contravention of the Corporation's strict ban on any form of advertising and its initiation must have caused some heartsearching. With gramophones, talkie films and radio all widely available, the sheer quantity of music falling upon middle class ears had greatly increased by around 1930. Not all of it was jazz and popular dance music; both the record companies and the BBC played an important role in bringing classical music to a wider audience. These new opportunities for musical appreciation were seized by the grammar and county secondary schools, whose pupils also enjoyed the sounds of a live orchestra in local theatres when these were visited in the 1930s by the touring Robert Meyer/Malcolm Sargent children's concerts.

Radio for home listening, a development of the early 1920s, remained a very middle class institution through its first decade and a half. In November 1922, the monopoly British Broadcasting Company started regular transmissions, at first somewhat precariously received on 'crystal sets', tuned by a 'cat's whisker' and brought to the ears by headphones, technology that had changed little since its adoption for marine morse code broadcasts in the early 1910s. This early home receiving apparatus, which required a long aerial hanging from a high post at the end of the garden, could be assembled and erected by amateurs for around five to ten shillings and the details of construction were widely dispensed in a selection of new specialist magazines.

In this early period radio was magic to child and adult alike, keeping families indoors almost every evening. By the end of 1926 it was reaching two million homes, the majority of them middle class, and one London railway was ascribing a reduction in evening traffic to its influence[6]. Two years later, about £5m worth of radio equipment (other than valves) was being sold annually, a sum which represented about twice the expenditure on photographic items, including cameras, and almost two-thirds that on sports gear[7].

In 1926 the British Broadcasting Company was converted to a public Corporation, at its head as director general the earnest and bluff public service missionary John Reith. Reith, who held the post until 1938, *was* the BBC; he created a cultural dictatorship, very middle class in tone, influence and outlook, which sought to broaden the listener's knowledge and appreciation of current affairs, serious literature, classical music and drama. Entertainment and popular music were tolerated but, it seemed, strictly rationed. Christianity was widely propounded, especially on Sundays and Holy Days. It was very much a matter of what Reith and his colleagues thought was best for the listeners, rather than what they might have wanted to hear. Announcers, and almost everyone else who broadcast, spoke in middle class accents, often in those slightly strangulated tones of the contemporary upper middle class which sound so strange to late twentieth century ears. Provincial inflexions were totally excluded, except in comic and documentary programmes, until World War 2. There can be no doubt that the BBC had some influence in standardising accents and speech patterns. Many were brought to conform to them slowly, hardly realising, whilst those actively seeking to consolidate their middle class status with socially acceptable vowel sounds and correctly-formed consonants were provided with a readily available guide day after day.

News was read only in the evenings, a response to pressure from newspaper proprietors fearing competition, which also explained an almost complete lack of editorial treatment on the radio. News readers and other announcers working after 6pm added to the general middle class atmosphere by wearing dinner jackets in front of their unseen listeners, an ostensibly eccentric practice officially explained as a courtesy to non-professional evening broadcasters, who might arrive at the studios similarly attired, coming straight from dinner at home or at their clubs. Reith's puritanical influence produced daily religious services and caused Sunday secular radio to be postponed until after morning church hours. Even so, Sunday broadcasts were largely serious music, ponderous 'talks', religious addresses and dramas, and church services.

Such a dry diet caused many to turn their tuning dials, and by the early 1930s the more powerful sets then available were bringing into the middle class home programmes in English sponsored by British commercial firms, broadcast from European transmitters such as Radio Luxembourg and Radio Normandie. Stung by this competition, the BBC began to unbutton just a little, broadcasting more light music, comedy and variety, though Sunday programmes still remained rather too dreary for popular taste. By 1939 there were five million sets in British homes, the majority of them probably middle class, since cost still made radio something of a luxury. At ten shillings a year, a radio receiving licence represented about one-sixth of the weekly pay of those on the very lowest rung of the middle class ladder and it was not until the late 1930s that factory-made sets brought prices down to just over twice the top working class weekly pay packet.

From the middle of the twenties horn loudspeakers and valve receivers began to supersede the crystal set and earphones but amateur assembly of receivers from parts was still very prevalent. Factory-made sets became more widely available around 1928, the receiver and cone moving-coil loudspeakers often sold as separate items. In 1929 a four-valve receiver said to be capable of receiving up to forty European stations cost £29.6s complete with loudspeaker, though there were two-valve receivers (without loudspeaker) available at this time for as little as six pounds. The loudspeakers, mostly in wooden cabinets with fancy fretwork designs, sold at £1.12s.6d to around seven pounds. In the early 1930s factory-made sets with cone speakers fully integrated into the cabinet flooded on to the market, prices falling as mass production got under way. Battery sets in 1931 were eight to nine pounds each but as much as £15.15s might be spent on a powerful all-mains receiver. The famous circular Ekco superhet with its plastic (bakelite) cabinet designed by the Canadian architect A. Wells Coates, appeared in 1934 at £10.12s6d. A four-valve version followed a year later at £8.8s. By 1938–9 four-valve battery superhets could be had for £6.15s–£7.15s and all-wave five-valve mains sets for seven to eight pounds.

At the end of 1936 the BBC started television transmissions for a few hours daily from north London's Alexandra Palace, using the Marconi-EMI system. The general tone and the accents of those participating were still predominantly middle class. Receiving sets, which had very small (twelve and fourteen inch) screens and required a 'booster' at additional cost for houses more than twenty miles from the transmitter, were sold at prices between £45 and £126, although there were table models at around £25. The more expensive models had elaborate hand-crafted cabinets which included radio receivers for the many empty hours between transmissions. By the time outbreak of war brought the broadcasts to a sudden end in September 1939 there were about 20,000 television sets in use, almost all in middle class homes in and around London. Whilst the content of the Alexandra Palace output was slightly more relaxed in tone than that of the Reithian radio, the influences of that tradition were by no means undetectable. When the broadcasts were resumed at the end of the war, there was no really significant change in their content and area of reception before the end of the 1940s.

## Middle Class Reading

Reading occupied a major place in the leisure activities of the middle classes. They were heavy buyers of newspapers, which reached the height of their circulation and influence in the period 1904–40. Most families took in at least two dailies, one to be read on the journey to work or at the lunch interval, the other, usually lighter fare, left for those at home all day. Commuters returning from the large cities would purchase an evening paper, with its local as well as national news, but an earlier edition of this was delivered to many suburban homes around tea time. Of the dailies, the most 'serious' were the long-established Conservative trio *The Times*, *The Morning Post* and *The Daily Telegraph*; the latter, the newspaper of the middle class businessman, absorbed the *Post* in 1937. Those inclined towards Liberalism or otherwise mildly radical took the *Daily Chronicle* or *Daily News*, (amalgamated as *The News-Chronicle* in 1930) or perhaps *The Manchester Guardian*, one of the few survivors of the once widespread provincial dailies. Middle class women favoured the zestful *Daily Mail*, only five years old as the century opened, or the clean-cut, pithy presentation of the still younger (1900) *Daily Express*; both were strongly Conservative. Others preferred the small format picture papers, which did not demand too much intellectual effort to digest: *The Daily Sketch* (1909) and *The Daily Mirror* (1903), again generally Conservative and middle class in comment and tone. *The Daily Mirror* went downmarket in the 1930s, adopting some aspects of US tabloid presentation with a more radical editorial policy, losing much of its middle class readership in the process. *The Daily Mail* of the first decades of the century seems to have set out to appeal to the burgeoning suburban lower middle class and its consistent jingoistic, imperialist tone in the 1900s and 1910s played upon the contemporary prejudices and attitudes of that readership. It organised the annual Ideal Home Exhibition, an institution which both led and reflected lower middle class suburban taste in housing, furnishing and domestic gadgetry from 1908 onwards (stopped by the two World Wars, the Exhibition was revived in 1920 and again in 1947).

Magazines and books read by middle class women and children have been noted in earlier chapters. Men tended to buy magazines catering for their leisure or other special interests such as political comment, investment, golf, motoring or railways. With some notable exceptions, general interest male-oriented periodicals such as *The Strand Magazine* (which sold around 400,000 copies a month in the 1900s and 1910s), *Blackwood's* and *The Windsor Magazine* (somewhat lower middle class in tone) tended to decline in popularity in the 1920s and 1930s, perhaps because of competition from radio and cinema.

Solace for men unable to achieve adequate fulfilment of their libido and hungry for some expression of their sexual fantasies (not an uncommon dilemma for the English middle class male of the period, married and single) became increasingly available in the 1930s and early 1940s, when the long-established and offbeat *London Life* blossomed out more strongly, and US imports such as *Silk Stocking Stories*, *Movie Humour* and *High Heel* with their slightly coy photographs of wholesome middle class American girls unable or unwilling to control their skirts (or without them) were sold by many small newsagents. A launching advertisement for C. Arthur Pearson Ltd.'s new pocket-sized shilling monthly *Men Only* in December 1935 announced that it was 'devoted entirely to men's interests. It doesn't want women readers. . . won't have them!' Popular with expatriates, this magazine offered a diet of demure nudes, mildly 'naughty' cartoon humour and hints on how to dress well, spiced with macho adventure, both reportage and fiction. Much of the latter had an overseas slant and a phrase taken from a 1938 issue, 'Tommy Atkins and Johnny Gurkha think the world of each other', suggests the general flavour. Writers and artists such as A. P. Herbert, A. G. Street, W. Barribal and Eric Fraser were among the early contributors. The tone was very strongly middle class, the advertisements mainly concerned with such items as best quality pipe tobacco (at 11½d to 1s2d an ounce) and cigarettes (a shilling for 20), shaving soap (a shilling or 1s6d a stick), male corsets (£2.2s–£4.4s), silk ties (three for 18s6d), hair creams (a shilling and 1s6d), motor car accessories, and cures for baldness.

A brilliantly innovative arrival of October 1938 was the illustrated weekly *Picture Post*, created by the Hungarian refugee Stefan Lorant. Its vivid photo-journalism owed much to pioneering Continental European precedents. With its mix of current affairs, social comment and other documentary features, this exciting newcomer set out to appeal to adults of both sexes and offered a sharp contrast to the then very staid, worthy and long-established *Illustrated London News*, widely available in middle class clubs and the waiting rooms of private doctors and dentists. Circulation of *Picture Post* soon reached two million and it was popular with the younger middle class, their elders mostly regarding it as a trifle too upbeat for their taste. In the late 1930s and early 1940s, *Picture Post* and its stable companion, the pocket-sized *Lilliput*, which contained a mixture of light prose, photographs and humorous drawings, together mounted a much-needed attack on contemporary political and social complacency and a self-satisfied Establishment, an attack reinforced by the Penguin Special paperbacks to be mentioned in a moment.

Slipped inside an ornamental leather or embroidered canvas cover, *The Radio Times* was to be seen in most middle-class sitting rooms. Founded by the BBC in 1923, this weekly's main purpose was to provide fully detailed advance programme information. Efficiently carried to the furthest corners of the kingdom by the railways, its wide circulation attracted much advertising directed at the middle classes. This brief survey of middle class periodicals would not be complete without mention of the venerable *Punch*, which faithfully continued to reflect most middle class attitudes, modes and manners, particularly in its humorous illustrations. If not taken at home, it was always available

281

in doctors' and dentists' waiting rooms, where it struggled gamely but hopelessly to relax the patients' tension and fears.

Throughout the five decades, books sold widely and well to a mainly middle class readership. From some 8,700 in 1914 the annual total of newly published titles rose to almost 15,000 by 1939. Sales of new books increased from just over seven million annually in the late 1920s to almost twenty seven million in 1939. First editions of hardback novels, costing six shillings before 1914 and 7s6d or more in the next three decades, sold almost entirely to the middle classes, whose favourites were mystery, humorous fiction, crime and detective stories. Healthy sales of these made it possible to produce cheap (3s6d) editions between the wars. Among the most popular authors were Agatha Christie, Margery Allingham, Ngaio Marsh, Edgar Wallace, Josephine Bell, Dorothy L. Sayers, P. G. Wodehouse and Richmal Crompton, all of whom faithfully reproduced their own middle class backgrounds, values and attitudes in the fictional worlds they portrayed. When Josephine Bell died, her obituarist in *The Daily Telegraph* observed that the real strength of her literary output came from 'a grasp of middle class values (and sometimes of their perversion)'.

Several efforts were made to give wider circulation to established classics. Shilling hardback 'pocket' editions appeared in the 1900s and 1910s; The Oxford University Press World's Classics from 1901; Collins' Illustrated Pocket Classics from 1903; Everyman's Library from 1906; and Cassell's Popular Library from 1909. All found a wide sale amongst the increasing ranks of the literate lower middle classes and in their more expensive, gilt-edged, leather bound editions were often given by them as presents. To encourage collections, some of these publishers sold custom-made bookcases. There were also cheap pocket-sized hardbacks such as Newnes' Sevenpenny Stories of 'powerful novels by authors of repute', first published in the 1900s. Pocket reprints of non-fiction works, often with a religious or rationalist theme, also found a ready sale at sixpence in the same period.

In the 1920s Woolworths' produced a Readers' Library of sixpenny classics and cheap hardbacks of popular contemporary fiction were again published. At the beginning of the 1930s, Watts launched its 'Thinker's Library' of cheap reprints of rationalist and anti-Christian works, eagerly consumed by the many middle class youngsters beginning to question received dogma as they entered a cynical adult world.

1935 saw a revolutionary new development, well timed to satisfy an expanding market: Allen, Richard and John Lane's sixpenny Penguin paperbacks, which were followed in 1937 by the Pelican series at the same price, covering social issues and scientific and historical subjects. In 1938 Penguin Specials appeared, each devoted to a major political or social issue of the day. All sold readily, largely to a middle class youth seeking to understand their frightening, war-threatened inheritance and also impatient to expand their knowledge of subjects such as economics, politics and architecture which had not been part of their formal education.

Although the middle classes made good use of the burgeoning public library facilities, many over the age of thirty or so, particularly women, favoured the more flexible circulating libraries operated by W. H. Smith, Boot's The Chemist, and some of the large London department stores, since these tended to offer a more attractive environment and a wider selection of the latest escapist romantic, crime and adventure fiction that formed a large part of their reading diet[8]. In the new suburbs of the 1920s and 1930s, especially those predominantly lower middle class, the commercial Twopenny Libraries (twopence per book per week) operated by newsagents and other shops thrived for much the same reasons as the circulating libraries and were usually in position well before public libraries had managed to extend into the new areas. In one such district in 1935, there were two such facilities operating whilst the new houses were still going up, one of them receiving 100 new titles every month from Foyles, the well-known London booksellers.[9]

## Dancing, Rinking, and Drinking

After the cinema and theatre, perhaps the most popular indoor pastime was dancing, which was socially important as a principal means of finding partners of the opposite sex. From the late 1910s public and private dances were increasingly attended by unchaperoned middle class girls though many parents still had misgivings about this. Modern dance music, mainly originating in the USA, had reached Britain in the early 1910s, soon spreading widely through sheet music and gramophone records. British dance and jazz bands proliferated in the 1920s, performing in dance halls, hotels, restaurants and on the BBC, which had its own 'Radio Dance Band' from 1926. This encouraged a boom in home-produced songs. Some of the early (1912–14) US dances, which rejoiced in such names as *The Bunny Hug, The Turkey Trot, Hitchy Koo* and *The Chicken Scramble* proved short-lived but the athletic *tango* of the same period did survive, its complications doing much to create a new custom of dancing with same chosen partner for a whole evening. Also enduring was the *foxtrot*, arriving around 1920, to be followed by the *Charleston* in 1925–27. Dixieland Jazz was imported from the USA in

1919. The leading British dance bands, under the batons of Jack Payne, Bert Ambrose, Victor Silvester, Carroll Gibbons, Jack Hylton, Harry Roy, Henry Hall, Roy Fox and Jack Jackson achieved great popularity through their radio broadcasts and gramophone records in the late 1920s and the 1930s. Whatever their social background (and it was quite often working class), the new dance band leaders and their vocalists (many of them Jewish) cultivated heavy and smooth middle class accents, knowing these would make them socially acceptable to their live audiences and their BBC and record company paymasters. Lower down the scale of skill and popularity were hundreds of small bands, mostly composed of young part-time musicians performing more or less acceptably on saxophone, trumpet, drums and piano.

Middle class parents encouraged their daughters (and much more rarely) their sons, to learn tap, ballet and Greek dancing from private tutors, who charged 15s to a pound for a term of twelve lessons between the wars. In their early teens children went on to learn 'ballroom dancing', principally the waltz, the veleta, the foxtrot and perhaps the tango. Some co-educational council secondary schools provided such tuition in preparation for an annual *soirée* for senior pupils and old students. In the larger middle class houses, at tennis and golf clubs and in small halls, young people danced to the music of the radio and the gramophone or small amateur band. But the 'real thing' was to dance to a good professional live band. For the lower middle class this was achieved at the local *palais de danse* such as that at Wimbledon in south-west London, where in 1928 there was dancing on 'the largest spring floor in the world' every evening from 7.30 to 11.30 for 2s6d admission (on Fridays 3s6d, in evening dress only). Wimbledon also offered a weekly tea dance on Wednesdays from 2.30 to 5.30 pm at an inclusive charge of 1s6d, and there were 'professional dancing partners' and a free car park. For those a little higher in the social scale, the usual resort was a tea, dinner or supper dance in one of the large city hotels and restaurants, where the famous dance bands were frequently engaged (dancing between courses at restaurants had become customary in the 1920s). Inclusive admission to *thé dansant* at London's Savoy hotel in the 1920s and 1930s was five shillings and at the Café de Paris, four. The lower middle class could taste the same delights in slightly less smart company at the Regent Palace Hotel, where tea dance admission was a mere two shillings. A supper dance at this hotel or at Appenrodt's nearby, from 10 pm to 12.30 am could be enjoyed for 3s6d, including the meal. To prepare their youth for such adult pleasures, the new middle class suburbs of the 1930s, such as London's Stoneleigh and Petts Wood, offered weekday dancing

284

classes in the ballrooms of their new 'superpubs', where at weekends the suburbanites flocked to tea and supper dances.

In contrast to dancing, rinking (roller skating) in a purpose-built hall with maple wood floors, enjoyed only a brief flowering, its participants largely confined to the lower middles and the better-off working class. Stimulated by developments in skating surfaces and the introduction of ball bearing roller skates, it surfaced in 1908, reviving an 1880s craze, and following the initiative of the American promoter, C. P. Crawford[10]. An entry ticket normally cost sixpence and roller skates could be hired. By 1910 interest was fading, largely due to the competition of the cinema, for which the rinks lent themselves to easy conversion.

Little or no alcoholic drinking took place at dances and virtually none at skating rinks or the cinemas, although most theatres had bars. Until the 1930s the middle classes tended to take their alcoholic refreshment either at home, in their golf clubs (golf club drinking was very popular), or in restaurants. Although they did not often frequent ordinary public houses or other specialised licensed premises (except railway station bars and the occasional country pub) these establishments did normally provide the usual segregation. Any middle class customers would usually be found in the lounge or saloon bar, paying a little more to be free of irksome contact with the rough *hoi polloi*.

This situation then changed. At the outskirts of cities and in the countryside, especially in the south east, a new building type began to appear. Very largely a response to the spread of private motoring and encouraged by the building boom, these 'roadhouses', incorporating features of Continental European practice, were in a sense a new generation of the traditional roadside inn. Sited at important road intersections, their spacious premises, in neo-Tudor, neo-Georgian or (more rarely) International Modern style were designed to welcome families. As well as large bars, they contained restaurants, gardens, and entertainment and dance halls. Some also had heated and floodlit swimming pools ('lidos'), tennis courts, bowling greens, or even golf courses and riding schools. Large car parks were seen as essential. A contemporary magazine defined the newcomers as 'a sort of public country club where one may call on the one hand for a "half-a-pint of mild", and on the other for a *filet de sole Normand*, and a bottle of *Veuve Cliquot*'[11]. At the 1932 *Berkeley Arms Hotel* at Cranford, Middlesex, designed in French chateau style by E. B. Musman, there was one wing with a public bar 'where one may play darts in the company of the local lads, and on the other wing there is the delicate sophistication of a Mayfair restaurant, complete with jazz band, skilful chef, and noiseless, long-tailed waiters'[12].

Contemporary with the roadhouse but on a slightly smaller scale were the new 'improved' public houses or 'superpubs' erected by the brewery companies, mostly in neo-Tudor or neo-Georgian styles, to meet the needs of the new middle class suburbs of the inter war period. Often strategically sited just outside the commuters' railway station and not far from their contemporaries the super cinemas, these also had facilities for eating and dancing, banquets and stage performances. George Orwell did not approve of either roadhouses or superpubs, seeing them as a threat to working class drinking traditions. He thought them 'dismal sham-Tudor places fitted out by the brewery companies and very expensive. . . for the working class population. . . it is a very serious blow at communal life'[13].

# Drama; and Beauty to Music

Almost every established middle class area had its amateur dramatic, operatic or literary society, if not all three. Such organisations were haunts not only of the enthusiast but of the lonely and unappreciated. The operatic and drama groups particularly, with their rehearsals, play readings and dressing-up, encouraged legitimate and extra-marital flirtation.

An entirely wholesome diversion for ladies of the middle classes appeared in 1930 when Mrs Molly Bagot Stack founded the Women's League of Health & Beauty, a movement reflecting the new interest in physical culture that was spreading out from Germany and Scandinavia. The League's slogan 'Racial Health' proudly displayed on the armband, was in tune with the times, if doomed to become something of an embarrassment as time passed. Members, of all ages, but mainly in their late twenties, thirties or forties, and mostly but not entirely middle class, were taught that 'the trained body can supply the secret of a simple, happy life'. To this end the enrolled ladies indulged in rhythmic drills, full of leapings and stretchings, performed in unison to music, dressed in a uniform of white satin sleeveless V neck blouse and black sateen shorts designed by Mrs Stack's sister, a West End couturier. Normally this activity took place in the decent privacy of halls of various kinds but the climax of the year was the mass demonstration before an admiring public at the Albert Hall, Hyde Park or Wembley Stadium. By the end of the 1930s, now led by Mrs Stack's daughter, Prunella, the League boasted some 100,000 active UK members, no doubt all in trim for the trials to come in the testing 1940s. That the League fulfilled a need is demonstrated by its survival today, largely unchanged in character, if inevitably more classless, its members still wearing the classic uniform of sixty years ago.

## Open Air Pursuits

Two outdoor games, golf and tennis, should certainly be regarded as quintessentially middle class during the first half of the century and as such deserve extended consideration. A few others, including croquet (which had virtually disappeared by 1920), were largely confined to this social grouping. Although there may be scope for a specialised thesis on social snobberies and class distinctions within the major county clubs, and in particular the MCC, cricket in general has always welcomed anyone showing skill at hitting a hard ball with a slab of wood, throwing it, or catching it, no matter what his class origins. It therefore calls for no particular mention here.

In England and Wales, if not in Scotland, golf was the premier middle class sport. A piece contributed to *The Sketch* in December 1934 by Sir Guy Campbell Bt., features an aristocrat investigating middle class views on the game and its facilities. Sir Guy very reasonably suggests that his bourgeois interviewees, two retired officers (a colonel and naval commander – the absence of the RAF is interesting), 'a businessman and a professional man' well represent the 'average golfer'. We shall return to them in a moment.

Not much played until the last two decades of the 19th century, when many new clubs were founded, golf experienced a surge in popularity in the 1900s and 1910s following the 1902 invention of a rubber-cored ball, which greatly increased the striking distance. The decade and a half to 1915 saw many new courses laid out. Normally it was necessary to join a golf club if one wished to play regularly. This introduced a structure providing many opportunities for maintaining class (and sex) segregation, for keeping out perceived undesirables and generally cultivating exclusivity and snobbery. Club entrance fees of five pounds or more and subscriptions ranging from £8.10s to as much as fifteen pounds between the wars, together with the cost of gear, caddies, and drinking and other activities in the clubhouse were in themselves an effective deterrent for many with modest incomes and family commitments. Some indication of the social status of golf is illustrated by a 1902 rule of the Dorking Golf Club about temporary membership, which it was suggested, might be drawn from 'schoolmasters, curates and doctors' locums temporarily employed in the neighbourhood'. When it was proposed by a member of the same club eighteen years later that the subscription be lowered to encourage *tradesmen* to join, the committee did not even bother to give the matter the dignity of discussion[14]. Some clubs relaxed sufficiently to allow a form of apartheid – an 'artisans' section, segregated in its own modest clubhouse and playing at pre-ordained times.

The club house of a golf course was typically a place totally redolent of the English middle class, where its heart beat strongly, and where its tastes, customs and manners were seen on open display. Sir Guy's little group of 1934 'average golfers' mentioned above considered that the club house should have well-proportioned rooms – 'the Georgian type of architecture, I gathered, was most favoured' – simply but comfortably furnished, the dining room arranged to give quick service, providing luncheons at 2s6d and teas at a shilling. Quick service was also thought a necessary feature of the general lounge, the men's smoking room, and the women's drawing room (note the careful segregation of the sexes). It was considered that the clubhouse should also have spacious changing rooms for men and women, each equipped with efficient drying room and a bathroom. Ideally there should also be a reading and writing room.

Middle class businessmen were among the most passionate adherents of a game which provided convenient and leisurely opportunities for making contacts, advancing new speculations and proposals and clinching deals. Golf had the advantage that it could be played long after advancing age had made it necessary to give up other sports. Comparatively undemanding in physical and mental effort, it could be pursued with contentment and reasonable skill by the ageing and overweight, especially so in a period when caddies were readily available to carry the bag of clubs and rescue or locate errant balls[15]. At the same time it was an entirely acceptable and respectable pursuit for middle class women. By the end of the 1920s there were 1,300 clubs in all parts of England and Wales with a total membership of over 352,000[16].

Sensitive to the popularity of the game amongst their clientele, housing developers at the upper end of the market sought to locate their building activities near existing golf courses, even in a few cases providing new ones. At Ifield, Sussex, in 1925, British & Continental Estates Ltd, promised 'an 18-hole golf course will be laid out'[17] whilst the Upminster, Essex, Garden Suburb was advertised in 1927 as having 'a miniature 9-hole golf couse'[18]. A 1937 advertisement for detached four and five bedroom houses costing £1,950 and £2,250 on the Goring Hall Estate at West Worthing and the nearby Ham Manor Estate at Angmering, Sussex, announced that they were 'planned around two superb golf courses on which residents are offered preferential terms'. At Dorking, between the wars, Park Copse, a small development of large detached houses, had its own private footpath on to the adjacent golf course and there were many other examples of this sort of facility.

Until the mid-twenties, most golfers travelled to their course by train. From about 1905, with golf enjoying a boom, the railways became alive to this new source of traffic, much of it likely to be First Class and therefore lucrative. An article in *The Railway Magazine* in 1910[19] spoke of the 'general policy' adopted by the railway companies 'in encouraging the formation of golf clubs in the most suitable and popular areas of their respective systems, and generally in encouraging golfers, as an influential class of the community, to travel far afield in search of opportunities to enjoy their favourite recreation'. This writer went on to note, 'it has become almost an axiom that where golf links are found, there speedily arises a growing and influential body of residents. Places like Beckenham, Bickley, Bexhill, Chipstead, Deal, Eltham, Walton Heath, Hythe, Littlestone, Rye, Limpsfield, Sevenoaks, Sidcup, Sundridge Park, Sydenham and Epsom, owe, for example a great deal of their growing prospects to the proximity of excellent golf links.' At this time many railway companies were issuing golfers' cheap return tickets (usually at single fare, or single and a quarter for the return journey) on production of a form signed by the club secretary or a club membership card. To encourage the others, club officials were given half-rate seasons and even free passes[20]. There were also special combined tickets; in 1924 the Great Western Railway advertised a package at specially reduced rates which included rail travel from London to Sonning (Berkshire), green fees, hotel accommodation and motor transport between railway station, hotel and golf course[21].

Golf featured strongly in railway publicity material. Seeking to attract golfers to Aldeburgh, Southwold, Frinton, Yarmouth, Sheringham and Hunstanton, the Great Eastern Railway in 1912 distributed pictorial score cards for these courses depicting a young lady at the end of what was described as 'a brassy stroke'. These cards were shortly followed by a free booklet, *Golf in East Anglia*, which contained illustrations of all the links served, details of the playing characteristics of each, subscriptions, green fees, and fares from London[22]. Similar guides were put out by the Great Northern and other railways.

Some companies went much further. The North Staffordshire Railway actually owned golf courses and club houses at Rudyard Lake, leasing them to clubs. Although Scotland is outside the main scope of this book, it is interesting to note that in that country, railway companies built and operated large hotels (Turnberry, Gleneagles and Cruden Bay) each equipped with magnificent eighteen-hole courses and designed in large part to attract the English middle class tourist. Before car ownership was widespread amongst the middle classes, some links were difficult of access by any means but rail and there were many instances of the railways opening special halts or platforms for the convenience of golfers, mostly in the period 1901–14. When a new 18-hole course was laid out at Moor Park, near Rickmansworth, Hertfordshire in 1908 the Metropolitan Railway agreed to provide a station to serve what were to be the nearest links on sand beyond the London clay belt north of the Thames. Old railway sleepers were helpfully supplied by the railway company for the construction of bunker faces and other features. The new station was opened to regular traffic in May 1910 and the promoter was awarded a free pass to and from London[23]. Other examples of golf clubs given rail facilities were Beaconsfield Golf Club, Buckinghamshire, (1906); St. Bee's Golf Club, near Whitehaven (1910); Bishop's Stortford Golf Club, Essex, (1910); Bessacar, near Doncaster (1912); Denham, Buckinghamshire (1912); Bramshot, near Farnborough, Hants, (1913); Dyke Golf Club, near Brighton, Sussex (about 1914); Purley Downs Golf Club, near Croydon (about 1914); and Carpenders Park, near Watford, (1914). At Bramshot, the train service had deteriorated by the late 1920s to only two services a week, restricted to members only; both calls were made on Sundays, timed to ensure that those travelling by rail were obliged to lunch at the clubhouse. At least the club treasurer was happy.[24]

Tennis, the one game in which women enjoyed equal status to men right through to the Wimbledon championships, was a very middle class sport, although it was often ignored by schools because it was not a 'team' activity, and for boys, since it offered little or no threat of physical injury, it was not considered 'manly'. Annually reinforced by the glamour and publicity of Wimbledon, it was a game which remained popular throughout the period.

Gardens of the larger middle class houses often contained at least one tennis court, a facility which allowed private tennis parties to become a regular part of the owners' summer social life. Those without access to such luxury played at the tennis clubs to be found in most middle class areas, including the speculatively-built estates of small semi-detached houses. For the lower middle classes living in the more thickly built-up older suburbs there were the courts in municipal parks. In each case, though perhaps least so in the last, tennis had the special attraction of providing opportunities for meeting socially acceptable members of the opposite sex.

At Hadley Wood, in north London, a tennis club started in the 1890s 'made a most important contribution to summer social life' and

290

nearly every family belonged. Teas were served in the pavilion and the summer gymkhana run by the club was followed by an informal Flannel Dance[25]. And in Wallington, Surrey, tennis girls in white dresses and young men in long white flannel trousers 'socialised' in the club pavilion, where on Saturday nights they would dance to the music of amateur local bands[26]. At Dorking, a Surrey town with a large middle class element, the first tennis club, with its four grass courts, was founded in 1901 with an annual subscription 'including balls' of thirteen shillings. Another club was started in this small town six years later and a third in 1913. The latter had a subscription of £1.11s6d for men and £1.1s for ladies, presumably more difficult to attract. There was also a hefty ten pound entrance fee, an effective means of excluding those from families of modest means. Furthermore, applicants for senior membership were required to state their father's 'profession' and this was taken into account when considering admission. Tradespeople were not encouraged and if they did succeed in being admitted, they tended to be left to play amongst themselves. This club's five grass courts were increased to seven after closure of the by then less popular croquet court in 1921. Sunday play, from 2 pm to dusk, was allowed for the first time in 1924. Three years later, two Ferndon hard courts were laid down. Tea and biscuits were dispensed to members in a wooden pavilion, whose draughty open-sided and rose-bedecked verandah sheltered players waiting for the summer rain to cease[27].

House builders, particularly in the 1920s, believing that such amenities added tone, were fond of advertising that there were tennis courts either on their estates, or nearby, or that their houses overlooked them. At Pavilion Gardens, Staines, Middlesex, in 1935, every house was alleged to overlook the tennis courts, where there were tea gardens, shrubbery and a pavilion 'exclusively for the use of residents'[28], although it is not clear for what purpose they were to use the shrubbery. In 1911, at Brockenhurst Gardens, Mill Hill, Middlesex, an advertisement for 'contract-built houses for gentlefolk' talked of the estate's own private tennis club[29] and on Laings' Colindale, (Middlesex), development of the late 1920s, 'estate tennis courts' were 'reserved for purchasers'[30]. The establishment of tennis clubs was encouraged by builders, who would donate strips or corners of land unsuitable for house plots.

Some other ball games should be mentioned briefly since they were predominantly middle class in character. Except in South Wales, Cornwall and the Anglo-Scottish borders, rugby football, in the version played to Rugby Union rules, was primarily a middle class game. It was popular in the universities and in the public schools, where it had superseded soccer after that had become a working class sport. Rugby Union was consequently adopted for winter compulsory games by many grammar and county secondary schools, copying the public school example. It followed that the spectators at Twickenham and other RU grounds were throughout the period largely middle class and the social life attached to RU and its clubs closely paralleled that of golf in providing suitable opportunities, in a relaxed atmosphere, for making business contacts and deals.

Hockey, netball and lacrosse were similarly middle class in tone. Popular at the universities, teacher training colleges and girls' public schools, they were taken up by many grammar and county secondary schools for the compulsory games syllabus as suitable for the young ladies of the lower middle class. Ladies' hockey clubs were established all over the country in the 1900s, their players awesome and unlovely in skirts six inches from the ground, cricket caps and ungainly boots. By the 1910s schoolgirls were playing the game in white shirts and navy blue box-pleated gym slips, their black-stockinged legs protected by cricket pads. Mixed hockey was comparatively rare, but at some co-educational schools there were occasional contests between staff and senior girls in which masters participated.

The Continental cult of athleticism and the open air which had led to the formation of the Women's League of Health & Beauty also provided a new boost for the pastime of walking in the countryside. This had been a popular recreation amongst the urban lower middle and respectable working class since the late 19th century and in the 1910s and 1920s the railways, in their search for lucrative off-peak traffic, had sought to encourage rambling by offering special 'out to one station, back from another' tickets, publishing guides with details of suggested walks. The inspiration for the revival came from Germany, where since the end of World War 1 many young men had taken to roaming the countryside in short-sleeved shirts, long socks and *lederhosen*. Young people, mostly from the suburban lower middle class, enthusiastically embraced the new craze for 'hiking' when it arrived in Britain in 1930–1. Unlike the earlier 'ramblers', the 'hikers' adopted a special garb, though the German leather shorts were rarely seen. Both sexes wore short-sleeved shirts and heavy cotton shorts with long woollen socks, but the more conservative girls preferred a pleated tweed skirt with rayon or silk stockings. A canvas haversack slung across the back carried refreshments, rain gear and maps. The men, frequently seen with tobacco pipe in mouth, often went hatless, whilst the girls tended to favour berets. Thus attired, they set out at weekends and holiday times in parties varying in size from half a dozen or less to small armies, passing along footpaths and across fields in single file, chattering and laughing. Since very few had the use of a private car to reach the starting point, the railways received a welcome increase in business at weekends. They again offered special ticket facilities which allowed return from alternative stations and published new series of walks guides. The Southern Railway booklets by S. P. B. Mais were illustrated with photographs and easily-followed sketch maps. Mais, the son of a clergyman, was a typical middle class figure of the period; educated at private schools and Oxford University, he had posts as games master at various schools. In the interests of drumming up as much railway business as possible, his guides suggested winter as well as summer, spring and autumn walks. Newspapers circulating widely amongst middle class office workers, such as the London *Evening News* also published details of walks based on railway stations.

At Easter 1932, with the new craze at its height, the Great Western Railway put on 'Hikers' Mystery Expresses' from London (Paddington). Over 1,500 turned up for the Good Friday train, making it necessary to run a duplicate[31]. Other companies copied. The railways, in cooperation with the Ramblers' Association, also operated special trains on Sundays to suitable stations from which there were guided walks of varying physical endurance to suit all comers, the schedules being handed out on the train. All walks ended at a tried and trusted tea place. With a break during World War 2, these ramblers' special trains continued until the early 1960s, by which time some of the users had taken to the private car as a means of reaching walking country and railway operators were paying more attention to the economics of such marginal operations.

Predictably, the arrival of the hiking era saw the ever-vigilant middle class guardians of sexual morality growing alarmed at the prospect of young people of both sexes dressed in skimpy clothes wandering off into the fields and woods. Somewhat illogically, day trips were not condemned, the anxiety concentrating on hiking holidays away from parental supervision[32].

Another outdoor activity, in contrast to the situation today, does not justify much attention here. Only a minority of middle class people were totally absorbed by gardening as a regular pastime. The working class and some lower middles recently moved up from it cultivated their allotments, an institution imposed by middle class influences and further encouraged by the food shortages of the two world wars. Other middle class men, mostly those with modest incomes, had vegetable patches in their suburban gardens and this equally became temporarily more popular during wartime. The statistical survey of middle class expenditure in

1938 referred to in earlier chapters tends to confirm the impression that gardening generally was far less widespread as a leisure activity than it is now, showing an average outlay on this item of less than a shilling a week or about the same as that on biscuits.

Whilst the proud owner of a new house in the suburbs would be much occupied for a year or two in forming a garden from the fenced patch of rough grass and builders' rubble that came with his purchase, after that, like the rest of the middle classes, he would probably do little more than keep the grass, shrubs and few flowers tidy, expending the very minimum in effort and enthusiasm. Those a little higher up the income scale employed as much of the readily available and low-cost outside help as they could afford and were content to enjoy their large gardens passively. Of course there were always a few fanatical enthusiasts, but most of these did little more than direct hired labour, reserving for themselves the more congenial tasks of paper planning and recording, pottering about, deadheading and looking to see what needed to be done by others.

# Less willingly to Church

By the 1930s and 1940s, under mounting assault, first from cycling, then from pleasure motoring and motorcycling, hiking and golf, the former middle class Sunday leisure activity of two or three church attendances, already falling away before 1914[33], had diminished to a trickle. Others were opting out because it was easier and more comfortable to absorb a religious service or sermon at second hand, through the new medium of radio. There were those too who had lost their faith in the traumas and social mixing of World War 1, or soon afterwards in delayed reaction to the awful loss and suffering inflicted. Since the urban proletariat, the poor and the upper classes had never been very enthusiastic attenders, church congregations shrunk to a core of middle class faithful, mainly women and the elderly, as the Victorian Sabbath gave way to the one and a half day secular weekend.

Until 1914 a fine church had always been a central feature of any new middle class suburb, erected with, or very soon after the houses themselves, its construction costs largely met by the developers or the enthusiastic new residents, anxious for the respectable cachet it would give their new district. But by the mid 1920s provision of churches in new middle class areas was beginning to lag far behind completion of other buildings. Although developers would frequently provide a site, many 1930s suburbs did not get their permanent church until after World

War 2, making do meantime with wooden huts or what was eventually to be the parish hall.

Despite a significant decline in regular churchgoing, formal observance continued unabated in such institutions as the armed services, and most middle class people went on using the church for baptisms, weddings and funerals, perhaps also retaining a nominal grip on their faith by attendances at Easter and Christmas Holy Communion. Many continued to send their children to Sunday Schools, vaguely recalling baptismal promises and trusting this indoctrination would provide some useful behavioural conditioning and sound moral principles whilst they enjoyed a couple of hours of relaxation on their own. Those able to send their children to boarding schools rested content that they would be certain to be in church or chapel every Sunday.

In one respect the Anglican Church in particular fulfilled a role similar to that we have noticed when talking of the local authority secondary schools. Those children at the lower margins of the middle class, or pressing up against them, who were persuaded by one means or another to take church life seriously from about the time of their Confirmation would find themselves associating closely with the characteristically middle class clergy, at meetings in the vicarage, serving at the altar and attending retreats and social functions. With this regular exposure to middle class manners, ways and lifestyle, they tended to absorb the class attitudes and aspirations alongside their religious education and development. In this way they were subtly directed towards their adult class status, whatever their background. Bourne noticed this process at work at Farnham Common in the 1900s, finding that some young artisans and labourers approved of the church's ideas and decorous life:

> It is a school of good manners to them, if not of high thinking, with the result that they begin to be quite a different sort of people. . . A pleasant suavity and gentleness marks their behaviour. They are greatly self-respecting, their tendency is to adopt and live up to the middle class code of respectability[34]

In social and political influence the churches remained powerful through the 1920s and 1930s, especially in such areas as secularisation of Sundays and resisting increasing pressure for Sunday opening of cinemas, places of amusement and shops. They worked successfully for suppression of any tendencies for publications, films or stage shows to be even mildly pornographic; in the control of drinking hours; and in opposition to divorce and contraception. These expressions of so-called Christian 'middle class morality' were also particularly pervasive and pronounced in parliament and local councils, where the often forcefully-expressed views of the elected and mainly middle class representatives, hypocritical and otherwise, backed by other self-designated moral guardians, were usually more extreme than those of the nation as a whole, or even the majority within their own social group.

## NOTES

1. Connell, J., in note to *Old Ordnance Survey Maps, London Sheet 29, Upper Holloway 1914*, The Godfrey Edition (1988).
2. Prices of goods quoted in this and subsequent paragraphs are taken from contemporary advertising in magazines, newspapers and shop catalogues.
3. Anon., *Sell to Britain Through 'The Daily Mail'* (n.d. but 1929 or 1930).
4. Cole, Oswald, 'The Quest for Cameron Corbett; a Study of an Eminent Edwardian', Lewisham Local History Society, *Transactions* 1973, 45.
5. Anon. op cit, (note 3).
6. GLRO ACC 1297 MET 10/483.
7. Anon, op cit, (note 3).
8. Never very profitable but traditionally regarded as useful in enticing customers into the shops, these libraries lasted until 1961 (W. H. Smith) and 1966 (Boots).
9. *The Resident*, Stoneleigh (Surrey) Residents' Association, December 1935.
10. EN 4 January 1909.
11. *Building*, April, 1932.
12. id.
13. Orwell, George, *The Road to Wigan Pier*, (1937).
14. Holland, Coffey, (in) Newbery, Celia, (ed.) *A History of Sports in Dorking* (1985).
15. Caddies, often youths as young as twelve, received ninepence a round in the 1920s (Cunnington, Mrs W., 'Barn Hill, Uxendon and Preston', *Harrow Miscellany* (1975). Older men got more, perhaps a shilling to half-a-crown (2s6d).
16. Anon, op cit (note 3). Quoting *The Alliance Yearbook 1936*, Saunders and Jones, op cit (note 3, chapter 1), give a slightly lower figure for 1930 of 957 clubs and 294,000 members.
17. EN 6 March 1925.
18. EN 4 November 1927.
19. Robertson, A. J., 'The Railways and Golf', *The Railway Magazine*, October 1910.
20. GLRO ACC 1297 MET 10/125.
21. *The Railway Magazine*, November 1924.
22. id, June and July, 1912.
23. GLRO ACC 1297 MET 10/125.
24. Kidner, R. W., *The Waterloo–Southampton Line*, (1983).

25. Clark, Nancy, *Hadley Wood, its Background and Development,* (1968).
26. Whiteing, Eileen, *Anyone for Tennis? Growing Up in Wallington between the Wars,* (1979).
27. Mercer, Miss D., (in Newbery, Celia, (ed) op cit (note 14).
28. EN 17 May 1935.
29. EN 20 April 1911.
30. Laing brochure, n.d.
31. *The Railway Magazine,* May 1932.
32. See eg sermon of Father F. Woodlock, SJ, reported in *The Daily Mail,* 4 May 1931 and subsequent comment and letter from Woodlock (7 May 1931).
33. In his *The Condition of England,* (1909), Masterman several times avers that the middle classes, once 'the centre and historical support of England's Protestant creed', were drifting away from their religion. An investigation carried out by *The Daily News* in London between November 1902 and November 1903 fond that of a total population of 6.25 million, only 1.25 million were attending the churches regularly, most of them lower middle class. The numbers of regular attenders continued to decline right through to 1950, with the middle classes, particularly the middle class women, remaining the bulwark of the Anglican congregations. Throughout the period middle class churchgoers were predominantly Anglican in their religious allegiance.
34. Bourne, George, *Change in the Village* (1912).

# CHAPTER 11

# SUMMER BY THE SEA

## Amongst One's Own Kind

Summer Holidays, usually taken at the seaside, had been an established feature of middle class life for most of the last half of the 19th century. Treated very much as a family occasion, they were regarded as a means of benefiting the children's health whilst the adults built up their energies to attack their regular occupations with renewed vigour. Unlike the working class, who used their brief respites as often orgiastic escapes from toil, the middle classes tended to have purposeful, sober holidays, pursuing recreation rather than relaxation and release. Whilst some went off to explore local churches, old towns and the countryside, others studied the local geology, botany or birdlife. Literary and artistic associations of the holiday area were carefully noted, the appropriate books read. Guides to middle class resort districts such as the excellent Ward Lock series made gestures towards this pursuit of cultural, scientific and general intellectual improvement whilst on holiday by incorporating suitable information.

At first the middle and upper classes had most places almost entirely to themselves, although there were a few centres such as Brighton where from quite an early date they were obliged to retreat from contact with the *hoi polloi*, imported in large crowds for a few brief hours by the railways' cheap excursion trains. As the new century opened, the working classes were appearing in greater numbers on day trips, even taking several days' holiday in the larger resorts, some of which, such as Blackpool, New Brighton and Southend, they were making very much their own. The middle classes responded by using their larger disposable incomes to go further afield, seeking out locations where they could enjoy quiet and be among their own kind, even if it did take them a week or so before they spoke to fellow-holidaymakers they saw several times daily. By the turn of the century small towns and communities at considerable distances from London and the other large centres were attracting middle class holidaymakers, whilst those who remained loyal to the older, more accessible resorts were patronising newly-developed middle class enclaves or satellites growing up in places secure from the noisy excursionists and other working class holidaymakers. Thus by 1901 Southend had its

Westcliff, Brighton its Hove, Hastings its Bexhill, Margate its Westgate and Birchington, Whitby its Sandsend, Cromer its Sheringham, Black-pool its St Anne's, Weston-super-mare its Clevedon, Ilfracombe its Woolacombe and so on. An octogenarian friend of the author, recalling holiday journeys by train to the Sussex coast in the 1910s and 1920s, remembers that his parents would claim they could forecast which passengers would alight at Bexhill and which would go on to Hastings simply by listening to their voices. These social distinctions between the older resorts and their middle class progeny were also underlined by the writer of a 1901 guide to Southend, who took great care to reassure any middle class readers that in Westcliff they would be quite safe from any contact with the Cockney working class[1]:

> . . . 'Arry and 'Arriet . . . don't, like the superior person, go hankering after new places every season. Year after Year they turn their eager faces in the direction of Southend's East-End, and once there think not of poaching on the superior person's preserves west of the Pier Hill. Westcliff, the new part of Southend, with its terraces and lovely shrubberies . . . its lounging chairs, bandstand and flagstaff has no attraction for 'Arry and 'Arriet. They have even been known to term it 'dead and alive'. . . The atmosphere of calm and repose depresses, and should curiosity tempt them to stray into this region, they speedily return to the old town. . . Both remain, after numerous visits, sublimely unconscious of the smart people, who of late years have taken up their abode in the smart residences west of Pier Hill. That region is an undiscovered country. . .

During the 1920s plebeianisation of the established major seaside resorts was greatly accelerated by the motor cycle and motor coach. These widely extended both the range and quantity of "'Arrys and 'Arriets' and their provincial brothers and sisters. The new invasion was further swollen when, in response to the new competition, the railways laid on more and cheaper excursion trains. This development caused the beleagured middle classes to range still further afield, to Devon and Cornwall, west and north west Wales and the Highlands and Islands of Scotland, or to strengthen their hold on existing bastions such as Frinton, Southwold, Aldeburgh, Sheringham, Seaview, Sidmouth, Deal and Rye. Also, from the 1910s, the same pressures caused increasing numbers of the more affluent to desert Britain altogether for the Normandy and Brittany coast, or even to follow the upper classes into Switzerland, Austria, the Rhineland, the Black Forest, northern and central Italy and Scandinavia.

This traffic had grown sufficiently by the early 1930s to encourage the nine leading tour operators jointly to charter trains in Europe, securing fare reductions of up to forty per cent per seat and enabling the British middle classes to explore the limits attainable in twelve to fifteen or even twenty four hours by rail and sea. Once the tourists had arrived at the chosen resort, they often found living costs noticeably lower than in the United Kingdom. During the thirties the exchange rates to most European countries were highly favourable; ten days all-inclusive at the Caux Palace Hotel, Montreux, cost no more than £12.10s in 1934, whilst Belgium was even cheaper than Switzerland, with all-in rates as low as 11s6d or 12s6d a day at The Continental Palace, Blankenberghe and the Hotel Britannique, Spa. At this time nine days in Italy including rail fare was offered at under eight pounds and a week in France and Germany for five pounds, including fares, was practicable. Cut-price short sea cruises to the Baltic, North Germany and the French Atlantic Coast, organised by shipping companies with surplus capacity caused by the trade depression, were very popular. After the financial crisis of 1931, when the government sought to discourage the spending of foreign currency, these cruises offered a way of holidaying abroad and paying most of the bill in sterling. By the mid 1930s, air transport, usually by Imperial Airways from Croydon Airport, was beginning to become a means of holiday travel to be considered by the middle classes, although as yet it was not a serious threat to the much more heavily-patronised rail and sea routes. Although Thomas Cook first advertised holidays by air in 1937, train chartering was to continue for many years after the interruption of World War 2.

In face of the onslaught from plebeian excursionists and short stay visitors, resorts with middle class pretensions fought hard to retain their exclusiveness, banning amusement parks and open-fronted booths peddling seaside rock, fish and chips, cockles, winkles and jellied eels, teas on the beach, ice cream and the like. Rigorous exclusion of the sort of amenities found in profusion on the promenades of Blackpool, New Brighton, Porthcawl, Skegness, Rhyl, Southend and Margate was usually enough to keep away the dreaded excursion trains, tripper motor coaches and motor cycles and sidecars. To be doubly sure, Frinton imposed a strict ban on both buses and motor coaches in the area between the railway and its sea front. At the latter there were no shops of any kind. In World War 1, finding it easy to overlook the sacrifices being made on their behalf a few miles across the North Sea, the residents of this town had even objected to the presence of wounded common soldiers on its clifftop greens, presumably because they looked untidy and could not be trusted to behave in a seemly Frintonian manner. For many years Bournemouth refused to have donkey rides on its beaches, fearing its image would be spoiled. In his *England for Everyman* (1933), H. A.

Piehler notes that at Thorpeness, a middle class seaside colony started on the north side of Aldeburgh in 1912, 'Jerry-built bungalows, piers, pierrots etc.,' were barred.

Two other devices were used to preserve selectivity and class separation at resorts. Artist-drawn picture postcards served not only as valuable publicity but could also be arranged to intimidate the prospective tripper by depicting smartly-dressed middle class visitors, perhaps also showing landaus with liveried coachmen against a background of imposing hotels. In their own publicity the larger hotels were fond of picturing expensive limousines ranged outside the main entrance. And at places like Scarborough, Llandudno and Folkestone there were private scenic roads and drives imposing a toll on pedestrians and vehicles.

## House, Hotel and Camp

Until World War 1 the wealthier middles continued the Victorian practice of going on holiday with their servants in attendance, thus ensuring there was always someone available to look after children, clothes and luggage, all of which might otherwise be tedious. For the summer break of a month or more, many families took a house of similar type to their own in which life proceeded very much as at home. It was not unusual for the father to leave the family on holiday, returning to London during the week after taking his own shorter break. 'Fathers' Boats' plied between London Bridge and the East Anglian and Thanet resorts in the summer, specifically to accommodate this traffic, whilst other fathers took advantage of the highly-discounted long distance season tickets offered by some railway companies, finding these cheaper than the purchase of six or so weekend tickets when the family was spending the summer by the sea. Some of the more affluent families stayed in the large hotels, most of which had suitably austere accommodation for the servants of their middle class residents or, if this were not convenient, they would hire out a servant at around 10–15s a day.

During the closing twenty years or so of the 19th century and in rapidly growing numbers after that, the new lower middle class began to join those already taking an extended summer holiday, though they could not of course afford to have their family at the seaside for more than a week or so. At first most went to the larger, established resorts, but by the late 1920s they were exploring more widely and were to be found alongside the wealthier middles in many of the remoter places mentioned above. Economical accommodation was available in the form of 'apartments', where the landlady would cook food purchased by her visitors; otherwise they would stay in a boarding house where they would be served three meals a day. At these establishments conditions in the 1900s and 1910s tended to be regimented and somewhat spartan. Guests would be seated at a long communal table covered with white linen cloths and furnished with the ritual middle class table napkins. This arrangement provided an enforced social contact not always welcome, but costs were low and even those on quite modest salaries could afford a week away. Thus a London-based girl typist in 1909 with an annual income of £66.18s including two weeks' paid holiday, needed only just over £4.10s for her fortnight by the sea. This purchased full board for two weeks (£2.10s), railway fare and cab (18s), and pleasure trips (just over a pound) leaving two shillings for tips.[2]. Before 1914 charges for full board ranged from £1.5s to around four guineas a week, the latter providing the best bedroom, a three-course breakfast, three-course lunch and six-course dinner[3]. Third Class rail fares averaged about one old penny and First Class two old pennies a mile.

After World War 1, many of the small boarding houses gradually upgraded themselves, introducing 'separate tables' instead of the communal board as well as 'running hot and cold water in all bedrooms', improvements which, with the increased cost of living, raised the full board charge per person per week from a minimum of £1.15s to around five pounds. 'Apartments', now charging £1.4s to £1.10s per bed per week, were much favoured by the lower middle class. Then, as now, it was customary to impose high rates in July and August when business peaked steeply owing to the seemingly immovable feast of school summer holidays. After rising in the war period, ordinary railway fares were fixed at 2½d a mile First Class and 1½d a mile Third Class from 1923 to 1937, then increasing slightly, but from mid-1933 until World War 2, 'summer' or 'monthly return' tickets were widely available at a penny a mile for the out-and-back journey and there were penny a mile Weekend Tickets and other special offers from the early 1920s.

'Boarding house' had become an increasingly down-market term by the 1930s, with more and more such establishments describing themselves as 'guest houses' or 'private hotels'. Any house employing staff outside the immediate family of the owners was thought to justify reclassification as a private hotel, a cachet which enabled slightly higher prices to be charged.

The long-established large seaside hotels lost much of their wealthier middle class trade after World War 1. If visiting the traditional resorts, such families no longer brought with them retinues of servants, but many were now cruising or holidaying abroad. They were replaced to some extent by *nouveaux riches*, the people who had done well out of the war. Most big seaside hotels (and inland ones at places such as Tunbridge Wells, Malvern, Bath and Dorking) also enjoyed a stable, if barely-remunerative year-round business accommodating long-stay elderly middle class ladies (and a few men) of the rentier or privately-pensioned retired groups. Draining away the ends of their lives in shabby gentility supported by small private incomes, pensions and investments, these 'permanent' residents of the large hotels were allowed substantial discounts on the normal charges of from £4.10s to £7.10s for a week's full board in the between-war years. Significant numbers of the 'unoccupied' rentier/retired groups, most of them over forty years of age, were also to be found living in flats and houses, mainly concentrated in south east Kent, Sussex and the other counties along the Channel coast as far as Devon and Cornwall. For them life was one long holiday.[4]

Until the end of the 1930s an annual holiday of a week or longer was a luxury largely confined to the middle and upper classes. From 1920 there was a steady growth in the numbers taking a week or more away from home until the figure reached what one source estimated to be fifteen million (of a forty six million population) in 1937[5]. This increase was related almost entirely to the extension of the holiday habit amongst the lower middles. Although by this time there was a substantial minority contributing to holiday savings schemes or enjoying paid holidays which provided some assistance towards achieving a week's break, most working class families managed little more than visits to relatives or extended day trips. A parliamentary committee on paid holidays reported in April 1938 that whilst there had been a considerable growth in the numbers receiving paid holidays since the early 1920s, there were still just under eleven million (seventy two per cent of the waged) who did not get them. But holiday pay or not, total income was the major deciding factor. A family man earning less than £3.10s–£4 a week had no margin for even the cheapest form of holidaymaking involving a week away from home even if he did receive holiday pay, so it was not surprising that the railways and lodging house keepers reported no perceptible increase in business arising from the holidays with pay movement of the late 1930s. In June 1939 *The News-Chronicle* published the results of a survey which showed that of those earning four pounds a week or more (ie broadly the middle classes) ninety per cent could afford an annual holiday away from home of at least a week, but amongst those earning less than this (almost entirely working class, but including some lower middle class) only just over a third could manage one.

It was for this reason that when Billy Butlin established his first holiday camps[6] (at Skegness in 1936 and at Clacton two years later) it was the lower middles, not the working class that formed the bulk of his initial clentele. The Industrial Welfare Society reported in 1938 'the commercial holiday camp seemed to be hardly used at all by the average worker. . . very few go abroad or to the country'. Even the Workers' Travel Association was obliged to admit that its guest houses were occupied mainly by middle class people.

It is interesting, though perhaps not surprising, that the urge to get away on holiday was unabated even during the worst years of World War 2, despite stern government discouragement of 'unnecessary' use of the strategically vital rail system by the public. Since the beaches of the east and much of the south coat were militarised and barricaded against the possibility of German invasion the pressure fell on the west country. With pockets well filled from the proceeds of long hours of war work, large numbers of the working class augmented the crowds of war-weary middle class besieging the railway stations serving that area. On the Saturday before August Bank Holiday 1941, the *Cornish Riviera Express* from Paddington to Penzance was run in no less than five sections, carrying in all 4,522 people to Devon and Cornwall, 1,089 on one train alone[7]. Similar pressures continued through each wartime summer peak and once the war was over, the late 1940s saw a boom in holiday traffic for the railways, the road coaches and the holiday resorts[8]. By this time over eighty per cent of the working population were enjoying holidays with pay and with their finances benefiting from wartime earnings and the regular incomes of the vastly increased number of their women in work, the working class now formed a far higher proportion of those taking one week or more for a summer holiday. At the end of the 1940s, the middle classes' near monopoly of a residential annual seaside holiday had disappeared. These years and the 1950s saw an almost unmanageable pressure on the railways and the road coaches in July and August, until it was relieved in the next decade by two new features: a vast extension of car ownership and the development of air travel for the masses. Had these not come about, some form of compulsory staggering of holidays would have become a national necessity.

# The Train Holiday

Throughout the half century it was the railway that provided the magic carpet to middle class holiday territory. It is true that from the mid twenties, some did drive to their holiday resort by car, or took motor touring holidays, but motoring long distances over a road system little changed from the horse-and-cart era in the primitively-built small saloon cars of the period could be tiring and frustrating. Many who could afford motoring preferred to travel by train and hire a car in their holiday area. Where the motor car was used, it extended the catchment areas of the holiday zones far beyond the limited trunk flows along the rail routes and also made it possible for the holidaymakers to stay at farms or in small places away from train and bus routes.

Whilst a few lower middles patronised the cheaper but much slower road coaches to reach their holiday destination, the predominant users of this mode in the twenties and thirties were the minority of working class people taking a few days' holiday away from home. For the middle classes, in the between-war years, motor coaches were more important for adding to the variety and interest of their holiday by opening up for day and half-day excursions inland attractions and 'beauty spots' inaccessible by rail and difficult to reach by local buses.

The significance of the predominantly middle class holiday traffic for the railways was evident in the spacious new station facilities provided at Llandudno in 1892, at Bexhill in 1901 and 1902 (by two competing companies), at Bognor in 1902, at Worthing in 1911, at Margate and Ramsgate in 1926, at Clacton in 1929, at Hastings in 1931 and at Seaton in 1939. It was also seen in the construction of a special branch line and four-platform terminal to serve the new Butlin Holiday Camp at Filey in 1947, two other new stations for holiday camps in the same year (Pen-y-chain and Heads of Ayr), and in the cooperation between the railway companies and the resort authorities in holiday publicity matters, which lasted from 1913 to 1962. The London & North Eastern Railway paid half the advertising costs for Butlin's pioneer holiday camp at Skegness and Butlin chose other resorts served by that company for his second and third ventures.

The time-hallowed custom of booking hotel and boarding house accommodation from Saturday to Saturday meant that the railways were under intolerable pressure on that day in July and August each year. 'It is no secret', noted *The Railway & Travel Monthly* in 1918, 'that the condition of the principal railway routes on Saturdays in pre-war summers was most unsatisfactory. The line was congested, expresses were overcrowded and unpunctual, and chaos prevailed at the principal junction stations.'[9] Until the early 1960s, large numbers of mainly elderly railway coaches were kept idle in sidings for most of the year simply to provide the extra capacity needed in the summer holiday peak from late July to early September, a period when locomotives were often diverted from freight to passenger use and much additional overtime had to be paid. In the late 1930s the railways were still having to cope with twenty million or more additional passengers in the late summer peak (some on day trips)[10] and as we have seen, this situation was to persist until the end of the 1950s.

In the early years of the century, holidays involved much preparation. As the departure date approached, one or more cabin trunks would be taken down from loft, attic or landing, to be filled with the family's newly-washed and ironed summer clothes, all carefully packed between layers of tissue paper. Placed around the edges were walking shoes and beach sandals, books and bathing costumes. Remembering wet holidays past, umbrellas and rainwear would not be overlooked, whilst a parasol might be thrown in too, with an optimistic smile. Were servants employed in the household, much of this work would fall upon them but as they also had something to look forward to, it would be done with a light heart. There was even more labour if a house were to be taken, since sheets, pillow cases, towels, table silver, china and glass might have to be packed as well, increasing the number of large trunks to perhaps half a dozen or more, including the servants' personal luggage.

Most families took away far more than was necessary and the quantity of luggage entrusted to the railways was prodigious. Some of the old-fashioned round-topped cabin trunks required two or even four men to lift them and it was not uncommon for one household's holiday luggage to occupy the whole of one or more large wooden four-wheeled platform trolleys. Allowances of ten minutes or more had to be inserted into summer timetables for loading and unloading the trunks and other impedimentia at principal intermediate stations, allowances that in practice were often exceeded by as much again. This loading of gigantic piles of accompanied luggage into the vans of passenger trains caused chronic unpunctuality, aggravating the chaotic conditions mentioned above. Eventually the situation led the railway companies to introduce schemes for sending luggage in advance at a nominal charge. In return for a shilling for each item, these arrangements, established between 1896 and 1912, provided collection from the holidaymaker's home, conveyance by rail to the holiday station and delivery to the holiday house or hotel. Cab drivers and porters, deprived of rich pickings, were not well pleased but the public quickly adopted the procedure once its reliability had been proved, learning that travelling light and finding their luggage waiting for them at the other end was altogether less stressful, especially when changes of train were involved. Suspended during World War 1, the scheme was revived in 1920 for a charge of three shillings per item, soon reduced to two shillings.

If the absence was to last more than a fortnight or so, other pre-holiday tasks included placing dust covers over the furniture and depositing the family silver and other valuables in the vaults of the local bank. On the appointed day, with the children worked up to a great state of excitement, one or more cabs would be taken to the railway station. In London, if the family were large and travelling with luggage and servants, some railway companies would supply a horse-drawn omnibus for the journey from the house to the main railway terminus, a facility also available for holiday parties crossing from one London terminus to another.

Tickets were normally taken for the First Class, which not only ensured the desired segregation from the lower orders but secured more space and the maximum attentiveness from railway officials and platform porters. The less affluent lower middle class (but not the servants) would sometimes travel Second Class until this facility was withdrawn[11].

Once settled in the carriage, it was a question of amusing the children until the great moment came when the sea was first glimpsed, perhaps many hours later, only just before sunset. Any change of train or journey across London would involve great confusion and anxiety, including much counting and recounting of family members, servants and pieces of luggage to ensure that none had been left by the wayside.

One diversion as the journey proceeded was the man with a hammer who walked along the outside of the train whilst it halted at a main intermediate station, tapping the wheels to detect cracks and examining the axle boxes of the carriages for signs of overheating. Another was the great pleasure of moving along to the restaurant car to take lunch and, a couple of hours later, afternoon tea, as the train steamed on at a leisurely forty to fifty miles an hour towards the destination. In its atmosphere and menus, the railway restaurant car was strongly middle class in tone, a feature which persisted well into the 1950s. For the children, a final excitement might be the change into a fussy little branch line train that would amble in relaxed fashion along a single track, often enough following a wooded valley or estuary to a holiday resort at the river's mouth.

The quantities of luggage and bevies of servants which still accompanied many middle class families going on holiday in the 1900s and early 1910s, together with competition for holiday business between the several large railway companies prompted the introduction of through coaches and through trains between the main provincial centres and the major resorts. These facilities, involving as they did much shunting and re-marshalling, not to mention much cautious negotiation of busy junctions around the metropolis, were no faster than the alternative and indeed were often significantly slower. But it is doubtful whether the extra journey time bothered many holidaymakers. Above all, the husband and wife appreciated the avoidance of the strain of dragging children (and often several servants) accompanied by piles of luggage across London to seek and load a second train to complete the journey. The best-known of these through services was *The Sunny South Express* (originally *The Sunny South Special*), started by the London & North Western and London, Brighton & South Coast Railway companies in March 1905[12]. This provided through carriages, including a dining car for much of the journey, from Liverpool, Manchester, Birmingham and Coventry to Brighton and Eastbourne. It ran every day of the year, catering for winter as well as summer holiday traffic (the wealthiest element of the Midland and Northern middle classes were persuaded, with limited success, to spend some part of the winter months in the milder climate of the south and south-west). There were convenient connections into this train from many large towns in Lancashire, Cheshire and Yorkshire. Later, through coaches were added, providing undisturbed journeys between Liverpool and Manchester and Bournemouth and Weymouth and also between these two cities and Deal via Ramsgate. Suspended in World War 1, the service was reinstated in 1921 and extended from Eastbourne to Bexhill and Hastings four years later. It ceased in September 1939 with the outbreak of war and after 1945 was not seen again in its old form, although from 1949 numerous through services were worked for some years across London, mostly on summer Saturdays. The *Sunny South* and its sister trains were the precursors of the many daily, all year round, through trains between the south and south west and the main provincial cities that British Rail runs today.

Another example of the railway companies' concern with middle class comfort was the provision of ladies' maids and valets on the *Cornish Riviera Express* from Paddington to Penzance in the summer of 1905. The maids, 'neatly attired in a black alpaca dress with white linen collar and cuffs, a nurse's bonnet, fancy apron and a badge in silver thread inscribed "GWR Ladies' Attendant" ', constantly patrolled through the train, alert to 'render services to ladies and children and they will especially watch over ladies travelling without an escort'. An Edwardian equivalent of the modern air hostess in fact, except that they did not serve food and drink, these being taken at table, in civilised fashion, in the train's dining car. The valets, dressed in a 'smart serge uniform' would 'do everything for the male passenger's comfort and at a pinch, are prepared to clean his shoes'[13]. One better indeed than the modern air steward, who would not do this, pinch or no.

For those travelling First Class on holiday or business between

Scotland and London, special luxuries were available on the London & North Eastern Railway's *Flying Scotsman* when a new train was introduced in 1930. This was equipped with more spacious lavatories than those ordinarily provided on trains, featuring fittings and wash-basins 'of the type found in *hotels de luxe*', a small dressing table, and a full length mirror. The floor of these luxurious toilet compartments was in green terrazzo, inlaid with mother of pearl. Since 1928 this train had also included a special ladies' retiring room with en suite w.c., dressing table, washbasin, chair, mirror, and cabinets and drawers from which the ladies' attendant would supply perfumery and toilet articles. Next to this haven of feminine luxury and comfort was a unisex hairdressing saloon with its own waiting room. This train was patrolled by W. H. Smith & Son newsboys selling magazines, books and papers from shoulder-slung baskets. Its Louis XIV style restaurant cars were served by all-electric kitchens and, after 1932, there was a cocktail bar. In the 1930s the same railway company provided some of its main line trains with cinema coaches and radio headphones receiving BBC broadcasts.

## Holiday Occupations

Arrived at the holiday resort, the middle classes followed well-established routines. Sea bathing was a holiday tradition, doggedly pursued whatever the weather. Few would be prepared to return home without being able to say they had been in the water at least once. Until the early 1930s, in the interests of preserving the modesty so precious to the middle class female, most of the bourgeois resorts continued to offer bathing machines. These were wheeled huts, towed out into the sea by horses, concealing the lady bathers from the prying male eye until they stepped down into the water, and affording some protection even then. Mrs Peel describes[14] how girls wore a loose trousered garment, covering most of the thighs 'and even when so clothed, hurried into the sea and, our bathe finished, hurried out again, and into the dank-smelling, sandy-floored bathing machine'. In the 1900s and 1910s, once the bathing ritual was over, everyone dried themselves quickly, returning to full holiday rig, the ladies in large shady hats, cotton frocks, stockings and shoes, taking up parasols to give further protection from the sun, the men in open-necked shirts, grey or white flannel trousers, blazers or jackets, heads shaded by panama hat or soft felts or straws.

But by 1930 all this was changing fast. The sun cult had reached Britain from Europe[15] and most holidaymakers under middle age were

Home from the Holidays, 1928

starting to indulge in new rituals at the seaside, exposing faces and bodies to the full glare of the sun for as long as possible, in search of the tan which they were assured would give them additional physical attraction and health. Equally important, it provided tangible evidence on their return that the holiday had been successful. With the sun cult came more attractive and briefer bathing costumes (often never wetted by the sea) as well as special accessories and fashions. Amongst the latter were round-lensed sunglasses with very dark tints and white or brown horn rims; creams and oils; beach pyjamas; and sunsuits. Resorts began to add sunshine recorders to their weather stations, vying with each other as to which had the longest number of hours of sunshine each day. Middle class holidays became somewhat less active, with more sitting and lying around on sunny days, although many did try to read books whilst they sunbathed.

In the early years of the century the children of the more affluent middle class families would often be left on the beach in the care of nanny or maid whilst parents indulged in golf or tennis or cultural activities. Most middle class families would seek out resorts with sandy beaches which formed ideal playgrounds for their children, who were never at a loss for something to do provided the rain kept away. There were sandcastles, moats, pits and elaborate canal systems to be constructed to defy the incoming tide, rockpools to be explored with nets, and at the larger resorts, sandcastle competitions and professional sand designers, existing on pennies and the occasional sixpences thrown down from the promenade. Punch & Judy shows and pierrots, with their shoes scratching the sand on the low wooden platforms serving as a stage, delighting child and adult alike, were found at even quite small resorts.

Although they usually had no car with them, the smaller middle class family parties at the seaside between 1920 and 1950 were more mobile than their Edwardian predecessors. A plenitude of local motor coach proprietors offered a wide variety of day, afternoon and evening trips to places of interest and beauty within a range of fifty or more miles, beginning the process of environmental ravaging and overcrowding at these locations which was to be much extended by mass motoring from the mid-1950s. There was also a close network of cheap and reasonably frequent country bus services to be made use of; some of these copied the railways by selling bargain 'rover' tickets allowing unlimited journeying for a week in holiday areas.

After the evening dinner, the adults would visit the theatre, the concert party on the pier, or the cinema, leaving the children in the care of their servants or of the hotel or boarding house staff. Cinemas were provided from the mid 1910s even in quite small resorts such as Shanklin, Ventnor, Grange-over-Sands, Dawlish and Castletown and of course did good business in the afternoons as well when the weather was poor. Other evenings might be spent indoors, writing letters and postcards to relatives and friends, reading novels or playing cards, and making plans for the next day. After that it was usually early to bed, healthily tired, windows flung wide open to admit the rhythmic sound of the sea rolling on to the beach.

For the lower middles, there was often a additional pleasure in holidays since they could bring the same glow of temporary elevation in the social scale which we have previously noted as generated by visits to the West End cinemas and Corner Houses. Holidays in well-selected hotels could afford experience of standards of domestic accommodation, meals and service superior to those to which they were accustomed through the rest of the year. Indeed some private hotels were conversions of large houses formerly owned by the affluent upper middle class, retaining much of their old atmosphere and environment. Thus the annual holiday often served to stimulate an already powerful motivation to rise further up the ladder.

## NOTES

1. Derbyshire, H., *Derbyshire's Guide to Southend-on-Sea* (1901).
2. Anon, *Accounts of Expenditure of Wage Earning Women and Girls*, Board of Trade Labour Department, (Cd 5963), (1911).
3. Hotel and boarding house charges quoted in this chapter are taken from advertising in holiday guides of the period.
4. For some tentative statistics on the distribution of the middle class rentiers and retired, see Brunner, Elizabeth, *Holidaymaking and The Holiday Trades*, (1945).
5. For this and some other information in this paragraph I am indebted to Brunner, op cit (note 4).
6. Sir Billy Butlin (1900–80), a South African by birth brought up in Canada, did not invent the idea of the holiday camp. On a small scale similar institutions, largely designed for the lower middle class, had existed since at least the early 1920s. Among the pioneers were the Civil Service Clerical Association, whose camp at Corton, near Lowestoft, was opened in 1924. Butlin was however the first to develop the concept on a large commercial scale, providing all the amenities of a seaside resort within the boundary of the camp: accommodation, huge communal restaurants, lavish amusement equipment and well-organised all-weather entertainment. His slogan was 'A week's holiday for a week's wage' and the inclusive weekly charge in the 1930s for three meals a day, accommodation and entertainment was £1.15s to three pounds, according to season. Butlin's camps were a great commercial success and were soon followed by imitators. After World War 2, the majority of those using commercial camps quickly became working class, although some lower middle families were always to be found in them, old habits dying hard, whilst others were just experimenting.
7. Nock, O. S., *History of The Great Western Railway: Volume 3: 1926–47* (1967).
8. In 1938, 104,595 passengers left London (Paddington) by long distance trains in the third week of August; in 1941 the corresponding figure was 178,421; in 1945, 255,756; and in 1946, with some involuntary staggering of holidays resulting from demobilisation, 202,270. (Figures from Barman, Christian, *Next Station*, (1947)).
9. *The Railway & Travel Monthly*, September, 1918.
10. Brunner, op cit (note 4).
11. The old intermediate Second Class had largely disappeared by 1914 and the last facilities (apart from some suburban and boat trains) were withdrawn in 1923.
12. Many other similar services were started about the same time, including

a working which combined through coaches from Derby, Leicester, Manchester, Leeds and Sheffield, dispersing them to Folkestone, Dover, Deal, Portsmouth and Southampton. A Birkenhead–Birmingham–Folkestone/Dover train ran daily all year for most of the period covered by this book as did the *Pines Express* from Manchester/Liverpool to Bournemouth, which started in 1910 although it was not named until 1927. Other through trains, avoiding London, like *The Devonian*, between Bradford and the west of England, were started in the 1920s, reflecting the continued growth in middle class holiday traffic across the country as well as to and from the capital.

13. *The Railway Magazine* August 1905.
14. Peel, Mrs C. S., *Life's Enchanted Cup: An Autobiography 1872–1933*, (1933).
15. The modern sunbathing cult seems to have originated in the 'school in the sun' clinic established by the Swiss Dr. Auguste Rollier in the Vaudois Alps in 1923. Rollier's book *Heliotherapy*, published in an English version in the same year, attracted widespread interest and did much to encourage the idea that exposure of the body to the solar radiation was thoroughly beneficial. During the 1920s the French Côte d'Azur, formerly a winter resort for the wealthy, became a popular summer residence for artists and intellectuals, most of whom took up the sunbathing cult with enthusiasm. In Britain electric sun lamps were being advertised by 1928 along with 'Vitaglass' windows, designed to admit the desired ultra-violet rays. In 1930 this special glass could be fitted to new homes for an extra cost of only a few pounds ('£4 on a £1,500 house'). It was also used in the carriages of some prestige express trains. British holiday places came into the act about 1930–31. 'Sunbathing is to be a feature of the summer of 1931 and is to be encouraged at all the popular holiday resorts' declared *The Daily Mail* on 9 May 1931, giving sunbathing hints and details of 'special sunbathing stations, stretches of sand and bungalows' which were to be provided at various 'progressive seaside resorts'.

CHAPTER 12
# RETROSPECT

The first half of the 20th century saw the English middle classes in unprecedented expansion, enjoying new heights of prosperity, comfort and influence. Between the wars, at a time of relatively low taxation, the salaried classes in particular prospered; smaller in family size than their predecessors, they experienced growth in disposable income, which the prevailing economic conditions allowed them to use in the acquisition of new and improved houses that were low in real cost. An expanding range and volume of consumer goods and high quality consumer services supported by a vast pool of cheap and willing labour all flowed principally towards the middle classes.

Throughout the half century, the old class distinctions survived largely unchanged, especially marked in the sharp divide that continued to separate the manual workers and the very poor from the rest. Although this gap was very real, it did not prevent upward mobility, most of the new arrivals originating from an education in the publicly-financed secondary schools which had the effect of funnelling a majority of the students into white collar jobs. And as we have seen, the same educational process confirmed and strengthened the class status of the children of the lower middles. This reinforcement from below was not the only factor in the increase of middle class influence in society as a whole; class values and principles were widely promulgated in the media, the arts and popular entertainment. Middle class influence infiltrated the governing classes, notably in the increasingly pervasive civil service, whilst politicians of middle class origin entered ministerial ranks in growing numbers.

In this highly favourable situation the middle classes, in contrast to their equivalents in many countries abroad, did not feel unduly insecure, though they were not without their anxieties, as we shall find later. Between the wars Britain was not troubled by domestic political extremism, despite very real problems of large scale unemployment and the existence of deep-rooted social injustice. Once the 1926 General Strike had passed, society at all levels seemed to enter a period of stability; the mass of the population were orderly and generally law-abiding, some might say docile and subdued. Vandalism, thoughtless violence and riots were almost unknown.

In this final chapter an attempt will be made to look behind this state of affairs at the principal characteristics, attitudes, and anxieties of those whose lifestyle has been described earlier. We shall also consider the circumstances that generated the underlying sense of security just mentioned, concluding with some account of the process of change in social attitudes and circumstances which started before World War 2, only to be accelerated by it and by its aftermath. This will take us to the end of the 1940s, when the old order, more or less stable for many decades, including the fifty years covered by this book, was already beginning to disintegrate and transmute at several points, a process which was to continue through the second half of the century.

## Characteristics of the Middle Classes

In our preliminary overview of the English middle classes of 1900–1950, it was noted that they were distinguishable from the working class not so much by their level of income but by a characteristic lifestyle, with common attitudes, habits and tastes, principally founded on prospects of a stable long-term career of non-manual work. From this there emerged as dominant characteristics a rigid adherence to the concept of 'respectability' and a lifelong quest for stability and security. With these went a very real sense of belonging and contributing to what was perceived as the steady progress and beneficial development of society and the nation. Allied to all this and underlying it, was a strong belief in the importance of family and home as the only true source of personal contentment and fulfilment as well as a necessary element for the success and stability of society as a whole.

It was very much a male-dominated world, in which, despite growing employment opportunities, the granting of full suffrage and some statutory progress towards emancipation, women were still seen as having first a decorative and then a supporting role, mainly in nurturing the children, and creating and consolidating the family and the home in return for the security of lifelong marriage. Home-making and an ordered, secure private life in a comfortable home assumed great importance, justifying a role for most women to which their other aspirations had to adapt or give way. Very few kicked against this trend and after the excitements of the suffrage campaign and the heady freedom and heightened emotions of 1914–18, the cause of female emancipation entered the doldrums, middle class women in general settling down with remarkable passivity between the wars and again for some time after 1945 to conform to the stereotypes set for them, if not by them. They seem to have preferred it that way.

Family and social cohesion, accepted by the middle classes as essential constituents of society, were secured by widespread adherence to expected patterns of social behaviour, underpinned by a moral code that accepted marriage for life to a single partner as the norm and looked with disfavour on sexual consort outside marriage. This 'cleanliness of life' as Masterman called it, was perpetuated for most of the half century because middle class youth in general showed itself ready to conform to the standards assiduously passed down to it by its parents, absorbing the received moral code without question, albeit sometimes with a temporary revolt in early adulthood. As the second half of the century dawned, the hedonistic youth cult and youth culture, so strong amongst all classes today, was as yet unborn.

The whole way of life, particularly in the predominant suburban sections of the class structure, was inward-looking and often narrow, its leisure punctuated by what Masterman scornfully described as 'random and meaningless sociabilities' and 'vicarious sport and trivial amusements'. Although noting some mitigating features such as good nature, 'cleanliness of life' and unbroken family tradition in what he called 'The Suburbans', Masterman listed a formidable catalogue of negative aspects: a certain restlessness and disappointment; a 'communal poverty of interest and ideal'; obsessions with trivia and material accumulations; and deplorably low public spirit in local affairs. He even conjured up a poetic image of an empty soul, swept and garnished, waiting for other occupants.[1]. Not perhaps all that far from the truth, given the limitations of generalisation. Nor was he the only middle class writer of the period ready to criticise and contemptuously portray what were seen as the deficiencies of his own class. Arnold Bennett's 1923 novel *Riceyman Steps* for example concentrates on lower middle class meanness and its consequences. One especially interesting middle class author of the period was Eric Blair, who wrote under the name George Orwell. Coming from a family he described as 'shabby genteel' and educated at a preparatory school and Eton, Orwell served in the Indian Imperial Police in Burma in the 1920s, closely observing the English middle classes in the dying phase of their role as 'the frontiersmen of all the world' (Masterman). Later he worked for a time as a schoolteacher. He wrote disparagingly of English middle class life in his 1930s novels *A Clergyman's Daughter, Keep The Aspidistra Flying* and *Coming Up For Air*, finding it permeated by disabling boredom, restlessness, meanness and callousness, characteristics which in his view outweighed its merits. Anxious to shed middle class respectability and expiate his class guilt, in the early thirties Orwell had sought to share the experience of working class life in England and in mainland Europe, averring that he found in it true warmth, nobility and human decency and becoming a defender of the proletariat. By the end of the 1930s he had adopted a personal form of socialism as his creed. Later he decided that middle class values were not entirely irredeemable, at least as far as the lower middles were concerned, and in his 1941 work *The Lion and The Unicorn*, the suburban lower middle class were linked with the workers in the struggle against the plutocracy. Orwell was riddled with class-consciousness and after making allowance for his prejudices and his emotional revolt against the world he found himself in as a young adult immediately after World War 1, the reader of these books can distil out of them much of the largely immutable characteristics of the English middle classes of the first four decades of the century.

Light is also thrown on these characteristics by studying behaviour, which can sometimes be seen to be influenced by environment. Although the garden cities and garden suburbs managed to engender and sustain a community spirit and social activities of various kinds (which in reality seem to have been somewhat artificial and forced), these were untypical. The newly-built Edwardian and neo-Georgian suburbs in general initially lacked any amenities for social, intellectual and cultural life outside that associated with the churches. This deficiency, combined with a seemingly often innate difficulty in forming new social relationships, only served to stimulate further the development of the inward, home-centred lifestyle which had already been triggered by the desire to embellish and nurture the newly-acquired house and garden. In great contrast to the easy social mixing among the working class and the very poor, middle class families, the newly-established lower middles as much as the rest, were normally not in the least gregarious, keeping very much to themselves and a few chosen friends.

In this self-sufficient, inward-looking climate, relations with immediate neighbours often remained stiff and formal, even after the passage of several years in which they had lived alongside. A writer to the London *Evening News* in January 1909 noted that he had dwelt in a North London suburb for four years without coming to know more than four families in the same road, two on either side of his house, or more than a dozen in the whole neighbourhood and 'never once did I enter their houses on business or pleasure'. He considered that children were 'the only true missionaries'; from their prattle the suburbanite learned of the habits of his neighbours. Almost thirty years later, things were little changed: in the new suburb of Stoneleigh, in Surrey, the bulletin of the Residents' Association commented that women who had lived in the area for over a year (and it should be remembered almost all of them were at home all day) barely knew their neighbours' names. Contacts were minimal: 'People just nod, and pass on'. The writer went on to say that efforts had been made to form social clubs but these were sometimes frustrated by a lack of enthusiasm – or was it deliberate insulation? It has been suggested by some social historians that this withdrawal into the limited circle of the family and a few friends with common interests that is so characteristic of the suburban middle classes may have been attributable at least in part to uncertainties about social status in a new environment at a time when much importance was attached to upward mobility. But too much can be made of the social insecurity of the newly-arrived, new home-owning lower middle class. Those already established in an area and a little higher up the social scale exhibited the same attitudes, showing no enthusiasm to welcome new arrivals in their midst, even into church life. Maybe they also felt insecure.

The narrowness of the home-centred suburban life of the period was aggravated by the geographical separation of much of the new middle class housing from cultural amenities. For the more widely-dispersed suburban or rural/seaside-dwelling middle classes of the first half of the twentieth century, a visit to a theatre, art gallery, concert hall, opera house or museum required a deliberate effort, involving travel into a city centre, a journey associated with an often grimly tedious daily routine. In comparison the attractions and comforts of the home and family and the 'vicarious sport and trivial amusements' of the suburb, the tennis, the aimless 'pleasure motoring', the golf, the card-playing, exercised a strong pull. So the majority succumbed, losing contact with such urban culture as they had known before marriage and the suburb. However the picture was not permanently bleak; the arrival of radio broadcasting and the improved gramophone in the 1920s, and the gradual establishment of public libraries in the new middle class areas, did something to counter this increasing dominance of purposeless play as a means of filling leisure hours.

The unfavourable and prickly attitude of many middle class people to the working class in the early decades of the century provides evidence of feelings of insecurity and one aspect of the underlying anxiety we shall shortly consider. Allied with this attitude we may note the way in which the police were seen as agents of the middle class, keeping their established order and dignity in being and discriminating in their favour. For obvious reasons this culture clash seems to have been particularly intense in those rural and semi-rural areas being newly-colonised by the villa-building middle classes.

Thus Bourne, in his 1911 study of Farnham Common, observed that

> Jealousy, suspicion, some fear – the elements of bitter class war in fact – frequently mark the attitude of middle class people toward the labouring class. It seems to be forgotten that the men are English. One hears them spoken of as an alien and objectionable race, worth nothing but to be made to work.

The way in which they were treated by the invading leisured classes and the manner in which this invasion changed their environment evoked a negative response from the established cottagers. Bourne saw how the old 'peasant' community of his village had become cowed and intimidated; their children quailed before middle class superiority, lacked confidence, ran away when challenged, not standing their ground and risking adventure as middle class children did. The country people no longer wandered off the public roads, afraid to trespass on private lands; they did their best to keep out of the way of the newcomers. This was not unconnected with police behaviour, for it was they (in their eyes) the police were stationed to watch, they who were suspect, they who were searched for rabbit wires, they who were punished for drunken revelry: 'In theory,' Bourne wrote, 'the policeman represents the general public; in practice he stands for middle class decorum and the rights of property. . .'

## Middle Class Anxieties

Since the highly advantageous and comfortable position experienced by the middle classes through most of these fifty years was in such sharp contrast to that of the multitudinous poor, hardworking and otherwise, it was not surprisingly often accompanied, at least in the thoughtful, by persistent and deep-seated feelings of guilt and anxiety. The attainment of a full measure of middle class rewards and security sometimes brought with it a degree of spiritual restlessness and dissatisfaction, a feeling that the situation was not a natural one in a world so full of threat, deprivation and uncertainty. Those given to self-examination and contemplation might have doubts that in their perhaps selfish and often complacent comfort they were not being properly tested, and this could inspire excursions into fabianism and other forms of socialism, or perhaps attempts at good works and charity, in an effort to assuage the spiritual discomfort. But for the majority, always surrounded by their own kind in both leisure and working life, and well insulated, it was easy to ignore or forget how others less fortunate were living. If they thought about such things at all, it was only to acquire a vague feeling that they

319

had something worth defending, which would always be subject to threat, either from below or from the world beyond Britain's calm shores. For this reason the middle classes were always ready to support anything which seemed to afford them better protection and security, whether it be the police and the legal system or more expenditure on armaments. In addition, the lower middles, desperately trying to preserve their status and respectability on incomes that were barely above working class levels, threatened by the spectre of unemployment and consequent downward mobility, and frustrated and disappointed at the non-appearance of the long-anticipated advance up the social ladder, often nursed more immediate and tangible anxieties.

Middle class *angst* was assiduously exploited by Edwardian writers such as H. G. Wells (himself a product of the lower middle class) and by middle class journalists and social commentators like the Liberal politician and writer C. F. G. Masterman. In particular they selected and played upon an underlying fear of the underprivileged masses[2].

Another equally potent bogy was emerging at the same time. Newspaper proprietors such as Alfred Harmsworth (later Lord Northcliffe) had discovered that sales were boosted by the generation of excitement and fear about such things as a German invasion. Journalists in *The Daily Mail* and similar publications directing themselves at a predominantly lower middle class readership enthusiastically focussed feelings of anxiety and insecurity on German expansionism and love of war and that nation's preparation for 'Der Tag'. This theme also attracted writers and dramatists. Such novels as Erskine Childers' 1903 *The Riddle of The Sands* about German preparations for war, and the closely-researched *The Invasion of 1910*, by William le Queux, with its many topographical references and descriptions of a German advance on London through East Anglia, first published in *The Daily Mail* in 1906, did much to arouse middle class anxiety in this direction, incidentally widening middle class support for huge increases in public expenditure on the reinforcement of the army and the expansion of the naval fleet. The same purpose was served by plays on the same theme. In 1900 *The Invasion of Britain; or, The Siege of London* was performed at Dalston, London and in 1909 a West End play, *An Englishman's Home* by Guy du Maurier, portrayed the desecration of a quiet middle class home by the soldiery of a mainland European invader, discreetly unspecified. *The Play Pictorial* noted 'It has done more to arouse the spirit of the nation to the dangers of invasion than all the platform speeches delivered on the subject', adding that recruiting offices for the Territorial Army were established 'almost at the doors of the theatre' with sergeants 'in close proximity to take advantage of the patriotic enthusiasm of those who have been stirred by the visual object-lesson presented to them of what might occur if England were invaded by a foreign army'. The programme for this play announced a serial about to appear in *Answers* magazine entitled 'The Invaders' and was spattered with advertisements for rifle clubs and units of the Territorial Army). Later in the same year a one-act play, *Invasion; or, Wake Up England!* was staged at the less fashionable Canterbury Theatre on the South Bank.

The British film industry made its own special contribution to the hysteria with *England Invaded* and *The Invaders* (both 1909), *The Raid of 1915* (about an invasion of Britain and made in Norfolk in 1913), *England's Menace, An Englishman's Home* and *Wake Up; or, a Dream of War* (all 1914). Foreign spies (French, German and unidentified) and the associated threat were also a popular subject for British films; Gifford lists no less than twenty six made between 1909 and 1914 on this theme.

Even *The Queen*, a ladies' magazine dealing with the activities of high society and widely read by the middle classes, featured articles about the naval dockyards (in 1910) and reports of mysterious aircraft flying over England at night. And in December 1911, the editor of *The Railway & Travel Monthly* was already so brain-washed by it all that he wrote of 'the coming German invasion'. On top of all this war mania, middle class youth, as organised into the Boy Scouts and Girl Guides, was being indoctrinated with training well-laced with techniques and skills likely to be useful for national defence against a foreign invader. And, at school and at home, their imperialistic enthusiasm was kept at fever pitch with a diet of annual Empire Days and suitable fiction. From 1911 onwards the patriotic 'modern fairy tale' *Where the Rainbow Ends* was frequently staged in London and elsewhere, impressing upon young middle class audiences its interpretation of the seemingly unique virtues of the English master race to which they had the good fortune to belong and whose future leaders they would provide.

This conditioning, continued unabated right through to 1914, must have accounted in large part for the patriotic fervour which greeted the outbreak and opening phases of World War 1. Nowhere was the enthusiasm for the war seen to be stronger than amongst the lower middle class and the adjacent literate and 'respectable' elements of the working class. It was almost as if the tension had burst, the long-awaited moment had come, presenting an opportunity to be rid of anxiety, making threatened middle class England and all it stood for secure for all time. So strong was the emotion generated that the heedless rush to volunteer for the slaughter was not stemmed when it became clear that no quick conclusion was likely.

It has been credibly suggested that middle class value systems, reinforced by the influences on young people in the decade or so before 1915, principally through the Boy Scout and church youth movements and public school or public school type private education, played a significant part in sustaining in the British army's morale in the face of frequently inept or and often inert generalship and the increasingly desperate conditions of land warfare, especially in the early and middle stages of the World War 1. Whilst some intellectuals caught up in the fighting rapidly became cynical (R. H. Tawney talked of 'the soldier's internal life, the sensation of taking part in a game played by monkeys and organised by lunatics'), the general unquestioning acceptance of the need to fight and go on fighting, making sacrifices of quite horrendous proportions in terms of human suffering, was certainly remarkable, given the circumstances. That it persisted as long as it did in the conditions of trench warfare on the Western Front may well have owed much to the pervasiveness of middle class values amongst a significant vein of other ranks and throughout the junior officers with whom they were in daily contact. In this way Britain faced up to the enemy's iron discipline, so consistently maintained by the highly professional and ingrained Prussian militarism.

Every effort was made to imbue the lower classes with same spirit that came more naturally to the middles. Significantly a government poster bearing the slogan 'WOMEN OF BRITAIN SAY "*GO!*" ' portrays two women and a child looking through a window at marching soldiers, the taller of the two, a well-dressed blonde with purposeful expression, clearly superior and upper middle, has her arm encouragingly around the other, who, meant to be recognised as one of their own by the working class, has dark hair, is a good head shorter, and wears plain black and white, a shawl around her shoulders.

Although there was a very sharp divide between the upper and middle classes and the rest of society, this dichotomy was by no means as potentially explosive as some felt at the time. Both the proletariat and the very poor were largely apathetic and inadequately led in their misery, despite an unprecedented wave of industrial unrest which swept across the country in 1910–11. Two events also contributed to defuse the situation. The first was the Liberal Party's tentative approach towards the establishment of a welfare state in 1908–14, a positive if small scale advance towards social justice made amidst general recognition by all political parties of the need for social reform[3]. This can be read as a practical expression of middle class conscience, persuading those in the most desperate situations that they need not abandon hope. Then came the upheaval and trauma of World War 1, with its unifying appeal to all sections of society as symbolised in the poster mentioned in the previous paragraph. Most importantly the need of the war effort in Britain itself provided many new jobs, for women as well as men, putting much more money into working class pockets and anaesthetising class envy.

However the effect of the war was temporary in these respects and with the armistice, the social structure quickly reverted to very much its pre-1914 state. Although the upper and the more affluent middle classes suffered disproportionately in the loss of sons, fathers and husbands in the fighting[4], the suburban middle class in general soon recovered and there was great relief that the violent social clashes which defeat might have brought had been avoided. It seemed that life could go on much as before. Nevertheless, with some rumblings of discontent and revolt in the armed forces over slow demobilisation, the general post-war social unrest in Europe, and above all the triumph of Leninist Communism in Russia, the underlying angst of the middle classes was readily focussed on the new bogy. There was a real concern that armed communist revolution might cross the English Channel, a prospect voiced by Lloyd George, the firmly middle class wartime Liberal Prime Minister. With such fears in mind, an expensive programme of public funding of new housing for low income groups was put through parliament in 1919, principally to squash one likely cause of social discontent. At this time and for most of the next decade, as in the Edwardian years, the favourite newspapers of the middle classes played a prominent part in fanning anxiety about threats to their comfort. Even the strip cartoons featured bearded Bolsheviks with bombs to frighten the children. In 1919, down in the South Wales coalfield, at the Temperance Hall, Tredegar, a hurriedly-written propaganda piece by a middle class dramatist entitled *The Bolshevik Peril* was staged in a brave attempt to dampen any nascent revolutionary tendencies. How many miners attended is not recorded. Novelists also took up the theme. In his 1923 book *Middle of The Road*, Sir Philip Gibbs depicted a defence force of ex-officers to defend 'us' against a revolution fomented by 'Bolshies' and agents paid with foreign gold. The 'us' referred to was described as 'the Decent Crowd. Anybody with a stake in the country, including the unfortunate Middle Classes. . . we must get the Working Classes back to their kennels'. It is interesting to reflect that the doctrines and leadership of both Russian and International Communism were closely associated with middle class intellectuals, though of course these were *foreigners*, which was enough to explain what might otherwise have been difficult to grasp.

It was obvious that an antidote to the supposed communist threat from abroad, which would at the same time weaken the political muscle of the domestic extreme left would be the development of a gradualist, patriotic and moderate Labour Party which could safely assume office without too much disruption to the middle classes. And this became a reality. By 1922 Labour had overtaken the Liberals to become one of the two major British parliamentary parties. From then on, with a new constitution opening membership to anyone, it grew in strength and influence, achieving in 1924 and 1929 brief if largely impotent periods of government with a minority vote in the House of Commons. This development owed much to middle class assistance, active and passive, and many of the Labour Party's best and most influential leaders and intellectuals came from this source. Although few would have been prepared to admit it, no doubt a conversion to socialism did much to assuage a troubled middle class conscience and this would continue to provide motivation.

In the General Strike of 1926 the middle classes also rendered moral support to the constitutionally-elected Conservative Government, many of them actively seeking a role in preventing a complete stoppage of the railways and other essential services. After the collapse of this challenge, they felt able to relax, complacently perceiving an uninterrupted prospect of security for their way of life, underwritten by political stability at home. The splendidly stolid upper middle class and very English figure of Stanley Baldwin[5], one of the major contemporary Conservative politicians, neatly personified this attitude and his approach and influence helped to reinforce it.

## Political Vacillations and the End of an Era

That this post-1926 middle class complacency and sense of security was able to develop alongside large scale unemployment and social deprivation in the older industrial areas may seem surprising. How was it that Britain continued to be almost totally immune from political extremism, both left and right, avoiding the disturbances suffered by other European countries during the financial and economic upheavals of the 1920s and early 1930s? The reasons for this relative calm are several. The greatest deprivation was concentrated in isolated regions of heavy industry and coalfields such as South Wales, Clydeside and the North East, where it was unobserved by the general population. And the immediate needs of the victims were somewhat relieved by the regular, if inadequate payment of unemployment insurance (the 'dole'). Low in spirit and vitality and generally apathetic, the unemployed, in their millions, gave the authorities little trouble.

The channelling of a major part of working class and left-wing political expression and energy into a moderate and reasonably strong parliamentary Labour Party also did much to quieten middle class fears of revolution, at the same time nicely removing any foundation on which to build successful fascist parties of the type that came to power in Italy and Germany on the backs of a frightened and insecure middle class. Thus it was that the British Union of Fascists, emerging in the early 1930s under the charismatic leadership of the frustrated and impulsive yet dynamic and clear-minded Sir Oswald Mosley, failed to gain an effective power base. Such support as the BUF obtained did however come largely from the middle classes, mainly lower middles, many of them between sixteen and thirty[6].

Meanwhile, at Westminster in the 1930s, the reins of power remained firmly in the hands of ageing men devoted to preserving the way of life of the upper and middle classes. Between 1929 and 1935 the Prime Minister was Ramsay Macdonald, 'Gentleman Mac', a lower middle class Scot who on achieving high office, adopted the airs and life of a country squire, seeking and finding favour with the Establishment. Appointed leader of the Labour Party in 1922, he had set its tone through the 1920s, wanting to encourage the transfer into it of middle class Liberals and advocating what he liked to call 'organic change'. Macdonald, expelled from the Labour Party in 1931 for compromising with the Conservatives, but continuing as the head of the 'National' Government, was followed as Prime Minister in 1935–37 by the Conservative and quintessentially upper middle class Baldwin, whose policy was to work for tranquility and the cooling down of class conflict. And in 1937 Baldwin was succeeded by Neville Chamberlain, a Conservative businessman from Birmingham who found himself facing the renewed threat of international conflict arising from Hitler's fiercely enthusiastic revival of German nationalism and expansionism. None of the conventional British political leaders or their administrations, inspired much affection or interest amongst the middle class young, who at university, or on leaving secondary or grammar school, often drifted into the more exciting and dynamic attractions of the several forms of communism, Mosley's BUF, or the extreme margins of socialism. Pacifism, another alternative diversion for the young and thoughtful, declined somewhat in popularity in the face of the increasingly aggressive and expansionist stance taken after 1935 by Nazi Germany and Fascist Italy.

During the thirties, the anxieties of the middle classes were more widely apparent than ever, focussed as they were on the very real possibility of another and more terrible international conflict to disturb and threaten their comfort and security. Memories of 1914–18 were still fresh. From about 1935 the more sensitive and perceptive saw this second major war as inevitable but most wanted to pretend it would not happen, a hope that many middle class newspapers, in the interests of their advertising customers, did their best to sustain until the very last moment. This was why Neville Chamberlain's return from Munich in September 1938 was greeted in the suburbs and semi-rural villas with enthusiasm and relief, the middle classes in general, apart from some of the articulate younger generation, showing little cynicism or shame at the concessions made to Hitler. Their mood was clearly established in the West End theatre, where plays and references to planes, bombs and dictators such as *Official Secret* could not be sustained for more than a few performances. And even when, a few months later, it was all too apparent to the most determined optimists and wishful thinkers that Munich was merely a postponement and not a release from the inevitable, there was no repetition of the 1914 enthusiasm and jingoism, simply a resigned determination to go along with the war preparations in the interests of self-preservation. Indeed until France was directly attacked in the summer of 1940, there was a sense of unreality, little war-motivation and a significant residue of puzzled indifference amongst the traditionally patriotic and largely Conservative middle classes. In those strangely silent months of late 1939 and early 1940, many hoped they would wake up and find it was all just a bad dream.

Then it all started to happen, quite suddenly; first Dunkerque, then the Blitz; and this new war, unlike that of 1914–18, was to have a lasting effect on the rigidity of the English class distinctions, accelerating a process which had begun in the early 1930s.

We have noticed in previous chapters how by the end of that decade the dress and appearance of all classes was losing its distinctiveness (although this in itself must not be mistaken as a sign of class-merging) and we have seen how secondary education was nurturing upward mobility and broadening-out the middle classes between the wars. Another factor important in this weakening and blurring of class distinctions was the decline in servant-keeping, at first most apparent in the south of England in the 1930s. This had brought about important changes of behaviour and attitudes within the home. With many middle class women having to do much of their domestic cleaning and servicing, the advertising and literature of home-making and housekeeping was obliged to assume a more classless character, reflecting and at the same time strengthening what was happening on the ground. This was further reinforced by a growing tendency for the lifestyle of the 'respectable working class' to become more home-centred, in line with the established middle class trend, and for that class to seek the middle class lifestyles proselytized with increasing fervour in what were the opening years of the new consumer society. It was in the commercial interests of the new consumer and service industries to widen out the market to the maximum extent. Increased working class prosperity both during and after the 1939–45 war accelerated this process.

Behaviour patterns and domestic arrangements designed to emphasise class differences in the presence of servants were soon discarded or modified as irrelevant once the last maid had gone. From the late 1920s, the middle classes also shared with the working class the delights of those important new social institutions, the super cinema and the 'improved' public houses, though, as we have seen, some segregation persisted in the latter. Finally, the formation of civil defence units and the vast expansion of the Territorial Army in the years leading up to the outbreak of war encouraged renewed mixing of social classes and the breaking down of social barriers, foreshadowing what was soon to take place on a much larger scale in the hutted camps and tents, the factories and the air raid shelters and the middle class homes accepting working class evacuees. The beginnings of an erosion of the traditional class distinctions were noticed by some contemporary commentators as early as 1937[7].

What had started before September 1939 was much accelerated by the circumstances of wartime life and the effects of war, which tended to encourage social levelling. Middle class civilians found they no longer commanded special privileges; wartime rationing and controls, generally exercised with scrupulous fairness, imposed a rigid equality of treatment, whilst the 'Utility' schemes for clothes and other consumer items spread a standardised appearance in dress and (more slowly) in homes. Exercising petty power in rationed shops and on restricted public transport, the working classes in large cities and towns showed noticeably less subservience and politeness towards their 'betters', an attitude that was to persist after the war. Income differences narrowed as the real value of wages grew, whilst middle class salaries, fees and profits stood still or even declined in real terms. This too continued after 1945.

At the same time, under wartime influences, middle class attitudes were undergoing significant changes. The intelligent young, thoroughly disillusioned with the complacent and indolent Conservative governments of 1931–40, their class consciences stimulated by the activities of their peers, or by their reading, carried their often potent discontent and social guilt into the war years. For many of the lower middles, denied access to university, the conditions of wartime life in uniform offered something of a substitute. The same comradeship developed and there was time, a lot of time, for serious reading and for questioning and discussion, if not for lectures.

Although the old formality and rigid separation between officers and men persisted in the army and the navy, these barriers were less formidable than in World War 1 and were perhaps least evident in the RAF. This, the youngest of the three services, with its emphasis on science and technology, had many middle class rankers and mixed officer/n.c.o. aircrews drawn from backgrounds ranging from upper middle class to 'respectable working class'. In the long drawn-out periods of idleness between bouts of purposeful military activity non-commissioned middle class members of all three armed forces had time to get to know and understand the views, the outlook and the aspirations of the working class for the first time in their lives.

Formal discussion groups, which often chose social and economic problems as topics, were encouraged by the new (1941) Army Bureau of Current Affairs and other services education authorities, to an extent that upset the more reactionary senior officers in the defence departments in Whitehall and some Conservative politicians. Overseas for years and away from the influence of elders and the predominantly Conservative British press, the young middle classes in uniform, particularly those from lower middle class homes, found themselves becoming much more open-minded about socialism than their forebears. Some of course had already flirted with it before the war. In particular its British manifestation seemed to offer nothing that menaced their personal future and prosperity or that of their families. And because it had never enjoyed a sustained period of effective government, the Labour Party possessed a distinct advantage over its rivals. Many middle class servicemen came to believe it should be given its opportunity, finding it difficult to fault its aspirations for a planned economy and abolition of class differences on the basis of a general state welfare system sustained by taxing those able to afford a fair tithe. Indeed the Labour programme seemed to advance the prospect of remedying the social injustice of which they had become aware at first hand and which caused them genuine concern. By 1941 Russia was an ally, suffering far more than any other nation from the aggression of the common enemy, a development which made it difficult to continue to promote the fear of international communism amongst the middle classes or to associate domestic socialism with it. Many servicemen and women regularly read *The New Statesman & Nation* or *Tribune* and there was no shortage of these or other radical and left wing literature circulating to be absorbed and talked over in the many long hours of enforced leisure and interminable sojourns in transit camps. Apologists for past and current Soviet and Chinese communist attitudes and policies were able to address servicemen quite freely. School and peacetime conditioning had never been like this for the middle classes. One outstanding manifestation of this radicalisation of the British Armed Forces was the 'Cairo Parliament' of 1943. Regularly attracting hundreds of servicemen, this held debates on postwar policies in a structured democratic parliamentary format. It forecast what was to come by producing a substantial Labour Party majority and became so popular and successful that the authorities, taking fright, dispersed the organisers.

For many of the younger members of the middle classes, wartime experiences away from home were thus exercising a profound influence on their outlook and political views. In a passage recalling the late 1940s, one of those affected has succinctly summed up the feelings of many of his generation:

> I had not taken a great interest in politics in general, beyond a slight leaning towards the left, although I had come from a Conservative family. This was mainly because of my reading and my experience in the army. I began to see that there was more to political thinking than the rather narrow outlook of a middle class upbringing had led me to believe.[8]

Nor were the changes in middle class attitudes entirely confined to the young. In the small provincial towns and the countryside, schoolchildren evacuated from the great cities under the threat of bombing and adults who had suffered in air raids had been taken into middle class homes. Their hosts were frequently shocked by what this experience taught them at first hand of life and conditions in the deprived urban areas, so much so that many became more sympathetic to the ideas of social reform so strongly backed by the Labour Party. Alongside all this there was an outbreak of idealism, spread by articles and books on the subject of the post-war world, much of it encouraged by the Government. As the dreary struggle dragged on, there emerged a widespread feeling amongst all sections of the population that this war, perceived as a classless fight for survival against evil expansionist regimes, must be followed, once won, by social justice at home and a better life for all. Linked as it was with patriotism, this feeling ran strongly through the middle classes, challenging the old hegemony of Conservatism.

In an attempt to crystallise this new outlook, J. B. Priestley and Sir Richard Acland formed the Common Wealth Party, gaining seats from the Conservatives in wartime by-elections. But practical politics – the British version of democracy – loaded the dice against any new political grouping. As an established party, Labour was in the best position; its leaders had achieved respectability in middle class eyes and their wartime record was unassailable. When the wartime controls and systems of a socialist/collectivist nature were seen to work well, this in itself influenced many who were in a position to shape public opinion. The blueprints for some of the social reforms seen to be necessary were already on the tables of Whitehall. Following the 1942 publication of the radical Beveridge Report, the concept of a welfare state had taken shape in White Papers of the next two years which owed much to the efforts of Labour politicians. Conservatives went along with it all but showed a very low level of enthusiasm, and in the case of Churchill, virtually none. All this worked towards the success of the Labour Party in the 1945 General Election, for which, in contrast to the Conservatives' emphasis on their stewardship in the unregretted 1920s and 1930s, Labour's campaign, concentrating on fashioning a future on the basis of prosperity and social security for all, seemed forward-looking.

When in due course the new Labour Government, acting on a mandate which had much middle class support, introduced the welfare state provisions and also passed legislation which firmly controlled town and country planning for the first time, contemporary right wing observers such as Lewis and Maude felt able to suggest that there no longer seemed to be any rational basis for feelings of social guilt amongst the middle classes[9].

But middle class disillusion with Labour was almost immediate. Idealism about social equality was soon to be overtaken by resentment as the new government struggled desperately with severe economic and financial problems not of its making. Substantial elements of the middle classes began to smart under an unaccustomed sense of deprivation, seeing their real incomes continuing to fall whilst taxation remained high. Manual workers, in contrast, were still enjoying real increases as well as the benefits of supplementary income from the increasing numbers of their married women now at work. Some worried about a future holding nothing but increasing doses of government interference with the freedom of the individual, fearing a continuous socialist dictatorship and an ever more elaborate bureaucracy. Statements of Labour ministers that they were the masters at the moment and for a very long time to come (Shawcross) and in which the Conservatives were described as 'lower than vermin' (Bevan) or society other than the workers was dismissed as not mattering a 'tinker's cuss' (Shinwell) did not assist dispersal of this irrational anxiety. Although all were equally affected, it was the articulate middle class which reacted most strongly against the grey post war regime of continued rationing, shortages and state controls, all of which were largely a consequence of external factors.

Their bitterness at it all erupted not only in the daily grumbling in commuter trains or at the golf clubs, but in the mouths of actors on the West End stage and in novels such as the contemporary works of Angela Thirkell. Yet this rebelliousness was not organised and had little or no effect on the course of events in the remaining years of the 1940s – apart that is from one minor exception, which deserves brief mention.

In July 1945 a clergyman's wife organised a small non-political revolt, expressing the frustrations of married women in the austere postwar environment. From this low-key beginning, the British Housewives' League developed into a formidable feminist and largely middle class protest movement against state interference and controls. Within two years or so, it had been infiltrated by Conservative Party activists, who eventually shaped it into a Conservative 'front' organisation. As such it was enthusiastically welcomed and encouraged by the powerful Tory Press and in practical terms it achieved some limited success in modifying Labour Government decisions on the food front.

Rationing, shortages and queuing were by no means the only post-war irritants scratching at sensitive middle class skin. There were the statutory restrictions on private housebuilding and commercial construction work; the restrictions on restaurant meals; a temporary removal of the basic petrol issue, stopping all 'pleasure' motoring; severe overcrowding and poor service generally on the badly run-down railways inherited from private enterprise; severe exchange control regulations which at first prevented then restricted any attempt by the more affluent to find solace in holidays abroad; and the disturbance caused by the implementation of the 1944 Education Act. The latter changed the whole tone of the g ammar and county secondary schools by excluding those middle class children not bright enough to pass the entry test, at the same time admitting the more able working class youngsters. The quintessentially middle class and conservative doctors, greatly exercised by unreasonable fears of a regimented and salaried medical profession, at first strongly resisted cooperation with the proposed National Health Service only to be finally won over in sufficient quantity by compromises. Town & Country Planning also proved a major irritant. At middle class Stevenage, for example, there was a powerful manifestation of revolt at the proposal to build a New Town to be filled with working-class Londoners, a project pushed through by the Labour Government despite almost total local opposition. In the General Election of 1950, Labour succeeded in obtaining even more votes than in 1945 (and almost a million more than

331

the Conservatives) but the nature of the British electoral system ensured that many seats were lost, particularly in middle class constituencies, and the Party emerged with a very slender parliamentary majority.

As the half century ended, with the spirit of 1945 now almost suffocated by post-war problems at home and abroad, the middle classes as a whole were not only disillusioned but often feeling beleaguered and embittered. For them, the world was never to be quite the same again. They stood on the threshold of significant changes.

It is always tempting, if misleading, to compartmentalise history, but here we do seem to have a certain neatness in the development of events. For the British middle classes, much of the first half of the twentieth century saw little alteration in the pattern and basis of their way of life, such changes as there were usually only increasing their comfort and security within the familiar structure. But as we have tried to show, by the 1930s, and even more so in the 1940s, new attitudes were emerging and there were portents of an upheaval which would open out and strengthen in the following decades. The very nature and extent of the middle strata was altering. It was no longer a question of the old middle classes absorbing new recruits from below in a manner which left their established position and form more or less intact. Beginning in the 1940s and consolidating and accelerating after 1950, the general level of comfort, security and education of the formerly under-privileged and deprived masses was drastically uplifted. In the process many found themselves wanting to take up features of middle class lifestyle and were able to do so with relative ease. Social distinctions were to become more subtle and complicated but in general mattered less. Some aspects of the old would remain recognisable, and the great educational divide would endure, soon to be joined by the development of private health services. But the first decades of the second half of the century were to see the privileged and comfortable environment and lifestyle we have surveyed inevitably diluted and modified as it was increasingly appropriated by the majority. Something like a 'middle class' way of life was to become the norm to which most Britons aspired, although (some would hold) that did not necessarily make them *middle class*.

## NOTES

1. Masterman, C. F. G., *The Condition of England*, (1909).
2. Masterman in particular seemed to relish this theme: in his 1909 book (op cit, note 1), he drew a vivid pen picture of how he saw the middle class London commuter of his day:

Every day, swung high upon embankments, or buried deep in tubes underground he hurries through this region where the creature lives. He gazes darkly from his pleasant hill villa upon the huge and smoky area of tumbled tenements which stretches at his feet. He is dimly distrustful of the forces fermenting in this uncouth laboratory. Every hour he anticipates the boiling over of the cauldron.

Yet, despite the tone of this and other passages in the book on the same theme, his considered view seems to have been that the middle classes had more to fear from what he calls their own 'poverty of interest and ideal' than an uprising of the underprivileged.

3. Masterman, op cit (note 1) in his preface to the New and Popular Edition (1911).

4. Just over fifteen per cent of officers were killed compared with 12.8 per cent other ranks.

5. Baldwin of Bewdley, Stanley, 1st Earl, (1867–1947) was Prime Minister three times: 1923–4, 1924–9 and 1935–7.

6. The British Union of Fascists (BUF), formed in October 1932, was the strongest, but not the first of the British middle class fascist movements (the pioneer British Fascisti, copying the Italian precendent, was set up as an 'anti-communist force' as early as 1923). The BUF leader, Mosley, coming from an upper class background, had started his political career as a Conservative, but was soon looking for an alternative. He joined the Labour Party in 1924, resigning from it in 1931 after its leaders had shown no enthusiasm for his proposals for tackling unemployment, based on the theories of the economist J. M. Keynes. Mosley's new BUF was at first strongly supported by the press baron Lord Rothermere and his newspapers, including *The Daily Mail*, with its mainly middle class readership. This support was considerably weakened after Mosley's henchmen had afforded violent treatment to communist and other hecklers at the BUF Olympia (London) rally in June 1934. A further check on the movement's progress followed the passing of the Public Order Act, 1936, which banned the wearing of uniforms by private armies and gave the police increased powers to control public meetings and processions.

7. Saunders and Jones (op cit, note 3 Chapter 1) thought they recognised enough change to cause them to question the relevance of class distinctions: '. . . is it not a misreading of the social structure of this country to dwell on class divisions when, in respect of dress, speech and use of leisure, all members of the community are obviously coming to resemble one another?' This statement is perhaps more valuable for its indication of trends noticeable to intelligent social observers as early as 1937 than for its basic proposition.

8. Guilmartin, G. Harry, *Bare Empty Sheds*, (1986).

9. Lewis, Roy and Maude, Angus, (op cit, note 12 Chapter 5).

# APPENDIX A

# INCOMES AND EXPENDITURE

## 1. EXAMPLES OF MIDDLE CLASS ANNUAL INCOMES (BEFORE TAX) AT VARIOUS PERIODS:

**1900–1915** — **£**

| | £ |
|---|---|
| Managing Director London Underground Railways | 8,000 (in 1906) |
| Successful barristers | 5,000 upwards |
| High Court and Court of Appeal Judges | 5,000 |
| General Manager, North Eastern Railway | 5,000 |
| General Manager, Metropolitan Railway | 2,525 (in 1913) |
| General Managers of medium and small size shipping and commercial companies | 1,000–2,500 |
| Editors of Fleet Street newspapers | 1,000–2,000 |
| Chief Engineer, Great Central Railway | 1,500 (in 1912) |
| Assistant Secretaries, Home Civil Service | 1,150 (average) |
| Solicitor to the Metropolitan Railway | 1,000 (in 1909) |
| Principals, Home Civil Service | 855 (average) |
| Manager, Liverpool Corporation Tramways | 800–1,000 |
| Accountant, Metropolitan Railway | 500 (in 1913) |
| Small town bank managers | 200–600 (average 400) |
| Bank of England clerks | 500 (maximum) |
| Members of Parliament | 400 (from 1911) |
| General practitioners | 395 (average) |
| Dentists | 368 (average) |
| Sub-editors Fleet Street newspapers | 200–500 (average 350) |
| Chemists | 314 (average) |
| Captain, railway Cross-Channel steamers | 205–300 |
| Non-resident public schoolmasters | 200–300 (average 250) |
| Urban District Council Surveyor & Sanitary Inspector (Dorking, 1910) | 200 |
| Stationmaster, Baker Street, Metropolitan Rly | 200 (in 1913) |
| Reporters, Fleet Street newspapers | 150–200 |
| Executive Officers, Home Civil Service | 195 (average) |
| Senior clerks in lawyers' offices | 150–200 and upwards |
| Clearing bank clerks, London | 40–30 (average 170) |
| Second Division Clerks, Home Civil Service | 70–250 (average 162.10s) |
| Male teachers, council schools | 154 (average) |
| Post Office clerks London | 107.18s (average) |
| Female teachers, council schools | 100 (average) |

| | |
|---|---|
| Commercial clerks | 99 (average) |
| Country stationmaster | 91 |
| Floor walkers, London shops | 70–120 (average 95) |
| Junior hospital doctors | 60–100 (average 80) |
| Railway clerks, London | 30–120 (average 75) |
| Railway booking clerks, London | 20–100 (average 60) |

*Notes*: At this time average adult male industrial earnings were £75 a year, unskilled labourers £56–66, shop assistant, London £80, postman, London £88, railway passenger guard £80.

In 1909 clerks earning more than the minimum level for income tax (£160) were almost exclusively in banking, insurance or central government employ. Railway clerks and their families enjoyed fare concessions.

In all cases where London is specified, the same posts outside were paid at lower rates (eg the maximum for a Post Office clerk outside London was £145.6s against £169).

## 1924–1929

| | £ |
|---|---|
| Successful barristers | 10,000–20,000 or more |
| Managing directors, large industrial concerns | 10,000–15,000 |
| General Manager London & North Eastern Railway | 10,000 |
| General Manager Southern Railway | 7,500 |
| High Court and Court of Appeal Judges | 5,000 |
| General Manager, Metropolitan Railway | 4,500 |
| County Court Judges | 1,500 |
| Assistant Secretaries, Home Civil Service | 1,000–1,200 (average 1,100) |
| Principals, Home Civil Service | 700–900 (average 800) |
| General practitioners | 756 (average) |
| Urban District Council, Clerk to Council and Rating Officer (Dorking, 1929, population 10,000) | 715 |
| Dentists | 601 (average) |
| Urban District Council Surveyor & Sanitary Inspector (Dorking, 1927, population 10,000) | 600 |
| Chemists | 556 (average) |
| Railway Clerks, Special Class | 350–500 (average 425) |
| Stationmaster, medium size station | 400 |
| Members of Parliament | 400 |
| Male teachers, council schools | 353 (average) |
| Bank clerks | 280 (average) |
| Executive Officers, Home Civil Service (male) | 100–400 (average 250) |
| Railway clerks, London | 45–360 (average 202.10s)* |
| Commercial clerks | 182 (average) |
| Clerical Officers, Home Civil Service (male), London | 60–250 (average 155) |

*Note*: Unskilled labourers at this time earned £130–145.

* Very few reached the upper levels of this range.

**1930–1940**                                                          £

| | |
|---|---|
| Successful barristers | 10,000–25,000 or more |
| Chairman of London Passenger Transport Board | 12,500 |
| Vice Chairman and Chief Executive Officer, London Passenger Transport Board | 10,000 |
| Successful solicitors | 5,000–6,000 |
| High Court and Appeal Judges | 5,000 |
| County Court Judges | 2,000 |
| Assistant Secretaries, Home Civil Service | 1,150–1,450 (average 1,300) |
| General practitioners | 1,094 (average) |
| Principals, Home Civil Service | 800–1,100 (average 950) |
| Dentists | 676 (average) |
| Members of Parliament | 600 (from 1937) |
| Chemists | 512 (average) |
| Bank clerks | 368 (average) |
| Male teachers, council schools | 348 (average) |
| Financial officer to Dorking Urban District Council (population 10,000) | 300 |
| Executive Officers, Home Civil Service, London, (male) | 150–525 (average 337.10s) |
| Railway clerks/administrative staff | 224 (average) |
| Clerical Officers, Home Civil Service, London, (male) | 85–350 (average 217.10s) |
| Commercial clerks | 192 (average) |
| Clerical Officers, Home Civil Service, London, (female) | 85–280 (average 182) |

*Notes*: Unskilled Labourers at this time were paid £135 a year.
Civil Service Clerical Officers worked a seven hour day, Mondays to Fridays and three and a half hours on Saturday mornings; the rates shown were subject to deductions of £15 and £30 a year outside London.

Sources: Routh G., *Occupation and pay in Great Britain 1906–50*, (1965); Metropolitan Railway Board Minutes and General Manager's papers (GLRO); *Imperial Calendar and Civil Service List* (passim); Booth, Charles, *Life and Labour of the People in London: 'Industry'* Vol 4; Hughes, Geoffrey. *LNER*, (1986); Dow, George, *Great Central*, Vol 3, (1965); Barker, T. C. and Robbins, Michael, *A History of London Transport* Vol. 2, (1974). *Dorking and Leatherhead Advertiser*, passim.

## 2. EXPENDITURE: SPECIMEN BUDGETS

*October 1915: Salary £400 a year, two children:-*

|  | £ |
|---|---|
| Food, laundry, cleaning | 130 |
| Rent | 40 |
| Rates | 14 |
| Servant | 18 |
| Education (two children) | 12 |
| Coal | 12 |
| Light | 7 |
| Water rate | 4 |
| Clothes for four | 50 |
| Railway season ticket | 12 |
| Holidays | -- |
| Insurance | 14 |
| City lunches and tobacco | 40 |
| Income tax | 25 |
| Doctor, dentist, house repairs etc | 10 |
| Savings | 12 |

(Source: 'The Daily Mail', 19 October 1915)

*1913 and 1928: salary £300 a year, two young children:-*

|  | **1913** £ | **1928** £ |
|---|---|---|
| Income tax | not payable | not payable |
| Repayment of mortgage, repairs to house, fire insurance | -- | 70[1] |
| Rent | 30 | --[1] |
| Rates | 10 | 20 |
| Coal | 5.8s | 9[2] |
| Gas | 5.5s | 10.10s |
| Food and cleaning materials | 62.1s6d | 123.18s8d |
| Railway season tickets | 8.6s8d | 12.10s |
| Life insurance | 7 | 7[3] |
| Household contents insurance | 15s | 15s |
| Clothes and clothing repairs | 22 | 40[4] |
| Doctor, dentist, holidays etc. | 3.10s | 6.6s4d |

*Difference* £145.13s10d[5]

Notes:
1. £800 house being purchased after £200 cash deposit, mortgage repayable over

338

fifteen years at £5.10s a month. £4 allocated for repairs and fire insurance. An equivalent rented house in 1928 would be at least £100 a year.

2. Four tons of coal in each case.

3. Saving for children's school fees when older, producing £130 after fifteen years.

4. £10 a head.

5. The pre-1914 family would have spent some of this on more food, better clothes, school fees and a living-in servant.

*1913 and 1928: salary £500 a year, two young children. Assumes living in same house as the £300 family above:-*

|  | 1913 £ | 1928 £ |
|---|---|---|
| Repayment of mortgage, house repairs | -- | 70 |
| Rent | 30 | -- |
| Rates | 10 | 20 |
| Coal | 6 | 10 |
| Gas | 6 | 12 |
| Food, cleaning materials and living-in servant | 106.14s2d | 208 |
| Railway season ticket | 8. 6s8d | 12.10s |
| Life insurance | 14 | 14 |
| Fire etc insurance | 10s | 1 |
| Clothes and clothing repairs | 33 | 60 |
| Doctor, dentist, holidays etc | 28.8s | 56.12s |
| Savings bank/certificates | 9.18s | 9.18s |
| City lunches | 13 | 26 |
| *Difference* | £234.3s.2d | |

Source: Peel, Mrs. C. S., *How We Lived Then, 1914–18* (1929).

*Note*: Mrs. Peel notes that income tax is not included since it was 'paid by the employer.'

1938–39: Statistics compiled by Philip Massey, supplied by '1,360 British middle class households in 1938–39' (published in *Journal of the Royal Statistical Society*, cv part III, 1942).

nb: Massey's figures were shown as average weekly amounts in shillings and old pence, taken over four weeks, but here, for convenience, they have been converted to annual sums expressed in £ and decimals of £1. Massey's figures for clothing and education were, exceptionally, related to a whole year. The information given below represents only a very small part of the detail provided in the original paper.

NOTES: the sharp increase in taxation between the two lower and two upper bands will be observed.

Most of those in the higher income bands would have paid off mortgages and would have acquired a suitable accumulation of furniture and chattels; this would account for their proportionately lower expenditures on housing, clothing and household items. The low expenditure by the highest paid on house decoration is surprising and may indicate that many of the larger middle class houses were somewhat neglected in this respect. It is not clear whether the additional amounts spent on food by the higher income band relate to quality and greater variety (most likely) or to quantity.

The higher public transport expenditure by the better-paid groups no doubt reflects a tendency to live in pleasant semi-rural or rural surroundings at some distance from the workplace.

Unfortunately this survey does not offer any adequate analysis of holiday expenditure. The figures given above for food and fuel and light almost certainly need some adjustment in this respect.

| Income of Head of Family | Over £250 & up to £350 | £350 & up to £500 | £500 & up to £700 | £700 & over |
|---|---|---|---|---|
| Average payment of income tax by head of family | £3.195 | £6.50 | £27.14 | £85.64 |

Annual Net Expenditure per Household
(figures in brackets represent
percentage of total annual expenditure):-

| | | | | |
|---|---|---|---|---|
| Food (including meals away from home) | £92.46 (26.15%) | £109.47 24.28% | £136.77 (23.09%) | £167.86 (20.06%) |
| Housing (rents/mortgage incl, rates) | £49.4 (13.98%) | £52.11 (11.56%) | £66.95 (11.3%) | £90.62 (10.83%) |
| Clothing incl. repairs | £32.285 (9.13%) | £39.865 (8.84%) | £53.14 (8.97%) | £69.225 (8.27%) |
| Fuel and light | £21.99 (6.22%) | £26.27 (5.83%) | £33.475 (5.65%) | £42.035 (5.03%) |
| Household items & equipment | £28.22 (7.98%) | £34.56 (7.66%) | £43.55 (7.35%) | £54.76 (6.55%) |
| Tobacco & cigarettes | £7.205 (2.03%) | £8.505 (1.89%) | £10.075 (1.70%) | £11.05 (1.32%) |
| Public transport | £10.615 (2.875%) | £14.19 (3.15%) | £19.45 (3.28%) | £37.59 (4.49%) |
| Reading matter, stationery, postages, telephones | £8.56 (2.42%) | £12.19 (2.70%) | £19.06 (3.22%) | £32.61 (3.90%) |
| Entertainment & sport admissions | £5.20 (1.47%) | £6.715 (1.49%) | £10.56 (1.78%) | £13.49 (1.61%) |
| Education of children | £2.33 (0.66%) | £8.61 (1.91%) | £20.64 (3.48%) | £37.59 (4.49%) |
| Medical & dental | £12.84 (3.63%) | £19.12 (4.24%) | £22.96 (3.88%) | £32.39 (3.87%) |
| Insurance, pension, trade union | £27.085 (7.66%) | £41.275 (9.16%) | £40.68 (6.87%) | £35.965 (4.3%) |
| Licences (car, radio, dog etc) | £3.195 (0.9%) | £4.06 (0.9%) | £6.34 (1.07%) | £3.09 (0.37%) |
| Domestic help | £4.765 (1.35%) | £8.18 (1.81%) | £16.845 (2.84%) | £38.51 (4.6%) |
| Alcoholic drinks | £2.71 (0.77%) | £4.115 (0.91%) | £5.04 (0.85%) | £12.51 (1.5%) |
| Motorcars, motorcycles (excl. licences, tax and insurance) | £8.665 (2.45%) | £12.295 (2.72%) | £26.81 (4.53%) | £61.64 (7.37%) |
| Home decoration | £7.80 (2.20%) | £10.13 (2.25%) | £8.61 (1.45%) | £3.955 (0.47%) |
| Total Average Expenditure (including miscellaneous items not listed above) | £353.545 | £450.83 | £592.31 | £836.49 |

# APPENDIX B

# SERVANTS

## 1. SERVANT'S DUTIES

The following was suggested in 1928 as a timetable for a household employing a cook-general and house parlourmaid. It was emphasised that it was important for each servant to have her own brooms, pans, brushes, pails etc to avoid quarrelling.

### COOK

| | |
|---|---|
| 6.30–700am | Attend to kitchen stove and hot water heater; arrange kitchen for morning's work; prepare early morning teas |
| 7–7.30 | Front steps, front door and entrance hall cleaning |
| 7.30–8.10 | Cook and prepare breakfasts |
| 8.10–8.30 | Kitchen breakfast |
| 8.30–9.00 | Help parlourmaid with general work; clean servants' bedrooms |
| 9.00–10.00 | Washing up; reviewing larder; arranging meals with mistress |
| 10.00–11.00 | As arranged |
| 11.00–12.30 | Preparation and cooking of lunch and kitchen dinner |
| 12.30–1.00 | Kitchen dinner |
| 1.00–2.15 | Dishing up dining room lunch; washing up |
| 2.15–3.30 | Cleaning and arranging kitchen |
| 3.30–5.30 | Free time |
| 5.30–7.00 | Cook dinner |
| 7.15–8.00 | As arranged |
| 8.00–8.30 | Kitchen supper |
| 8.30–9.00 | Wash up and straighten kitchen |
| 9.00–10.00 | As arranged |

### HOUSE PARLOURMAID

| | |
|---|---|
| 6.30–7.00 am | Draw up blinds open windows; vacuum-clean dining room |
| 7.00–7.15 | Take round early morning teas and call household |
| 7.15–7.30 | Finish cleaning dining room and lay breakfast table |
| 7.30–8.00 | Clean stairs and landings; polish brass |
| 8.00–8.10 | Serve dining room breakfasts |
| 8.10–8.30 | Kitchen breakfast |
| 8.30–8.45 | Clear dining room and prepare for morning housework |
| 8.45–9.45 | General bedroom work |
| 9.45–12.00 | Special cleaning tasks |
| 12.00–12.30 | Dress for lunch; lay dining room table; attend to table service |

| 12.30–1.00 | Kitchen dinner |
| 1.00–1.45 | Wait at dining room table |
| 1.45–2.00 | Clear dining room |
| 2.00–3.30 | Free time |
| 3.30–5.00 | Front door attendance; prepare and serve afternoon tea |
| 5.00–6.00 | Clean silver and attend to other duties |
| 6.00–7.00 | Bedroom duties; dining room preparation |
| 7.00–8.00 | Serve dinner; wait at table |
| 8.00–8.30 | Kitchen supper |
| 8.30–10.00 | As arranged |

Source: *The Ideal Home* magazine, article by Mary Gwynne Howell, August 1929

In February 1930 the same magazine gave a timetable for managing a house with one maid. It was emphasised that all equipment should be modern, to reduce work to a minimum:-

| 6.30–7.00 am | Open up house; attend to water heater; clean shoes |
| 7.00–7.30 | Clean dining room; lay breakfast |
| 7.30–7.45 | Clean front door, hall and brasswork |
| 7.45–8.00 | Help mistress prepare breakfasts |
| 8.00–8.30 | Serve breakfasts and start on bedrooms |
| 9.00–10.00 | Clear breakfasts and wash up, then finish bedrooms with mistress |
| 10.00–11.00 | Attend to special cleaning tasks or wash clothes |
| 11.00–11.30 | Prepare lunch |
| 11.30–12.00 | Cooking and washing |
| 12.00–1.00 | Attend to kitchen work; eat own dinner and then serve lunch |
| 2.00–2.30 | Clear table, wash up and then tidy kitchen |
| 2.30–3.30 | Free time |
| 3.30–4.00 | Attend at door then serve afternoon tea |
| 4.30–5.00 | Clear tea, wash up and then clean silver or do ironing |
| 5.30–6.30 | Prepare and serve dinner |
| 7.00-7.30 | Eat own supper |
| 7.30–8.00 | Clear dinner, wash up, tidy kitchen |
| 8.00–9.00 | Free time |
| 9.30–10.00 | Attend to bedrooms, hot water and bells. |

In April 1938 in the same magazine the following dispositions were suggested for a household with one or two children:

*One maid; house of two living rooms ad four to five bedrooms, one a nursery:*
*Mistress*: undertakes care of children, marketing, bedmaking, preparation for weekly cleaning, washing clothes (or does daily cleaning whilst maid washes cloths on washday).

*Maid*: does meal preparation, daily and weekly cleaning, washing and ironing, cleaning silver, and cares for children as required.

*Cook-housemaid and nurse-housemaid, four to five bedrooms, one a nursery:*
*Mistress*: undertakes supervision, care of children in mornings and marketing.
*Cook-housemaid*: prepares all meals; cleans dining room; kitchen, hall and own bedroom; helps with washing and bedmaking and waiting at table.
*Nurse-housemaid*: undertakes care of children in afternoon; serves meals taken by whole family together; cleans rest of house; does some washing and all ironing; cleans silver.

*Three maids, five to seven bedrooms, two nurseries, two maids' rooms.*
*Mistress*: undertakes supervision, prepares menus and does marketing; undertakes some care of children.
*Cook*: all meal preparation; cleaning of kitchen, hall and dining room and own room; washes up breakfast.
*House Parlourmaid*: Cleans most of house; waits at table; cleans silver; washes up tea and lunch; washes and cares for children when nursemaid out.
*Nursemaid*: care of children, serving children's meals, washing of children's clothes and help with the rest; cleaning nurseries; children's and general mending; washing up dinner things with housemaid. Other duties on half days of other maids.

Each maid to have one half day off a week after lunch lasting to breakfast next day. Also each maid free on alternate Sundays after midday dinner. Each maid to have daily breaks of two to three hours with some free time in the evenings.

(For further suggestions as to servants' duties and the allocation of work between servants or between servants and mistress, see Troughton (op cit), Chapter XXV).

## 2. GEOGRAPHICAL DISTRIBUTION OF SERVANTS

The following statistics of female servants (including those in hotels and boarding houses) are taken from *Sell to Britain through 'The Daily Mail'* (1929):

|  | No. of families | Servants | Servants per family |
|---|---|---|---|
| Metropolitan area (London, Middlesex and parts of Essex, Herts and Kent and Surrey) | 1,975,080 | 298,400 | 0.15 |
| South Coast (Dorset, Hants, Sussex, Surrey (part), Kent (part)) | 705,780 | 149,300 | 0.21 |

| | | | |
|---|---|---|---|
| Cornwall & Devon | 252,075 | 43,350 | 0.17 |
| Gloucester, Somerset & Wiltshire | 377,860 | 58,500 | 0.15 |
| Thames Valley (Oxford, Bucks, Berks, Herts (part) | 241,365 | 47,500 | 0.20 |
| East Anglia (Bedfordshire, Cambridgeshire, Essex (part), Hunts., Norfolk, Suffolk) | 490,395 | 64,900 | 0.13 |
| South Wales (Carmarthen, Glamorgan, Monmouth) | 407,825 | 38,400 | 0.09 |
| Shropshire, Staffs, Hereford, Worcester, Warwick, Birmingham | 818,585 | 82,500 | 0.10 |
| Derby, Notts, Leicester, Northants | 557,330 | 48,400 | 0.09 |
| Lincoln & East Riding of Yorkshire | 255,100 | 34,530 | 0.14 |
| Yorks West Riding | 802,615 | 62,860 | 0.08 |
| Lancashire & Cheshire | 1,400,950 | 114,330 | 0.08 |
| Cumberland, Durham, Westmorland, North Riding of Yorks, Northumberland | 653,035 | 75,250 | 0.12 |
| Pembroke, Cardigan, Brecknock,          Radnor, Montgomerys, Merioneth, Caernarvon, Denbigh, Anglesey, Flintshire | 176,060 | 30,060 | 0.17 |
| Scotland | 1,108,290 | 122,300 | 0.11 |
| Northern Ireland | 273,670 | 21,200 | 0.08 |

# GIRLS' PRIVATE SCHOOL TIMETABLES AND UNIFORMS

1. Daily Timetable of a Surrey private school for girls, 1937:

| *Girls under age 10* | | *Girls 10–16* | |
|---|---|---|---|
| Rise | 0730 | Rise (1) | 0730 |
| Breakfast | 0800 | Breakfast | 0800 |
| Make beds; see Matron | 0830 | Make beds; see Matron | 0830 |
| Prayers | 0915 | Prayers | 0915 |
| Lessons | 0930 | Lessons | 0930 |
| Lunch (fruit or milk) (2) | 1100 | Lunch (fruit or milk) | 1050 |
| Lessons | 1130 | Lessons | 1100 |
| Free Play | 1230 | | |
| Lunch | 1315 | Lunch | 1315 |
| Rest on beds | 1345 | Lessons | 1400 |
| Lessons (3) | 1430 | Games | 1500 |
| Tea (4) | 1615 | Tea (4) | 1615 |
| | | Preparation | 1700 |
| Play | 1645 | High Tea | 1830 |
| Supper | 1800 | Bath and bed | 1930 |
| Bath and bed | 1830 | | |

(1) Girls over fourteen rose at 0700 for half an hour's preparation.
(2) Followed by games.
(3) Or dancing, eurythmics, handwork or singing.
(4) Tea and biscuits or milk and rusks.

---

2. Clothes List for the same school (this dates from c 1949 but is effectively little changed from the requirements of the 1930s):

(nb items marked * are 'Regulation Requirements', to be obtained from the appointed outfitters (Rowe & Co., New Bond Street).

1 Blazer*
1 Serge Tunic*
1 Green Mackintosh and Sou'Wester*

1 Green Pullover*
2 Green Overalls*
1 Green Beret*
1 School Tie*
3 pairs Green Knickers*
3 pairs Linings
1 Eurhythmic Tunic
1 Jersey and 1 Tweed Skirt (for Saturday wear)
1 Old Coat (for Garden use)
1 Dance Frock and 2pr. Silk Socks or Silk Stockings
3 pairs of Pyjamas
3 Vests
3 Liberty Bodices
6 pairs Brown Cashmere or Lisle Stockings (over 10's)
6 pairs of Brown Socks (under 10's)
2 pairs of Garters (under 10's)
2 pairs of Suspenders (over 10's)
18 Handkerchieves
1 Dressing Gown
1 pair Games Shoes
1 pair Gum Boots
1 pair Galoshes
1 pair Gym Plimsolls
1 pair Dancing Sandals
1 pair Bedroom Slippers
4 Bed Sheets
3 Pillow Cases
3 Large Bath Towels
3 Face Towels
3 Table Napkins
1 Table Napkin Ring
1 Rug/Eiderdown
1 Bible and 1 Prayer Book
1 Nightdress Case
2 Combs (one pocket) and Brush
1 Soiled-Linen Bag
1 Sponge Bag
1 Toothbrush and Paste
1 Small Sponge and Flannel
1 Face Flannel
1 Trunk
1 Comb & Brush Bag
1 Small Suitcase (for things required first night of Term)
1 Dark green Brush & Comb Bag for Cloak room

In addition the following were required:

# APPENDIX C

Winter term: 1 Green Tweed Coat*; 1 Stitched Hat to match*; 3 Flannel Blouses*; 1 Green Velvet Frock (for Sunday wear); 2 pairs Woollen or Fur Gloves; 1 Warm Scarf; 1 pair Bed Socks; 2 pairs Outdoor Shoes.

Summer term: 1 Green Gabardine Coat*; 1 Panama Hat with School Band*; 3 Cotton Frocks*; 3 pairs Cotton Knickers*; 1 Cotton Tunic*; 1 Cotton Piqué Sports Dress (Rounders and Tennis Team girls); 1 Racquet; 1 Bathing Suit, Cap & Towel; a pair yellow fabric Gloves; 6 pairs of White Socks; 1 Cotton Hat; 3 Cotton Frocks and 3 pairs Cotton Knickers for Saturday wear; 2 pairs of Outdoor Shoes (of which one pair could be Sandals).

# SOURCES AND
# SELECT BIBLIOGRAPHY

## 1. General Historical and Social Background

Addison, Paul, *Now The War is Over, A Social History of Britain 1945–51*, (1985)

Bedarida, Francois, *A Social History of England 1851–1975* (1979)

Bourne, George, *Change In The Village* (1912)

Branson, Noreen & Heinemann, Margot, *Britain in the Nineteen Thirties* (1971)

Carr-Saunders, A. M., and Jones, D. Caradog, *A Survey of the Social Structure of England & Wales as Illustrated by Statistics* (1937)

Cecil, Robert, *Life in Edwardian England* (1969)

Chapman, Agatha L., *Wages & Salaries in the United Kingdom 1920–38*, (1953)

Cole, G. D. H., & Postgate, Raymond, *The Common People, 1746–1946* (1949)

Crossick, Geoffrey (ed), *The Lower Middle Class in Britain 1870–1914* (1977)

Cross, Colin, *The Liberals in Power 1905–14* (1963)

Graves, Robert & Hodge, Alan, *The Long Weekend: A Social History of Great Britain 1918–39* (1940)

Gregg, Pauline, *A Social & Economic History of Britain 1760–1966* (1966)

Halsey, A. H. (ed), *Trends in British Society since 1900* (1972)

Hill, C. P., *British Economic & Social History 1700–1939* (1961)

Lewis, Roy & Maude, Angus, *The English Middle Classes* (1949)

Marcus, Geoffrey, *Before the Lamps Went Out* (1965)

Marriott, Sir J. A. R., *Modern England 1885–1945* (1948)

Marsh, David C., *The Changing Social Structure of England & Wales 1871–1971* (1965)

Marwick, Arthur, *The Deluge: British Society & The First World War* (1965)

Marwick, Arthur, *Britain in the Century of Total War* (1968)

Marwick, Arthur, *Britain in Our Century* (1984)

Masterman, C. F. G., *The Condition of England* (1909)

Montgomery, John, *The Twenties* (1970)

Mowat, Charles, Loch *Britain Between The Wars 1918–40* (1956)

Nowell-Smith, Simon (ed.), *Edwardian England 1901–14* (1964)

Ogilvie, Vivian, *Our Times: A Social History 1912–1952* (1953)

Peel, Mrs C. S., *How We Lived Then, 1914–18* (1929)

Peel, Mrs C. S., *Life's Enchanted Cup: An Autobiography 1872–1933* (1933)

Priestley, J. B., *The Edwardians* (1970)

Roebuck, Janet, *The Making of Modern English Society: From 1850* (1973)

Saunders: see Carr-Saunders

Stevenson, J., *British Society 1914–45* (1984)

Stevenson, J., and Cook, C., *The Slump; Society & Politics during The Depression* (1977)

Taylor, A. J. P., *English History 1914–45* (1965)

Thomson, Paul, *The Edwardians* (1975)


## 2. Budgets and Expenditure

Jones, D. Caradog, 'The Cost of Living of a Sample of Middle Class Families', *Journal of The Royal Statistical Society, xci part iv*

Massey, Philip, 'The Expenditure of 1,360 Middle Class Households in 1938–9', *Journal of the Royal Statistical Society, cv, part iii, (1942).*


## 3. Housing, Home-making, Suburbs and Suburban Life

Anon. *Brochure for Morrells' Estates* (n.d., c1935)

Anon, *Brochures for Clements Wood (Ilford), Grange (Ilford) and St. German's (Lewisham) Building Estates* (n.d. c1896–1901)

Anon, *Cranbrook Park Estate* (Ilford), (1904)

Anon, *Garden City Houses and Domestic Interior Details*, (1913, 1915, 1919 and 1924)

Anon, *Harmsworth's Household Encyclopedia* (six-volume part-work, concluding in 1924)

Anon, *The Home of Today – Its Choice, Planning, Equipment & Organisation* (n.d. c1935)

Anon, *Mrs Beeton's Household Management* ('New Edition', n.d., c.1921)

Barron, P. A., *The House Desirable* (1929)

Bateman, R. A., *How to own & Equip a House* (1926)

Betham, E., (ed.), *House Building 1934–36* (1934)

Bowley, Marian, *Housing and The State 1919–1944*, (1945)

Briggs, Martin S., *Building Today* (1944)

Burnett, John, *A Social History of Housing 1815–1985*, (1986), Part II,7; Part III,9.

Byers, Anthony, *Centenary of Service: A History of Electricity in The Home* (1981)

Duff, Charles, *Anthropological Report on a London Suburb* (1935)

Edwards, Arthur M., *The Design of Suburbia: A Critical Study in Environmental History*, (1981)

Green, Frank, & Wolff, Dr Sidney, *London & Suburbs Old & New: Useful Knowledge for Health and Home* (1933).

Humphrey, Mrs C. E., *The Book of The Home*, six volumes, (1912)

Jackson, Alan A., *Semi-Detached London: Suburban Development, Life & Transport, 1900–39* (1973)

King, Anthony, *The Bungalow: The Production of a Global Culture* (1984)

McGrath, Raymond, *Twentieth Century Houses* (1934)

Myles Wright, H., *Small Houses £500–£2,500* (1938)

Oliver, Paul; Davis, Ian; and Bentley, Ian, *Dunroamin: The Suburban Semi and Its Enemies* (1982)

Osborne, John, *A Better Class of Person; An Autobiography 1929–1956* (1981)

Peel, Mrs C. S., *The New Home: Treating of the Arrangement, Decoration and Furnishing of a House of Medium Size, to be Maintained by a Moderate Income.* (1903).

Phillips, Randal, *The £1,000 House* (1928)

Richards, J. M., *The Castles on the Ground: The Anatomy of Suburbia* (1946)

Sparrow, W. Shaw, (ed.) *The Modern Home* (1905)

id. *The British Home of Today: A Book of Modern Domestic Architecture and the Applied Arts,* (1904)

id. *Flats, Urban Houses & Cottage Homes* (nd but c1907)

Spencer, Christopher, & Wilson, Geoffrey, *Elbow Room: The Story of John Sydney Brocklesby, Arts & Crafts Architect,* (1984)

Turner, Mark; Ruddick, William; and Dalling, Graham, *The Decoration of the Suburban Villa 1880–1940* (1983)

Whiteing, Eileen, *Anyone For Tennis? Growing Up in Wallington Between the Wars* (1979)

Periodicals: *The Builder* 1901–45 passim; *The Ideal Home* 1929–39 passim; *Our Homes & Gardens* 1922–39 passim.

## 4. Servants and Servant Keeping

Anon, *Mrs Beeton's Household Management* ('New Edition', n.d. c1921)

Davies, F. V., *Not in Front of the Servants; A True Portrait of Upstairs, Downstairs Life,* (1984)

Gathorne-Hardy, Jonathan, *The Rise and Fall of the British Nanny,* (1972)

Troubridge, Lady, [Laura], *The Book of Etiquette,* (1926), Chapter XXV

Periodicals: *The Ideal Home,* 1929–39 passim.

## 5. Fashions and Dress, Consumer Goods, Department Stores

Adburgham, Alison, *Shops and Shopping 1800–1914,* (1964)

Adburgham, Alison, *Shopping In Style: London from The Restoration to Edwardian Elegance,* (1979)

Anon, Gamages Catalogues 1911, 1913, as reprinted in *Gamage's Christmas Bazaar 1913* with introduction by Alison Aldburgham (1974)

Anon, *The House That Every Woman Knows* [for Harrods Ltd.] (1909)

Anon, Harrods General Catalogues, 1920–39

Anon, *A Story of British Achievement: 1849–1949* [for Harrods Ltd] (1949)

Byers, Anthony, op cit (Section 3)

Caldwell, Doreen, *And All was Revealed; Ladies' Underwear, 1907–80* (1981)

Ferry, John, William, *A History of The Department Store* (1960)

Laver, James, *Taste and Fashion: From the French Revolution to The Present Day*, new edition, revised and enlarged, (1945)

Page, Christopher, *Foundations of Fashion; Corsetry from 1856 to the Present Day* (1981)

Pound, Reginald, *Selfridge* (1960)

Pritchard, Mrs Eric, *The Cult of Chiffon* (1902)

Stevenson, Pauline, *Edwardian Fashion* (1980)

Troubridge, op cit, (section 4), Chapter XXVIII

Voller, Madame W., *Efficient Corseting* (n.d. c1908)

Williams, A. H., *No Name on the Door* [Selfridges] (1956)

Newspapers and Periodicals: advertisements (1900–1950) in *Britannia & Eve; The Bystander; Dorking Advertiser** and various Dorking area church magazines* and concert etc. programmes*; *The Evening News* (London); *The Play Pictorial; Theatre World; The Tatler; The Sketch; The Sphere.*
(* ie those of Charles Degenhardt Ltd. Dorking, 1930–70, filed in albums at R114/1/1–5, Dorking & District Museum).

## 6. Childhood and Adolescence

Anon, Gamages catalogues (see section 5)

Anon, Hornby Trains and Meccano Catalogues 1920–39

Betjeman, John, *Summoned By Bells*, (1960)

Dahl, Roald, *Boy: Tales of Childhood*, (1984)

Kerr, Rose, *Story of the Girl Guides 1908–1938*, New Edition, (1976)

Newsom, John *The Education of Girls*, (1948)

Osborne, John, op cit (section 3)

Reynolds E. E., *Boy Scouts*, (1944)

Smith, Joanna, *Edwardian Children* (1983)

Springhall, J. O., 'The Boy Scouts, Class and Militarism in Relation to British Youth Movements 1908–1930'. *International Review of Social History, XVI*, 1971, Part 2, pp.125–158.

Troubridge, op cit, (section 4), Chapter XXVII

Wade, E. K., *Twenty-one Years of Scouting: The Official History of The Boy Scout Movement from its Inception*, (1929)

Whiteing, op cit (section 3).

## 7. Leisure, Entertainments & Holidays

Atwell, David, *Cathedrals of the Movies: A History of British Cinemas and Their Audiences*, (1980)

Brunner, Elizabeth, *Holidaymaking and The Holiday Trades*, (1945)

Elwall, Robert, *Bricks and Beer: English Pub Architecture 1830–1939* (1983)

Eyles, Allen & Skone, Keith, *London's West End Cinemas* (1984)

Gifford, Denis, *The British Film Catalogue 1895–1985: A Reference Guide,* (1986)

Hern, Anthony, *The Seaside Holiday* (1966)

Nicoll, Allardyce, *English Drama 1900–1930: The Beginnings of the Modern Period* (1973)

Pearsall, Ronald, *Edwardian Life & Leisure* (1973)

Pimlott, J. A. R., *The Englishman's Holiday* (1947)

Richards, Jeffrey, *The Age of The Dream Palace: Cinema and Society in Britain 1930–1939* (1984)

Saunders, Ruth Manning *Seaside England* (1951)

Sharp, Dennis, *The Picture Palace and Other Buildings for the Movies,* (1969)

Short, Ernest, *Theatrical Cavalcade* (1942)

Troubridge, op cit (section 4), Chapters XXI, XXII

Walvin, James, *Beside The Seaside* (1978)

Periodicals: *The Play Pictorial*, 1902–1939; *Theatre World*, 1925–39, passim; *The Sketch*, 1934–35, passim.

Letters to the author from J. H. Price, formerly Managing Editor, Thomas Cook Timetables.

## 8. Commuting & Journeys to Town

Jackson, Alan A., op cit (section 3), Chapter 10.
   id *London's Metropolitan Railway* (1986)

Periodicals: *The Railway Magazine*, 1900–1950, *Railway/Transport and Travel Monthly*, 1910–22, passim.

# Index

nb All general references relate to the middle classes unless otherwise stated. There may be more than one reference on the page given.